BEDE AND AETHELTHRYTH

MEDIEVAL EUROPEAN STUDIES XVIII
Patrick W. Conner, Series Editor

OTHER TITLES IN THE SERIES:

Isidorean Perceptions of Order: The Exeter Book Riddles and Medieval Latin Enigmata
Mercedes Salvador-Bello

Beowulf and the Grendel-kin: Politics and Poetry in Eleventh-Century England
Helen Damico

The Book of Emperors: A Translation of the Middle High German Kaiserchronik
Edited and translated by Henry A. Myers

The Old English Poem Seasons for Fasting: A Critical Edition
Edited by Mary P. Richards with the assistance of Chadwick B. Hilton Jr.

Sir Gawain and the Green Knight
Translated by Larry Benson
with a foreword and Middle English text edited by Daniel Donoghue

Perspectives on the Old Saxon Hêliand:
Introductory and Critical Essays, with an Edition of the Leipzig Fragment
Edited by Valentine A. Pakis

Cross and Cruciform in the Anglo-Saxon World:
Studies to Honor the Memory of Timothy Reuter
Edited by Sarah Larratt Keefer, Karen Louise Jolly, and Catherine E. Karkov

The Cross and Culture in Anglo-Saxon England
Edited by Karen Jolly, Catherine E. Karkov, and Sarah Larratt Keefer

Cædmon's Hymn and Material Culture in the World of Bede
Edited by Allen J. Frantzen and John Hines

The Power of Words: Anglo-Saxon Studies Presented
to Donald G. Scragg on his Seventieth Birthday
Edited by Jonathan Wilcox and Hugh Magennis

Innovation and Tradition in the Writings of the Venerable Bede
Edited by Scott DeGregorio

Ancient Privileges: Beowulf, Law, and the Making of Germanic Antiquity
Stefan Jurasinski

Old English Literature in its Manuscript Context
Edited by Joyce Tally Lionarons

Theorizing Anglo-Saxon Stone Sculpture
Edited by Catherine E. Karkov and Fred Orton

Naked Before God: Uncovering the Body in Anglo-Saxon England
Edited by Benjamin C. Withers and Jonathan Wilcox

Hêliand: Text and Commentary
Edited by James E. Cathey

Via Crucis: Essays on Early Medieval Sources and Ideas
Thomas N. Hall, Editor, with assistance from Thomas D. Hill and Charles D. Wright

Bede and Aethelthryth

An Introduction
to Christian Latin Poetics

———

Stephen J. Harris

WEST VIRGINIA UNIVERSITY PRESS
MORGANTOWN 2016

Copyright 2016 West Virginia University Press
All rights reserved
First edition published 2016 by West Virginia University Press
Printed in the United States of America

ISBN:
pb: 978-1-940425-93-1
epub: 978-1-940425-94-8
pdf: 978-1-940425-95-5

Library of Congress Cataloging-in-Publication Data available at the Library of Congress
Cover image: MS49598 90v ("The Benediction of St. Aethelwold") used by permission of the British Library.

Nihil Obstat
Reverend Mark S. Stelzer, S.T.D.
Censor Librorum
Imprimatur
Most Reverend Mitchell T. Rozanski, D.D.
Bishop of Springfield
November 6, 2014

virgo triumphat ovans
—Bede

Contents

Preface	ix
Note on Orthography	xv
Abbreviations	xvii
1. On Beauty	1
2. Metrical Arts	33
3. Rhetoric	60
4. Sources	88
5. St. Aethelthryth in the *HE*	126
Hymn to Aethelthryth (English)	158
Hymn to Aethelthryth (Latin)	161
Hymn to Aethelthryth (Edition)	164
6. *Hymn to Aethelthryth*, A–G	167
7. *Hymn to Aethelthryth*, H–R	203
8. *Hymn to Aethelthryth*, S–end	243
Works Cited	273
Index	295

Preface

For a long time, I found Christian Latin poetry extremely dull. I wondered how anyone enjoyed it. Yet people had enjoyed it, century after century. And since taste is more often developed than inborn, I was compelled to learn why. What precisely did educated readers find beautiful about Christian Latin poetry, specifically Bede's poetry? What did they look for? What did they remark on? Eventually I came not only to appreciate Bede's poetry, but to stand in awe of it. It offered an aesthetic pleasure that I was only dimly familiar with, one that I had not associated with poetry. In about 1825, Saint John Henry Newman described that pleasure in a sermon on blessedness. Newman was speaking on the highest pleasure humans might possibly know, the pleasure of Heaven. He wrote that in this world "every man can do his *own* pleasure, but [in Heaven] he must do *God's* pleasure." Inheritors of the Western tradition of political and religious liberty are trained to balk instinctively at "must," but for a devoted Christian, the obligation to do God's will does not diminish, but rather fulfills the self. The pursuit of happiness is not denied, but refined. Newman writes, "Heaven then is not like this world; I will say what it is much more like,—*a church*." And in Heaven, as may be dimly and fleetingly seen in a church, the blessed will enjoy "an endless and uninterrupted worship of the Eternal Father, Son, and Spirit."[1] Christian poetry also strives to meet the challenge of an uninterrupted worship of the Trinity. It offers the pleasure of worship, the pleasure one finds in a church. Just as worship prepares the Christian to engage Christ, so the literary

---

1. Newman, "Sermon 1," p. 7.

aesthetic of Christian Latin poetry asks a reader to recognize the spiritual goal of literary beauty, its function as a path to the ultimate good. We recognize here the old Greek triad of the Good, the True, and the Beautiful. But the age-long repetition of this commonplace threatens to denude it of meaning and to obscure its far-reaching consequences. It is, I have learned, a key to reading Christian Latin poetry. Contemporary literary criticism spends much of its effort on the good, some effort on the true, but less and less effort on the beautiful. Christians of Bede's day were similar. I would like to know something about those who concentrated on the beautiful.

If poets respond to their audiences, then it seems to me essential to learn as much as possible about the expectations of their audiences. When Tatwine or Bede read the poems of their predecessors, what elements of a poem did they find engaging? On what basis did they judge a poem successful or unsuccessful? My aim in this book is a commentary on grammatical and critical *expectations*. Following in the line of Hans Robert Jauss, I am asking after the "horizon of expectations" of Bede's ideal reader—which is another way of saying the limits and history of a reader's expectations. It is exceedingly important that we recognize the fact of Bede's allusions to Virgil's *Aeneid*, but it is equally important to understand what the larger implications of such allusions are.[2] Invocations of authors were not only to the authors *per se*, but also to the genres in which they wrote, and to the reams of commentary that accompanied those authors. Commentary told readers what was important or unique about a poem. Bede's ideal reader would have known that commentary. It served as a kind of secular catechesis for elite readers. As well as recognizing allusions and commentary, Bede's ideal reader operated within a Hellenized Christian aesthetic. Following, among others, Umberto Eco, Calvin Kendall describes that aesthetic:

> For the earlier Latin Middle Ages, the sense of beauty was inextricably linked with, and a reflection of, divine order. Beauty derived

---

2. For example, with respect to expectations of genre among medieval readers, see Jauss, *Towards an Aesthetic of Reception*, p. 79.

from the relationship in space and time between the parts of the whole.... Beauty had to do with proportion, with harmony and balance, with number, and with licensed deviation from the norm. The perception of beauty brought the mind closer to God.[3]

What Kendall describes is known as the Great Theory of Beauty. I describe it more fully in my first chapter. Allusion, meter, vocabulary, rhetorical figures—these were not mere decoration, but an orderly means of approaching God through language. Bede's poetry was used as well as appreciated within an intellectual environment that considered the closest, achievable point to God to lie not as much in a feeling or personal sensation of God, but in the *Lôgos*, in Wisdom (*sophia*), Reason (*ratio*), and Knowledge (*scientia*).[4] One of the first questions I ask of Bede's poetry is not what it expects you to *feel*, but what it expects you to *know*.

When we learn about poetry today, we are taught that it is supposed to be more about feeling than knowledge. What makes a poem beautiful, we learn, is the intensity of its feeling and the author's style. Readers of more recent English poetry quickly become familiar with the stylistic particulars of Keats or Wordsworth, for example. But stylistics—the study of an author's vocabulary, grammar, and syntax—is not always useful for distinguishing poetry from prose. So style becomes for us an accessory to feeling. We look primarily for emotion or for an authentic experience in a poem. If a poem achieves heightened emotion in heightened style, as did those of Shakespeare and Goethe, then we tend to judge it to be successful. Scholars after the Enlightenment tend to read medieval Latin verse as if it had attempted what Goethe achieved. That is their "horizon of expectation." To take but one example, F. J. E. Raby, author of two authoritative histories of medieval Latin poetry, praises those verses in which he finds emotional and experiential authenticity. (He does not dismiss style, of course. We cannot fall into an either/

---

3. Kendall, "Introduction," in *Libri II*, p. 20.
4. Holder, "Introduction," in *The Venerable Bede*, p. 13: Christ is the Wisdom of God.

or fallacy.) Nevertheless, authenticity is a poetic quality whose virtue is decidedly modern.[5] Bede, Alcuin, or Wulfstan did not praise it; I am not sure that they would have recognized it as a quality of poetry at all. And it is essential to recognize that Raby does not describe why a particular poet appealed to medieval audiences, but rather why he (or she) might appeal to Raby's readers. Bede did not appeal to those readers. As Raby wrote of Bede, "His was not a poetic nature."[6] The phrasing tells us that Raby thought a poet was a person whose very nature was different from that of others. In such a view, a poet is a Byronic hero, or a sophisticated radical, or a sensitive flower musing on life's nuances in delicate phrases. But in Bede's world, a poet did not have a different nature, only different abilities. He was a craftsman, like a carpenter or a goldsmith. As Bede explains, the Anglo-Saxon poet Caedmon got his material from Abbess Hild, and then formed it into poetry. Eduard Norden, too, was not awed by Bede's verse, "a stylistically uncultivated but grammatically correct Latin."[7] Norden was exceptionally alert to the distinguishing features of poetic style, gauging Bede against authors like Virgil and Fortunatus, preeminent Latin stylists. As a craftsman of hymns, Bede was not building Chippendale chairs, but Shaker stools. While critics today try to avoid declarations of aesthetic standards for a number of reasons, Raby did not. Luckily, neither did schoolmasters like Bede. So we have a long record of aesthetic judgments from the early Middle Ages that are mixed in with moral claims and theological observations. With a lot of digging, we can recover what early medieval Latin authors valued in their models and then strove to reproduce or to refashion.

I wrote this book to serve not only as a primer to early Anglo-Latin aesthetics, but also as an introduction to Bede's Christian, Latin verse. In the process, I found so much to say about one poem that

---

5. See Trilling, *Sincerity and Authenticity*.
6. Raby, *CLP*, p. 146; cited by Bonner, "Bede and Medieval Civilization," p. 76.
7. Cited and translated by Winterbottom, "Aldhelm's Prose Style and its Origins," p. 39.

I had to abandon the rest. I hope readers will find Bede's *Hymn to Aethelthryth* as fascinating as I have. I planned this volume as a propaedeutic to the forthcoming edition of Bede's poems by Michael Lapidge—as a struggling pseudo-Sergius to his Donatus, although I flatter myself greatly in the comparison. I am extremely grateful to Professor Lapidge for his guidance and encouragement as I wrote this book. What faults remain in this book—and they are not few—result from having followed his advice poorly. I am also extremely grateful to Professor Calvin Kendall, who was tremendously helpful and generous with his comments and suggestions. He saved me from many errors not only in Latin but also in my understanding of Bede as a poet. I must admit to feeling a bit like the dragon in the first book of the *Faerie Queene*, spewing error relentlessly on these two Latinists in their battle-scarred armor. E. J. Christie was extremely generous as a reader for the press. Patrick W. Conner, Hilary Attfield, and Jason Gosnell at West Virginia University Press kindly allowed that enough readers of Bede would appreciate a general overview of medieval Latin poetry. The anonymous copyeditor at West Virginia also made a number of extremely helpful suggestions, for which he or she has my thanks. Medievalists and classicists capable of scanning a line of Virgil have already internalized most of the material that I present here. A sense of meter, of propriety, of innovation, of allusion is part of learning Latin, and has been so for generations. But much of that sense is not codified, or is scattered throughout libraries or dedicated studies of Latin literature, and is tricky for non-specialists to find. Perhaps in collecting a little of it here, I can offer an introductory guide to the sorts of aesthetic considerations mulled over in the Anglo-Saxon classroom. I am extremely grateful to West Virginia University Press for their support of this project and for their long-suffering indulgence.

My most profound debts are to my colleagues and predecessors. One achieves very little on one's own. We know that the study of Anglo-Saxon England is sometimes a progression, sometimes a clarification, and sometimes a salutary obfuscation of an existing debate. And the student of Anglo-Saxon England is always responding to the work of others. I have been honored to respond to brilliant scholars, and whatsoever of my work is worthwhile is reflected light. Many of those scholars are listed in my Works Cited rather than in a bibliography. Lapidge's forthcoming edition will undoubtedly provide a far better bibliography than I could manage. A bibliography to 1991 can be found on bede.net, compiled by Scott DeGregorio and me. Although I have read more widely than is suggested in my list of works cited, I wanted to provide readings accessible to my intended audience, which is not professional Latinists. So I have cited editions from the CSEL, which are available to readers free online, when they do not differ significantly from Brepols's CCSL. I have also used editions that are accompanied by a translation into a modern European language in order to encourage readers to pursue further some of these Latin authors. Those major authors whose work I have cited can be found in the table of abbreviations. Readers will find that citations from the Latin Vulgate and Greek Septuagint are from the Stuttgart editions; translations are from the Douay-Rheims. For their help on this volume I would like also to thank for their generosity, suggestions, and many kindnesses Pat Conner, Tom Hall, Brian Breed, Scott DeGregorio, George Hardin Brown, Allen Frantzen, Andrew Scheil, Mary Dockray Miller, Michael Drout, Sharon Rowley, Don Scragg, Linda Moore, Trent Maxey, Craig Nicolson, Damien Fleming, the Rev. Dr. Christopher Carlisle, Fr. Gary Dailey, William Roundy, and all the "Bede-niks," as Faith Wallis puts it with characteristic good humor, at Kalamazoo. For innumerable suggestions, face-saving advice, and her keen editorial eye, I am extremely grateful to my wife Marian, who also patiently suffered the long march of this book to press. This is ultimately a book about beauty, so I am thankful for the opportunity to dedicate it to my daughters Grace and Lillian, whose beauty exceeds description.

—SJH
August 28, 2014
Feast of St. Augustine of Hippo
Amherst, MA

Note on Orthography

I distinguish between u/v unless citing from a source that does not—I do not edit sources. I do not use the e-caudata (ę) unless citing from a source; all are changed to *ae* or to the preferred form cited in the *Oxford Latin Dictionary*.

Words in quotation marks are taken directly from a source and therefore keep their inflections. Words in italics are changed into the nominative case or infinitive form. Thus Bede's Hymn includes "ridet" (l. 21), in quotations, which is the third-person singular present active indicative form of the verb *ridere*, in italics.

Translations of phrases are in parentheses and double quotation marks, translations of words in single quotation marks. Thus "sobria corda" ("sober hearts") but *cor* 'heart.'

Printer's marks make it difficult to indicate that all diphthongs are long. So I have marked the first vowel of a diphthong long, and left the second vowel unmarked: thus *animāe*, where –*ae* is long. Juxtaposed vowels that do not form diphthongs are both marked: thus *dĕŭs*. I trust this will not cause confusion.

Elision is marked with parentheses. Thus "Orta patr(e) eximio" ("Born from a distinguished father").

Hiatus is unmarked. It would crowd the text too much and tax the reader more than I already have.

Feet are separated by a single bar, |.

Caesura, if marked, is marked with a double bar, ||. The central caesura of a pentameter is marked this way in each of Bede's elegiac strophes.

To avoid an overly convoluted apparatus, I place a macron over all long vowels, failing to distinguish between vowels long by nature and vowels long by position. For that reason, I do not mark the final syllable of the hexameter.

Proper nouns are capitalized: thus Heaven and God. Populist orthography sometimes equates lowercase letters with the quotidian, so we now get "the president of the United States" and "US senator," rather than President and Senator, which are the proper nouns naming the offices. Thus Pope not pope, and Church when referring to the Catholic Church.

Abbreviations

Latin Authors

Aldhelm
  CDV   *Carmen de virginitate*, ed. Ehwald, MGH AA 15 (Berlin, 1919), pp. 350–471.
  PDV   *Prosa de virginitate*, ed. Ehwald, MGH AA 15 (Berlin, 1919), pp. 211–323.
Ambrose
  Expositio   *Expositio psalmi CLVIII*, ed. M. Petschenig, CSEL 62 (Vienna, 1913)
  Hymnes   *Ambrose de Milan: Hymnes*, ed. Jacques Fontaine (Paris, 2008); cited by hymn number and editor. Note that each hymn is edited independently.
  Lucam   Ambrose, *Expositio evangelii secundum Lucam*, ed. C. Schenkl, CCSL 32.4 (Vienna, 1902)
Augustine
  Conf.   *Confessiones* (CSEL 33); *Saint Augustine, Confessions*, trans. Henry Chadwick (Oxford, 1991)
  DDC   Augustine of Hippo, *De Doctrina Christiana*, ed. Green, CSEL 80, pp. 3–169; *On Christian Doctrine*, trans. D. W. Robertson (New York, 1958)
  Enn.   *Enarrationes in psalmos*, PL 36 & 37, cited by column
  Exposition   Augustine, *Exposition on the Psalms*, trans. Maria Boulding, 6 vols. (Hyde Park, 1999)

Bede
- DAM   *De arte metrica et De schematibus et tropis*, ed. Calvin B. Kendall, CCSL 123a (Turnhout, 1975); *De arte metrica*, ed. and trans. Calvin Kendall, *Bede: Libri II De Arte metrica et de schematibus et tropis* (Saarbrücken, 1991)
- DDI   *De die iudicii*, ed. J. Fraipont, CCSL 122 (Turnhout, 1955), pp. 439–44.
- DO   *De orthographia*, ed. Charles W. Jones, CCSL 123a (Turnhout, 1975)
- DST   *De arte metrica et De schematibus et tropis*, ed. Calvin B. Kendall, CCSL 123a (Turnhout, 1975); *De schematibus et tropis*, ed. and trans. Calvin Kendall, *Bede: Libri II De Arte metrica et de schematibus et tropis* (Saarbrücken, 1991)
- HA   *Abbots of Wearmouth and Jarrow*, ed. and trans. Christopher Grocock and I. N. Wood, Oxford Medieval Texts (Oxford, 2013)
- HE   *Historia ecclesiastica gentis Anglorum*, ed. and trans. Bertram Colgrave and R. A. B. Mynors, Oxford Medieval Texts (Oxford, 1969)
- Hymn   Hymns of Bede; *Liber hymnorum*, ed. J. Fraipont, CCSL 122 (Turnhout, 1955), pp. 406–38. Cited by Fraipont number
- *Martyrology*   ed. by Quentin; coordinated against Jacques Du-Bois, *Edition pratique des martyrologes de Bède, de l'anonyme lyonnais et de Florus* (Paris, 1976).
- VSC   Werner Jaager, *Bedas metrische Vita Sancti Cuthberti* (Leipzig, 1935), cited as verse *VSC*

Cassiodorus
- *Explanation*   Cassiodorus, *Explanation of the Psalms*, trans. P. G. Walsh, 3 vols., Ancient Christian Writers 52 (New York, 1991)
- *Expositio*   Cassiodorus, *Expositio in Psalterium*, PL 70:9–1056

Fortunatus, *Poems*   *Venance Fortunat: Poèmes*, ed. and trans. Marc Reydellet, Collections des universités de France, 3 vols. (Paris, 2002)

Hilary, *Commentaire*   Hilaire de Poitiers, *Commentaire sur le psaume 118*, ed. and trans. Marc Milhau, Sources Chrétiennes 344, 2 vols. (Paris, 1988). Latin edition is Hilary of Poitiers, *Tractatus super psalmos*, CSEL 22 (Vienna, 1891)

Isidore, *Etym.*   Isidore of Seville, *Etymologiarum sive originum libri xx*, ed. W. M. Lindsey, 2 vols. (Oxford, 1911); *The Etymologies of Isidore of Seville*, trans. Stephen A. Barney et al. (Cambridge, 2006)

Prudentius   *Prudence*, ed. and trans. M. Lavarenne, Collections des universités de France, 3rd ed., 4 vols. (Paris, 2003)

Apoth.   *Apotheosis* in Prudentius, vol. 2

Cath.   *Cathemerinon liber* in Prudentius, vol. 1

Contra Symm.   *Contra Symmachum* in Prudentius, vol. 3

Hamart.   *Hamartigenia* in Prudentius, vol. 2

Hymn   see *Cath.*, cited by hymn

Peri.   *Peristephanon liber* in Prudentius, vol. 4

Psych.   *Psychomachia* in Prudentius, vol. 3

Sedulius, *CP*   *Carmen Paschale* in *Sedulii Opera Omnia*, ed. J. Heumer, CSEL 10 (Vienna, 1885); Springer, *Sedulius: The Paschal Song and Hymns* (Atlanta, 2013), cited by book and line

Servius, *Commentarii*   Servius, *In Vergilii Carmina Commentarii*, ed. George Thilo and Hermann Hagen, 3 vols. (Leipzig, 1884)

Sources and References

AH   *Analecta hymnica medii aevi*, ed. Clemens Blume and Guido Maria Dreves, 55 vols. (Leipzig, 1886–1922)

AS   *Acta sanctorum*, ed. Joannes Bollandus, 68 vols. (Paris, 1863–1948)

ASE   Anglo-Saxon England

ASE   *Anglo-Saxon England* (Cambridge, 1974–), journal

BHL   *Bibliotheca Hagriographica Latina*, ed. J. Bollandus, 2 vols. (Brussels, 1898–1900)

Brown, *CB*   George Hardin Brown, *A Companion to Bede* (Cambridge, 2009)

Brunhölzl, *LLMA*   Franz Brunhölzl, *Histoire de la littérature Latine du Moyen Âge*, 3 vols. (Turnhout, 1990)

CCSL   Corpus Christianorum Series Latina (Turnhout)

CPL   Clavis Patrum Latinorum, ed. Eligius Dekkers, 3rd ed. (Turnhout, 1995)
CSASE   Cambridge Studies in Anglo-Saxon England
CSEL   Corpus Scriptorum Ecclesiasticorum Latina (Vienna)
De Bruyne, *Études*   Edgar De Bruyne, *Études d'esthétique médiévale*, 2 vols. (Paris, 1998)
DeGregorio, *CCB*   *The Cambridge Companion to Bede*, ed. Scott DeGregorio (Cambridge, 2010)
DMA   *Dictionary of the Middle Ages*, ed. Joseph L. Strayer, 13 vols. (New York, 1982)
DuCange   *Glossarium mediae et infimae latinitatis*, ed. DuCange et al. (Niort, 1883–)
EETS   Early English Texts Society
Famulus Christi   *Famulus Christi: Essays in Commemoration of the Thirteenth Centenary of the Birth of the Venerable Bede*, ed. Gerald Bonner (London, 1976)
Fontaine, *Études*   Jacques Fontaine, *Études sur la poésie latine tardive: d'Ausone à Prudence* (Paris, 1980)
Gneuss, *Handlist*   Helmut Gneuss, *A Handlist of Anglo-Saxon Manuscripts* (Tempe, AZ, 2001)
HBS   Henry Bradshaw Society
Innovation and Tradition   *Innovation and Tradition in the Writings of the Venerable Bede*, ed. Scott DeGregorio, Medieval European Studies 7 (Morgantown, WV, 2006)
Jarrow Lectures   *Bede and His World: The Jarrow Lectures 1958–1978*, vol. 1, and *Bede and His World: The Jarrow Lectures 1979–1993*, vol. 2 (Burlington, VT, 1993)
JML   *Journal of Medieval Latin*
Keil, *GL*   Heinrich Keil, *Grammatici Latini*, 7 vols. (Leipzig, 1857)
Kendall, *Libri II*   see above Bede, *DAM* and *DST*
Knappe, *TKR*   Gabrielle Knappe, *Traditionen der klassischen Rhetorik im angelsächsischen England* (Heidelberg, 1996)
Laistner, *Handlist*   Max Ludwig Wolfram Laistner, *A Hand-list of Bede manuscripts* (Ithaca, NY, 1943)

Lapidge
    ALL   Michael Lapidge, *Anglo-Latin Literature, 600–899*, 2 vols. (London, 1996), cited by volume and item number
    APW   *Aldhelm: The Poetic Works*, trans. Michael Lapidge and James Rosier (Cambridge, 1985)
    APrW   *Aldhelm: The Prose Works*, trans. Michael Lapidge and Michael Herren (Cambridge, 1979)
    BP   "Bede the Poet," Jarrow Lectures, 1993, pp. 929–956
    Library   Michael Lapidge, *The Anglo-Saxon Library* (Oxford, 2006)

Manitius, *Geschichte*   Max Manitius, *Geschichte der lateinischen Literatur des Mittelalters* (Munich, 1976)

Mantello and Rigg, *ML*   *Medieval Latin: An Introduction and Bibliographical Guide*, ed. F. A. C. Mantello and A. G. Rigg (Washington, DC, 1996)

Marouzeau, *Traité*   J. Marouzeau, *Traité de stylistique latine* (Paris: Belles Lettres, 1962)

MGH   Monumenta Germaniae Historica
    AA   Auctores antiquissimi
    PLAC   Poetae Latini Aevi Carolini

Milfull, *Hymns*   Inge B. Milfull, *The Hymns of the Anglo-Saxon Church*, CSASE 17 (Cambridge, 1996)

Mohrmann, *Études*   Christine Mohrmann, *Études sur le Latin des Chrétiens*, Storia e Letteratura 65.1, 65.2, 103, and 143, 4 vols. (Rome, 1961–77)

Norberg, *Introduction*   Dag Norberg, *An Introduction to the Study of Medieval Latin Versification*, trans. Grant C. Roli and Jacqueline de La Chapelle Skubly, ed. Jan Ziolkowski (Washington, DC, 2004); French edition is *Introduction à l'étude de la versification latine médiévale*, Studia Latina Stockholmiensia (Stockholm, 1958)

Norden, *AK*   Eduard Norden, *Die antike Kunstprosa: vom vi. Jahrhundert v. Chr. bis in die Zeit der Renaissance*, 2 vols. (Darmstadt, 1974)

OEN   *Old English Newsletter*

OHMLL   *Oxford Handbook of Medieval Latin Literature*, ed. Ralph J. Hexter and David Townsend (Oxford, 2012)
OLD   *Oxford Latin Dictionary*
Orchard, *PAA*   Andy Orchard, *The Poetic Art of Aldhelm*, CSASE 8 (Cambridge, 1994)
PL   *Patrologia Latina*, ed. Jacques-Paul Migne, 217 vols. (Paris, 1844–64)
Raby, *CLP*   F. J. E. Raby, *Christian Latin Poetry*, 2nd ed. (Oxford, 1953)
Raby, *SLP*   F. J. E. Raby, *Secular Latin Poetry*, 2 vols. (Oxford, 1934)
Quentin, *Martyrologes*   Henri Quentin, *Les Martyrologes historiques du Moyen Âge* (Paris, 1908)
Stotz, *HLSM*   Peter Stotz, *Handbuch zur lateinischen Sprache des Mittelalters*, 5 vols. (Munich, 2000)
Szövérffy, *Annalen*   *Die Annalen der lateinischen Hymnendichtung*, 2 vols. (Berlin, 1964).
TLL   *Thesaurus Linguae Latinae* (Berlin), online at http://www.degruyter.com/view/db/tll, cited by volume and page
TTH   Translated Texts for Historians
Walpole, *Hymns*   *Early Latin Hymns*, ed. A. S. Walpole (Cambridge, 1922)
White, *ECLP*   Caroline White, *Early Christian Latin Poets* (New York, 2000)
Wilkinson, *GLA*   L. P. Wilkinson, *Golden Latin Artistry* (Cambridge, 1963)

CHAPTER ONE

On Beauty

A significant decline in the study of Latin and the widespread secularization of the Western university have resulted in very few readers being prepared to appreciate the Christian Latin poetry of the Venerable Bede. He wrote at a time when educated readers knew something of both classical and liturgical Latin. More importantly, all of Bede's poetry engages with the Latin Vulgate Bible, and Bede's readers knew the Vulgate well. Christians today read Scripture in dozens of English translations, some of which are far removed from the terminology and syntax of the Vulgate. Translations of Bede, even into Old English, tend to obscure allusions to classical and Scriptural traditions, which are at the heart of Bede's literary art. This is especially true of his poetry. Most of Bede's prose has been translated: Bede's *Historia ecclesiastica gentis Anglorum* (c. AD 735, hereafter *HE*) is available in English translation, as are most of his commentaries on Scripture and his works on grammar and time. However, apart from a few snippets here and there and a pamphlet printed in Lincoln, Bede's poetry remains available only in Latin.[1] Why? Perhaps because tastes have changed in 1300 years. Or perhaps because Bede is no Shakespeare. But then Shakespeare is no Bede: they wrote to different audiences and to different purposes. If we are to appreciate Bede's poems, then understanding his audience

---

1. We await the edition of Bede's poems by Michael Lapidge. The pamphlet is Jackson, *The Hymns of Bede*, and is intended for singing (p. vi).

and his purpose is an essential first step. But how to empathize sufficiently with his readers? Typically, one tries to imagine an ideal reader, an avatar who is sensitive to the historical and cultural cues contemporary with a poem. But imagining as accurately as possible a reader in seventh-century Anglo-Saxon England is exceptionally difficult. We would have to imagine what she (not we) would notice in Bede and, if she were a teacher, what she would ask her students to notice. She would have to be a cloistered Christian, subject to a convoluted mixture of monastic rules. She would have to live in a monastery connected to a school and scriptorium.

Perhaps she might be a nun who lived at Barking, an abbey in London that was part of Bede's audience. One of Bede's sources for his *HE* was a book written at Barking,[2] which housed a monastic school. She would have trained in the best grammatical traditions available in Britain, as Bede did. She would have had access to an extensive library, such as existed at Bede's twin monasteries of Wearmouth and Jarrow. Barking's abbess Hildelith taught the trivium, and she and nine other nuns or abbesses, to whom Aldhelm dedicated his prose *De virginitate*, were capable of parsing Aldhelm's very difficult Latin. (The importance of female readers of Bede's work will become apparent in later chapters.) Still, however successfully we might construct this reader, we could not reasonably reconstruct her psychology or her tastes. At best, we could try to recover what she and her contemporaries recommended to each other as beautiful in the art of poetry. That is the subject of this chapter: beauty in the eyes of an educated, orthodox, Christian nun in the seventh century. Once we know a little about seventh-century beauty generally, we need specifics. Which particular elements of a poem would she have seen as beautiful? As a response to that question, a review of Bede's reading and tastes comprises chapters two through four. The last four chapters cover Bede's *Hymn to Aethelthryth*. If all that sounds

---

2. See Hollis, "Barking's Monastic School," 33–55. The Barking *liber* or *libellus* treated of the conversion of the East Saxons, one of the *gens Saxonum*, as the *HE* treated of the *gens Anglorum*.

tentative, provisional, and imaginative, it is. Still, it may provoke some interesting questions.

First, if indeed our nun of Barking sought out Beauty in Bede's verse, what might *beautiful* mean to her in regard to poetry? Did she conceive of Beauty as an observable phenomenon, something that she could segregate out of a poem like a vein of gold in a rock? Or was beauty just a word—a nominal category—something everyone says but no one really understands? If Beauty is real, where do we find it? Is it a quality found in things like paintings or poems, or is it a capacity of an observer? If Beauty is in the eye of an observer, is it intuitive or learned? Second, if Beauty is not real but nominal, then perhaps we can discover how people talked about it. Yet we find that, although there is a vague core of meaning, definitions change. The term *beauty* has to be treated in historical context. The term might be like an evolving organism, adapting as aesthetic opinions changed. If it was, then how could we fix on one definition, or even several? Would our nun of Barking have a historical sense of the shifting meaning of *beauty*? Or the shift in meaning between languages? Even if *beauty* were sufficiently defined, would it be translatable across languages and cultures, or is it semantically limited by them? Third, if both philosophical and philological descriptions of Beauty are elusive, then is there a way to recover a lived experience of Beauty?[3] We seem so far removed from the early Middle Ages that we rely on a simulacrum that we have built from what few shards survive. It is like trying to navigate a video game with most of the polygons missing. How would recovery of an experience of Beauty be possible with such partial evidence? Fourth, picking a point in history and in geography to solve these problems of shifting meaning might be an illusion to calm our fear of uncertainty. Would our composite nun of Barking be unrecognizable to Bede? Her reading must be reconstructed. But how? The extensive library of Wearmouth-Jarrow is a library of the imagination, its contents having

---

3. See Carruthers, *The Experience of Beauty in the Middle Ages*, which has shaped much of the following discussion.

been assembled over the centuries by scholars and source-hunters. Works known to have been at Jarrow have since lost their historical and local peculiarity in the necessary compromises of modern, printed editions.[4] Moreover, whatever the putative training of our nun, she would need interests, desires, or expectations to drive her reading. They would likely coordinate with the interests and desires that drive a person to lifelong service to Christ. But an ideal reader constructed by a twenty-first-century academic would probably look a lot like an academic. (Could we imagine, for example, an ideal reader with whom we would disagree or whom we are incapable of understanding?) What then would justify the historicized characteristics of any proposed ideal reader? Is there a well-tried method for establishing such a reader?

Not only is the meaning of Beauty a conundrum, but so too is a method of analyzing the topic of beauty. Beauty in literature is usually treated as a province of aesthetics. However, it is impossible to know whether Bede or his contemporaries would have recognized aesthetics as a discrete area of inquiry. A thousand years later, Immanuel Kant initially thought it beyond the reach of philosophy.[5] Moreover, current topics in aesthetics range far beyond our seventh-century monastic quarry. Among these topics are aesthetic experience, a psychology of aesthetics, language and aesthetics, and the ideological function of aesthetics. These topics, each of which promotes a set of methodologies, range loosely around a set of fundamental questions that arise from complicated philosophical debates, many of which reach back centuries. To flit from one debate to another would be jejune; but to choose one debate and trace it

---

4. I am thinking of Katherine O'Brien O'Keeffe's important study, *Visible Song*. She reminds us "that a text exists in the world as a written object, that important elements of its meaning are fixed in the visual array by which it is presented on a page, and that each realization of the text depends on a unique act of scribal repetition," p. 190.

5. Kivy, "Introduction: Aesthetics Today," pp. 1–4. In 1790, Kant published a critique of aesthetic judgment, part one of his *Critique of Judgment*. The topic is too vast for anything but a cursory overview.

backwards in time would risk excluding much medieval material—Biblical commentaries, for example, or the Catholic liturgy—that is largely beyond the scope of current aesthetic debates. What makes angels beautiful? What is attractive about the bride in the Song of Songs? Can terrible suffering be beautiful? Even a study of Latin or Old English terms that imply aesthetic qualities is of little help. The terms are strangely disposed in early medieval texts and do not map from one language to another. Bede called hexameter meter *pulcher* 'beautiful', the same word used in Genesis 41:26 to describe the cows of Pharaoh's dream. Beautiful cows? Surely, one use of *pulcher* had a bearing on another, but what Modern English term would connect the syntax of hexameters to attractive bovines?[6] To make sense of that wide semantic scope, we would have to presume a deep connection between aesthetics and Scripture; but that presumption would confound contemporary academic departmentalization. It would be more in keeping with current academic trends to apply poetics to Scripture, to treat Scripture as another text to be explicated aesthetically—the Bible *as literature*, for example. All this being said, there is nevertheless a fruitful line of inquiry into Bede's aesthetic practices that focuses on religious devotion, even if that line of inquiry is not strictly in the province of modern aesthetics. Furthermore, that line seems particularly germane because of the *locus in quo*, the monasteries in which Bede prayed and taught.

Bede lived a very traditional and conservative life. It was a peaceful life of order and repetition, governed by a complicated monastic rule. That life still exists today, and if we were to stretch a golden thread between Bede's past and our present, its modern end would fix firmly to a contemporary monastery. As in many monasteries today, Bede's monastic life was shaped by a visual and aural aesthetic. Based ultimately on Scripture, that aesthetic was derived in part from the Magisterium—the tradition of Scriptural commentary and Church teaching that was integral to a formal life of Catholic faith. The Magisterium is not a list of doctrine and rules, but rather

---

6. Compare Carruthers, *Beauty*, pp. 181–87.

a vast sea of revealed truths that come in the shape of debates, investigations, proposals, and stipulations that help to prepare a Christian for his own encounter with Christ. A Catholic's encounter with Scripture is tutored by the encounters of inspired readers who preceded him. It was therefore within a monastic environment informed by the Magisterium that Bede found his audience. The limits of that audience's expectations were drawn by Scripture, Catholic tradition, Church liturgy, the Breviary, hymns, homilies, and the Latin and vernacular literature they read. Bede was not writing for modern, secular scholars in research universities, but for devoted men and women religious in Britain.

This chapter describes an aesthetic common to that monastic environment; it is generally known as the Great Theory of Beauty. The divine attributes of order and due proportion sit at its center, and they help to define an ideal reader whose literary tastes can be suggested by assessing early medieval reading habits.[7] As we will see, those tastes were considered mature if they confirmed the valuations of order and due proportion that had been observed in nature and in Scripture. Bede, who observed and described the order of the tides, of time, of the Latin language, and of English ecclesiastical history, was devoted in his intellectual and spiritual efforts to natural, right, and just order.[8]

The Great Theory: Greek

The story of Beauty begins in Greece. We are concerned here with a story, not with historical fact, and the story gets retold from

---

7. Constructing an ideal reader is not the same as defining an extant audience. For the latter, see Gunn, *Bede's Historiae*, chap. 1.

8. Rowan Williams, recently Archbishop of Canterbury, writes that Bede's historical works "are part of a greater intellectual enterprise, the unfolding of God's enterprise in creation itself, in the progression of natural times and seasons . . ."; "Introduction," in *Bede's Ecclesiastical History*, trans. Williams and Ward, p. 6. See especially Thacker, "Bede and the Ordering of Understanding," pp. 37–63.

generation to generation. It becomes the grounds of our continuing inquiry into Beauty. This story shapes our encounter with art; it tutors us in our efforts toward refined, sophisticated appreciation of literature; it is codified in books, in the layout of museums, and in the college curriculum. Very, very generally, it goes like this. In early Greek life, beauty was not an autonomous idea, but, as Umberto Eco says, was "always associated with other values, like 'moderation,' 'harmony,' and 'symmetry.'"[9] In part, this multiple association is reflected in vocabulary. The words used for *beautiful* in demotic Greek are *eueidēs*, meaning well-shaped, and *kalos*, meaning good and beautiful. Earlier Attic Greek distinguished between *kalos* and *agathos*—the former meaning physically beautiful, the latter morally beautiful—but in later Greek the two terms elide into *kalos*, which comes to mean both good and beautiful. Another term that arises is *kalokagathía*, a combination of *kalos*, *kai* (and), and *agathos*. So in the Greek language, beauty is literally synonymous with morality.[10]

Demotic Greek is the language of the New Testament and thereby influences Christian conceptions of beauty—or at least limits how Christians can express beauty. Greek theories of beauty tend to describe it as a bridge between the body and soul. For Plato, and equally for Sappho and Praxiteles, beauty lay in both the physical form and the goodness of the soul.[11] Plato explains that relationship in his *Phaedrus*. The soul experiences true Beauty before it is embodied here on earth. When a man sees the beauty of the earth, Plato writes, he "is transported with the recollection of the true beauty." True Beauty is somehow innate, built into every human soul. The heavenly light of Beauty even shines in earthly bodies. Plato writes that these lights "are seen through a glass dimly."[12] This idea would resurface in Paul's First Letter to the Corinthians 1:12: "For now we see through a glass darkly, but then face to face." (Paul

---

9. Eco, *History of Beauty*, p. 37.
10. See De Bruyne, *Études*, 2:387. In this paragraph, I capitalize Beauty when it refers to a Platonic form.
11. Eco, *History of Beauty*, p. 45.
12. Plato, "Phaedrus," in *The Dialogues of Plato*, trans. Jowett, vol. 7, p. 126.

was speaking in Greek to Greek-speaking philosophers.) The soul finds pleasure in Beauty, because in looking even on the dim light of earthly beauty, it returns, as if on wings, to the illuminated condition of its origin. The metaphor of Beauty as light, we should note, is an ancient association carried resolutely into Christian hymnody. St. Ambrose of Milan would use that association as the governing metaphor of his famous hymn, "Splendor paternae gloriae" (the radiance of the Father's glory). God's glory is "Light of light and source of all light, / Daylight, illuminating days."[13] Prudentius, whom Bede calls "nobilissimus scolasticus" (most celebrated scholar, *DAM*, 153), would use the image of a monk waking at dawn as a metaphor for the soul waking to Christ. Above Bede's tomb in Durham, cast in light-reflective metal, are words from his commentary on Revelation: "Christ is the morning star who when the night of this world is past brings to his saints the promise of the light of life and opens everlasting day."

So what does the Greek soul perceive besides light? Primarily order, proportion, and harmony. Pythagoras sowed the seeds of this idea. He held that the origin of all things lay in number. Number and order are distinguished from Chaos, a distinction that was assured by heavenly protectors. Harmony and order were under the protection of Apollo, and Chaos was associated with Dionysus, a dyad famously pursued by Nietzsche. Pythagoras found numerical order everywhere in nature. He listened to the sounds of variously sized hammers as they struck anvils and wondered why smaller hammers had a higher pitch. He thereby correlated pitch with weight, demonstrating that the world is not as discrete as our senses suggest, but that even sound and weight are subject to a common order. He then developed his numerical theory of musical notes, which exist both as effects of specific physical objects such as flutes and lyre strings, and as mathematical ratios. In other words, abstract mathematics describes harmonies in physical bodies. The abstract world and the physical world were governed and correlated by a

---

13. Ambrose, *Hymnes*, p. 185; trans. White, *ECLP*, p. 47.

mathematical order. Given a string of length x, ½ x is an octave, ¼ x is a fifth, and so on. This proportion obtains for the length of a column of wind in a flute or a trumpet. It also underlies the difference between the weights of strings on a lyre.[14] Proportions also govern sound and vision in Greek art. The mathematical proportions between the notes in a column of wind are the same proportions one finds between the columns of a Greek temple. And they were applied to the human form in the pursuit of beautiful statues. The Romans later adopted this notion of a governing mathematical order. Illustrated in a famous drawing by Leonardo, Vitruvius set the proportions of the ideal human body. Given a body of the height x, ¼ x is the height of the torso, 1/10 x is the height of the head, and so forth. Art and sculpture present idealizations of form, idealized according to divine proportion. One finds another description of the numerical order of the universe in Cicero's *De re publica*, specifically in the Dream of Scipio Africanus that was commented upon by Macrobius. From the Greeks comes the fundamental aesthetic principle of the Middle Ages: a perfect, rational, abstract, describable mathematical order underlies all physical reality.

Pythagoras said that Zeus gave order to the cosmos, a just measure and limit, too. Number, proportion, and harmony governed the disposition and movement of the cosmos. The Greeks therefore believed, and rightly, that the interrelation of bodies can be described mathematically. Bede, the scientist who reorganized the calendar to better accord with his astronomical observations, knew it, too. So would our nun of Barking. Juvencus, a Spanish poet who influenced Bede, described the Magi as "a people far away that knows the secrets of the rising sun. / Skilled at noting the risings and settings of the stars."[15] Science was considered beautiful. Its beauty and the beauty of art reflected the orderly, proportional, and harmonious movement and disposition of creation. And it is this claim that is

---

14. For an Anglo-Saxon like Caedmon to make and tune a lyre, he would have to have known something about such proportions.
15. Lines 224–25; trans. White, *ECLP*, p. 36.

known as the Great Theory of Beauty.[16] The Pythagorean view was distilled into a belief that could be carried easily from generation to generation: that the numerical order of the universe governs both the physical world and the human soul.

Now, while mathematical government of the physical world will be no surprise to modern readers, mathematical government of the soul is not so well appreciated. We tend to think of our minds and our imaginations as unfettered, free to roam at will. But in the Pythagorean view, the mathematical order of the universe does not stop at our eyes; the mind is not immune from physical laws. This means that the mathematical harmonies outside of us correlate to mathematical harmonies inside of us. (So the closer your thoughts correlate to the structure of observable nature, the more beautiful they are.) Pythagoreans thought that the universe was composed of intercalated spheres, like Russian dolls. Each of the seven spheres of the universe makes a particular note as it spins, and the result is the music of the spheres. That music, a harmony of the universe, also governs the human soul, if one is capable of hearing it well. This view influenced Milton and Shakespeare and helped to explain the relation between music (or meter) and feeling. Why should the musical intervals of a minor key feel sad? Or a dactyl feel fast? As an extreme example, Eco reports, "Pythagoras is said to have restored the self-control of a drunken adolescent by having him listen to a melody in the Hypophrygian mode with a spondaic rhythm."[17] Modes and rhythms describe the seriated disposition of sound, disposed proportionally according to precise algorithms. They would come to be used as the basis of Gregorian chant as well as the songs of the Beach Boys.

As the Middle Ages dawned, Greek convictions about beauty traveled via Plato and the Neoplatonists, through Greek translations of Scripture, through commentary, into Rome, Latin Catholicism, and the Renaissance.[18] With some modification, these convictions

---

16. Begbie, "Created Beauty," p. 20.
17. Eco, *History of Beauty*, p. 63.
18. De Bruyne, *Études*, p. xvii.

correlated well with the revelation of Scripture. Scotus writes concerning the homology between music, language, and nature:

> the beauty of the whole established universe consists of a marvelous harmony of like and unlike in which the diverse genera and various species and the different orders of substances and accidents are composed into an ineffable unity.[19]

Here and elsewhere the visually beautiful and the sonically beautiful are connected to a greater ontological harmony. Again, that harmony subsists in the divine order, which Christians describe as the *Lôgos*, Christ. Christ, no longer Apollo, provides a governing mathematical order, one that also governs music. Paulinus compared Christ to a lyre or cithara, as did Aldhelm; Honorius of Autun said that the universe is organized like a giant cithara. And the analogy goes further. Just as the order of the universe is dispersed into physical species, so is the order of the universe dispersed into certain harmonies, rhythms, and meters, each of which has a particular effect on the soul. Not just Hypophrygian spondees, but iambs and trochees, too, affect the soul—a claim that we will return to shortly.

The wide variety of specific effects results from difference, not similarity. Scotus and Honorius are not claiming that each note is homologous to the whole—a microcosm of the macrocosm, if you will—but that each plays its different part, like differently tuned strings. The idea of harmony is not to force everything to be the same, but instead to coordinate a variety of opposites and contraries. Diversity is the key. After all, if every note on a piano were a Middle C, there would be no music. Paul writes in 1 Corinthians 12:4–6, "Now there are diversities of gifts, but the same spirit. And there are differences of administrations, but the same Lord. And there are diversities of operations, but it is the same God which worketh all in all." Wise man and fool, dark and light, good and bad, rich and poor, loyalty and betrayal, love and hate—each is coordinated and balanced within the whole. Prudentius, one of Bede's favorite

---

19. *Periphysion* 6.1, in Thiessen, *Theological Aesthetics*, p. 72.

poets, calls it harmonious disorder; Gregory the Great disposes his *Pastoral Care* according to the varieties of human nature and their opposites; Prudentius's *Psychomachia* is arranged similarly. Opposites coalesce in Christ, the center of all harmony. Paulinus of Nola—student of Ausonius of Bordeaux, a contemporary of St. Augustine, and a poet known to Bede—describes God the Father hanging his lyre ("cithara") on the Cross.[20] That lyre is Christ, who produces "innumeris uno modulamine linguis, / respondentque deo paribus noua carmina neruis" (one melody out of innumerable tongues, / While the new songs respond to God with matching strings).[21] Harmony requires variety and diversity.

What does that necessary diversity and variety imply for poetic judgment? One thing it means is that a medieval work of religious art may be trying to achieve fidelity to a universal harmony of differences, to a grand act of balance. While modern readers are conditioned to seek unity, a central theme, medieval literary texts may consciously work against unity, purposefully striving for contradictions and contraries, and multitudes of insurmountable cruces. Seamus Heaney promoted this aesthetic in his Nobel address. Good poetry, he said, does not preach a theme; instead, it comprehends contradictions.[22] We should therefore revel in the indissoluble contradictions of an Anglo-Saxon poem. To take an example, Michael Roberts writes concerning the Late Antique poet Ausonius, "The brilliance of an expression is derived from its setting, from the relationship of equivalence or opposition it bears to its fellows, from the play of variation and concinnity that invests it with a multi-faceted jewel-like quality."[23] Early medieval poetry, or some of it at least, sought to balance opposites. Just as a painter will balance her colors—orange with blue, red with green, and so forth—so will a poet balance her lines, images, and stanzas. Roberts calls this the

---

20. Paulinus of Nola, poem 20, line 51; CSEL 30.2: p. 145.
21. Paulinus, poem 20, lines 60–66; trans. White, *ECLP*, p. 63.
22. Heaney, *The Redress of Poetry*.
23. Roberts, *The Jeweled Style*, p. 20.

jeweled style, and he illustrates it through many of the poets that Bede read and taught.[24]

As an example of the necessary antitheses of this style, one might profitably read Chaucer not to seek out a single theme, but to observe the interplay of contradiction and contrariety, and to draw from one's observations some *sentence*, or meaning: Palamon and Arcite's animal urges contend against their idealization of civilized order; the Prioress's provincial superficiality and vulgar anti-Semitism contend against her deep, honest devotion; the Miller's rustic simplicity and strong *moralitée* contend against the Knight's romantic sophistication and superficial *moralitée*. These oppositions are harmonized but never dissolved. Not only characteristics, but also motifs, images, and connotations can be balanced. *Beowulf*'s funeral pyre on land is balanced by Scyld's funeral on water; the cold, wet monsters of its first half with the hot, dry monster of the second; a young, brash warrior with an aged, measured king. Some have called this balance of contradictions irony. Irony, like the Greek stock character *Eiron* from which it derives, is another way of describing a reader's observation of contradictions and contrariety unknown to the participants in a story. We see contradictions that they do not. As Christian readers observe the contentions and contradictions playing out in a text, they can better appreciate and reconcile the comprehensive harmonies of creation. Composing by means of contradictions seems to be a guiding aesthetic principle for Bede.

What motivates a desire for comprehensive contradiction? Postmodern readers, steeped in the methods of scientific inquiry, might be satisfied by an explanation of serial, efficient causes (that is, by tracing a series of efficient causes to an origin). An efficient explanation demonstrates that something is the case because an earlier stage made it so. But that explanation only defers the question of final cause or purpose, so that an efficient explanation becomes turtles all

---

24. Roberts, *The Jeweled Style*. There is a direct correlation between color and rhetoric in the vocabulary of style during the early Middle Ages. See his chap. 2.

the way down. To use a mechanical example, one could explain the movement of billiard balls thus: a black ball was hit by a white ball because a white ball was hit by a cue, which was moved by an arm, and so on. But a chain of efficient causes does not explain the larger purpose of the movement of billiards: finally, they move because that's how you play a game of billiards.[25] An efficient explanation of literary change, while comprehensible and certainly useful, was not sufficient to Christian Latin poets who sought to orient their verse to a larger purpose. It wasn't enough to know that you write a hexameter a certain way because your teacher wrote it that way, as her teacher did, and so on back to the first poet. There had to be some larger justification to tradition. The Great Theory offered a final cause, a blueprint: namely, the purposeful hand of God, which disposes opportunities for change in a rational, orderly way.

Furthermore, because Christianity was not seen as a newcomer to the world, but as a revelation of the world's fundamental order since the beginning, a mechanical chain of causes could be viewed as part of a comprehensive plan. One footprint follows another not only because that's how feet work, but also because whoever made the prints had a destination in mind. Changes in poetic form were more than a chain of pagan causes and Christian effects. There was a grand purpose to changes in poetry and poetic form. The Roman poet Proba wrote an account of the Gospels using only hemistichs (half-lines) from Virgil. Her poem is not a pagan poem, although it uses Virgil exclusively, any more than Hadrian's Wall is a field of stones. Virgil is a material and efficient cause of her poem, but not a final cause, which is Christian devotion. Like pagan stones in a church wall, pagan literary forms such as the hexameter and colors such as the chiasmus provide material that can be reused for Christian devotion. While other, less influential arguments rejected all pagan poetic devices entirely, such arguments failed to dominate

---

25. Cf. Augustine, *DDC*, II, xxxiv. Bede may have known this passage through Rufinus; see Ray, "Who Did Bede Think He Was?," p. 24, n. 36. On causality, see Falcon, "Aristotle on Causality."

Christian thought at its highest registers because of the overwhelming conviction that the final cause of Christian poetry—that is, divine order—trumps efficient and material causes. To see divine order in Virgil is not to co-opt Virgil to Christian use, but to recognize the divine in all things, to find God's beauty even in the songs of pagans. Nevertheless, the *translatio literarum* was not simply a matter of making an argument about cause.

Poetic form could not be cloven from its pagan past. Traditional, pagan religion in the Roman Empire was long associated with particular literary forms, and literary interrogations of Roman life had progressively shaped literary form. Those interrogations and pagan religion comprise in part the history of a genre, a history invoked each time the genre is employed. A pastoral poem, for example, invokes Theocritus, Lucretius, and Virgil as well as Pan; by doing so, it invites readers to consider more generally the role of poetry in mediating past and present, human will and divine caprice.[26] Christians sought poetic expression within the same legacy of classical languages and literary form, but sufficiently distinct from it to constitute themselves as a *tertium genus*. So the generic invocations of something like the pastoral, steeped as they are in pagan tradition, were seen to conflict with Christian content. Jerome therefore reacted strongly against using these forms in the liturgy,[27] and Jacques Fontaine writes that pagan poetry appeared to early Christians as "a sort of bastion of Satanism" due to its mores, mythic content, and vanity.[28] Indeed, one constant in the early production of Christian Latin poetry was a debate about the propriety of particular literary forms to the expression of Christian faith. The *loci classici* of this debate are well known—Jerome, Gregory, and so forth. The debate is not superficial; it proceeds from the Greek idea that content is

---

26. Breed, *Pastoral Inscriptions*, pp. 95–97.
27. Mohrmann, *Liturgical Latin*, p. 42.
28. "une sorte de bastion satanique"; Fontaine, "Le poète chrétien nouveau psalmiste," p. 131. Eduard Norden writes that the war between Greek classicism and Christianity was considered a war between form and content. Norden, *Die antike Kunstprosa*, 2:458.

always congruent with form. The external, physical, written ode, for example, resolves "die innere Öde" (an inner desolation).[29] Accordingly, the internal disposition of the poet to transcendent reality was inextricable from the formal particulars of external, formal expression. Christians who worried about the formative influence of classical poetry attempted to distinguish internal disposition from its external form, in part by imagining an idea to exist independently of its Hellenistic clothing.[30] In its nascent and unformed state, the newly independent inner idea was conceived of as effecting new literary forms.[31] At the same time, older forms were being reshaped by Christian poets. (Form and content, of course, are not so easily separable, but such is the bane of a simplified history of beauty.)

While Augustan poetry was being imitated and partially transformed in this manner, the stylistic particulars of the Gospels were being carefully scrutinized. Educated Christians saw that the literary style of the Gospels was relatively unpolished, but they believed it to be a vehicle for Truth—and thereby for Beauty. This apparent contradiction between polished pagan Latin and rough Scriptural Latin strained the rationalizing capacity of educated Christians. After all, one's social status was in part based on the ability to speak and write at the highest registers. And the highest register of speech was poetry. Juvencus writes, "Multi sunt quos studiorum saecularium disciplina per poeticas magis delicias et carminum voluptates oblectat" (There are many for whom the special delight of secular education lies in the charms of poetry and the pleasures of verse).[32] But how to speak like a Christian in a world where polished Latin marked

---

29. Norden, *Die antike Kunstprosa*, 2:459.
30. Ibid., 2:466. This sartorial figure distinguishing between the internal disposition (body) and external form (clothing) can be seen in Bede's description of Aethelthryth, whose fine clothes cannot mask her humble, corporeal sanctity.
31. Stotz, *Handbuch zur lateinischen Sprache des Mittelalters*, vol. 1, §10.5, p. 37: a new *Gefühlswelt* 'emotional world' and *Denkweise den Christen* 'Christian form of thought' needed a new Latinity, a sociolect.
32. Friesen, "The *opus geminatum* and Anglo-Saxon Literature," p. 132.

status? It was not obvious—nor is it today. There were various responses to differences in style between Christian and pagan Latin. Minucius Felix and Lactantius avoided any Christian vocabulary or idiom entirely, while Tertullian did otherwise.[33] Between these positions, and in something of an apologia, St. Jerome observed that among all the Evangelists, Luke was the most erudite writer in the most proper of styles.[34] He joined in wider praise of an Evangelical style that was considered to have achieved a studied artlessness. Paul's Evangelical style was akin to Greek epistolary style, which was directed capaciously at an audience that is *idiōtēs tō logo, àll' où tē gnōsei* (rude in speech yet not in knowledge).[35] In this very important Christian transformation of Latin style during the fourth and fifth centuries, Paul's carefully wrought artlessness was observed to mask a profound knowledge of rhetoric and a careful handling of allegory and verbal ornament. Similar observations of Paul's style were made by Paulinus of Nola, Augustine, Origen, and Eusebius. John Chrysostom (the name means "golden-mouthed") recommends Paul's style as a model for medieval sermons, and Jerome sees something of Paul in Seneca's style.[36] Studied simplicity became the basis of a style that Christians appreciated and cultivated. It is commonly called *sermo simplex*. Ambrose and Augustine widened that appreciation to many of the simpler styles in Scripture. In his prose, Bede seems to have been influenced by the studied simplicity of Evangelical style; his poems explore the styles of Scripture a little more deeply.

But the compromise with Augustan Latin that the Evangelical style represents did not erase the allure of Virgil, Ovid, or Horace.

---

33. Mohrmann, *Liturgical Latin*, pp. 47–49.
34. Cited in Norden, *Die antike Kunstprosa*, 2:482.
35. Ibid., 2:492, citing 2 Corinthians 11:6.
36. Ibid., 2:501. Note that the particulars of Greek style were available to Theodore and Hadrian, whose Latinity shaped all subsequent Anglo-Latin authors. See Bischoff and Lapidge, *Biblical Commentaries*; and Law, *The Insular Latin Grammarians*, p. 9. Ambrose called Paul's style "historic-historico stilo"; Ambrose, *Lucam*, p. 8; Prudentius calls it a sacred style, "sacri . . . stili"; *Contra Symm.* 2.60.

Neither was it sufficient for classroom purposes, since some of the most important Biblical commentaries had been written by highly polished rhetors—Jerome and Augustine especially. By the seventh century, Roman Christianity dominated the upper echelons of Latin society, no longer the religion of a persecuted minority. For his classroom, Bede replaced with examples from Scripture the pagan Roman exempla that stood like busted statues in handbooks of Latin grammar. But he did not reject the classical tradition. A recognition of God's plenty (of the varied and diverse world of letters), an appreciation for the beautiful language of classical Latin poetry, and a respect for the place of Roman and Greek traditions kept a wide variety of literary styles in play during the seventh century. The Irish would explore the baroque potential of Latin, yielding the Hiberno-Latin style (also called Hisperic or Hermeneutic). Its many convolutions continue to amaze and frustrate Latinists. At the same time, Augustan style provided Christian writers with the ability to write affective, resplendent texts. Hilary of Poitiers wrote in the fourth century that "a beautiful and dignified style gives honor to God."[37] Monastic scriptoria copied classical Latin poems, amid raging debates about their place in a Christian monastery. Those debates reached the height of their partisanship in the fourth and fifth centuries, when they were frozen into written polemics, inscribed into manuscripts, and bound into codices. Those codices made their way into transalpine Europe and into monastery libraries.

Thereafter, whatever the state of conflict actually was on the ground, the textual record remained frozen at a consistently high pitch. Combatants reached for their old books and perpetually wielded tradition. Newly converted portions of northern Europe shaped similar debates by means of ancient arguments found on the shelves of their libraries. In some instances, a portion of those arguments was either inappropriate or immaterial to the conflicts arising during the Christianization of northern Europe. This said, a caveat:

---

37. Mohrmann, *Liturgical Latin*, p. 49, who cites Hilary of Poitiers, *Tractatus super psalmos*, p. 49.

the easy polarities of historical summary lead me inappropriately to set ideational content against literary form. Neither is possible without the other, and neither is sufficiently fixed at any point in time to be used properly as comparanda. Moreover, the tension between physical form and intellectual content is always at issue in the upper registers of Latin poetry, Christian or pagan. Literary interest in that tension descends from classical poets like Virgil and Catullus, whose interrogation of literary form in the expression of ideas is well known. Bede would take up the question of form in his *Hymn to Aethelthryth*. Questions of form and content also pervade medieval Christian Latin poetry—and our own.

The Great Theory: Latin Christianity

The next stage in the story of beauty jumps a century and assumes an untroubled continuity throughout late Antiquity. That said, the Great Theory made its way into seventh-century Britain in the writings of the Latin fathers, and it was also observable in Christian Latin poetry. But not all of it is good. One of its most distinguished chroniclers writes that Christian Latin poetry "exhibits an immense variety"; it "has come down to us in a vast bulk, in which good and bad are mingled, the tentative along with the complete achievement."[38] Well-made orthodox poetry comprises only a small portion of that bulk, one that survived barbarian fire, time, and the censorship of fashion. Yet again a smaller portion held the constant attention of devout Christians. That smallest of portions begins and ends with the reality of Christ, in whom Christians live and move and have their being. David Lyle Jeffrey writes that Christian readers acknowledge "the persistent presence of Christ in the literary imagination down through the centuries, even while candidly confirming the evident complexity of response to that presence by individual writers."[39] The presence of Christ is a difficult gauge by which to measure literary

---

38. Raby, "Preface to the First Edition," *CLP*, n. p.
39. Jeffrey and Maillet, *Christianity and Literature*, p. 28.

quality; nevertheless, some Christians consider the spiritual sensitivity of a reader to be a viable critical faculty. Among other things, it is a means of uncovering abstractions that are approachable through the reading process. Grace, salvation, sacrifice, charity, love—none of these can be sensed. Although one can see examples of love, love itself is invisible. In seeking after invisible and intangible realities, medieval Christian Latin poetry, Jean-Yves Tilliette explains, "takes up a project that is not only aesthetic but cognitive in nature—that of revealing objects that are inaccessible in rational discourse."[40] Christian poetry both reveals reality, by making visible what is invisible (like grace), and reproduces reality, by imitating the world around us. In the Great Theory, Beauty resides in the transcendent perfection to which revealed objects refer: a poem is beautiful insofar as it participates in that transcendent Beauty. Conversely, participation makes the abstract physical. Truth, like Beauty, is an ideal form that exists prior to and outside the world. We cannot see Truth, but Truth is brought into physical being through a poem: the poem's very words connect Truth to physical existence. By means of her eyes or ears, a reader senses a physical word, a sign, and through a complex of mental and corporeal reactions, recognizes within that word traces of a transcendent form, a transcendental signified. Somehow, she can see Truth dimly in the word "truth." And when she does, Truth makes "truth" beautiful.

The relationship between a word and a transcendent form is metaphorical—a *carrying across* (Gk. *meta* 'across' + *phoréin* 'to carry'). A reader's intellection is carried across from sign to signified. She knows that the word "truth" is really just scratches on a page, and that its meaning somehow resides outside of it. Open to meaning, she revels in metaphor. Metaphor, a carrying-across of intellection, becomes, in the words of Peter Dale Scott, "the highest available mode of knowing."[41] St. Augustine of Hippo writes that though

---

40. Tilliette, "Verse Style," p. 259.
41. Scott, "Rhetorical and Symbolic Ambiguity," p. 127. On Christian Platonism generally, see Arnou, "Platonisme des Pères," pp. 2258–2392.

the Christian reader might delight in words, "it is a mark of good and distinguished minds to love the truth within words and not the words."[42] A discerning Christian reader can somehow see truth inside the word, and truth carries the prepared mind toward God. Discernment of Truth requires knowledge of how signs work.

Calvin Kendall has described clearly Bede's attempt to distinguish means of intellection in signs, symbols, and figures.[43] If a connection between a sign and the transcendent divine can be made, the connection brings the reader toward Beauty. Reading and writing are thereby a mediation of the abstract world, a bridge, a way of shaping access to the transcendent. While reading is about moving from sign to signified, writing works the other way round: Geoffrey of Vinsauf, the thirteenth-century author of the *Poetria nova*, a handbook on writing and reading, described "poetry's capacity to bring the superhuman reality of archetypal ideas into the perceptible world."[44] The physical words of books and songs are a sort of passage wherein transcendent realities are translated into sounds, and vice versa. When one accepts that premise—that literature is a bridge to a transcendent reality—then the arts become a means rather than an end, but no less important for their service. The author manipulates words, but in doing so he manipulates the bridge to the transcendent. It is not enough for an author to have good intentions: because all relationships to the transcendent are mediated precisely, an author is responsible to his readers to use words correctly, to properly lead a reader through language to the transcendent. But there are bad authors, and the medium can sometimes distort the message.

How trustworthy are media? Notwithstanding Augustine's influential discussion of language and signs, much medieval thinking

---

42. Augustine, *DDC*, IV, xi, p. 136; trans. Robertson.
43. Kendall, "The Responsibility of Auctoritas," esp. pp. 112–19.
44. Scott, "Rhetorical and Symbolic Ambiguity," p. 127. See also Stock, *The Implications of Literacy*, esp. chap. 4. A great deal has been written on neo-Platonic ideas of reading, and it is not the place here to survey the arguments; others have done that much better than I could. My aim is far more general.

about aesthetics concerned the visual arts. "Pulchra sunt quae visa placent" (Those things are beautiful which can please the sight), Aquinas writes.[45] However, the Carolingians were generally cautious about images, thinking them ill-defined and non-functional.[46] This was partly the case with Alcuin of York, the great court scholar of the Carolingians. His student, the ninth-century monk and author Hraban Maur, warned that the pleasure one gets from viewing an image is potentially misleading, vain, and false (although Hraban is known for his acrostic poems overlaid on stunning paintings).[47] An image may mislead, but writing was thought to direct our understanding more clearly.[48] Why? The immediate sensation provoked by images was decidedly worldly (images represent things of this world). While a painting of a tree might look like a particular tree, the word "tree" does not. Like the world, images are mutable—they belong to a changing reality. Because they are not permanent (like forms or numbers), images are insufficient grounds for wisdom.[49] Conflicts over the propriety of images and signs were thus part of Bede's intellectual environment. The Iconoclastic Controversy during Bede's lifetime raged over the proper role of images in approaching the Godhead.

Although images might deceive, sometimes they did not. The Forms of the Good, the True, and the Beautiful to which some images referred were fixed in their mutual participation in God's perfection.[50] Thus, physical or worldly beauty could be a visual

---

45. Literally, "Beautiful are those, which having been seen, are pleasing." My thanks to William Roundy.
46. The terms are from Chase, "Alcuin's Grammar Verse," p. 146.
47. On the iconoclastic controversies and Hraban's responses, see Wilhelmy, "Die Entstehung von *De laudibus* im Spannungsfeld von Bilderstreit und Glaubenswahrheit," pp. 23–32; and Noble, *Images, Iconoclasm, and the Carolingians*, esp. chap. 3.
48. Chase, "Alcuin's Grammar Verse," p. 147.
49. See de Bruyne, *Études*, 1:195, who cites Alcuin.
50. Aertsen, "The Triad «True-Good-Beautiful»"; Assunto, *Die Theorie des Schönen im Mittelalter*, p. 40.

manifestation of Truth and Good, a vehicle to the transcendent. That view is still a living, competing part of Christian ideas about beauty. Well over a billion Christians are exposed to it every day in the liturgical language of worship. But physical beauty could also be an allurement to evil. Distinguishing between physical allure and transcendent appeal means developing discernment in matters of taste and matters of beauty. Taste is suspect when it focuses on that which is transitory and local. A desire for beauty seeks in a particular thing a window, a bridge, a passage to the invisible, abstract world. Eco writes that medieval beauty

> was concerned neither with the autonomy of art nor the autonomy of nature. It involved rather an apprehension of all the relations, imaginative and supernatural, subsisting between the contemplated object and a cosmos which opened on to the transcendent. It meant discerning in the concrete object an ontological reflection of, and a participation in, the being and the power of God.[51]

While a physical experience might seem perfect, in the theology of beauty we are describing, an experience of perfection is never physical. The beauty of numbers, for example, lies not in the physical strokes on the page, the written "3," but elsewhere, in the immaterial transcendent reality of Three. To continue the metaphor, there is in fact no such physical, worldly thing as Three; there are only numerals or signs—"3," "iii," "٣," "Γ"—that manifest Three to us, that make it physical so that we can see, hear, or feel Three. Importantly, a desire for beauty does not alienate the need for pleasant sensation; the two are intimately connected, just as transcendence inheres in the physical world.

Transcendent order inheres in the physical world: this claim is essential to the Great Theory. Accordingly, all revealed things can

---

51. Eco, *Art and Beauty in the Middle Ages*, p. 15. John Scotus Eriugena (b. 828), writing on the celestial hierarchy, says, "Visibiles formas, siue quas in natura rerum, siue quas in sanctissimis diuinae scripturae sacramentis contemplantur . . . inuisibilis pulchritudinis imaginationes esse"; cited in de Bruyne, *Études*, p. 192.

be fit within a mathematical order. Henry of Avranche explains the received Patristic position in terms of the Book of Wisdom (11:21),

> according to which God has organized everything *in mensura et numero et pondere*: the world created by God is thus . . . a metrical (*metrum id est mensura*) or rhythmical (*rithmus id est numerus*) poem, and the voice of the poet, because of the particular formal constraints imposed upon it, echoes that of the Almighty.[52]

Bede will use the same phrases in his *Commentary on the Apocalypse*.[53] The world is thus a poem, but conversely, with a just and measured arrangement of images, words, sounds, and meters, a poet makes manifest the divine order. As a *vates*, he speaks the language of divinity. He arranges words to reproduce a transcendent order, making physical the invisible world. As the natural order of the world around us reveals the divine, so does the correct order of words reveal transcendent reality. In early medieval art, order, structure, and pattern were not conceived of as arbitrary, man-made aspects of art, but as the very nature of existence that makes art possible. Art is drawn out of the order of the world, not placed on top of it. Observing and then abstracting the systematic organization of nature, the musician brings order to sound, the sculptor gives shape to clay, and the poet gives pattern to language. Generally speaking, a medieval Christian artist was less someone who escaped order, like a Beat poet, and more one who intuited the immanent, natural order, like a Romantic poet. In the literary arts, formal patterning in language was a mark of a higher order of communication, a way of participating more emphatically in the divine. For the insular arts of Britain, Robert Stevick has shown how thoroughly images and texts "embody formal features,

---

52. Tilliette, "Verse Style," pp. 260–61. Similarly, Assunto, *Die Theorie des Schönen im Mittelalter*, p. 16. See Rodriguez-Herrera, *Poeta Christianus*, p. 10: "Der Dichter (poeta, ποιητής) ist ein Schöpfer und eben deshalb genießt er eine gewisse Verwandtschaft mit dem Urschöpfer des Weltalls" (The poet is a creator and for that very reason enjoys a certain relationship with the primary creator of the universe).

53. See Holder, "The Feminine Christ," p. 110.

both extensive and comprehensive, crafted from management of quantities, whether in two-dimensional designs or in linear compositions."[54] These features were not considered alienable from good poetry; they characterized good poetry like counterpoint in a Bach fugue. As mathematics and geometry were (and are) seen as more purely descriptive of natural order, so too did symmetrical, geometric design in image and language illustrate more clearly divine order and harmony. Such verbal and visual order permeates the poetry of Bede.[55] In the temporal order of meter, in the symmetries and controlled imbalances of phrase and line, and in the management of antithetical sounds and images lies the kernel of Bede's literary aesthetic. Christ the *Lôgos* offers order to Bede's language.

The Great Theory attempts to connect Christian artistic expression with Christian faith. The order of reality is thought to subsist in God, who is *se ipsum esse*, as Aquinas says, Being itself. God is Being (*ego sum qui sum*, Exodus 3:14). Not *a* being, but Being, that which causes all to exist. Humanity, simply by virtue of existing, participates in that greater Being. The order of Being is called the *Lôgos*, which means "Christ," "the Word," "language," "logic," and "intellect." In other words, existence is ordered, not chaotic. Because that order extends throughout existence, all manifested order is homologous; conversely, all order participates in a common Being. By "order" is not understood an arbitrary Borgesian order, like the Emperor's encyclopedia, but something akin to mathematical order. One might imagine a pervasive, uniform, and regular order to be something like the mathematics behind chemistry and music, behind colors and language. Numbers are not God, but they are a disposition of Being in time and space. Nothing escapes such disposition; everything exists within an orderly system, which is a basic assumption of logical, rational, scientific thought. This larger

---

54. Stevick, "Hunting the Anglo-Saxon Aesthetic." In the same volume, John Hill explores the "aesthetic of Anglo-Saxon geometric art" in *The Dream of the Rood*.

55. See Caviness, "Images of Divine Order."

argument was available to Bede. Its clearest proponent, pseudo-Dionysius, was not available in Latin until 862, when John Scotus translated him. Dionysius's description of the idea of order behind the Great Theory should still be consulted, if only because the idea is too complicated to describe otherwise.

Dionysius argues that the Beautiful "reveals a universal structure of Being, which . . . is manifested and unfolded in the sensible world, in such a way that it plays the role of mediator between the idea and the sensible reality."[56] A beautiful poem, the Periodic Table of Elements, a Bach fugue—all are windows through which are revealed the universal, orderly structure of Being. Everything and everyone participates in Being through its temporal disposition. That temporal disposition is called the *Lôgos*. Thus, the argument runs, Christians seek the grounds of their own being in the Christian Scriptures, which reveal and share in the ordered reality of Christ. Faithful Christians do this because of a common desire to assimilate imperfect humanity to the perfection of the rational and natural *Lôgos*. *Lôgos* is central to the experience of Christian poetry, which in part is a recognition of rational form (*Lôgos* as logic) and humane content (*Lôgos* as the suffering and salvific Christ) in patterned speech (*Lôgos* as language). Some version of this aesthetic theory runs from Antiquity to the present day. I contend that it undergirds the horizon of expectation of Bede's Christian audiences as they read his poems in the cloister and in the classroom. Of course, it was not the only aesthetic theory available to antique and medieval readers, and in some periods and for some authors it was not even in play. But it was pertinent to Bede and to our imaginary nun of Barking.

Modern readers tend to be dissuaded from the pertinence of this view for a number of reasons. One is simply that it is impossibly abstract, far removed from the act of poetic composition. Yet one can write, compose, paint, and sculpt contemporary art without being able to articulate fully the *Zeitgeist* or Foucault's episteme or the regnant

---

56. Koutras, "The Beautiful According to Dionysius," p. 32. A helpful translation of all of Dionysius's known works is by Luibheid, *Pseudo-Dionysius*.

ideology. Another reason is far more important, and concerns the role of the Great Theory in our own assessment of the poetry of Bede. Bede's reputation as a poet seems to have had its ups and downs, something that would be unlikely if his poems resonated so well with a dominant aesthetic. So we need to ask whether or not Bede was a good poet. Earlier, modern opinions of Bede as a poet, described in the Preface above, held that he was not especially good; he was competent, if derivative. That view changed significantly when Michael Lapidge gave his Jarrow Lecture in 1993. Lapidge pointed out how popular Bede was in the Middle Ages, and then opined, "Bede was a poet of great refinement and subtlety." Lapidge compared Bede to George Herbert, saying that both possessed what Eliot called a "masterly simplicity."[57] (Do we see traces here of the Evangelical style?) Lapidge also praised Bede's "distinctive poetic voice." While that is a quality I prize in poets, too, Lapidge raised an important question: would Bede aspire to a distinctive poetic voice? Richard Sharpe thinks he did not. Sharpe writes of Bede that "the notion of a personal style was quite alien to him."[58] The autobiographical impulse of a distinctive style might compromise his humility, real or pretended. Notwithstanding my untutored instincts, Lapidge has rightly compelled us to ask whether or to what degree Bede would have prized individuation as a component of style. And that points up a modern prejudice that filters our appreciation of Bede.

Rosario Assunto warns that we ignore a radical distinction between modern artistic-poetics (*Künstler-Poetiken*) and a medieval theory of beauty. Modern poetics, Assunto argues, is entirely subjective, militantly taste-oriented, and has a more explicitly empirical origin.[59]

---

57. Lapidge, BP, pp. 943–45.
58. Sharpe, "The Varieties of Bede's Prose."
59. Assunto, *Die Theorie des Schönen im Mittelalter*, p. 64. Thus, Mary Carruthers explores the physical components of beauty, its sensuousness and sense-derived intellection. See her *Experience of Beauty*. While I am compelled by her project, I have reservations about charting experience through literary vocabulary. I see literary vocabulary offering at best a proposal that an actual, historical reader may or may not adopt.

I would temper that claim significantly, but it agrees in essence with René Wellek's famous account of the decline of Neoclassicism and a shift from the formalism of earlier literature:

> But by far the strongest and most obvious change in the middle of the 18th century was the shift of critical concern to the reaction of the audience, which led to a dissolution of neoclassicism into emotionalism and sentimentalism. . . . It shifted attention to the emotional effect of art, and . . . it became destructive of the essential feature of art: its appeal to contemplation.[60]

Whether or not Wellek was correct in his assessment of the concomitant disintegration of art, he rightly observed a shift of dominant critical interest. Both Assunto and Wellek indicate that the emotions and sentiments of audiences took the fore in critical assessment, a subset of what Alisdair MacIntyre called "emotivism."[61] This tectonic shift in Western culture affects the current reception of medieval Latin poetry.

Critical assessments of medieval Latin poetry during the last century have thus been grounded, not unsurprisingly, on post-Enlightenment assumptions about the high value of the sentimental effect of lyrics. F. J. E. Raby is perhaps the best-known historian in English of medieval Latin poetry. He tends to praise sentimental effect, typical of poetry of his own day, in medieval Latin lyrics. Raby writes that the Christian poetry of the Middle Ages improves as it adopts Scripture's "more romantic imagery" and gives to classical Latin "an emotional and symbolical quality which had been foreign to its nature." From the Book of Zephaniah, for example, "was to issue the poetry of the future, the poetry in which the Catholic emotion was to discover its final expression." And from that Catholic emotion, perhaps denuded of its drier religious mission, came "the romantic poetry of the modern world."[62] Raby's insistence on

---

60. Wellek, *A History of Modern Criticism*, 1:26.
61. MacIntyre, *After Virtue*.
62. Raby, *CLP*, pp. 11 and 27.

lyric emotion may derive from a similar approach to faith, suggested by his laudatory mention of "the emotion of Western Christianity," whatever he might have understood that to mean. Raby recommends poets not only for their technical mastery, but also for the feelings they evoke in refined readers, especially emotional authenticity. Damasus, an important fourth-century Pope, wrote verses that "contain many sins against pure prosody and show little or no poetical feeling."[63] Nevertheless, Raby recommends the epigrams of Damasus, who became Pope in AD 366, because they describe the suffering of martyrs, something sure to fire the emotions of readers.[64] Raby lists in support of his views Karl Borinski, who in 1914 saw lyrical expressions of modern *Empfindungsleben* originating in the music of medieval lyric. Borinski posited a kinship between German literary criticism in the Renaissance and that of his own era. Gustav Ehrismann, the great German literary historian, fixes the point of transition in Germany from medieval to Renaissance in the work of Niclas von Wyle and his heightened emotional self-awareness.[65]

Raby finds most praiseworthy the medieval poetry that issued from the "Franciscan religious revival," which

> breathed a new spirit into the old doctrinal hymnology, and, using the perfected verse forms of the twelfth century, filled them with an emotion hitherto unknown, an emotion of personal pathos and pity which was destined profoundly to influence the lyrical poetry of the modern world.[66]

At one point, Raby adduces the tears of St. Augustine (*Conf.*, IX, vi) in evidence of the quality of Ambrose's hymns.[67] That may be so, but only to a point. We would not want to fall into an either/or

---

63. Ibid., p. 18. Similarly, Lapidge calls Bede's epigram on a church in Lindsey "conventional and traditional"; "Bede the Poet," p. 2.
64. Raby, *CLP*, pp. 18–19.
65. See Borinski, *Die Poetik der Renaissance*; Ehrismann, *Geschichte der deutschen*, 4:660.
66. Raby, *CLP*, p. 28.
67. Ibid., pp. 32–33.

fallacy, foolishly pitting reason against emotion. Emotion is certainly part of the effect of Christian Latin poetry, but according to the Great Theory it is only a means to a higher end. Truth is the ultimate quarry, emotion only its proximate effect. In Augustine's account, Ambrose's hymns provoke devotion, but only because their truth becomes manifest to Augustine: "The sound[s] flowed into my ears and the truth was distilled into my heart. This [i.e. truth] caused the feelings of devotion to overflow. Tears ran . . ."[68] Truth, *veritas*, is the primary quarry of the appreciative listener; refined feeling is its consequence. Raby seems to elide truth in his praise of emotional authenticity, but truth is the *raison d'être* of Christian poetry. Music and rhythm can provoke or intensify feelings that accompany truth,[69] and feelings are best intensified by employing the proper modes and genres of poetry. Augustine writes that "because of their diversity, all the feelings of our spirit have their proper modes in song and voice, according to which they are stimulated, due to some mysterious relationship."[70] So Truth, along with particular modes of poetic form, brings on particular feelings. Although I can imagine an argument that human emotion and suffering portrayed in poems are the truths that inspired Raby's attendant feelings, I do not think that is the argument Raby is making. Nevertheless, beyond his aesthetic claims, Raby cannot easily be gainsaid. He is rightly considered one of the great historians of medieval Latin poetry. But with respect to aesthetic judgment, Raby's assumptions about literary value are

---

68. Trans. Henry Chadwick, p. 164 (CSEL 33.1: p. 208): "uoces illae influebant auribus meis et eliquabatur ueritas in cor meum et exaestuabat inde affectus pietatis, et currebant lacrimae, et bene mihi erat cum eis."
69. Wulfstan of Winchester seems to have been the first Anglo-Saxon to propose in writing that certain modes either of music or of rhetoric intensify certain feelings. See Zeeman, "The Theory of Passionate Song," p. 241. To distinguish between the affective and contemplative function of lyric is beyond the scope of this chapter and beyond my expertise. A good guide to the complexity of the question is Bestul, "Devotional and Mystical Literature"; and, in the same volume, see McDonough, "Lyric."
70. Zeeman, "The Theory of Passionate Song," cites Augustine, *Conf.* 10.33.49, p. 240.

in keeping with those of literary historians who certified the canon of medieval Latin poetry during the nineteenth and early twentieth centuries.[71] These literary historians include Gustav Gröber, Adolf Ebert, and Max Manitius. They wrote in an environment where lyrical poetry was associated with an overflow of emotion, an association not obvious during the Anglo-Saxon period.[72] (In fact, Bede will disparage passion in the Hymn's final strophe.) Raby was as much a Victorian critic as Matthew Arnold. He was engaged in many of the same debates that animated Victorian literary criticism, although his interests lay in medieval Latin.

Whatever the precise contours of the debate, and unable as I am to step outside of it, I do want to emphasize two points. The first is that Bede's poetry was devotional, centered on Christ. Judgments of its quality depend on one's view of the precise role that emotions play in Christian contemplation. For Bede's audience, it is not clear that emotions were epistemologically distinct from reason, as became the case during the Enlightenment.[73] There was no disembodied mind chanting *cogito ergo sum*. Emotions were part of the complex process of intellection, not distinct from it. Feeling was part of thinking. Moreover, it's not clear that putting one's feelings on display was the high-water mark of Anglo-Latin poetry. Neither was testifying to one's existential angst. Bede's poetry is less like *The Waste Land* and more like prayers. It may interest Christian readers today, not because it competes with Auden or Eliot, but because it is a vehicle for Christian devotion.

And that raises a second point. Bede wrote poems that were to be used in a Christian community. They had a liturgical and devotional use, like collects, "The Prayer of St. Francis," or Prudentius's

---

71. For a list of such histories, see Ziolkowski, "Towards a History of Medieval Latin Literature." For a meta-history of emotion as a motivating factor in literary criticism, see Fuchs and Strümper-Krobb, *Sentimente, Gefühle, Empfindungen*.
72. Cf. Zeeman, "The Theory of Passionate Song," p. 233.
73. See Lockett, *Anglo-Saxon Psychologies*.

Peristephanon.[74] They were no place for Bede to assert his individuality. Each monk or nun who took up his poems, who channeled his or her devotion through Bede's words, would hear his or her own voice less the more Bede's interfered. So, as objects of contemplation and devotion, Bede's poems champion a monastic ideal of losing one's self—one's distinctive voice—in the divine order. *Lôgos* first, poet last. There is a gentle anonymity to Bede's poems. To my ear, Bede's anonymous style is improved by his interaction with the Latin poetic tradition. One hears in his lines snippets of other poets, like snatches of songs while changing radio stations, or a hundred whispered prayers before the onset of Mass.[75] Bede's voice is dimmed in the murmuring tides of tradition. Much of his art lies in the control of these many pieces, in the precise patterns in which those pieces are arranged, and in the sensations and intellections prompted by those patterns. He is a master of mosaic. As Lapidge says, what makes Bede such a gifted poet is his consummate control of language. That control extends from sounds and meter to his magnificent, preternatural control of allusion. Part of Bede's art is learned, and in the next chapter I review some of the sources of his art.

---

74. The "Prayer of St. Francis" is a Catholic prayer first published in 1912. See Christian Renoux, "The Origin of the Peace Prayer of St Francis." On the devotional use of Prudentius's *Peristephanon*, see the outstanding book by Anne-Marie Palmer, *Prudentius on the Martyrs*, p. 3.

75. Lapidge calls this phenomenon Bede's "rapid and unobtrusive allusion to the diction of earlier Latin poetry"; "Bede the Poet," p. 13.

Chapter Two

Metrical Arts

The Great Theory of Beauty compels a poet to properly dispose sounds, words, and meter in a poem. The technical particulars of that art comprise poetics. Two of Bede's textbooks concern poetics directly: *De arte metrica* (On the metrical arts, hereafter *DAM*) and *De schematibus et tropis* (On Schemes and Tropes, hereafter *DST*). Extant in whole or in part in 96 manuscripts and written sometime after 709,[1] they are some of the first textbooks to organize material for non-Latin speakers, much improving on earlier, if more prominent

---

1. A third textbook, *De orthographia* (On Orthography, Bede, *DO*), dedicated to grammatical information about particular Latin words, does not concern me in this chapter. The editions of *DAM* and *DST* are found in *De arte metrica et De schematibus et tropis*, ed. Calvin B. Kendall, CCSL 123a (Turnhout, 1975); translated with new preface by Kendall in *DAM* and *DST*. All translations are Kendall's unless otherwise noted. On dating, I follow Franklin, "The Date and Composition of Bede's *De Schematibus et Tropis* and *De Arte Metrica*," who also provides an overview of the arguments and evidence. On early dating, see Laistner, "The Library of the Venerable Bede," p. 241; and Knappe, *TKR*, p. 234, n. 4. On later dating, see Kendall, *Libri II*, pp. 28–29; and Irvine, "Bede the Grammarian," p. 43. On manuscripts, see Kendall, *Libri II*, p. 29; Laistner, *Handlist*, s.v. An extremely informative study of *DAM* and *DST* is Heikkinen, "The Christianization of Latin Meter," available free online. Heikkinen examines prosody; my concern in this chapter is stylistics. Where we overlap, I have not coordinated references, but I recommend the reader to Heikkinen for all technical aspects of Bede's prosody.

grammarians.² Some of Bede's methodological innovations were introduced by necessity. Unlike Aelius Donatus or Fabius Quintilian, Bede was not writing for students whose native language was Latin. Latin, although once native to Britain, was not native to Anglo-Saxons. Bede taught his students to analyze Latin poetry grammatically and stylistically. Before moving on to the particulars of decorous syntax and semantic play described in *DST*, I begin where Bede begins: sounds, syllables, letters, inflections, and conjugations. For Anglo-Saxons, all of it had to be learned from scratch, and all of it concerned style at some level. Only after a long tutelage could they hope to produce Latin verse. However difficult it was to produce technically correct Latin verse, still more difficult were sound judgments of literary taste. Correct verse was not always good verse.

Composing verse for highly literate Christians was no simple task. Some Latin poetry is built on the natural stress patterns of Latin—on syllabic quality (louder or softer)—and is called *qualitative* or *rhythmic* verse. A good deal of medieval Latin poetry is rhythmic. But *quantitative* verse, perhaps an inheritance of Greek, is another matter entirely; it is built on the syncopation of Latin—on syllabic quantity (whether the vowel of a syllable is long or short).³ The classical Latin verse of Virgil and Ovid, for example, is quantitative. Although contemporary with Virgil's quantitative verse, rhythmic or stress verse was considered rustic and unsophisticated, but in the following centuries rhythmic verse had firmly established itself in

---

2. See Law, *The Insular Latin Grammarians*. Knappe, *TKR*, p. 235, praises Bede's lucidity and precision, a phrase that rightly echoes Palmer, "Bede as Textbook Writer," p. 573.
3. More precisely, Greek meter is based on syllable weight. See Golston and Riad, "The Phonology of Greek Lyric Meter," pp. 79–80; and Allen, *Accent and Rhythm*; Allen points out that "in Greek classical verse there appears to be no attempt to achieve agreement between accent and metre in any part of the line in any spoken meter" (cited in Golston and Riad, 79). But see the arguments of Parsons described in Clackson and Horrocks, *The Blackwell History of the Latin Language*, §5.2.1, pp. 132–38. A brief, clear guide to quantitative verse can be found in Lapidge, *APrW*, pp. 19–24.

centers of Western literary production, and by the seventh century Bede reported that quantitative and rhythmic verse were both valued: as Eva Castro writes, "A popular poet created rustic, rhythmical poems, a cultivated poet wrote them in a learned manner."[4] Both means of composition grew from properties inherent in Latin. Except in the very early period, Latin verse always existed at the intersection of a natural-stress language and a highly formal artifice. In any given quantitative poem were found both Latin's natural stress patterns and Greek's adopted (and modified) metrical formulae. Bede's first task in his textbooks was to make students conscious of the phonemic value of letters and the correct length of syllables. Only with this grounding could students come to appreciate the *metricae artes* (metrical arts) as the masters had practiced them.[5] Then they might go on to learn various poetic forms and come to understand some of the aesthetic expectations of their readers.

The metrical arts are not merely tools of classification and form; they are part of a poet's aesthetic palette. In practical terms, Latin poems require readers to draw out long vowels for metrical reasons and for semantic ones. But aesthetic considerations also apply. The texture of a verse depends in part on the phonic effects of vowels, and on the syncopated cadences of alternating longs and shorts. A quick succession of short *i*'s or an elongated, ponderous series of long *o*'s might, for impressionistic reasons, heighten the emotional effect of a verse. A poet hoping to stimulate a sympathetic reaction in his reader might affect gravity by using first-declension inflected plurals, such as *–ārum* or *–ās*. More abstractly, grammatical categories might be used for subtle implications—for example, modifying a noun either with a genitive noun or an adjective. In "chair

---

4. *DAM*, xxiv; Kendall, *Libri II*, p. 160. For Castro, see Caridad, "La poesía rítmica," p. 630. But see Heikkinen, "Bede's *De Arte metrica*," pp. 176–77.

5. *DAM*, I. Heikkinen, "Bede's De Arte metrica," p. 178, points out that Bede was unaware of the Greek metrical prototypes that inspired earlier Latin verse, and so he was unaware of the aesthetic aims of poetic liberties taken by classical poets. On Greek origins, see Raven, *Latin Metre*, p. 17; and Halporn, Ostwald, and Rosenmeyer, *The Meters of Greek and Latin Poetry*, p. 59.

of gold," the successive order of images in a reader's head runs: first chair, then gold. In "a golden chair," the order is reversed (a rhetorical figure called *antiptosis*). In an inflected language, the words can be placed out of normal order to manipulate this succession (a rhetorical figure called *hyperbaton*, an excess of which is called *synchisis*). William Fitzgerald calls this successive order "the way in which the sense unfolds" and "the temporal experience of accumulated meaning."[6] That temporal experience is an essential component of the Latin literary experience.

Temporal experience may include not only successive images and sensations, but also a series of more abstract entities. Oddities of inflectional systems, for example, might suggest oddity more broadly. The fifth declension is an oddity among languages of the Roman Empire; it has no correlative in any Proto-Indo European language.[7] A fifth-declension word may have suggested subtly to poets and readers the idiosyncrasy of Latin. Grammatical gender might also play a role in a work's subtler, unfolding implications. *Philosophia* and *anima*, both feminine nouns, may suggest that higher intellectual faculties are somehow feminine, as Boethius does by portraying *philosophia* as a woman in his *De consolatione philosophiae*. Gregory Nazianzus was thought to have had a vision of two spectral women, *Sapientia* 'Wisdom' and *Castitas* 'Chastity'.[8] Bede writes that the wisdom of God "consoles us as a mother."[9] Or, knowing that *musa* is a feminine noun and that *vates* is masculine allows one to postulate

---

6. Fitzgerald, *How to Read a Latin Poem*, p. 34. It is a wonderful introduction to Latin aesthetics. Augustine makes a similar case on behalf of semantics in his *De dialectica*; see Stock, *Augustine the Reader*, p. 144, on *magnus*. Hearing the adjective *magnus*, students have an ambiguous sense of its meaning since they await the noun it modifies, which will presumably disambiguate the adjective. Perhaps similarly, Carin Ruff suggests that Bede understood metrics linearly: "It is described in terms of the reader's experience of scanning the verse"; Ruff, "The Place of Metrics," p. 152.
7. Clackson and Horrocks, *Blackwell History of the Latin Language*, p. 18.
8. *Old English Martyrology*, ed. Herzfeld, EETS o.s. 116 (London, 1900), pp. 40–41.
9. See Holder, "The Feminine Christ," pp. 110–18.

that a muse inspiring a poet may play with sexual implication. In pursuit of an aesthetic that celebrates variety, early Latin poets sometimes suggested profusion or abundance through a variegated disposition of grammatical gender, case, and inflectional type. The idiosyncrasies and details of grammar were part of the Latin poet's artistic toolkit—grammatically trained readers wrote for other grammatically trained readers.[10]

My operating assumption is that Bede's classroom offers us a window on his verse. Clearly, those characteristics of verse that Bede emphasized in his textbooks were meant to prepare his students to appreciate the artful, grammatical subtleties of Latin poetry.[11] More specifically, Bede made a fundamental connection between grammar and the Christian Scriptures, which is demonstrated in part by the examples that he adduces for rhetorical figures. My primary aim in this chapter is to pursue that connection to Scripture and, in doing so, to dig a little deeper into Christian Latin poetics. In emphasizing a Christian poetics, I follow Michael Roberts, who cautions, "To appreciate late antique poetry properly, it is necessary to view it on its own terms rather than from the perspective, conscious or not, of classical aesthetics."[12] He rightly cautions against supposing "a single aesthetic that is characteristic of late antiquity."[13] We ought to allow that literary experiences of Christian readers in the seventh century were as catholic as the many churches that comprised Catholicism. Correlatively, and in terms of method, Erich Auerbach suggested "selecting characteristic

---

10. See Ward, *The Venerable Bede*, pp. 20–26; Brown, *CB*, chap. 2; Love, "The World of Latin Learning." More generally, see Irvine, *The Making of Textual Culture*; and Shockro, "Reading Bede as Bede Would Read," chap. 1.
11. The point is made by Werner Jaager in *VSC*, p. 17. More generally, see Thornbury, *Becoming a Poet in Anglo-Saxon England*, chap. 2. Thornbury divides those who had access to manuscripts into four categories of people most likely to become poets; teachers are one of her categories. On Bede's classroom, see Kendall, "Bede and Education."
12. Roberts, *The Jeweled Style*, p. 3. Roberts cites Henri-Irénée Marrou as a guide. DeGregorio makes a similar point about the context in which to approach Bede; see Brown, *CB*, p. 18, n. 6.
13. Roberts, *The Jeweled Style*, p. 6.

particulars" of a literary period rather than attempting a synthesis of them.[14] For that reason, I am concentrating on Anglo-Latin poetry in the age of Bede, rather than ranging wider afield. In terms of evidence, Martin Irvine suggests that grammatical culture can be revealed through medieval textbooks, pedagogy, and literature. By grammatical culture he means the "textual competencies that were preconditions for participation in literary culture throughout medieval Europe." My scope is not Europe, though, but Wearside in northern England at the turn of the eighth century, an area Irvine calls "the leading center of grammatical culture . . . in the Western world."[15]

In this chapter I have two ancillary aims. First, I want to reaffirm a distinction between early Anglo-Saxon reading habits and Late Antique Roman ones. In terms of the Latin language, I follow Peter Stotz in seeing strong continuity between the Latin of Bede and the Latin of the fourth and fifth centuries. Like his insular contemporaries, Bede writes a Latin relatively free of idiomatic influence.[16] In terms of reading habits, though, Bede is not a fifth-century Roman, but an Anglo-Saxon and a professed Christian monk during an age when Christianity has achieved broad, cultural respectability.[17] That leads to a second ancillary aim of this chapter: to investigate the manner in which Bede's poetry was meditated upon as an act of monastic reflection. I pursue these ancillary aims largely by means of selection and implication. The scope of my evidence is fairly narrow: I am concerned with the poetry of Bede and with the Latin poems that monks and priests, nuns and female religious shared with each other

---

14. Auerbach, *Literary Language and its Public*, p. 18.
15. Irvine, *The Making of Textual Culture*, pp. 1–2 and 273.
16. Stotz, *HLSM*, 1:11 and 1:29.
17. I follow Bonner, "Bede and Medieval Civilization," p. 78: "too much stress should not be laid on the alien character of Bede's Latinity." His is the learned Latin of the living Church. For obvious reasons Bede's written Latin is formal, rather than idiomatic. The classical style in Anglo-Latin is so-called, not because it is particularly Augustan, but in order to distinguish it from the hermeneutic style. See Alistair Campbell as noted in Lapidge, "Three Latin Poems," p. 86.

during the early Middle Ages. The distribution list of such poems is fairly small, the community of adept readers equally so. Among the servants of Christ in Anglo-Saxon England, only a small number at any given time were capable of appreciating well the Latin poetry of their predecessors, an observation that Aldhelm himself makes.[18] My own competence is such that I cannot offer the kind of subtle and informed commentary that a classicist might.

How did Anglo-Saxon students come to understand the Latin language? What resources did they have at hand? Bede's textbooks were far less comprehensive than those of Marius Victorinus or Donatus. Bede seems to have deliberately chosen a more selective approach than did Donatus. Why? A story Bede tells in the *HE* about Bishop John of Beverley is instructive in this regard. John heals a dumb boy and then teaches him to speak, first the names of letters, then syllables, words, and longer sentences.[19] This is the same path that Bede takes with his young students. He seems to think of Latin education not as translating a foreign language into a native one, but as rebirth into a new language. The mechanics of his teaching can be inferred from grammatical handbooks that circulated in ASE, from class texts like Aelfric's Latin *Colloquy*, and from school exercises. Yet they cannot reveal a full panorama of the living pedagogical tradition. For example, Anglo-Saxon students were encouraged to distinguish between the sounds they heard and the letters they saw. Meter was marked by the ear, not on the page.[20] Bede emphasizes this distinction: "Whoever

---

18. See Lapidge and Rosier, *APW*, p. 20.
19. Bede, *HE*, 5.2, pp. 457–59; also noted by Irvine, *The Making of Textual Culture*, p. 277.
20. On voice, *vox*, see Henderson, *The Medieval World of Isidore of Seville*, pp. 31–40. Henderson's book is a terrific guide to the major assumptions and perspectives of literary culture in the seventh century. Irvine, *The Making of Textual Culture*, argues that *vox* and *littera* are "convertible terms," p. 92. On Bede specifically, see de Bruyne, *Études*, 1:152. Stock, *Augustine the Reader*, p. 32: "The line between the spoken and the written was finely drawn"; nevertheless, Augustine prized written words for their relative permanence. See also Stock's chapter 6, "Speaking and Reading."

desires acquaintance with the metrical arts, he first must attentively acquire knowledge of the difference between letters and syllables."[21] Bede writes, "This *ma-* that one says in 'mater' occupies twice as much time as does *pa-*, that one says briefly in 'pater.'"[22] Although the written vowel of *ma-* and *pa-* looks the same to the eye, <a>, the syllables are spoken differently, /ā/ and /ă/ respectively. Augustine makes a similar point about the word *os* in Psalm 138:15, which can be pronounced /ōs/ (mouth) or /ŏs/ (bone); the written word, he says, can be disambiguated only through speech or by checking against the Greek.[23] Vowel length is something one hears, something one learns by hearing—rarely do length marks appear in manuscripts.

Oral competence was extremely important. It mattered whether <ae> was pronounced /ai/ or /ei/, or <c> was pronounced /s/ or /k/.[24] Apparently, Bede's students had difficulty discerning terminal /d/ from /t/; in *De orthographia*, Bede reminds them that "*apud* is written with a *d*, *caput* with a *t*, which gives *capitis*."[25] Moreover, there is an aesthetic component to the physicality of oral performance, what M. H. Abrams calls "the fourth dimension of a poem."[26] Artful ambiguity in a poem, for example in the poems of Catullus, awaits oral

---

21. Bede, *DAM*, I, i; Kendall, *Libri II*, p. 27, translation modified. Again, Bede, *DAM*, xvi; Kendall, *Libri II*, pp. 140–41, distinguishes between an audible dactyl that correlates to a written spondee.
22. Bede, *DAM*, II; Kendall, *Libri II*, p. 43. On length of syllables, Bede, *DAM*, I, ii (CCSL 123a: p. 86).
23. Augustine, *DDC* III, 3, 7.
24. Allen, *Vox Latina*, on the pronunciation of early Latin and the nineteenth-century controversy. Isidore, *Etym*, I.iv: <k> "is also called superfluous because the ancients wrote all such sounds with a C," p. 41. Marouzeau, *Traité*, p. 2, notes that proper pronunciation was for the ancients an essential element of the aesthetics of Latin. C. Marius Victorinus, one of Augustine's teachers, dedicates a section of his *Ars Grammatica*, a book that Bede knew, to enunciation; he begins with stress and the effort of forming vowels "in ore" (in the mouth); see Keil, *Scriptores artis metricae*, p. 32.
25. Bede, *DO*, p. 12. The confusion of *d* and *t* is a characteristic of medieval Latin. See Lapidge, "Colloquial Latin," p. 413.
26. Abrams, *The Fourth Dimension of a Poem*.

performance for possible disambiguation. More mundane facets of the classroom environment encouraged a distinction between reading letters and hearing sounds.[27] Textbooks were not produced in vast numbers (students were unlikely to have had a common text before their eyes). Dictionaries did not exist (students were unlikely to have had immediate access to reference works). Scansion marks were unknown (students were unlikely to have experienced Latin scansion as a written phenomenon). If we pause to consider the pedagogical ramifications of a spare classroom, then we can develop some suggestive hypotheses. First, without textbooks, students would have had to memorize long portions of texts. Second, without dictionaries, students would have had to memorize long lists of words, such as those that Aldhelm prepared. And third, without the paraphernalia of the modern classroom, students would have spent much of their time reciting, repeating, scanning, and composing orally.

The Art of Christian Latin: Letters

Poems in our own time can be identified as poetry by their intensity of thought or emotion, whether or not they rhyme or scan. By contrast, early medieval Latin poetry was defined very simply as writing that was rhythmical or in meter.[28] It was distinguished from prose not by its content, but by its form. Meter intensified expression, even in a piece of prose. Bede defines meter in *De arte metrica*: "[M]etrum est ratio cum modulatione, rithmus modulatio sine ratione" (meter is order with modulation, rhythm is modulation without order).[29]

---

27. Tilliette, "Verse Style," p. 245. More generally, see Kendall, "Bede and Education"; and Riché, *Education and Culture in the Barbarian West*.
28. Tilliette, "Verse Style," p. 240.
29. Bede, *DAM*, XXIV, p. 160; my trans. On *modulatio*, see Kendall, *Libri II*, p. 99, n. 40. In his *De musica*, Augustine writes that "musica est scientia bene modulandi," *PL* 32:1083; but he differentiates verse and music by noting that a *grammaticus* judges verse by authority while music is judged from reason and the senses. See also Ambrose, *Explanatio psalmorum xii*, ed. Zelzer, p. 4, lines 9–12.

Meter was no mere ornament, although it could be ornamental; moreover, it constituted the chief literary manifestation of number, proportion, and order found in nature. Meter was thought to be a material cause of poetry's beauty. Augustine wrote that "everything is beautiful that is in due order."[30] As we saw in chapter one, the claim was echoed by innumerable Christian authorities, some of whom also found beauty in the meters of Scripture. Seppo Heikkinen writes that "much of the Old Testament was believed to have been composed in various meters, which, accordingly, came to be seen as reflection of Divine Order."[31] Jerome explained that Hebrew versions of the hexameter and elegiac meters could be found in the Old Testament. Bede was thereby authorized to use these meters for Christian literature not by Virgil or Horace, but by the Bible. This distinction matters because it suggested to Christians that these meters—these measured dispositions of sound in time—were more "natural," more divinely ordered, than the artificial meters of pagan antiquity.[32] These meters were also considered an authorized means of expression in the three holy languages—Hebrew, Greek, and Latin. Thus, these particular meters could better express Christian content and help a Christian to meditate on things divine.

In the regular movement of metrical time, as in the regular movement of liturgical time, the ideal Christian reader might sense divinity. Emily Thornbury reports that Aldhelm's view was that "the entire cosmos was organized according to numerical patterns, and that meter provided one window into that rational organization."[33] Christian literary aesthetics operates within a continual, bivalent

---

30. Beardsley, *Aesthetics from Classical Greece to the Present*, p. 94. Kendall, *Libri II*, p. 20: "the sense of beauty was inextricably linked with, and a reflection of, divine order. . . . Beauty had to do with proportion, with harmony and balance, with number, and with licensed deviation from the norm."
31. Heikkinen, "Bede's *De Arte metrica*," p. 178.
32. The distinction between natural, divinely ordained time and artificial, man-made time is explained by Faith Wallis in her commentary to *Bede: The Reckoning of Time*, p. 264.
33. Thornbury, *Becoming a Poet*, p. 45.

comparison between meter as it unfolds in language and its idealized divine source. This comparison is akin to John Scotus's "harmony of like and dislike" from his *Periphyseon*.[34] In this view, individuals participate, sometimes antagonistically, in a larger unity. Edgar de Bruyne writes that Irish poetry in this period embraced balanced antagonism as a means to depict "beautiful chaos."[35] We shall see balanced antagonism at play in Bede's *Hymn to Aethelthryth*. Available in seventh-century Wearside was an aesthetic that prized variety integrated into an ultimately unknowable unity, "the harmony of divine and human existence."[36] Within that unknowable unity, a degree of disorder and individualization made a poem human, local, and (very literally) comprehensible. Comprehension is a gathering together of many elements in time, as occurs in metrical poetry. An imperfect reader may find a potentially improving order in the metrically regular disposition of narrative.[37] As a form of ordering a reader's inner life, meter serves faith.

As music is made up of tones, so is meter made up of letters. Bede believed, according to Robert Palmer, "that in any discussion of prosody it should be recognized that letters have specific *potestates*

---

34. "John Scotus Eriugena, from *Periphyseon*," in Thiessen, *Theological Aesthetics*, p. 72. Bede cites Augustine, *De Trinitate*, "It is necessary that many men make many books, in a different style, but not in a different faith"; *Bede: The Reckoning of Time*, p. 4.
35. See De Bruyne, *Études*, 1:140–41.
36. Von Balthasar, *The Glory of the Lord*, 2:13. Jan den Boeft offers a reading of Ambrose, "Aeterne rerum conditor," in which the use of *temporum* and *tempora* indicate "the alternating succession of times . . . by a most efficiently used polyptoton, which by its twofold use of the plural of *tempus* emphasizes the multiple temporariness of creation, in contrast to the uniform eternity of the Creator"; see his "Ambrosius Lyricus," p. 81.
37. Von Balthasar, *The Glory of the Lord*, 2:98. The soul seeks God, the true light, and "the whole multiplicity of both sacred and profane exists as a unity within this single light which transcends all plurality, and which consequently, for the soul, lies rather in the extension of its illuminated subjective act of seeing (inwards) than in the direction of the external multiplicity of objects. . . ."

which can and should be discussed independently of their *potestates* in syllables."³⁸ A musical note has its own potency (as C or E or G, for example), but in combination it offers a distinct potency (as a third or a fifth). Bede begins his textbook on Latin poetic composition, *De arte metrica*, by introducing the twenty-one letters of the Latin alphabet (Donatus, Sergius, and Pompeius counted twenty-three). Five, he says, are called *vocales*, vowels. In order to spell borrowed words from Greek, Latin speakers adopted a sixth vowel, <y>. Latin-speaking Christians also borrowed Greek letters spoken of in the Bible, such as *Alpha* and *Omega* in the phrase from Revelation 1:8, "I am the Alpha and the Omega." Borrowings from the Greek bring the total number of letters to twenty-seven. The vowels, Bede says, are eight: <a, e, i, o, u, h (*eta*), y, and o (*omega*)>. <i> and <u>, though, are sometimes used as consonants, as in *uinum* (which modern editors will sometimes spell *vinum*). <i> is unusual because like <x> and <z>, as a consonant it is a *duplex*, or double consonant. So, <i>, though a single letter, can produce multiple sounds.

One of Bede's sources, Isidore of Seville, dedicates two chapters of his magisterial *Etymologiae* to letters. Hebrew, Isidore explains, is "the mother of all languages and letters,"³⁹ and has twenty-two letters in its alphabet. Greek has twenty-four. And Latin, "falling between these two languages," has twenty-three, an increase from Old Latin's original seventeen (which is the number Donatus gives). Isidore appears to count <i> and <u> once as vowels and once as consonants. The earliest extant manuscript of *DAM*, St. Gall 876, includes these alphabets, presumably added by the St. Gall scribe.⁴⁰ Bede concludes that Christians use twenty-seven letters. Palmer reports, "As far as I know, this is the first attempt to add up all of

---

38. Palmer, "Bede as Textbook Writer," p. 576.
39. Isidore, Etym., I.iii, p. 39.
40. St. Gall, Cod. Sang. 876, pp. 208–77, at pp. 278–80; circa AD 800. Kendall bases his edition on St. Gall 876, available at http://www.e-codices.unifr.ch/de/list/one/csg/0876. Most Anglo-Saxon manuscripts contain a Greek or Hebrew alphabet.

the letters of the Christian alphabet."[41] In support of Christian exceptionalism, one might infer that Bede has distinguished Christian Latin from classical Latin even at the level of letter.[42] We shall see the importance of these counts later, when the topic of alphabetic poems is introduced. (Bede will employ twenty-three letters in his alphabetic *Hymn*, but will add four stanzas in an acrostic to give twenty-seven.) For the moment, the characteristics of these letters are important metrically, since what metricists call liquids (m, n, l, and r), sibilants (s, z), mutes (b, p, t, d, c, g), and aspirates (h) have different effects on vowel length. Moreover, medieval judgments concerning sonority and euphony depended on a knowledge of the phonetic classes of consonants.

In Latin, a vowel is articulated for either a single moment of time or two moments of time. One moment of time is called a *mora* (delay, space of time). A syllable is a vowel alone (e.g., a, e) or in combination with another sound. And a combination of syllables makes up metrical feet. Isidore wrote, "Feet are what last for a certain timespan of syllables."[43] I want to emphasize again that meter is a way to measure language in time; in fact, Aldhelm calls morae *tempora*. A hexameter line is made up of six feet measuring twenty-four morae. Each foot measures four morae (a dactyl or a spondee). The last foot is also four morae; it may be either a spondee or a trochee, but if it is a trochee, the last syllable is considered to be common and treated as two morae.[44] A musical analogy is six measures of four beats.

---

41. Palmer, "Bede as Textbook Writer," p. 579. And see Jones, "Bede's Place in Medieval Schools," p. 269.

42. Perhaps the influence of Canterbury's Antiochene exegesis or views on Genesis led Bede to conceive of a connection between the letters of the Christian alphabet and the elements of creation. See Love, "The World of Latin Learning," p. 41. See also Irvine, *The Making of Textual Culture*, p. 100. On the Antiochene school and its relation to early Anglo-Saxon England, see Bischoff and Lapidge, *Biblical Commentaries*, pp. 20–27.

43. Isidore, *Etymologiae*, I, xvii; trans. Barney, p. 47. Victorinus compares the length and brevity of vowels in meter to those in music; Keil, *Scriptores*, p. 39. On Aldhelm, see Ruff, "The Place of Metrics," p. 156.

44. Bede, *DAM*, X; Kendall, *Libri II*, pp. 96–97.

Additionally, the fifth foot should not be a spondee (Bede was adamant on the point), and the last foot cannot be a dactyl.

Syllables are called *long* or *short*. But a syllable's length is not always equivalent to the length of its vowel. Vowel length is natural to a word, but syllable length can change depending on its immediate phonic context.[45] So *năm* (on account of) contains a naturally short vowel, and on its own is a short syllable. But in another context, *năm tumet* (on account of [it] swelling),[46] the syllable is made long by position. In other words, the consonant cluster <mt> at the junction of the two words lengthens the preceding syllable: *năm* becomes *nām*. Vowel length is a difficult concept if alien to one's native language. Already in the fourth century, St. Augustine had remarked that his African students could not hear syllable length. But in the vernacular Anglo-Saxon language, vowel quantity was phonemic. Anglo-Saxons distinguished, for example, between *god* (God) and *gōd* (good). In both words, the position of the vowel in the mouth is identical: a mid-back vowel, /o/. But *god* is one mora, and *gōd*, two morae in duration. Theoretically, *god* took less time to say that *gōd*. Perhaps, then, speakers of Anglo-Saxon were better prepared to appreciate quantitative verse than are speakers of Modern English. In *De arte metrica*, Bede offers a brief list of minimal pairs that follow the pattern of *god* and *gōd*: words spelled identically, but distinguished semantically by vowel length. Some are *līber* (book) and *līber* (free), *plăga* (region) and *plāga* (blow, stroke), *pŏpulus* (people) and *pōpulus* (poplar tree).[47]

Diphthongs also matter in meter. *Foedus* begins with a long syllable—long because it contains, not two consecutive vowels, but

---

45. See Raven, *Latin Metre*, pp. 22–30. "Greeks and Romans attached little importance to 'tempo', at least as we understand it in modern music," p. 23. A clear and pleasant guide to metrical composition is Califf, *A Guide to Latin Meter*.
46. VSC, line 84.
47. *DAM,* IV; Kendall, *Libri II*, p. 67. Note that although long vowels attract accent, all the examples here are accented on the first syllable, whether it be long or short. Accent is only a rough guide to syllable length. See Fränkel, *Iktus und Akzent*.

a diphthong <oe>, and all diphthongs are long by nature. (Bede uses *fēdus* in the *Hymn*, reduced from a long diphthong to a long vowel, line 5.) Not all consecutive vowels are diphthongs—*mea* contains two short vowels, not a diphthong. *Eo-* in the verb *deōsculor* (to kiss warmly) is not a long syllable because here *de-* is a prefix, and in scansion must be recognized as such. Further complicating the example of *deōsculor*, the /ō/ of *ōs* (mouth): the second vowel of *deōsculor* is long by nature. In *deōsculor*, the /ō/ is long by nature since it derives from *ōs*, but also long by position, since <o> precedes <sc>, two consonants. Making sense of this confusing set of phonological rules is one of Bede's great pedagogical feats. In *De arte metrica*, Bede begins with phonemic classes of letters. To determine the length of a vowel by position, it is imperative to know the difference between a double consonant like <x> (double because it is made up of the two sounds /ks/) and a semi-vowel like <u> or a continuant like <f>. So, *ĕt* but *ēx*, since <x> is composed of two consonant sounds. It is somewhat comforting to know that even Bede himself was sometimes confused.[48]

In the tradition of quantitative verse, alert poets (and readers) had to be acutely aware of the phonological configuration of words. Indeed, strict metrical rules sometimes limited one's vocabulary. Some words were difficult to use in the epic hexameter, for example a *tribrach* or three consecutive shorts. Bede points out some of these words: *Ĭtălĭă, băsĭlĭcă, rĕlĭgĭŏ, rĕlĭquĭæ*.[49] Nevertheless, some of these words were used on the authority of classical and Christian poets—Virgil lengthens the first <i> of *Italiam* in *Aen.* 5.629. The last two in

---

48. Lapidge, "Bede's Metrical Life of St. Cuthbert," p. 343: *nec* "has been wrongly scanned as a naturally long syllable" in Bede's early draft, corrected later. To the rules of long and short syllables, there are exceptions, such as common syllables, whose length is either long or short depending on a poet's preference, and words such as *mox*, whose vowel is short by nature but long by position. Bede explains common syllables in his *DAM*, and describes nine ways in which syllables can be lengthened or shortened. Shortening a long vowel or diphthong that precedes a vowel is called *correption*.
49. Bede, *DAM*, XV; Kendall, *Libri II*, p. 133.

Bede's list are cretics (long-short-long), *vērĭtās* and *trīnĭtās*, impossible to place in a hexameter line. Aldhelm lists a number of cretics which, again but for the license afforded by canonical poets, deprived Christian hexameter poets of essential vocabulary such as "truth," "Trinity," and *cārĭtās* (love, charity).[50] Michael Lapidge notes that a characteristic of Anglo-Latin verse is its more intensive use of "distributive numerals and multiplicative circumlocutions," developed because "numbers such as *duodecim* and *quattuordecim* would not scan."[51] Hexameter poets thus could not speak directly of the twelve apostles! Poets had to be alert first to the lengths of stem vowels peculiar to the five nominal declensions, to the three adjectival declensions, to pronouns, and to gerunds and participles; second, to the length of vowels in verbs and adverbs; and third, to the length of vowels in inflectional and conjugational suffixes. Poets memorized long lists of words useful for particular metrical feet.[52]

Fifth-declension nouns like *dies* (day) have short *i* as a root vowel but are inflected with long vowels (with the exception of the accusative singular). Thus, the nominative singular *dĭēs* is syllabically divided *dĭ-ēs*, with a short root syllable and a long syllable as the inflection. As a subject, *dies* is an iamb; as an accusative object, it is a pyrrhic. That fact affects how a poet speaks about a day in an iambic line, such as in Bede's hymn "Primo Deus coeli globum," where he speaks of the second day of Creation in the iambic ablative singular

---

50. Aldhelm, "De metris et enigmatibus ac pedum regulis," pp. 168–69. Aldhelm notes other examples: *unitas, orbitas, sanctitas, claritas, dignitas, quantitas, civitas, falsitas, vanitas,* and *pontifex*. Aldhelm nevertheless allows them in a hexameter on the authority of Virgil and Ovid. See below, chapter 4. Metrically illegal terms significantly compromise philological conclusions based on poetic evidence; e.g., see Thornbury, *Becoming a Poet*, chap. 1, where the metrical value of *poetae* in Alcuin's sixth foot (as well as *vates* and *vatorum* in other lines) mitigates against inferring Alcuin's semantic intent.
51. Lapidge, "Three Latin Poems," p. 86.
52. Lapidge describes Aldhelm's lists of such words and their uses. "Aldhelm's Latin Poetry and Old English Verse," *ALL* 1, §9.

("Dĭē secunda," line 18).⁵³ Because it is an iamb, *dies* cannot stand at the head or foot of a hexameter line, such as those found in Bede's metrical *Life of Cuthbert*. Other inflections amenable to the iambic line include *dĭēs* (n.pl.), *dĭērŭm* (g.pl.), and *dĭēbŭs* (ab.pl.). As an aside, in this hymn, during the first days God decorated the world ("ornavit orbem," line 7), in much the same language that Caedmon uses ("after teode"). Because the only place in a hexameter line that an iamb fits is between the end of a dactyl and the beginning of another foot, fifth-declension nouns are excellent for bridging feet— like the fifth and sixth. Aldhelm, perhaps following Virgil in his *Georgics* or Paulinus of Nola in his *Carmina*, uses *dĭērŭm* twice in *De virginitate* to bridge the fifth foot (ll. 673, 1270). *Dĭēmque* and *dĭēsque* are also used widely in that position by classical poets (e.g., Statius) and once by Aldhelm (l. 1305). Anglo-Latin poets show "an extreme tendency to use nouns in *–amen* declined in the ablative singular or accusative plural to fill the requirements of the dactyl in the fifth foot of a hexameter."⁵⁴ Such nouns would also bridge the fourth foot and thereby "bind the [final, two-foot] cadence more tightly to the hexameter."⁵⁵ In short, certain positions in the hexameter line welcome particular words (thus, the ideas or qualities they signify) and particular inflections. This characteristic of meter means that poems are experienced as unfolding in fairly uniform syntactic patterns. With so many lexical, morphological, and syntactic constraints at play, the experience of reading a Latin poem was suffused with a sense of order and form.

Bede divides his lessons on vowel length into initial, medial, and final syllables. He recommends that a budding poet examine

---

53. Note, too, that Bede accurately distinguishes between *dies* as a masculine for a definite date and as a feminine for an indefinite date. See Druhan, *The Syntax of Bede's Historia Ecclesiastica*, p. 1.
54. Lapidge, "Three Latin Poems," p. 87. Lapidge suggests that Anglo-Latin poets may have been inspired here by Ovid and then Aldhelm. On *–men* and *–amen*, see Stotz, *HLSM*, 2:313–15, §63.1–63.6. Examples include *iubilamen, narramen,* and *revolumen*.
55. Observed by Lapidge and Rosier, *APW*, p. 21.

"attentively the syllables of all words at the beginning of heroic verses," because a hexameter line must begin with a long syllable.⁵⁶ For example, as Bede points out, *de-* is long while *ab-* is short. His students might remember this lesson when reading his metrical *Life of Cuthbert*, where he writes, "ut usque morari / Defessus" (too worn out to linger, line 190), from the deponent verb *dēfĕtīscī* (to be worn out).⁵⁷ When considering medial and final syllables, a student would know that of sixty-five singular nominal inflections, thirty-seven are likely to end in vowels. In Latin verse composition, one must be especially attentive to words ending in vowels because, if the next word begins with a vowel, the two risk merging—a process called *elision*. It was used delicately by classical poets, as in the opening of the *Aeneid*—"mult(um) ill(e) et terris," (1.3)—"to vary the flow of syllables," as Lapidge explains.⁵⁸ (This line's *–um* is also suppressed in pronunciation, which is a form of elision called *ecthlipsis* 'squeezing out'.) Avoiding elision was a challenge: Cicero said of Latin-speakers that "we cannot keep our vowels apart even if we wish."⁵⁹ A pause between words occasioned by adjacent vowels is called *hiatus*, often spurned, and in fact Bede avoids it.⁶⁰ Other aesthetic considerations pertained to diphthongs, which were especially prized as markers of the grand style (as were Greek names).⁶¹ Some of these aesthetic

---

56. Bede, *DAM*, IV; Kendall, *Libri II*, p. 63.
57. Bede, verse *VSC*, p. 72.
58. Lapidge, *APrW*, p. 22. Medieval authors tended to avoid elision. See Norberg, *Introduction*, pp. 32–33.
59. Cicero, *De oratore*, 152; cited by Wilkinson, *GLA*, p. 21. The opinion was not universal in the classical world; see Wilkinson, pp. 20–24. Marouzeau, *Traité*, pp. 37–38, reports that Quintilian did not find hiatus a notable fault. Neither did Cicero, who saw it as expressive, although he warned against hiatus that caused misunderstanding. Isidore warns, "In letters, their adjoining should be apt and proper [*apta et conveniens*], and thus care must be taken to ensure that the final vowel of the preceding word is not the same as the initial vowel of the following word, as *feminae Aegyptiae*" (*Etym.* II, xix); trans. Barney, p. 75.
60. Bede, verse *VSC*, p. 20.
61. Marouzeau, *Traité*, p. 14.

markers are characteristic of classes of words. All first-declension *a*-stems are inflected with a long syllable or a closed syllable, except in the nominative and vocative singular. Thus, first-declension nouns are good for most feet of a hexameter, since the first five feet admit dactyls. In *De arte metrica*, Bede discusses such classes. For example,

> Final ES, when it is found in nouns of the fifth declension, is long, as, *dies*. When it is found in nouns of the third declension, it is long when the genitive singular has the same number of syllables as the nominative, as, *labes, tabes, cedes, pubes, plades, fames, vulpes, claves, aedes, sedes, strages, proles*, and *nubes* (although some prefer to pronounce the nominative *nubs*).[62]

Of course, a good poet also pays attention to consonants (stops, fricatives, affricates, and so forth), not only insofar as they affect syllable length, but also as they affect alliteration, assibilation, assonance, elision, hiatus, and poetic sonority generally.

Bede was part of a generation of poets for whom metrical verse was first learned with the eyes and rhythmical verse was learned with the ears.[63] Jean-Yves Tilliette writes that "in Cicero's day, even the uneducated public was well aware of syllable quantity and would copiously heckle an actor who pronounced a short syllable as long, or vice versa."[64] This vivid example is probably not representative of republican Latin speakers generally. Latin was always in a state of change, due in part to a constant influx of Latin speakers from the far reaches of Empire, and in part to the great range of dialects on the Italian peninsula. In light of Latin's diversity, Joseph Farrell asks for "a history [of Latin literature] that emphasizes the play of voices against one another, always and everywhere, rather than attempting to construct successive, homogenous periods of better or

---

62. *DAM*, VI; Kendall, *Libri II*, p. 75. On this passage and its idiosyncrasy, see Heikkinen, "The Christianization of Latin Meter," p. 53.
63. Tilliette, "Verse Style," pp. 243–45; De Bruyne, *Études*, 1:151.
64. Tilliette, "Verse Style," p. 241.

worse latinity . . ."⁶⁵ Some of these voices would grow into different Romance languages. In the meantime, as the Empire wore on, and then wore out, vowel length was not at all obvious to an increasingly larger numbers of speakers.⁶⁶ Tilliette reports that in the centuries preceding the birth of Bede, "even the most educated [were] deaf to the music of antique verse."⁶⁷ That music had to be learned by rote, not only through scansion, but also through composition. Latin composition was taught largely through imitation, as it still is today. (My father used to recall anxiously reading his Latin compositions while his teacher waited with an eraser thick with red chalk, ready to douse the boy who misconstrued his prose.) A good deal of Latin poetry that survives from the Middle Ages seems to have had its direct or indirect origin in school exercises. For example, writes Tilliette, "in the Ottonian empire, the most gifted students are set the task of transposing the life of a venerated saint into verse, as a final record of the end of their studies."⁶⁸ Those academic origins should temper our distaste for various categories of medieval Latin verse. A *vita* that results from a school exercise may not exhibit—and its author and reader may not have sought—the kind of originality of expression or authenticity that critics like Raby looked for. The art of a composition was often borrowed art. Its ultimate measure was not so much the artful originality of the poet, important as that was, but the degree to which a poet elaborated the learned traditions of Latin verse.⁶⁹

---

65. Farrell, *Latin Language and Latin Culture*, p. 123.
66. See Meyer, *Gesammelte Abhandlung*, 1:3–16.
67. Tilliette, "Verse Style," p. 241.
68. Ibid. See also Szövérffy, *Secular Latin Lyrics*, 1:9, and Stotz, "Dichten als Schulfach," pp. 1–16. Such exercises are collected in St. Gall ms 381; see Raby, *SLP*, 1:253. Bede wrote a prose account of Paulinus of Nola's life of St. Felix.
69. Thus, Norden, *AK*, 1:12, "Der Stil war im Altertum nicht der Mensch selbst, sondern ein Gewand, das er nach Belieben wechseln konnte" (Style in ancient times was not the man himself, but a garment that he could change at will). See Hays, "Prose Style."

Along with meter, another aspect of the art of quantitative verse is the interplay of meter (*metrum*) and ictus (*rithmus* or accent). The combination of the two systems in Latin poetry provided aesthetic opportunities for poets. T. S. Eliot famously remarked,

> I cannot help suspecting that to the cultivated audience of the age of Virgil, part of the pleasure in the poetry arose from the presence in it of two metrical schemes in a kind of counterpoint: even though the audience may not necessarily have been able to analyse the experience.[70]

Eliot imagines the pleasure of an audience, but we must also imagine the anguish of the poet. A difficulty of merging the two schemes is that a word's ictus does not always coincide with the metrical quantity of its vowels. The adjective *vetus* 'old' has *veteris* (g.s.) and *veterēs* (n.pl.), both of which carry the main accent on the antepenult (*ve-*), although only the latter is quantitatively an anapest. To coordinate vowel length with metrical position seems extraordinarily difficult. The results are, from my perspective at least, sometimes too nuanced to appreciate fully. Wilkinson judges a hexameter by Virgil to be "melodiously narcotic": "spárgens úmida mélla sopóriferúmque papáver" (sprinkling liquid honey and soporific poppy-seed, *Aen.*, iv, 486).[71] Perhaps in appreciation of such steady and euphonious lines, Archbishop Theodore developed a verse form of continuous octosyllables, in which ictus and meter coincide.[72]

Furthermore, idiosyncrasies of the dialects of spoken Latin magnify the difficulty of coordinating ictus and meter. Stress shifted in various areas of the Empire, which resulted in changes in pronunciation and in the length of vowels. So the hexameter line ending

---

70. Eliot, *On Poets and Poetry*, p. 20; Wilkinson, *GLA*, p. 120. C. Day Lewis made a similar remark; Wilkinson, p. 93. And Nussbaum, *Vergil's Metre*, p. 38: "The idea that ictus and accent interact in Latin . . . is now well established, and forms the basis of much sensitive appreciation of Vergil's poetry."
71. Wilkinson, *GLA*, p. 72.
72. See Lapidge, "The School of Theodore and Hadrian," pp. 46–47.

Metrical Arts 53

"datas a summo" by the African poet Commodian would have been illegal to Cicero due to its fifth-foot bacchius (Cicero would read, "| dătās ā | sūmmo"), but was acceptable to Commodian given changes in African pronunciation. Commodian assumed vowel length based on stress, and so he likely stressed the words "dátas a súmmo" and scanned them "| dātăs ă | sūmmo."[73] Inscriptions in Pompeii and Herculaneum demonstrate the distinctive orthographic and grammatical features of non-literary (or Vulgar) Latin even in the first century.[74] Similarly, pronunciation of imported Greek terms changed throughout the classical period, sometimes Latinized in the popular pronunciation while Graecized among the literati.[75] In short, given the variety of dialects of Latin at any given point in time, proper scansion, as it were, was largely a matter of register. To appreciate verse from the various regions of the Latin-speaking world, one needs to appreciate overlapping registers of Latin, including Church Latin, classical Latin, and Vulgar Latin (itself too varied to constitute a unified phenomenon). Any given poem may operate within one or more of those registers. They differ in vocabulary and syntax—for example, in clausal subordination—as well as in pronunciation.[76] The overlap of registers means that we cannot chart cause and effect easily. Elite style may become common, common style, elite. Peter Stotz asks whether or not medieval Latin prose rhythms are attributable to a collective Greek and Italian *Volkskunst* 'popular art',

---

73. Herman, *Vulgar Latin*, p. 29. On changes in vowel length and stress in Africa, see, among others, Meyer, *Gesammelte Abhandlung*, 1:13–15. On "African style" and "African Latin" as a Humanistic creation and a misunderstanding of provincial sound changes, see Norden, *AK*, 1:588–631. Norden writes that the idea of "African Latin" should be abandoned for a more precise description of sound change and syntactic particulars, a recognition of the prime role of Africa in innovations of Christian Latin and of the influence there of native Greek.

74. See Wallace, *An Introduction to Wall Inscriptions from Pompeii and Herculaneum*, §2.

75. Marouzeau, *Traité*, pp. 8–12.

76. Herman, *Vulgar Latin*, pp. 87–88. See also Blaise, *A Handbook of Christian Latin*.

which is on a continuum from classical literary arts. He notes that this continuum is to be distinguished from the larger Christian Latin *Sprachsphäre* 'linguistic sphere', which had attained a certain cultural validity by the fifth and sixth centuries.[77]

Of the various aspect of the art of quantitative verse, some are more objectively judged than others. Meter can be discerned largely irrespective of critical opinion.[78] But rhythm and euphony are far more subjective; nevertheless, they were codified and taught. From the classical period onwards, euphony became an illusion regularly nourished by literary critics.[79] So one aspect of the art (rather than the science) of quantitative verse is a poet's attention to the phonological quality and position of a vowel. For example, a poet may employ a series of back vowels, or alternate between front vowels and back vowels. Simply put, these vowels sound differently in the mouth. Some sounds were thought expressive of particular ideas. Marouzeau calls this "a sort of aesthetic of sounds."[80] Socrates

---

77. Stotz, *HLSM*, 1:45–47. The point was made by Gaston Paris in 1866; see Meyer, *Anfang und Ursprung*, p. 4.
78. But Dag Norberg begins his famous study of medieval prosody with the sentence, "La métrique est un des sujets qui offrent le plus de prise à la controverse" (Meter is one of the subjects that offers the greatest opportunity for controversy); Norberg, *Introduction* (French), p. 5. For Aldhelm, though, meter was not a matter of opinion. See Ruff, "The Place of Metrics," p. 162.
79. Marouzeau contends, "La stylistique ne doit pas être conçu comme un art, encore moins comme un code de règles scolaires" (Stylistics should not be conceived as an art, and again less as a code of academic rules); *Traité*, p. xi. For Marouzeau, style is "une sorte de psychologie linguistique du sujet parlant" (a sort of linguistic psychology of the speaking subject, p. xviii). See Herescu, *La Poésie latine*, p. 12: "Presque sans exception, les grands poètes insistent sur l'importance du son, sur l'essence musicale de la poésie" (Almost without exception, the great poets insist on the importance of sound, on the musical essence of poetry).
80. "une sorte d'esthétique des sons"; *Traité*, p. 17. Marouzeau also reports that Cicero thought <f> was an "insuauissima littera" (most unpleasant letter), a judgment that Quintilian sought to explain by physiological means.

thought the letter Rho expressive of motion or rapidity.[81] The sound /s/ is not demonstrably unpleasant, but classical and medieval readers of Greek and Latin were trained to think so. Renaissance writers, steeped in the same sources as their medieval predecessors, were inclined to think so, too. Tennyson rid his poems of sibilants that bridged words (like Virgil's "solebas strident"); he called it "kicking the geese out of the boat."[82] Yet Bede begins his prose *Life of Cuthbert*, "Principium nobis scribendi." Long vowels were considered grave, and thereby expressive of ponderous thoughts.[83] Aulus Gellius, author around AD 170 of the *Attic Nights*, believed that long vowels pleased the ear more than short, so that Virgil's *urbēs* (here, gen. sing.) was better than his *urbis*, which he thought bloodless. Cicero and Quintilian recommended the alternation of vowels and consonants, avoiding consonant clusters if possible, unless for comic effect.[84] These metaphoric associations of sound and thought, although arguably illusory, were also nourished by literary critics even into our own time. The sound of a verse was extremely important to its successful reception.[85]

---

81. Wilkinson, *GLA*, p. 46. See Clayman, "Sigmatism in Greek Poetry." Clayman notes an "association of excessive sigma with bad style" even in the fifth century BCE, p. 69. My thanks to Professor Calvin Kendall for this reference. See also Marouzeau, *Traité*, p. 25. This is not onomatopoeia, an example of which is Ovid's description of men who had turned into frogs, "quamuis sint sub aqua sub aqua" (*Met.* vi, 376); *Traité*, p. 26. In French, frogs say "koax" or "koa," derived from *coasser* 'to croak' and L. *coaxare*, Gr. *koax*; not to be confused with Fr. *croasser* < L. *crocitare*, the croaking of ravens. Persius called <r> the *littera canina* (dog letter), since it reproduced the growling of dogs; *Traité*, p. 27. Bede calls <r> harsh, *dura*; *DAM*, XVI; Kendall, *Libri II*, p. 140.
82. Wilkinson, *GLA*, p. 14.
83. Ibid., p. 63: "Quintilian remarked that long syllables represented *gravia, sublima, ornata*, and that colloquial passages needed more short vowels." He follows Marouzeau, *Traité*, p. 19.
84. Marouzeau, *Traité*, pp. 19 and 20–21. Augustan rhetors had no disdain for consonant clusters in Greek words. See also p. 35. On Gellius and grammatical culture, see Irvine, *The Making of Textual Culture*, pp. 80–83.
85. Tilliette, "Verse Style," p. 245. Marouzeau argues that we must be

Sound is germane to hymns, too, since as Bede notes in *DAM*, a writer of hymns is obliged to meet the needs of choirs.[86] To appreciate the care authors took with sound, consider Bede's hymn on the six days of creation and the six ages of the world. It begins, "Primo Deus caeli globum . . ."[87] In this brief opening line, Bede alternates between front and back vowels—/i/ to /o/, then /e/ to /u/; he then alternates between low or mid-vowels and high vowels—/ae/ to /i/, then /o/ to /u/. There is some symmetry in his disposition of vowels. Bede is also making use of open and closed syllables. Each word in this line begins with a stop and ends with a continuant—a vowel, sibilant, or nasal. Alternate words end in vowels. Vowel variation and placement may be significant figuratively (as an illustration of variation generally), but it is certainly important as a practical matter.[88] Variation in vowel position modulated the phonic qualities of a verse as it was intoned. One imagines that any vowel echoing off the choir walls or one held in harmonic sustain would not duplicate the vowel being sung; harmonies would thereby be more fully differentiated in their multiple voicing.

Compare Bede's varied verse to one by Virgil, analyzed by N. I. Herescu. In *Georgics*, 4.466, Virgil writes,

Té, dulcis coniunx, te solo in litore sécum,
Té ueniénte dié, te décedénte canébat.

([Orpheus] sang of thee, sweet wife—of thee, to himself on the lonely shore; of thee as day drew nigh, of thee as day declined.)

---

attentive to distinctions in style between written and spoken language, *Traité*, p. xx.
86. Bede, *DAM*, I, xi; Kendall, *Libri II*, p. 113.
87. Hymn 1. Lapidge and Kendall consider this hymn genuine. A similar alternation of vowels occurs at the onset of Bede, *HE*: "Britannia Oceani insula" (1.1, p. 14).
88. Isidore, *Etym.*, II, xxi, p. 75: "Because a straight and continuous oration makes for weariness and disgust as much for the speaker as for the hearer, it should be inflected and varied into other forms, so that it might . . . deflect criticism with a diversity of presentation and hearing" (trans. Barney). For a similar analysis of a verse of Ovid, see Herescu, *La Poésie latine*, pp. 22–23.

Herescu writes that this prolonged chain of /e/ (in bold, with ictus marked) mimics the incessant call of Orpheus to his lost Eurydice.[89] He offers numerous similar examples from Virgil's work; each is a matter of critical judgment.

Other characteristics of the art of quantitative verse include the judicious use of extrametrical lines, the phonological context of syntactic pauses (in the middle or at the end of lines), phonological enjambment (in which the sound that terminates one verse line resonates with the sound that begins the next), disposition of word classes in a line and between lines, and many more. Though they may be relatively subjective considerations, they proved resilient characteristics of the literary arts. These many devices were learned by English poets and used in their poetry—Shakespeare, Sidney, Milton, Pope, Johnson, Shelley, Keats, and Tennyson are only some of the poets whose inherited ideas about Latin style were made native to the poetry of England and its colonies. Milton took a great deal from Virgil, as did virtually every English poet before the teaching of Latin disappeared from school curricula. Samuel Johnson was considered an extraordinarily accomplished Latin poet. Tennyson was perhaps one of the last major poets who would write to an audience capable of appreciating the classical origins of his style. "It is sometimes said that Tennyson is the most Virgilian of modern poets," wrote Wilfred P. Mustard in 1899.[90] Could such a judgment be made today? Hallam Tennyson, the poet's son, writes of his father reading Catullus in Latin, "His finger moved from word to word, and he dwelt with intense satisfaction on the adequacy of the expression and of the sounds, on the mastery of the proper handling of quantity, and on the perfection of the art."[91] This image of Tennyson reading would not surprise medieval Latin poets. Slow, methodical, appreciative, close to the language, grammatical, intensely sensitive to sound and

---

89. Herescu, *La Poésie latine*, p. 24.
90. Mustard, "Tennyson and Virgil," p. 186. See more generally, Farrell, *Latin Language*, chap. 4; and Murray, *The Classical Tradition in Poetry*.
91. Cited in Pavlock, "'Frater Ave atque Vale,'" p. 366.

implication—theirs was the difficult, acquired art of reading well. In seventh-century Wearside, appreciation of Latin verse was taught in part through grammar and in part through the rhetorical arts, such as they were, and to which we now turn.

Chapter Three

Rhetoric

Bede was not a rhetorician *per se*, but a *grammaticus*—a philologist, as it were, and a teacher. His interests lay less in enumerating rhetorical tropes than in employing them to understand Scripture. He understood the need for both a *scientia interpretandi* (science of interpretation) and a *ratio recte scribendi et loquendi* (system of proper writing and speaking)—the two branches of *grammatica*.[1] Christians had long-standing concerns about the potential corruption of a rhetorician's power of persuasion. That power manifested itself most clearly in his ability to elicit emotional responses (*pathos*), sometimes to the detriment of reason and morality. But it seems to me that Bede would have thought ignorance of rhetoric an intellectual shortcoming. More importantly, I think that he would have distinguished sharply between the use of rhetoric for Christian purposes and the study of rhetoric for its own ends.

Bede is thought to have had indirect access to about twenty-eight authors of rhetorical and grammatical handbooks, many secondhand through Isidore.[2] But, as Martin Irvine points out, *DST* is not

---

1. Irvine, "Bede the Grammarian," p. 25. For Bede's wariness, see Brown, *CB*, pp. 20–21. Kendall is not of the same opinion; see his "Bede's *Historia ecclesiastica*."
2. See especially Law, *Insular Latin Grammarians*; Irvine, "Bede the Grammarian," p. 32; Laistner, "The Library of the Venerable Bede"; *CPL*; and Lapidge, *ASL*. See also Wright, "Bede and Virgil," pp. 361–62. A list of cited sources is collated by Harris, "The Library of the Venerable Bede,"

a rhetorical treatise. "The purpose of the work," Irvine writes, "is exegetical."[3] Bede wrote *DST* for the practical use of his Christian students—and possibly for the nuns of Barking (the real ones, not our imaginary one). It is a selective list of seventeen figures or schemes and thirteen tropes useful for interpretation and composition.[4] Cassiodorus had named ninety-nine in his *Exposition of the Psalms*, a book Bede knew. Most were listed in the Leiden-Family of glosses that derive from the Canterbury school of Theodore and Hadrian, which may have influenced Bede.[5] Knowing figures is not the same as using them, though. In composition the rhetorical arts were not capriciously applied to a poetic thought, but always with an eye to propriety, what Cicero called *decorum*. Decorum concerned genre, speaker (or voice), audience, and topic. In Christian rhetoric,

---

online at oenewsletter.org. Brown, *CB*, p. 19, is wary of supposing any major rhetorical texts were at Wearmouth-Jarrow.

3. Irvine, "Bede the Grammarian," p. 36; and Brown, *CB*, pp. 23–24. A ninth-century *Accessus ad auctorem Bedam* confirms its role in early education: Bede wrote *DAM* "ad erudiendos pueros"; CCSL 123c, p.701.

4. Those "rhetorical concepts which are used for interpretation" Knappe calls "grammatical rhetoric"; "Classical Rhetoric in ASE," *p*. 9. On the absorption of rhetoric by grammar, see Vickers, *In Defence of Rhetoric*, p. 221. This modified grammatical tradition is to be distinguished from the rhetorical arts *per se*, as Brown suggests, *CB*, p. 19. Knappe notes also that the insular rhetorical tradition established by Theodore and Hadrian studied figures for use in exegesis (*TKR*, p. 143). Byhrtferth of Ramsey selected portions of Bede's *DAM* to translate into Old English; Knappe compares the two authors. See also Murphy, "The Rhetorical Lore of the *Boceras* in Byhrtferth's *Manual*." On utility as Bede's guiding principle, see Bonner, "Bede and Medieval Civilization," *p*. 81.

5. Knappe, "Classical Rhetoric," p. 17; *TKR*, pp. 237–39. Cassiodorus's *Expositio psalmorum* is cited in *DAM* and *DO*. For his complete list, see Knappe, *TKR*, Appendix B, pp. 491–99. Knappe reports that Cassiodorus's exposition must have had some impression on Bede, notwithstanding Bischoff's suggestion that Bede remained independent of the glosses of the school of Theodore and Hadrian; TKR, p. 147. The glosses are to the first fifty psalms only, and list fourteen figures; Knappe, *TKR*, p. 226, n. 2. I count only one overlap with Bede's list, *polysyndeton*.

decorum also implies divine beauty: when God rebukes Job, He directs Job to "circumda tibi decorum" (clothe thyself in beauty), as can the Lord. Later in *DAM*, and again in his commentary on Luke, Bede comments that David was a man beautiful in wisdom and virtue ("hominem decorum quidem sapientia et virtute").[6] Decorum implies elegance rather than glamor, perhaps in the way a mathematical proof can be elegant. Decorum called for discernment in the use of figures. Some but not all rhetorical figures were thought to produce specific emotional or intellectual effects in an audience; the effects in turn were considered proper to certain verse forms.[7] For example, a syndetic catalogue does not offer the same subtle force as an asyndetic one. Thus, *veni, vidi, vici* is thought to strike an ideal, attentive reader as three forcefully juxtaposed actions, rather than as three carefully serialized ones, as might be suggested by *veni et vidi vicique*. When would such forceful juxtaposition be decorous? No medieval rhetorician tells us outright. But we can infer an answer from celebrated poems. A catalogue will serve as an example.

Asyndetic catalogues appear in a number of Christian poems. Bede mentions Fortunatus, *De virginitate*, as containing especially pleasing examples.[8] Bede's recommendation comes in a discussion of dactylic verse, the optimal form of poetry ("optima carminis forma"). The context of Bede's discussion implies that the catalogue is associated with a high style, proper to heroic poems, epideictic verse, and formal prose. Fortunatus also uses the high style in his letter to Pope Gregory the Great. He begins that letter with a catalogue of qualities of Latin prose and poetry that were highly valued:

> Acuminum suorum luculenta ueteris aetatis ingenia qui natura feruidi, curatura fulgidi, usu triti, auso securi, ore freti, more

---

6. Job 40:10. Kendall, *Libri II*, p. 196. On voice as persona, Bede writes of the *Song of Songs* in which "uox alternans C[h]risti et ecclesiae"; Bede, *DAM*, XXV.

7. See Carruthers, *The Experience of Beauty*, p. 29. These figures are not the same as *topoi*, such as the *ubi sunt* motif.

8. Bede, *DAM*, XI; Kendall, *Libri II*, pp. 104–5.

festiui, praeclaris operibus celebraturi posteris stupore laudanda reliquere uestigia, certe illi inuentione prouidi, partitione serii, distributione librati, epilogiorum calce iucundi, colae fonte proflui, commate succiso uenusti, tropis paradigmis periodis epichirematibus coronati pariter et coturnati, tale sui canentes dederunt specimen ut adhuc nostro tempore quasi sibi postumi uiuere credantur etsi non carne uel carmine.[9]

(In their acumen, the brilliant geniuses of ancient times who, ebullient in temperament, sparkling in culture, proven in taste, controlled in audacity, self-assured in eloquence, cheerful in character, celebrated through splendid masterpieces, left to posterity astonishment and praiseworthy footsteps; these men surely were prophetic in invention, earnest in classification, balanced in division, pleasant in the reckoning of an epilogue, flowing in a fountain of phrases, beautiful in brief clauses, wreathed together and elevated by the grandeur and nobility of tropes, examples, periods, syllogisms— their singing gave such an ideal that still into our time one believes it to be alive, if not in flesh then in song.)

Fortunatus not only catalogues valued qualities, but also demonstrates them. We see prolepsis, an anticipation of a referent, which is described by Bede in *DST*. The third word, *luculenta* 'brilliant', causes a reader to anticipate a referent that then arrives three words later, *ingenia* 'geniuses, qualities, talents'. In prolepsis, the grammatical anticipation of a reader is carefully managed through an alternation of grammatical discord and resolution. Pronouns await referents, nouns await verbs, adjectives await nouns, phrases await balance, until the whole composition resolves itself (sometimes in perfect antithesis or faulty parallelism).[10] Augustine wrote that God "governs human history as though with the trope of antithesis." Another figure of anticipation is zeugma, or a yoking of many words with a single verb or clause, found in Fortunatus's set of phrases that

---

9. Fortunatus, "Praefatio," in Fortunatus, Poems, 1:2; my translation.
10. In Carruthers, *The Experience of Beauty*, p. 23, n. 11.

resolves in the verb *dederunt* 'they gave'. The first set of phrases, a catalogue of qualities describing the ancients, is balanced numerically (seven items) and phonetically (-/i/) with a second set of phrases, a catalogue of qualities of their work. Fortunatus balances both catalogues further by resolving each with an elaborate phrase containing a perfect active verb (*reliquere, dederunt*). There are a dozen more rhetorical figures besides. As befits an opening paragraph, Fortunatus has written a balanced, artful, ordered sentence in which grammatical tension provides energy and flavor.

To describe Fortunatus's ordered art requires rhetorical training. Like any mechanical art, rhetoric requires a knowledge of parts. But to compose such ordered art requires a knowledge of the proper deployment of figures. When is a catalogue appropriate? Why ought a poet to employ zeugma? What effect does hirmus have on a reader? Answers to these sorts of questions seem to be largely impressionistic. But again, readers were trained to accept those impressions as the basis of cultivated reading. Although Anglo-Saxons of the early period were unlikely to have been schooled in the *ars bene dicendi* (art of speaking well) as it was codified by Quintilian and others, that tradition "subtly entered the field of grammar," as Gabrielle Knappe writes, and became the "tradition of rhetoric within grammar."[11] Basic rhetorical training became part of the grammar school curriculum. Moreover, the rhetorical tradition of ancient Greece was recalibrated to a distinct Christian style, which in turn developed during the fourth and fifth centuries.[12] Readers were trained from a young age to react positively to that style. Poets and readers were trained to admire, for example, a combination of substantives, adjectives, and verbs in a parallel sequence. It was called the golden line (adj-1 | adj-2 | verb | noun-1 | noun-2). Thus Aldhelm's "LUCIDA **stelligeri** qui condis CULMINA **caeli**" (literally, "BRIGHT, **starry**, [you] who make HEIGHTS **heavens**"). Wilkinson says of the golden line that Horace

---

11. Knappe, "Classical Rhetoric," p. 7.
12. Mohrmann, "Augustine and the Eloquentia," 1:356.

"reserved its monumental quality for special purposes."[13] A verb between two nouns and two adjectives is rarer, but not unknown.[14] One sees it in Virgil, Juvenal, Lucan, Sidonius, and others. In some Irish texts the figure may be more frequent. For example, text A of the *Hisperica Famina* shows 180 specimens in 612 lines. The figure seems to have been widely known and used in the British Isles.[15] Aldhelm employs the figure, but, as Michael Winterbottom argues, likely borrowed it from classical models or perhaps Spanish ones.[16]

But just how sensitive are our antennae to these structures? How responsive are our palates to their monumentality? Indeed, how appreciative or responsive were Anglo-Saxons? Latin poets employed the golden line sparsely in hexameters, but it appealed to Irish writers.[17] Bede reported it to be "optima . . . versus dactyli ac pulcherrima est positio" (the best and most beautiful arrangement of a dactylic hexameter verse).[18] It is difficult to tell whether we are hearing a description of Bede's untutored tastes or the result of his trained literary palate—if such things can be or ought to be differentiated. Mary Carruthers suggests that "medieval aesthetic experience is bound into human sensation"; one wonders whether a refinement of taste increases the discernment of one's senses.[19] Perhaps. That question aside, as a consequence of these serial prejudices, associations, and impressionistic judgments, a tradition of cultivated literary taste develops and is cherished. That tradition is sustained through the careful and appreciative study of canonical authors. It shows itself occasionally in glosses, commentaries, and grammatical and rhetorical handbooks.

---

13. Wilkinson, *GLA*, p. 216.
14. Kerlouégan, "Une mode stylistique," p. 278. He reads from Marouzeau, *Traité*, pp. 319 ff.
15. Kerlouégan, "Une mode stylistique," pp. 276 and 293.
16. Winterbottom, "Aldhelm's Prose Style and its Origins."
17. Orchard, *PAA*, p. 97. Wilkinson, *GLA*, p. 216, offers statistics.
18. Bede, *DAM*, XI; Kendall, *Liber II*, p. 102. See especially Kerlouégan, "Une mode stylistique," pp. 275–97. He discusses variants on pp. 277–78.
19. Carruthers, *The Experience of Beauty*, p. 8.

Bede is not a nineteenth-century aesthete, but a devoted Christian monk and priest, and his aesthetic reflexes are part and parcel of that devotion. He was trained to develop those reflexes as a component of his evolving Christian vocation, especially in light of Scripture.[20] He explains that not only should students understand that Scripture is authoritative, divine, and useful in leading one to eternal life, but also that it "praeeminet positione dicendi" (excels in its presentation of speaking). *Positio* is, among other things, a grammarian's word; Aldhelm uses it almost exclusively in descriptions of syllables and meter. *Dico* likewise, to some degree and in combination: the *ars dicendi* are the rhetorical arts. Cassiodorus called them the arts of "pulchre loquendi" (gorgeous speaking).[21] The implication that readers have drawn from Bede's phrase is that Scripture is the best teacher of grammar and rhetoric, of the art of speaking well. One need not study rhetoricians' rules; Scripture will suffice. Augustine, too, saw in Scripture the model of sacred eloquence.[22] In the first instance, Bede is being practical: to understand the language of Scripture, a reader has to recognize unusual locutions. In the second instance, there is more to Scripture than a collection of facts or moral lessons, or even aesthetic principles and paradigms. Scripture models Christian speech. In Scripture, Bede explains, the order of words sometimes differs from common usage. Why? For decorousness,

---

20. Brown, *CB*, p. 18. On Christian literary aesthetics in this period more generally, see Mohrmann, "La langue et le style." Mohrmann writes that what set early Christians against pagan poetry was not a general antipathy toward art, but a hostility to decadence: "La gravité et l'enthousiasme des premieres chrétiens, l'heroïsme des martyrs, la conviction et la certitude intérieure des apologistes des premiers siècles ne trouvaient pas une expression adéquate dans une poésie qui vivait seulement dans les cercles des grammairiens et des rhéteurs" ("The gravity and enthusiasm of the first Christians, the heroism of the martyrs, the conviction and interior certainty of the apologists of the first centuries did not find adequate expression in a poetry that lived only within circles of grammarians and rhetoricians") 1:153.
21. In Knappe, "Classical Rhetoric," p. 11. Cassiodorus notes that they are collected from illustrious poets.
22. Augustine, *DDC*, 4.7.11. Also Evenepoel, "The Place of Poetry."

"causa decoris," in Bede's phrase. *Decor, decoris* 'beauty, grace' points to the primary aim of classical rhetoric: *decorum*. The meaning of that primary aim shifts under Christian aegis and through Augustine's influence to describe a factor of evangelization.[23]

As has been proposed, effects of schemes—that which caused them to be useful for evangelization and exegesis—were vaguely and impressionistically codified in literary practice. But there exists no chart of direct correspondences between figures and effects. Hilary of Poitiers wrote, "The Christian message ... requires a dignified phrasing," but what dignity entailed precisely is a difficult issue, especially given the *sermo humilis* of the Gospels. The fisherman's Latin of God challenged Ciceronian eloquence to its exclusive claim to dignity, and Bede describes his own prose style in his prose *Life of Cuthbert* as *sermo simplex*.[24] The convoluted issue of stylistic decorum significantly affected Christians who defend the faith "in hoc opere sermonis" (in this labor of words, *DDC*, IV, iv). In a cloistered world that values words so highly, tropes are more than capricious decoration: "The sweetness of scriptural tropes disentangles readers from worldly enjoyments and delights them with 'sweetness that would make us blessed.'"[25] Rhetorical pleasure is transformed by

---

23. Murphy, *Rhetoric in the Middle Ages*, pp. 58–59. Augustine wishes to use rhetoric "in the active service of the ministry," p. 59. This repurposing of the rhetorical arts dissolved the relation between matter and form that motivated the classical, Ciceronian hierarchies of style. For Augustine, the Christian writer's subject is revelation, the highest of matters. See Auerbach, *Literary Language*, on the *sermo humilis*, esp. pp. 36–39; and Evenepoel, "The Place of Poetry," p. 40.
24. *In Psalm*. 13:1 (CSEL 22: pp. 78–79); cited in Evenepoel, "The Place of Poetry," p. 43. On *sermo simplex*, see *Two Lives of Saint Cuthbert*, ed. Colgrave, p. 144. Also Norden, *AK*, 2:668.
25. Olmsted, *Rhetoric*, p. 40, quoting Augustine, *DDC*, 4.7. She continues, "Delightful style is not cultivated for its own sake, but so that listeners may 'feast delightedly on truth'"—p. 40; *DDC*, 4.26. In a very useful essay, W. Evanepoel cites Lactantius, who writes, "Itaque si voluptas est audire cantus et carmina, Dei laudes canere et audire iucundum est. Haec est voluptas vera quae comes est et socia virtutis" (And so if it is a pleasure to

Augustine into a cultivated form of spiritual delight. But among clerics and *grammatici*, whose lives are spent working with words, that pleasure threatens to be an end in itself rather than a means to higher things. George Hardin Brown notes that in Bede's commentary on Samuel, Bede warns "that Christians should neither love nor pursue too ardently the sweetness of secular eloquence."[26] Here, critics have long concentrated on "secular," but "eloquence" is equally at issue. The spiritual utility of eloquence leads Bede to advocate its mature appreciation and careful employment. Likely following Augustine, whose work *De doctrina christiana* he had excerpted (perhaps on the model of Eugippius), Bede is preparing his student to appreciate the clearer, if syntactically uncommon, passages of Scripture before introducing tropes of figurative expression like metaphor and metonymy.[27] More importantly, Bede prepares his students to appreciate the grace of Scripture and the power of its words to open the heart to truth. The techniques of its persuasive power can be discerned and employed by the Christian *grammaticus*; Scripture offers lessons not only in terms of actions, but also in terms of language. To put

---

hear chants and songs, let it be a joy to hear and sing the praises of God. This is the true pleasure which is the companion and associate of virtue); in Evenepoel, "The Place of Poetry," p. 42, trans. M. F. McDonald. One must be moderate in that delight, Bede warns in his commentary on Samuel; see Ray, "Bede and Cicero," pp. 4–5. Alan Thacker puts it well: "For [Bede] education, moral teaching and spiritual understanding were inextricably linked. Taking what was available, he selected and integrated Christian and classical learning, to shape a new educative framework. He also produced an oeuvre designed to meet its needs"; Thacker, "Bede and the Ordering of Understanding," pp. 62–63. See also Bonner, "Bede and Medieval Civilization," pp. 86–87.

26. Brown, *CB*, pp. 19–20. On the centrality of *grammatica* to Bede's work generally, see Irvine, "Bede the Grammarian," p. 38.

27. See Augustine, *DDC*, 3.2.2; trans. Robertson. On Augustine, see further Olmsted, *Rhetoric*, pp. 34–37. Bede's excerpts are collated by Hurst, *Bede the Venerable*. Augustine's connection to the opening of *DST* is described by Holtz, "Bède et la tradition grammaticale latine," p. 15.

it another way, Christian literary style is learned from the Word to better preach the Word.

Which figures does one need? Bede names the "eminentiores" 'more noteworthy' (I.i) of figures: prolepsis, zeugma, hypozeuxis, syllepsis, anadiplosis, anaphora, epanalepsis, epizeuxis, paranomasia, schesis onomaton, paromoeon, homoeoteleuton, homoeoptoton, polyptoton, hirmus, polysyndeton, and dialyton. He describes each one in a brief paragraph and illustrates it with a passage or two from Scripture. Bede's list parallels exactly the list in Donatus, *Ars Maior*, III, v, and (with three slight exceptions) the list compiled by Isidore of Seville in his *Etymologiae*.[28] What differentiates Bede's list from his sources are the examples. While Donatus and Isidore use classical authors, Bede uses only Scripture. Those Scriptural examples recommended his grammar to later Christian readers. Yet why ought these particular figures occupy Bede, aside from their easy availability in Donatus and Isidore? Donatus names seventeen he thinks "necessaria" (necessary). But necessary to what? To understanding classical poetry, one assumes. Isidore says the seventeen are "inveniuntur" (found). But where are they found? In the works of pagan poets, as both Donatus and Cassiodorus suggest? Although one may be satisfied to imagine Bede simply passing on information, to list what both Donatus and Isidore had listed seems redundant. Bede's full coordination of schemes with Scripture suggests more.

Bede does not merely replace pagan citations with Christian citations; he displaces the rhetorical authority of Augustan Latin by finding the origins of all rhetoric in the Holy Word. Although he follows Augustine in "using secular learning for Christian purposes," Bede demonstrates the Christian origins of that learning.[29] He jokes

---

28. Keil, *GL* 4, pp. 397–98; Isidore, *Etym*, 1.36. See Holtz, "Bède et la tradition grammaticale latine," p. 17. Isidore replaces Donatus's epanaphora with epanalepsis, reverses homoeoptoton and homoeoteleuton, and adds hypallage.

29. The quotation is from Knappe, "Classical Rhetoric," p. 14, and a commonplace in Christian rhetoric. Holtz, "Bède et la tradition grammaticale latine," writes that Bede hopes to "christianiser la grammaire," p. 13. But

that the Greeks boast that they invented figures and schemes, but Augustine had observed figures in Scripture.[30] Augustine moreover had famously encouraged Christians in his *De doctrina christiana* to instruct others "by rousing the emotions of the heart through appropriate stylistic devices."[31] Augustine wonders why Christians would abandon a worthwhile tool. And again, Bede seems to be responding profoundly not only to Augustine's suggestion (raised most clearly in his *De ordine*) to separate grammar and rhetoric from its service to pagan poetry, but also to Augustine's caution about idolizing signs. In *DDC* III, ix.13, Augustine writes,

> He is a slave to a sign who uses or worships a significant thing without knowing what it signifies. But he who uses or venerates a sign divinely instituted whose signifying force he understands does not venerate what he sees and what passes away but rather that to which all such things are to be referred. Such a man is spiritual and free, even during that time of servitude in which it is not yet opportune to reveal to carnal minds those signs under whose yoke they are to be tamed.[32]

---

the point is that Bede is not baptizing an existing tradition so much as revealing its birth certificate. See Irvine, "Bede the Grammarian," pp. 35–36.

30. Augustine, *DDC*, 3.19, and Kendall, *Liber II*, p. 40. Augustine's revolutionary point in *DDC* 4 is that eloquence must be a means, never an end. Mohrmann writes that "he is here in opposition with the spirit of his time, and with age-old tradition"; Mohrmann, "Augustine and the Eloquentia," 1:359. Again, "For Augustine the Christian orator serves not the spoken word but truth, and this truth is in the first instance to be drawn from the Scriptures, which he must read over and over again and which must be his model and source of oratory," 1:362.

31. Cipriani, "Rhetoric," p. 724.

32. Trans. Robertson, pp. 86–87; "Sub signo enim servit qui operatur aut veneratur aliquam rem significantem, nesciens quid significet. Qui vero aut operatur aut veneratur utile signum divinitus institutum, cuius vim significationemque intellegit, non hoc veneratur quod videtur et transit, sed illud potius quo talia cuncta referenda sunt. Talis autem homo spiritalis et liber est, etiam tempore servitutis, quo carnalibus animis nondum oportet signa illa revelari, quorum iugo edomandi sunt"; *PL* 34:30. On Augustine in *De*

The carnality of the Word is at issue. Bede wrote that he gave himself entirely to the study of Scripture ("omnem meditandis scripturis operam dedi," *HE*, 5.24, p. 566). Bede, a worker in the field of words, seems to be pointing out to his students that their intense study of rhetoric is not idolatrous. Instead, rhetorical schemes and their particular effects are here authorized by their origin in Scripture. They are things divinely instituted, for Scripture "divina est, vel utilitate" (is both divine and useful). The argument, if I read Bede correctly, seems to suggest that schemes could thus be justifiably employed in one's pastoral or pedagogical role without fear of idolizing one's own fluency.

Bede connects rhetorical figures to his Scriptural examples in two ways, and both bear on poetics. The first, which concerns Bede's Old Testament examples, is focused on rhetorical effect. I shall review these before turning to the second, which concerns New Testament examples and is focused on theme. The connection Bede makes is not merely one of citation, but of allusion—of the letter and the spirit, if you will. Allusion is a more complex matter than a simple index of A to B. Andy Orchard points out that it is not enough to identify an allusion, to say this or that quote is from Prudentius. One must understand the larger implications of an allusion, to ask what Prudentius meant to seventh-century readers of Anglo-Latin, which Orchard does at some length in his study of Aldhelm's poetic art.[33] In short, allusions also invoke an author's reputation. Rhetorical texts cited Virgil on account of his masterful Latin and his place in the pantheon of Latin writers. But with respect to specific citations, such as line 161 of Book Twelve of the *Aeneid*, which specific implications were on offer? What was the scope of such an allusion?

---

ordine, see Irvine, *The Making of Textual Culture*, p. 89. Bede did not have access to *De ordine*; see Lapidge, *Library*, s.v., Laistner's *Handlist*, and Bonner, "Bede and Medieval Civilization," p. 89. Augustine makes the same point elsewhere in his writings.

33. Orchard, "'Audite omnes amantes,'" p. 165. Helen Conrad O'Briain writes, "How they [citations] were understood and used is as important as where they were found"; see her "Bede's Use of Classical Poetry," p. 46.

One of the more widely used textbooks in the seventh-century classroom was a commentary on Virgil by Servius, like St. Jerome a student of Donatus. Book Four of the *Aeneid* begins with Dido longing for Aeneas. Servius comments,

> Apollonius wrote the *Argonautica* and in the third book portrays Medea in love; this book [of the *Aeneid*] was carried over entirely from there. It is, moreover, almost wholly concerned with feelings [of love]. . . . Of course the entire book is concerned with plots and contrivances, for its style is nearly comic; and not surprisingly where the subject of love is treated.[34]

The commentary tells us something very important about the reception of love stories and of the role of *consilium* 'plot' and *subtilitas* 'contrivance' in them. When Dido is said to feed her veins in IV.2, Servius explains that "love runs through the veins just like poison (*venenum*)," playing with the word for vein, *vena*. As this example illustrates, words, phrases, lines, passages, and whole books are given an authoritative *accessus*, a guide to readers that shapes the reception and later use of classical passages. One might note in this regard that Jerome wrote an *accessus* for each book of the Bible. Implications of specific Christian allusions—the first verse of Psalm 1, for example—can be traced in commentaries. To speak of the *beatus vir* is to invoke not only Psalm 1, but also the received understanding of what *beatus* means in Patristic and liturgical tradition. Just as a citation of a Virgilian line carries with it a received understanding of that citation, similarly a verse of Scripture carries with it a received understanding of that verse. In coordinating grammar with Scripture, Bede seems to be coordinating the received understanding of a classical citation to the received understanding of a Scriptural citation. He is coordinating allusions. We can observe it in his discussion of prolepsis.

Prolepsis, an anticipation, is demonstrated by both Donatus and Isidore with a citation of Virgil, *Aeneid*, 12.161, "Interea reges ingenti

---

34. *Servius' Commentary on Book Four of Virgil's* Aeneid, trans. McDonough et al.; their translation.

mole, Latinus." In his commentary on Virgil, Servius notes the convoluted order of these words, a long hyperbaton.[35] The line comes early in Book Twelve as the armies of Aeneas and Turnus draw together before the city gates in anticipation of battle. Juturna, sister to Aeneas's foe Turnus, weeps for her brother. Juno, who is standing on the summit of a mountain, counsels Juturna to try any stratagem to save Turnus. Next, writes Virgil proleptically, they ride forth, the kings. Then he names them. First comes Latinus, king of the city; behind him, Turnus; and in the distance, Aeneas "Romanae stirpis origo" (source of the Roman stock).[36] Here is an especially decorous moment for prolepsis, grandly heightening audience expectation, and delaying a full description and naming of kings. In its place, Bede adduces an example from the Psalms. Why the Psalms? And why this verse of all the thousands he might have chosen? One possibility is that Bede was led to it by the mountain on which Juno stands and the city gates before which Virgil's battle takes place: "Fundamenta *eius* in montibus sanctis; diligit Dominus portas Sion" (The foundations *thereof* are in the holy mountains: [2] The Lord loveth the gates of Sion, Psalm 86:1–2; my italics). "Thereof" anticipates "the Lord," giving us prolepsis. Like the passage from the *Aeneid*, the psalm speaks of "writings of peoples and of princes," of foreigners and of battles. Cassiodorus explains, "In the first part of [Psalm 86], the prophet speaks to the faithful, proclaiming the heavenly city. In the second, the Lord Saviour by citation of different names announces that this city will come to believe." He continues by noting, "Though the prophet has previously said nothing of the city of God, he seems to discuss the foundations of it as if he has already said something about its summit." Cassiodorus says that the rhetorical figure "is called *anastrophe* or inversion, when what ought to have been expressed first is placed second."[37] In this case,

---

35. Servius, *Commentarii*, 2:594.
36. Trans. Fairclough, *Virgil*, p. 311. All further translations of Virgil are by Fairclough. Note that *origo* (and the origin point, Aeneas) comes last rather than first.
37. Cassiodorus, *Expositio;* trans. Walsh, 3:336–38.

the verse is also proleptic. Cassiodorus comments that this psalm proclaims the City of God; Virgil had proclaimed the city of Rome. A comparison between the eternal Christian city and pagan Augustan Rome is central to Bede's *Hymn to Aethelthryth* in his *HE*, which speaks of the relation of Christian to pagan verse. For Bede and his readers, prolepsis is a Scriptural scheme, illustrated in the Psalms, and only afterwards a scheme adopted by pagan rhetors. In both examples, it appears in formal, dignified descriptions.

Also germane to Bede's example is Augustine's commentary on Psalm 86, especially his discussion of the role of Christ in the image of Zion. If the foundations of the holy mountain are in Zion, did the apostles build upon that foundation? In other words, asks Augustine, do the Gentiles, not being Jews, have any place in Zion?[38] Might we imagine, too, that the question nagged at Christian poets, anxious that their own efforts built upon pagan literary forms. Bede has already answered that anxiety by illustrating the historical primacy of Scripture. He also indicates the salvific power of Scripture. Like Augustine, Bede held that "Christ is the first and greatest foundation," upon whom all later traditions were built.[39] And perhaps speaking to those who imagine the literary primacy of the Virgilian line that Bede has effaced, Augustine writes that the Lord "loves the spiritual city more than all those that prefigured it, more than those earthly ones which hinted at the city that abides forever, the eternal, heavenly city of peace."[40] Virgil's line is used in part by Cyprian of Gaul, so-called, whose poetic *Heptateuch* Bede knew and cited in his various grammatical works. During the early fifth century in southern Gaul, Cyprian wrote hexametrical paraphrases of the Old Testament. His aim, according to Roberts, "is to bring the scriptural text into conformity with the standards of poetic excellence, in particular of Virgilian epic, as understood by late antiquity."[41] In his paraphrase

---

38. Augustine, *Exposition*, 4:247.
39. Ibid., 4:248.
40. Ibid., 4:251.
41. Roberts, *The Jeweled Style*, p. 9. See also McBrine, "The English Inheritance of Biblical Verse." And for Bede's opinion, see verse *VSC*, lines 20–21.

of Genesis 26:26, at a moment when Isaac seems to be threatened by his enemies, Cyprian writes, "Interea reges veniunt Abimelus et Ozas" (l. 860). The Vulgate reads, "Ad quem locum cum venissent de Geraris Abimelech, et Ochozath amicus illius" (literally, with phrases demarked, "to which place | when came | from Geraris | Abimelech and Ochozath his friend"). The anticipation evident in the syntax of the Vulgate correlates with the proleptic phrasing of Cyprian. A threefold correspondence in style and matter is suggestive: in the Vulgate, Cyprian, and Virgil, the figure of prolepsis heightens anticipation in a description of an assembly just before imminent conflict. Bede has found an example that has the same effect in Scripture as it does in Virgil. In a number of other schemes, Bede connects rhetorical figures to Old Testament examples through their rhetorical effects.

A second strategy of connection involves New Testament examples and concerns coordinated themes. Bede wrote that Scripture takes primacy on account of both its antiquity and its ability to lead one to eternal life. In figures with New Testament examples, the second sort of primacy seems to obtain. The New Testament, after all, cannot show the relative antiquity of Scripture, since Virgil wrote before Christ. Consider one of Bede's two examples for zeugma. Zeugma, as we have seen, is another figure of grammatical anticipation, a scheme in which a series of words or phrases is concluded by a single verb or clause. Anticipation arises while the reader awaits syntactic completeness. Some rhetors see zeugma as a form of ellipsis, in which a verb is omitted from one or more phrases. There's no practical difference between these views, but Bede's view allows one to see more clearly how the figure embodies the theme of multiplicity in unity. A multiplicity of words, phrases, or ideas is unified (but not erased) through a single element like a verb or a phrase. As an example of this figure, Donatus cites his favorite source, Virgil's *Aeneid*: "Troiugena, interpres diuum, qui numina Phoebi, / qui tripodas, Clarii laurus, qui sidera SENTIS" (O son of Troy, interpreter of the gods, who the will of Phoebus, / the tripods, the laurel of the Clarian, the stars [all] KNOWS, 3.359–60; trans. modified). This verse is spoken during a banquet given to Aeneas and his homeless

Trojans as they make their way around northwestern Greece toward Italy. On landing, they meet Andromache, who has been married off to Helenus, a fellow Trojan, king of Epirus, and a *vates* 'poet, seer'. This small portion of the Trojan diaspora lives in a city built to look like Troy. Aeneas asks Helenus for a prophecy. Helenus then describes the trials awaiting Aeneas and his men on the long road ahead.

In replacing it, Bede could have used any of dozens of examples from the Old Testament.[42] Instead, he replaces Virgil with Ephesians 4:31,"Omnis amaritudo et ira et indignatio et clamor et blasphemia TOLLATUR a uobis cum omni malitia" (Let all bitterness, and anger, and indignation, and clamor, and blasphemy, BE PUT AWAY from you, with all malice).[43] The nouns are resolved by zeugma in the verb "tollatur." One connection between the examples from Virgil and Ephesians is the general topic of a diaspora that desires unity. Ephesians was written at a time before the foundation of the Papacy and the centralization of the Roman Church. The Christians of Ephesus, one of numerous widely disposed churches, sought immediate counsel from Paul and, ultimately, a true home. Perhaps that similarity led Bede from Virgil to Paul. More specifically, in this chapter of Ephesians, Paul is calling upon the fractured church of Ephesus to "keep the unity of the Spirit in the bond of peace" (4:3). In the unity of the Spirit and in Christ, writes Paul, men shall no more be "children tossed to and fro, and carried about by every wind of doctrine" (4:14). In a very literal way, Aeneas and his seafaring men are carried about by every wind. They are at risk from every malice of men and gods as they seek a home. Yet they struggle on.

A diaspora that desires unity is also germane to Bede's Christmas sermon on Luke 1:21. There, Bede also cites Ephesians 4. He reminds Christians of a common desire to find a heavenly home and advises in the words of Paul to "put off the old man . . . and put on the

---

42. E.g., Deuteronomy 18:10–11; 19:21; Psalm 25:7; Judges 12:19; though none are as extensive as the example Bede uses.
43. Bede, *DST*, p. 144; Kendall, *Libri II*, pp. 170–71.

new man."⁴⁴ Bede explains in his *De mansionibus filiorum Israel* of 716 that this phrase from Ephesians means "following the way of virtues," which is "the ascent of spiritual virtues seeking the sublime, to which the Church of Christ (and indeed, every faithful soul) hurries to climb in hope of being set free from this vale of tears to go up to the place laid out for it above (that is, to see *the God of gods in Zion* [Psalm 84:7])."⁴⁵ It is a familiar motif in Old English poetry: the wandering, homeless Christian seeking the peace and unity of a heavenly home. Bede explains Ephesians 4 similarly in his commentary on 1 Samuel 6:7, describing the unity of catholic peace that frees men from the yoke of sin.⁴⁶ And in his commentary on the Canticle of Habakkuk, Bede writes that Zorobabel and Joshua

> were once deported from Judea to Babylon but returned once more to their homeland. These scripture calls the children of the deportation, and tells how they restored by the enthusiasm of their great dedication the sacred things which the enemy had destroyed. This is the clearest figure of our own condition. For in our first parent we were removed from our heavenly homeland and brought into the Babylon, i.e. the confusion, of this world; but by the bounty of the Lord Jesus Christ, our king and high priest of whom Zorobabel and Joshua were a type, we were recalled once more to the homeland and vision of supreme peace. . . ."⁴⁷

As Aeneas and his men find themselves homeless, so do Christians. Both historically and thematically, Bede appears to relate the transcendent value of Aeneas's wandering to the situation in Ephesians. In the home that is Christ, bitterness and anger are put away. And perhaps to emphasize his point about a home in Christ, Bede also adduces an

---

44. Trans. Martin, in Martin and Hurst, *Bede the Venerable*, 1:109.
45. Trans. Foley and Holder, *Bede: A Biblical Miscellany*, pp. 34 and 33, their italics.
46. Bede, *In primam partem Samuhelis*, CCSL 119, p. 51. Bede's word for "yoke" is *iugum* and relates to his term for the effect of zeugma, *coniunctio*. *Coniugare* is to join in marriage, and is used of Aethelthryth.
47. §36. Trans. Connolly, *Bede: On Tobit*, p. 90.

example for zeugma from Psalm 14:2–5, "qui ingreditur sine macula et operatur iustitiam . . . qui FACIT haec non movebitur in aeternum" (He that walketh without blemish, and worketh justice . . . he that DOES these things shall not be moved for ever). He who wanders in Christ, who is led beside the still waters in the paths of righteousness, can be planted finally in a true home. Such at least is one possibility among many to explain Bede's very specific choices here. My aim here is not as much to choose among them, as it is to indicate that Bede's choices are possible subjects of contemplation. One other consideration here is that the scene in the *Aeneid* is taking place in a replica of Troy, a simulacrum of the home that Helenus, Andromache, Aeneas, and his men have lost. Perhaps the implicit relation between a false home and the true one, between sign and signified, between a scattered Trojan diaspora and the foundation of pagan Rome, between scattered Christian churches and the foundation of Christian Rome, and between scattered pieces of grammar yoked together in zeugma all prompted Bede to recollect these Scriptures.

A last thing to be said about zeugma is its effect in a poetic line. Among other uses is enjambment. Virgil will hold substantives, adjectives, and so forth in suspension in a line until he yokes them together by a line-initial verb. The verb gives instant order to the previous line. For example, "in segetem veluti cum flamma furentibus austris / INCIDIT" (as when upon a corn-crop in a south-wind gale fire swoops).[48] This suspension of order first creates a sense of anticipation, of symmetrical disorder, of managed confusion, and then a sense of resolution and comprehension. It is a figure natural to formal Latin salutations. In the salutation of his Prologue to his prose *Life of Cuthbert*, Bede suspends a series of phrases naming Bishop Eadfrith, the Lindisfarne Brethren, and himself before resolving, as is typical, with "salutem" (I wish health to).[49] The salutation of his

---

48. Trans., Wilkinson, *GLA*, p. 66. Wilkinson recommends further examples in Marouzeau, *Traité*, pp. 307–8.
49. *Vita sancti Cuthberti*, trans. Colgrave, p. 142. On hyperbaton with non-verbal heads, see Devine and Stephens, *Latin Word Order*, pp. 563–67.

verse *Life of Cuthbert* is similar. And the first clause of his hexameter verse life is a zeugma: "Multa suis dominus fulgescere lumina saeclis / Donavit" (The Lord HAS GIVEN many lights to his world to glitter). The sense of this verse unfolds in a convoluted hyperbaton, literally: *many, his, the Lord, to glitter, lights, world, gave*. It is almost a golden line; but in the center sits the glittering light of the Lord rather than a single verb.[50] Readers are invited to be alert to these subtle sensations as they read. Grammatical anticipation and convolution are deflected and slowly resolved. Semantic ambiguities, such as the image of *lumina*—which could be the sun, the stars, or the Son—await clarification (which comes with "Christus / Lux" and "lucernae / Ecclesiae," lines 4–6, both enjambed, and with "nova lux fidei," line 9, as well as with the various saints). A poem thus becomes more than a list of statements; it becomes a series of sensations, each invoked seriatim. Some resolve what has passed; some anticipate what is to come. A reader responds not only to single words, but also to words and phrases in successive relation, like someone listening to a concerto who responds not to each note individually, but to notes in temporal relation to one another. Syntax, to continue the metaphor, yields a melodic line set within polyphonic counterpoint. Zeugma describes one pattern of that melodic development.

Other figures with New Testament examples also bear upon the poetics of Bede's verse. One can, if one wishes, search for connections between Donatus's examples and Bede's. To my mind, those connections exist, but it would be tedious to review them all. There are, nevertheless, a few items of further interest in some of Bede's figures. *Paromoeon* (alliteration) has always been a feature of Latin poetry, notwithstanding claims that it is an especially Germanic device.[51] It was used in legal formulas, proverbs, idiomatic doublets, and prayers—e.g., *in saecula saeculorum*. Caesar's famous line

---

50. See Wright, "The Metrical Art(s) of Bede," 1:164.
51. See Winterbottom, "Aldhelm's Prose Style," p. 49, n. 3. He gives a substantial number of examples from classical authors. One might add Corippus's hexameter poem on the Libyan War (MGH 3.2), 1.22, as just one of thousands of examples, but one noteworthy for its serial alliteration,

alliterates: "veni vidi vici." Alliteration was often deployed in early dactylic poetry, and it is necessary to certain figures like *adnominatio* or *polyptoton*. Donatus cites as an example a famous line from Ennius, one of the earliest Latin versifiers, who was reputed to have brought the dactylic hexameter from Greek into Latin: "O Tite, tute, Tati, tibi tanta, tyranne, tulisti" (O Titus Tatius, tyrant, you brought upon yourself such great misfortunes!). This line was intended, it seems, to emphasize pathos resulting from a disquieting dream.[52] In keeping with generations of classical scholars, Winterbottom suggests that alliteration in classical authors might be used to call notice to a particular passage.[53] Orchard points out a passage in a hymn to St. Patrick in which "the use of alliteration points up a conscious chiastic patterning of syntax."[54] Another use of alliteration is to suggest the comic, especially in describing a lover's infatuation, as Servius suggested above.[55] It is unlikely in Anglo-Saxon England, however, where vernacular poetry was built on alliteration, that paromoeon suggested humor.

Bede cautions that paromoeon is best sought in "ea lingua qua Scriptura est edita requiritur" (the language in which the Scripture was required to be published), that is, Latin.[56] Note the remarkable rhyme in this claim, and the consequent hiatus. Is Bede subtly indicating the artful, decorous capabilities of Latin? One of Bede's

---

"saeva superpositis plectuntur colla catenis." Marouzeau says, "L'allitération est un fait universel," *Traité*, p. 45.

52. Conte, *Latin Literature* p. 81, trans. Solodow.
53. Winterbottom, "Aldhelm's Prose Style," p. 42.
54. Orchard, "Audite omnes amantes," p. 156: "qui caeleste haurit uinum in uasis caelestibus" (l. 67). Jaager opines that alliteration played no meaningful role in Bede's poetry; *VSC*, p. 22.
55. The verse in Latin reads, "vulnus alit venis, et caeco carpitur igni" (IV.2); *Servius' Commentary*, pp. 2–3.
56. Kendall, *Libri II*, p. 176; my trans. Kendall translates, "the language in which the Scripture was first proclaimed." Although Kendall's meaning is clear, to my pedestrian mind the language indicated is ambiguous: Hebrew, Greek, or Latin. Bede seems to be referring to Jerome and his Vulgate, whom he perhaps trusted to maintain the alliterative patterns of the Hebrew.

examples, Psalm 117:26–27 in the *Vetus Latina*, or Old Latin, reads, "Benediximus vos de domo Domini; Deus Dominus et inluxit nobis."[57] We see in *Domini* and *Dominus* the figure of *polyptoton*, where a word is repeated with a different inflection, and in *domo* and *Domini* perhaps the figure of *paregmenon*, where two cognate words appear—such as "wisdom" and "wise." Polyptoton encourages alliteration, and examples in Christian poetry indicate an admiration of the ornament, if used judiciously. Still, some alliteration seems extreme. Poem 23 of the Latin Anthology (Codex Salmasianus), "Verba amatoris ad pictorem," begins "Pinge, precor, pictor, tali candor puellam." Venantius Fortunatus employed alliteration copiously. In his dedicatory poem to Bishop Vital of Ravenna, he writes that the Bishop occupies the basilica of the Lord, "per quem digna Deo est aedificata domus"; and then, "Sumpsisti a Domino culmen cui culmina condis . . ."[58] At a particularly emotional moment, *Ruodlieb*, an early eleventh-century German romance, reads, "Mi fili care, misere matris memorare / Quam, sicut nostri, discendens deseruisti" (see V. 251–58). The tricolon of increasing members connected alliteratively by /m/ is reminiscent of Cuchuimne's "Cantemus in omni die," in which he invokes, "Maria mater miranda" (l.15), whom earlier he described as the "virgo venerabilis" (l.9).[59] In groups of two or three, alliterated words are not uncommon features of insular poetry. Indeed, Aethilwald, a student of Aldhelm, in his *Carmina 3* writes often in tricola of increasing members,[60] and he seems quite

---

57. *Bibliorum Sacrorum Latinae*, 2:231. Both the LXX and the Hebraicos read "vobis" for "vos."
58. "Ad Vitalem episcopum," in Fortunatus, *Poems*, 1:20.
59. *Lateinische Lyrik des Mittelalters*, p. 64. Bernard and Atkinson, *The Irish Liber Hymnorum*, 1:15. Cuchuimne was an Irishman who lived at the time of Bede.
60. "Summum satorem solia" (1); "Cuncta cernenes cacumine" (5); *Carmina 4* includes "Facunda funde famine" (9), "Larem librant lucifluam" (19), "fumam furuam frigoribus" (23), "Titan tremet torrentibus" (27), "Noctem nigram nubiculis" (33), "Neque nocent nitoribus" (37), "Ruris rigati riuulo / Roscidi roris sedulo / Sed lutosam liquoribus" (39–41), "Glescunt, ut

taken by the figure. One wonders what he imagined his audience would infer from it.[61]

Homoeoptoton, says Bede, differs from homoeoteleuton by coordinating similar, not identical sounds. Some rhetoricians defined homoeoptoton as a repetition of inflectional endings, others as a repetition of case (words need not end in identical inflections); some distinguish it from homoeoteleuton by saying that the latter is rhyme in a tricolon.[62] Bede distinguishes homoeoptoton from homoeoteleuton by defining the former as assonance, the latter as rhyme. In terms of position, Bede says homoeoteleuton occurs when a word in the middle and one at the end of a verse have identical endings—the word preceding a medial caesura and the last word. This is called Leonine rhyme, which was reinvigorated by Gottschalk of Orbais after its partial abandonment by Carolingian poets.[63] Bede does not seem to have sought end rhyme, although it does appear infrequently.[64] But consider Bede's alphabetic *Hymn to the Apostles Peter and Paul*. There are eight sets of end-rhymes in the hymn until we arrive at the letter *x*. At that point, the hymn reads:

Xriste precamur, ut QUIBUS 21
Laudes ovantes dicimus,
Horum frui nos lucidis
Dones per aevum ASPECTIBUS. ||

Ymnis per aethram ac SUAVIBUS 25
Apostolorum LAUDIBUS [;] ||
Noster chorus hic consonet
Psalmis canorus DULCIBUS. ||

---

glebae germina" (45), "Sucorum sumunt saporem" (49), "Sic, sic sane sublimibus" (65), "Caeli ceu per culmina" (67); *Poetria Nova*.

61. This sentence is itself a tricolon of increasing members, three serial phrases, one longer than the last: "One wonders | what he imagined | his audience would infer from it."

62. Lanham, *A Handlist of Rhetorical Terms*, pp. 83–85.

63. Norberg, *Introduction*, pp. 40–41.

64. Bede, verse *VSC*, p. 21.

Zona benignus aurea
Nos cinge castimoniae,   30
Ut te videntes LAUDIBUS
Tuis vacemus perpetes. ||⁶⁵

Three stanzas are prompted by three letters of the alphabet. Six of twelve lines end in *–ibus*. The rhymes do not coordinate couplets, as in Wordsworth or Mother Goose, but they help to coordinate units of sense and to vary the structural effects of rhyme within those units. This is a hymn, so we must listen to the periods (independent clauses or sentences, marked with ||) rather than look at punctuation. In the tetracolon of Bede's first period (here, lines 21 to 24), the end of the first verse, *quibus*, rhymes with the end of the last verse, *aspectibus*. The rhyme emphasizes the end of the period and the end of the stanza. The close rhyme *dicimus* (l. 22) emphasizes the end of the period's first clause, arguably a period as well but here marked with a comma. In what I am calling the second period (here, lines 25 to 26), the ends of each verse rhyme loosely like a Leonine line. Again, the rhyme emphasizes the end of a period. In the third period, the second verse rhymes with the first and second periods, thereby closing the stanza. In the fourth and final period (lines 29 to 32), Bede returns to his unrhymed stanza, but picks up on the previous rhymes with *laudibus*, perhaps to emphasize that the hymn is a prayer.

Bede seems to have been very careful with his rhymes here. Norberg notes that in popular Latin by the end of Antiquity and in the High Middle Ages, <e> and <i> rhyme, as do <o> and <u>. So, "vinculo" and "paradisum" may rhyme.⁶⁶ Bede has avoided any such confusion here, ensuring that both spoken and written lines either rhyme or don't. Augustine had written rhymed sermons, perhaps because rhyme seemed to be popular in North Africa.⁶⁷ Medieval

---

65. Hymn 9, pp. 428–30. Kendall and Wallis believe this hymn to be genuine.
66. Norberg, *Introduction*, pp. 47–48.
67. Mohrmann, "Augustine and the Eloquentia," 1:365–66, who notes that "sermons without any rhyme at all are rare," 3:366; and 3:368. It is

Latin poetry more generally is no stranger to rhyme. Something like Gottschalk's prayer, "Christe, mearum lux tenebrarum," is comprised of twelve stanzas of six rhymed lines.⁶⁸ (Note here the rhyme of "mearum" and "tenebrarum.") Mohrmann points out that while rhyme can serve mnemonic functions and clarify syntax by pointing out parallelism, "It serves also a higher inspiration." It is used syntactically in Christian hymns, and also as "an element of uplifting, devotion and religious inspiration."⁶⁹ We see it in the Apostles' Creed: "Et in Iesum Christum, Filium eius unicum, Dominum nostrum," and in the chiastic rhymes of its close, "sanctor*um* communionem, remissionem peccator*um*."

One final element we will see in Bede's *Hymn to Aethelthryth* is a consequence of syntactic patterning. What has been called Visual Grammar describes how the order of words on a page (or in the ear) mimics their content. In Virgil's *Aeneid* we find in Book Four, "speluncam Dido dux et Troianus eandem / deuenient" (they went into the same cave, Dido and the Trojan leader, 4.165, cf. 4.124). Commentators note that Dido and Aeneas are physically and grammatically surrounded by the cave (*speluncam . . . eandem*). They sit next to each other on the line (*Dido dux*), and are divided neither by a verb, a conjunction (*et*) nor by the adjective that modifies Aeneas. That adjective is separated (ironically?) by the conjunctive *et*, which, one commentator has written, suggests the arms of Dido reaching around Aeneas for the conjunction. A. M. Young remarked on "Virgil's habit of 'representing pictorially in the arrangement of his words exactly what he relates.'"⁷⁰ He offers as example *Aeneid* 9.346: "sed magnum metuens se post cratera tegebat" (but for fear was hiding himself behind a huge bowl), in which "the little word 'se' for him [Young] is tucked away in the middle of the line under cover of the huge

---

interesting to note that Hadrian, abbot of St. Augustine's, Canterbury, and colleague of Archbishop Theodore, was born in North Africa.
68. *Lateinische Lyrik*, pp. 182–86.
69. Mohrmann, "Augustine and the Eloquentia," 1:367.
70. Cited by Wilkinson, *GLA*, p. 65.

bowl."[71] William Fitzgerald points to *Aeneid* 1.293–94, "dirae ferro et compagibus artis / claudentur Belli portae" (the grim gates of War, with their tight iron frames, will be closed). The *dirae . . . portae* (grim gates) enclose "the sentence like the doors themselves."[72] In the fifth poem of his first book of odes, Horace describes his former girlfriend Pyrrha, embraced by her new boy on a bed of roses, "Quis multa gracilis te puer in rosa . . ." Fitzgerald describes Horace's art:

> The pronoun *te* (you) in the accusative is the object of a verb for which we must wait. Around this *te* Horace interweaves two phrases *Quis . . . gracilis . . . puer* (what slender youth) and *multa . . . in rosa* (in much roses). But he does so in a way as to create concentric circles around the *te*: Quis **multa** GRACILIS TE PUER **in rosa**. **Multa . . . in rosa** forms the outer circle and GRACILIS . . . PUER the inner, with Pyrrha (*te*), appropriately, in the center. The effect is as much visual as aural: Pyrrha is embraced by the boy, and both are surrounded by roses.[73]

The same effect is found in Lucan and in Seneca, among others. Paul the Deacon seems to employ it in his short poem on the death of a boy, whose weight breaks through the ice of a river. The weight is in the middle of the line, and the hard water surrounds it: the boy "frigore CONCRETAS *pondere* **rupit** AQUAS" (through his cold *weight* **broke** the FROZEN WATER).[74] The point is not to argue that this

---

71. Ibid., p. 66. David Califf remarks on Virgil's *Georgics*, 1, "invitae propres anni spem credere terrae" (224), noting that the seeds, *anni spem*, "are metaphorically planted" within the *invitae . . . terrae*; see his *Guide to Latin Meter*, p. 38.
72. Fitzgerald, *How to Read a Latin Poem*, p. 166; his translation.
73. Ibid., p. 117.
74. The verb is in bold, the accusatives in small caps; "De puero qui in glacie extinctus est," in *Lateinische Lyrik*, p. 82. The line appears to be a modified "golden line," where a medial verb has been replaced by a noun (*pondere*). Grocock and Wood notice an instance of visual grammar in Bede's *HA*: "quod **ex meo** haec quae vobis statui decreta indoctus **corde** protulerim"; they write, "All the *decreta* are in his heart—in truth and in word order." See their *HA*, p. lxxxi.

Rhetoric

device is factually present in Latin poems, but that it was perceived to be present by both readers and writers.

The artistry of Anglo-Latin poets, their style, was resonant with aesthetic assumptions. Style is not merely a contingent affect, one style being as good as any other, but also an index of the relation between author and audience. Even at the most general level, such as a poet's choice of vocabulary, style is far more than an accessory to content. Readers of Chaucer are familiar with the issues surrounding his choice of English over French and Latin for his *Troilus and Criseyde*. Similar issues pertain to the early Middle Ages, as well. David Townsend asks about the social conditions that help to explain the tenacity of Latin in the face of the vernacular. He calls on critics to notice not only the sociolinguistic consequences of language choice, but also, within a particular language, that "certain stylistic markers function in a specific literary milieu."[75] As the corpus of seventh-century Irish poetry attests, Latin was not a necessary choice in composing poetry. It was a choice made with an eye to reception, authority, status, and literary inheritance. One might ask, for example, what consequences for reception might have followed from Bede's choice to compose his "Death Song" in Old English rather than in Latin, if indeed he did compose it. And the option of language is but one option that a poet has. Each choice a poet makes carries cultural weight and sets him in the company of other poets. A choice of genre, for example, carries weight: to write an epic is to admit oneself into the company of Virgil, Homer, and Statius; and to write an alphabetic hymn is to invite comparison with Psalm 118 (119). To use a hexametrical foot from Virgil is to announce one's literary inheritance, to declare the interleaving of one's work with the past, to announce one's poem as a worthy setting for the best of Latin poets. The fourth-century Latin poet Proba wrote a popular poem in which she used only lines from Virgil to retell the story of the Gospels.[76] Her

---

75. Townsend, "The Current Questions and Future Prospects," p. 10.
76. Proba, "Cento" (CSEL 16: 569–609); partially translated by White, *ECLP*.

work, like the mosaics of Ravenna, was prized for its artistry, rather than derided for unoriginality.

The arrangement of the content of a poem was stylistically meaningful. The disposition of adjectives and verbs was stylistically meaningful. The number of words per line was stylistically meaningful. Also stylistically meaningful was the consonance of meter and stress, and the use of classes of phonemes. Readers were trained to appreciate aesthetic effects, and writers were trained to reproduce them. Dionysius of Halicarnassus, author of the influential *De compositione verborum*, praised Sappho: "The words nestle close to one another and are woven together according to certain affinities and natural attractions of the letters."[77] Sappho's genius set the high mark for classical poetic style. It was the work of the Patristic age to understand both the beauty and the utility of that style in its relation to Scripture. The study of Latin style may seem a drily technical one, but Bede's textbooks suggest that he saw tremendous beauty in the Word of God. In the next chapter, we will try to discover what Bede thought was beautiful about the poetry of his Christian predecessors.

---

77. In Wilkinson, *GLA*, p. 22; from *De comp.*, xxiii.

CHAPTER FOUR

Sources

The Great Theory of Beauty provides a larger context for poetry and its genres. But how would our nun of Barking have connected the patterns of sound and syntax in a poem to divine order? For example, although Plato may have imagined a connection between certain modes of metrical composition and the arrangement (or derangement) of the humors, he does not describe a similar connection between, say, a chiasmus and a particular response by a reader. What effect does a chiasmus have? When ought it to be used? Why ought any particular figure to be used? How would its appropriateness, its decorum, be gauged? Before looking at Bede's style in the book's concluding chapters, I would like to survey some of the styles available to him as models.

First and foremost were the various styles of Scripture. They very likely recommended themselves to Bede as his primary models. Scripture is, in fact, an anthology of styles. As we have seen, the style of Paul is very important for early Christian Latin. Second, the most authoritative (non-Biblical) style on Bede's palate is known as the jeweled style, and was characteristic of some of Bede's favorite poets. They were composed during one of the most remarkable centuries in Christian letters: AD 350–450. These authors were as distant in time from Bede as Shakespeare and Milton are from us. They include Caelius Sedulius (fl. c. 450), Alcimus Avitus (d. 518), Juvencus (fl. 330), and Arator (fl. 544), all of whom retold Scriptural stories in classical Latin meter.[1] Venantius Fortunatus (c. 530?–609), Sidonius Apollinaris (mid-fifth century), and Prudentius (348–c. 410) treated Christian themes in classical meter. Third were the prose styles of St. Augustine (354–430) and St. Jerome (347–420), whose classical rhetorical polish was admired by Bede.[2] Augustine also wrote poetry. When it came to hymns, a plainer style, though by no means free of ornate decoration, is that of St. Ambrose of Milan (339–397). And fourth were the styles of the many and various classical Latin poets whom Bede knew and taught.

Along with these styles came questions of genre, which determined style. Certain meters were appropriate to certain genres. When Bede sat down to write his *Hymn to Aethelthryth*, for example, why did he choose the elegiac meter? Why not an iambic dimeter in which he wrote his other hymns? Was he making reference to the elegies of Ovid or Propertius? Did he have some more theological rationale in mind? What connotations did the elegiac form hold for him? Why did Bede ignore so many other meters? In *DAM*, Bede writes, "I have preferred not to deal with them because of their pagan nature."[3] But is the hexameter not pagan too? In order to gain some purchase on these questions, we need some sense of how early Christian poets translated and transformed classical style and poetic form. In the remainder of this chapter, I would like to look at those poets who were likely known to Bede.[4] What were they known for? How did they fit into the larger picture of Christian poetics? When Bede alludes to one of them, what connotations would have occurred to our nun of

---

1. An excellent introduction is Herzog, *Die Bibelepik der lateinischen Spätantike*; more recently, Green, *Latin Epics of the New Testament*; and McBrine, "The English Inheritance of Biblical Verse."
2. See verse *VSC*, p. 14.
3. Bede, *DAM*; Kendall, *Libri II*, p. 161.
4. Most of these same poets are surveyed by Orchard, *PAA*, chap. 4. Biographies and overviews of their works can be found in Manitius, *Geschichte*; Raby, *SLP* and *CLP*; and Szövérffy, *Annalen*. Other surveys can be found by consulting Mantello and Rigg, *ML*.

Barking? Some indication is given in Bede's overview of poetic forms in his *DAM*. In his overview, Bede cites distinguished Christian Latin poets as illustrations of particular forms. There, I hope to find what we seek.

Bede begins his description of meter with the dactylic hexameter, the meter of Virgil's *Aeneid*, the single most influential poem of the Latin west. Although in *DAM* Bede cites Virgil 33 times, it would have surprised our nun of Barking that Bede does not mention Virgil at this particular point, since there was no more important classical hexameter Latin poet. Bede mentions Homer instead, the ultimate rather than the proximate source of the meter's nobility. Bede calls the hexameter "more beautiful and loftier than all the rest" of the meters.[5] He reports that it had been used to sing "of the deeds of heroes, i.e., of brave men." For those reasons, Bede writes cryptically, it is suited to prolix works and to succinct ones, common or noble. I say "cryptically" because it is not clear which specific qualities of the hexameter make it more beautiful. Nor is it clear why its meter is peculiarly appropriate to the celebration of heroic deeds. Virgil and Homer had used it thus, and innumerable authorities repeated the claim, but what precisely about the meter provides loftiness? Bede does not say. To put it another way, there is no clear causal connection between style—in this case, a choice of meter—and a theory of beauty. Seppo Heikkinen suggests that the hexameter held its status because of its versatility and its difficulty; however, I don't understand why iambic dimeter is any less versatile, especially given Latin's many long vowels, nor the Sapphic any more difficult. Moreover, Bede points out the tremendous versatility of the septenarius and the Phalaecean dactylic pentameter.[6] I think we shall fail if we seek the cause of beauty in the disposition of meter, or equate beauty with versatility. Instead, a major cause of the hexameter's high status is its adoption by Homer and Virgil. Their facility

---

5. "ceteris omnibus pulchrius celsiusque est"; Kendall, *Libri II*, pp. 96–97.
6. Bede, *DAM*; Kendall, *Libri II*, pp. 159 and 145. Heikkinen, "*Quae non habet intellectum*," pp. 82–83.

with the meter suggested its versatility; authority and tradition lend it dignity. Its nobility derives more from the depth of its roots than from the arrangement of its flowers.

After describing the hexameter's composition, Bede gives an example. Again he does not cite Virgil, the obvious choice for a schoolmaster in the early Middle Ages. Nor does he cite Sedulius, author of one of the most celebrated hexameter poems of the early Middle Ages, *Carmen Paschale*, whom Bede cites thirty-three times elsewhere in the *DAM*. Instead, Bede cites an elegy by Fortunatus, Bishop of Poitiers and author of the famous iambic dimeter hymns *Pange, lingua* and *Vexilla regis prodeunt*.[7] Bede knew Fortunatus's *De virginitate*, and perhaps no more. The poem was a medieval school text and part of a larger collection that Aldhelm knew and that may have been unavailable to Bede.[8] The poem was composed a little after AD 576 on the investiture of Agnes as Abbess of St. Germain in Paris.[9] It is an elegy, a form reputed to have been invented by Archilochus, which is composed of couplets, themselves comprising a hexameter followed by a pentameter catalectic. Bede cites the first line:

Cūlmĭnă mūltă pŏlōs rădĭāntī lūmĭnĕ cōmplēnt

(Many worthies fill Heaven with radiant light)[10]

The rest of the couplet is "laetanturque piis agmina sancta choris" (and they take pleasure, the holy cohorts, in pious choirs). *Agmĕn*,

---

7. Raby, *CLP*, pp. 86–95. On dates and biography, see Roberts, *The Humblest Sparrow*, chap. 1. For knowledge of Fortunatus, see Hunt, "Manuscript Evidence"; and Michael Lapidge's Appendix to Hunt, "Knowledge of the Poems in the Earlier Period," pp. 287–95; on Bede specifically, pp. 291–92.
8. Book 8, poem 3. Orchard, *PAA*, p. 192.
9. Fortunatus, *Poems*, p. 129, n. 10.
10. Trans. Kendall, modified; Kendall translates, "Many mansions fill Heaven with radiant light." I take "culmina" to stand in apposition to "agmina," and therefore a reference to saints and angels, or "fratres et celsa caterua piorum" (line 15). I also hear the echo of Genesis 6:5, "multa malitia hominum" (great wickedness of men) in antithesis to the "culmina multa," suggesting those who have entered "in gaudium domini" (Matthew 25:21).

ăgmĭnĭs means a progressive movement, as a river's current, but is also a military word, meaning "troops," as in troops of angels.[11] Fortunatus's poem begins by describing song in Heaven, psalmody, and the echo of sung praise against the skies. "Here echo the melodious voices of the Patriarchs," Fortunatus writes. He names Abraham and Moses, Peter and Stephen. Then he praises the Blessed Virgin Mary, who stands amid a band of young women (*puellae*, line 27), just as the pious choirs of line 2, *piis . . . choris*, grammatically surround the holy cohorts, *agmina sancta* (visual grammar again). But the obvious question still remains: why cite this elegy by Fortunatus when Bede knew so many other heroic hexameters? What makes this line appropriate to illustrate the most beautiful, the loftiest of meters?

One can only guess. Fortunatus's line may have interested Bede for a number of reasons. The last foot of a hexameter can be either a spondee (two longs) or a trochee (a long and a short). Bede treated the last syllable as common, which meant that a trochee's short syllable could be counted as long. With his example of Fortunatus, Bede bypasses these metrical complications by offering two obviously long syllables, *cōmplēnt*. A second interesting feature is *lūmĭnĕ*, which inhabits the fifth foot of the verse. It is a dactyl. Seppo Heikkinen points out that Bede was dogmatic in his belief that the fifth foot ought not to contain a spondee, which had been allowed by classical poets, although it was unusual. Aldhelm was just as dogmatic. Aldhelm writes in a dialogue about the hexameter, "D: Quis est pes quintus? M: Dactilus" (Teacher: What is the fifth foot? Student: A dactyl). Heikkinen writes that in virtually outlawing a fifth-foot spondee, Bede's description of the hexameter "constitutes a redefinition of the dactylic hexameter itself."[12] In giving a heavily dactylic line as his primary example of the hexameter, free of a fifth-foot spondee, Bede reinforces his conviction. Moreover,

---

11. See *TLL*, vol. 1, pp. 1340 ff., s.v. "agmen"; DuCange, 1:143; for syllable length, Quicherat, *Thesaurus Poeticus Linguae Latinae*, pp. 42–43.
12. Heikkinen, "*Quae non habet intellectum*," pp. 82 and 84. The example is from Aldhelm, *De metris et aenigmatibus ac pedum regulis*, p. 83.

Bede seems to have wanted to distance Christian poetics from classical poetics, to the point where he tries to explain away Christian fifth-foot spondees as mutated dactyls, applying what Heikkinen calls a dubious "parasite-vowel theory." But why such animosity? The generic dogmatism of a textbook? An exaggerated certainty on Bede's part? Or was there some stylistic reason, perhaps one that Bede inferred from the relative absence of spondees in late Antique Christian poets? Unlike modern researchers, Bede could not electronically search the *Library of Latin Texts* for a thorough analysis of data. Instead, his conclusions were drawn from a far more limited body of evidence. Fortunatus, one of the most influential of Christian Latin poets, uses a fifth-foot spondee only once. It occurs in his hexametric *Life of St. Martin* (3.315) to describe "the slow wit and great weight" of a cow. The spondee, as numerous commentators have remarked, was perceived as heavy, hence Fortunatus's little joke about the heavy cow. Aldhelm had called the fifth-foot spondee *minus lenis* 'less smooth', artfully using an /s/, which was thought to hiss gratingly.[13] He warned against a fully spondaic line, calling that *durum et horrens* 'hard and rough'.[14] Aldhelm even asked in his verse *De virginitate* for protection against it, "Spondaei quintam contemnat sillaba partem" (Let the syllable of the spondee shun the fifth foot).[15] Can we surmise then that *lenis* 'light, smooth, mild' is an aesthetic quality highly sought after by a Christian hexameter poet? Perhaps a lightness near the end of the line was a valued characteristic of Christian Latin poetry.

For readers of Latin like me, for whom the innate lightness of a dactyl is not obvious, aesthetic assumptions like these require enumeration. Moreover, the terms used for aesthetic judgment are, to my mind at least, maddeningly imprecise. Although both Aldhelm and Bede seem to prefer the "lighter" dactylic line, 12 percent of Aldhelm's and 11 percent of Bede's hexameters are composed almost

---

13. See Heikkinen, "*Quae non habet intellectum*," pp. 88 and 89.
14. Ibid., p. 90, his translation.
15. Ibid., p. 91, his translation.

entirely of spondees.[16] Were they hoping with these spondaic lines to give an effect of *durum*? What might that mean? George Sheets, writing on the poetry of Catullus, calls the spondaic line "slow and stately" because it is longer in duration.[17] Wilkinson notes that the spondee was used by the Greeks while pouring libations during religious ceremonies; it was appropriate because "of the solemnity of slowness and because the smooth regularity reflected in the act of pouring."[18] (The connection to alcohol recalls Pythagoras, who as we saw used spondaic meter to quell the high spirits of a drunken lad.) So is the spondee unpleasantly hard, heavy like a cow, or pleasantly stately? What of dactyls? Dactyls are thought to provide a sense of speed. They gallop, as is commonly suggested in contemporary expositions of *Aeneid* 8.596, "quādrŭpĕdāntĕ pŭtrēm sŏnĭtū quătĭt ūngŭlă cāmpūm" (with galloping tramp the horse-hoof shakes the crumbling plain). In this verse, as George Duckworth writes, "the horses gallop with the dactyls across the plain." He comments on *Aeneid* 8.452, "illi inter sese multa vi bracchia tollunt" (They with mighty force, now one, now another, raise their arms), which contains five spondees. Duckworth explains that the disposition of spondees "enables us to hear the Cyclopes working at their anvils."[19] Likewise, Carl Springer, commenting on the *CP* of Sedulius, writes that Sedulius may have used spondees in his description of the placard over Christ's head at the Crucifixion in order to evoke "a hammering quality."[20] These aesthetic qualities of spondees and dactyls may not be scientifically demonstrable, but we can see how they become part of the process of learning to read Latin poetry. From at least the days of the early Republic, aesthetic characteristics of Latin dactyls and spondees were learned assumptions.

Duckworth suggested that aesthetic judgments about the

---

16. Orchard, *PAA*, Appendix 5.2, Table A7, pp. 296–98.
17. Sheets, "Elements of Style in Catullus," p. 202.
18. Wilkinson, *GLA*, p. 61. Also cited by Califf, *A Guide to Latin Meter*, p. 9, n. 10.
19. Duckworth, "Vergil's Subjective Style and its Relation to Meter," p. 3.
20. Sedulius, *CP*, trans. Springer, p. xli.

disposition of spondees in a hexameter line governed poetic composition generally. He reported "an amazing correlation of subject matter and meter" throughout the *Aeneid* concerning lines with four spondees arranged DSSSDC (D = dactyl, S = spondee, C = common), abbreviated *dsss*:

> although *dsss* is Vergil's favorite pattern in the *Aeneid*, with an overall percentage of 14.39 . . . , it shows a surprising variation according to style and subject matter, from zero to 5 or 6 percent in many passages, from 20 to 30 percent or higher in others. The *dsss* pattern has a low frequency in episodes and speeches which are dramatic, psychological, and emotional, where the style is subjective or "empathetic-sympathetic," and especially in scenes of death and laments for the dead. On the other hand, *dsss* appears with an abnormally high frequency in certain types of episodes: those in a more objective style, particularly scenes of mass fighting and individual combat; those in which divinities . . . appear and speak; those dealing with Rome and Augustus.[21]

This pattern is used to speak of war, divinity, and royalty—all highly dignified topics. Eleven percent of Bede's lines are *dsss*.[22] If we return to Bede's citation of Fortunatus, we scan "Cūlmĭnă mūltă pŏlōs rădĭāntī lūmĭnĕ cōmplēnt" (*ddds*). This contrastingly light dactylic line is not one of Bede's more preferred meters, comprising only eight percent of his hexameters. If Bede sensed what Duckworth did, then it would have struck him as odd that Fortunatus had failed to use *dsss*, earlier used by Virgil for divinities and battles, to describe troops of angels—that is, unless Bede thought that Fortunatus had selected a lighter, dactylic line to distinguish Christian Latin meter from its pagan antecedents as it presented these highly dignified topics. Although there has been a great deal of work cataloguing and

---

21. Duckworth, "Vergil's Subjective Style," p. 8. Also see Winbolt, *Latin Hexameter Verse*, p. 123. Duckworth notes the tripartite division of the arrangement: ds/ss/ds.

22. Orchard, *PAA*, p. 297: Aldhelm, 29.54 percent; Alcuin, 18.8 percent.

counting the various meters of early Latin poetry, we await a study of their disposition. It may be that some topics in Christian poetry were thought better suited to particular patterns of feet than others.

Another consideration about Fortunatus is the genre of Bede's citation. Fortunatus had written heroic poems comprised solely of hexameters. So had other Christian poets. Why would Bede choose to excerpt a line from an elegy on virginity rather than mine hexameter poems, such as Sedulius's *CP*? It would be akin to choosing to illustrate iambic pentameter with a line from T. S. Eliot's "Love Song of J. Alfred Prufrock": "And sáw|dust rés|tauránts | with óy|ster-shélls." Accurate, but a curious choice given the more obvious option of, say, Shakespeare. In the case of Bede's hexameter, the answer seems to be fairly pedestrian. Bede's next topic is the pentameter, which he illustrates with the second line of Fortunatus's couplet, a pentameter catalectic. Bede apparently made an efficient selection, killing two birds with one stone. But he has to qualify his selection by explaining the difference between the scansion of a pentameter and a pentameter catalectic. Although it may have been a practical choice, Bede's selection of Fortunatus perhaps will bear a little more scrutiny. Bede wanted to cite a Christian Latin poet of international renown, so his choices were not unlimited. He cites sixteen poets in *DAM*. Five were pagans. If a count of citations is anything to go by, Bede seems to have been drawn—in order—to Sedulius, Prosper of Aquitaine, Paulinus of Nola (whose verse *Life of St. Felix* he turned into prose), Fortunatus, and Juvencus. Given that Sedulius is cited three times more often than Fortunatus, and that Sedulius was highly esteemed as a hexameter poet, why opt for Fortunatus? Bede is giving the primary example of the most important classical meter, so his choice has to be more than incidental. Perhaps the answer lies in genre rather than in meter: perhaps the heroic epic did not enjoy the same status in seventh-century Christian poetry that it did in Augustan Rome. A glimmer of this possibility comes from Gerald Bonner, who writes that Bede was not comparing Christian poets to classical poets in terms of quality; he was more concerned with advancing a Christian poetics. Bede's attitude, explains Bonner, was not shared by the Carolingians, "who decided that Christian writing alone could not provide the norms of the Latinity which they desired."[23] But like Martin Irvine I do think that Bede was concerned with the relative quality of Christian poets.[24] I just don't think that Virgil or the heroic hexameter were Bede's only comparanda.

Bede cites a number of heroic epics. Foremost among them is the *CP* of Sedulius. It was "a Christian classic, cited by the grammarians, read as a model of style, and imitated by generations of versifiers," writes Raby.[25] Johannes Huemer, editor of the *CP* in 1885, reports that Sedulius's poem was highly praised very soon after its dissemination.[26] It was contemporary with Augustine's *De doctrina Christiana*.[27] Sedulius was imitated by Gregory of Tours and praised by Fortunatus, who called him "dulcis" (sweet).[28] Fortunatus also noted in his verse *Life of St. Martin* (l. 15) that Sedulius wrote in clear, radiant language. Isidore of Seville praised his incomparable verses. Sedulius seems to have been known for his rhetorical ability, the pleasing dexterity of his florid style. Ernst Robert Curtius, however, who was not a fan, calls it "magniloquent rhetoric in Christian

---

23. Bonner, "Bede and Medieval Civilization," p. 87. Similarly, Pierre Riché argued that "Bede read the classics but did not experience them as literary works"; cited in Irvine, "Bede the Grammarian," p. 33.
24. Irvine, "Bede the Grammarian," pp. 32-33. See Curtius, *European Literature*, p. 51, "All *auctores* are of the same value, all are timeless. This is and remains characteristic of the entire Middle Ages."
25. *CLP*, p. 110. Manitius does not distinguish in status among Bede's Christian Latin sources; see Manitius, *Geschichte*, 1:74-75. Brünholzl, *LLMA*, mentions Sedulius only in passing. An overview of Sedulius's reception in ASE, especially in Aldhelm, is in Orchard, *PAA*, pp. 163-66. Especially informative is Green, *Latin Epics of the New Testament*.
26. Sedulius, CP, ed. Huemer, p. ii.
27. Green, *Latin Epics of the New Testament*, p. 156.
28. Fortunatus, *Carmen* 8.1.57, cited by Huemer, in Sedulius, CP, p. iii. The citations that follow are also taken from Huemer. Isidore includes Sedulius in his *De viris illustribus* (*PL* 83:1094; *CPL* 1206). Also very useful is the introduction by Springer, in Sedulius, *CP*

Sources

guise" and Sedulius "grandiloquent and vainglorious."[29] Aldhelm called Sedulius *doctiloquus* 'learned in speech'. He was praised by Bede, Alcuin, Theodulf of Orleans, Ermoldus Nigellus, Smaragdus, Hraban Maur, and many others. Orchard writes, "For Aldhelm Sedulius was, after Vergil, the single most important verse influence." Aldhelm thought him "an outstanding poet endowed with metrical eloquence."[30] Hundreds of manuscripts of Sedulius's works can be found throughout Western Europe.[31] The *CP* can be found in eight Anglo-Saxon manuscripts, including CCC 173, an eighth-century copy of the poem with Latin and Old English glosses. It is also found in CUL Gg.5.35, a manuscript copied in England soon after 1035 and containing the major school texts of ASE.[32] In his *DAM*, Bede cites Sedulius as often as he cites Virgil. In fact, during Bede's discussion of the heroic hexameter, seven of his fourteen examples are from the *CP*. Many more examples from the poem populate the remaining chapters of Bede's textbook. Fortunatus's *De virginitate*, on the other hand, does not appear to have enjoyed similar estimation in ASE. No insular manuscripts survive.[33] Bede offers twelve examples from Fortunatus—compared to seventeen from Paulinus of Nola and nineteen from Prosper of Aquitaine. Once again, in demonstrating the hexameter, why cite Fortunatus's elegy rather than Sedulius's heroic epic?

It might seem absurd to suggest, but in terms of genre, Bede may have valued the elegy on par with the heroic epic. "Absurd" because to do so would be to upturn classical tradition then and now. Nevertheless, Bede is consciously writing in a "modern" Christian age, viewing the classical past as ancient and outdated. This is a standard literary trope, but no less relevant on that account.[34] One of the

---

29. Green, *Latin Epics of the New Testament*, pp. 152–53; Sedulius, CP, ed. Heumer, p. iii. Curtius, *European Literature*, pp. 460 and 148.
30. Orchard, *PAA*, p. 164 and p. 165.
31. See Sedulius, CP, ed. Springer, p. xvii, and his citations.
32. Gneuss, *Handlist*; Ziolkowski, *The Cambridge Songs*, p. xxvii.
33. See Lapidge, "Appendix" to Hunt, "Manuscript Evidence."
34. Curtius, *European Literature*, p. 251. On the status of the lyric genre in

chapters of *DAM* distinguishes between ancients and moderns on stylistic grounds, implying that ancients were far more casual—or perhaps freer (*liber*)—in their observance of rules (chap. 16).[35] Moderns, says Bede using a term popularized by Cassiodorus, are far more decorous, far more controlled. That the priority of Fortunatus and the elegy is not incidental is further suggested by Bede's short description of genre that follows his citation of Fortunatus:

> For scholars speak of elegiac poetry as sad, and the modulation of this verse, where the first line is a hexameter and the next a pentameter, is suited to the lamentations of the miserable. It is said that the Song of Moses in Deuteronomy and Psalms 118 and 144 were written in this meter in Hebrew, while the book of the blessed Job was written in plain hexameters [*simplici exametro*].

Jerome, in his preface to his translation of the Book of Job, says that the first part of the book, up to the point when Job first speaks, is in prose (*prosa oratio est*).[36] From 3:3 to 42:6, the book is in hexameters, running in dactyls and spondees (*dactilo spondeoque currens*), but in the idiom of Hebrew, in its own feet, not in those of Latin. Jerome was long considered to be correct. Neither the structure nor meter of Biblical Hebrew verse was adequately described until Lowth in 1753.[37] There is still no agreement about whether or not Biblical Hebrew verse is metrical, but there is a sense that it is somehow poetic. The epilogue and prologue of Job are rendered in prose in the modern Soncino edition of Job in both Hebrew and English, the

---

antique and medieval poetics, see Evenepoel, "The Place of Poetry," p. 35.
35. See Heikkinen, "Vergilian quotations in Bede's *De arte metrica*," pp. 102–3.
36. "Prologus sancti Hieronymi in libro Iob," *Biblia Sacra iuxta vulgatam versionem*, p. 731. See Curtius, *European Literature*, p. 447.
37. O'Conner, *Hebrew Verse Structure*, p. 32; on syllabic meter, 2:34–37. But see Fokkelman, *Major Poems of the Hebrew Bible*, pp. 325–81; and van der Lugt, *Cantos and Strophes in Biblical Hebrew Poetry*, esp. chap. 1 on the history of the study of Hebrew prosody. Van der Lugt says that about forty percent of the Hebrew Bible is written in verse, p. 1.

balance translated into a loose approximation of pentameters, the highest register of English poetry.[38] In terms of subject-matter, the verse portion relates the dialogues and interior thoughts of the players, while the prose portion relates a more distant historical view. Translating the poetic idiom of Hebrew into that of Latin, Jerome writes that all the songs of Scripture—including the Psalter, Lamentations, and Jeremiah—are like Latin elegies, odes, Alcaics, and Sapphics. Arator repeated it in his verse *Epistola ad Vigilium*.[39] Bede cites it in his *DAM*.[40] Further, as Bonner notes, Bede claimed that "Vergil's ninth eclogue is matched by the Song of Songs; to the *Georgics* and the *De rerum natura* of Lucretius are opposed Proverbs and Ecclesiastes; the *Odyssey* and the *Aeneid* have the book of Job as their Christian equivalent."[41]

In short, Holy Scripture authorizes a Christian poet to write both elegies and heroic hexameters. From the perspective of Scripture, Fortunatus's elegy is as compelling to the Christian reader as Sedulius's heroic hexameter. Given Bede's view of his place in a Christian modernity, the question of literary genre now becomes one of the relative status of genres in Scripture. An ideal reader like our nun of Barking might suggest that the forms of verse that comprised the liturgy and the hours—those presumably found in the Psalms, for example—were most amenable to monastic use. She may have read it in Sedulius, who makes a similar connection between the Psalms and Christian Latin verse in his *CP*, 1:13–28 (see below). I do not want to insist on a full-scale Christian revaluation of genre, but the status of the epic hexameter is not so easily established in

---

38. Reichert, *Job: Hebrew Text & English Translation*.
39. Arator, *Epistola ad Vigilium*, lines 23–26. See Jerome's *Preface* to his translation of Job found in the Vulgate noted above; repeated by Isidore, *Etym*. 1.29.11.
40. Bede, *DAM*, XVI; Kendall, *Libri II*, pp. 134–35. *DAM*, I, x. See Cassiodorus, *Expositio*, 118:2–26; Barney, p. 65. See Irvine, "Bede the Grammarian," p. 34; and Malaspina, "Tre meditazione salmiche di Beda il Venerabile." Also Luiselli, "Sul perduto *Liber epigrammatum* di Beda," p. 368.
41. Bonner, "Bede and Medieval Civilization," p. 86.

the multi-faceted world of Christian verse. The variety of contexts in which verse was used called for a variety of meters. Moreover, less lofty meters recall the ideal of *sermo humilis*, the more humble style of the Gospels, which Auerbach calls "the Christian form of the sublime."[42] That King David and Solomon had used the Hebrew equivalent of non-heroic meters in the Psalter would have lent those meters a very high status in Christian poetics. Psalms were the single most important influence in liturgical Latin. Christ recommends the study of psalms in Luke 24:44, and Paul commends the Ephesians to speak "to yourselves in psalms and hymns and spiritual canticles" (5:19).[43] Ambrose, who wrote some of the first hymns of the Western Church, said that the angels praised the Lord in psalms; he called the Psalter particularly sweet.[44] Lactantius in his *Divine Institutes* describes a series of psalm-like poems called the *Odes to Solomon*, extant in Latin in the fourth century, testifying to their early adoption as models of Christian praise.[45] Hilary of Poitiers composed a lyric in iambic senarius as the preface to his *Hymns*, "Felix propheta David primus organi / in carne Christum hymnis mundo nuntians" (Happy the prophet at the harp, David, who first announced to the world in his hymns Christ incarnate).[46] Further recommending the stylistic model of the Psalter to monastic use, Cassian writes that a monk should imbibe the Psalms to such a degree that he becomes like their author.[47] In short, the epic hexameter, however highly valued as a vehicle of Latin, is not always appropriate as a vehicle of Christian praise.

---

42. Auerbach, *Literary Language*, p. 22.
43. On this triplet, see Szövérffy, *Annalen*, 1:42–44.
44. Ambrose, *Explanatio psalmorum xii*, ed. Zelzer, pp. 3–4.
45. Jacques Fontaine, "Le poète latin chrétien nouveau psalmiste," p. 133, n. 8. See also Threade, *Studien zu Sprache und Stil des Prudentius*, p. 23.
46. Cited in Fontaine, "Le poète latin chrétien nouveau psalmiste," p. 134.
47. See Clark, "Medieval Latin Spirituality," p. 468. And Dyer, "The Psalms in Monastic Prayer," p. 62, on similar phrasing in the rules of Augustine and Caesarius, and in the *Rule of the Master*.

What did Bede prize in these poets? Bede next describes an optimal hexameter. He gives many examples from Sedulius. Fortunatus makes three appearances, Prosper two, and Arator and Lucan, pagan author of the historical *Pharsalia*, one. These five authors apparently offered the best hexameters for the task at hand. What struck Bede as most pleasing (*gratissima*) about the style of these authors was, first of all, enjambment. He cites Arator and Sedulius as frequent practitioners. Bede warns not to go on too long—five or six lines will do—since enjambed verses quickly become "distasteful and wearisome."[48] While enjambed hexameters read well, enjambed hymns do not. Verses must be arranged, says Bede, so that the sense ends at a line-ending, allowing antiphonal choirs to trade verses back and forth. After enjambment, Bede is especially taken with word position in the hexameter line. He describes variations of word order in which syntax is carefully disarrayed, a phenomenon called hyperbaton. (Anglo-Saxons sometimes glossed Latin manuscripts with letters and dots to indicate which Latin words went where.[49]) The most prized hyperbaton in classical verse is called the Golden Line (as we saw above), which runs abCAB, where "C" represents the verb, and adjectives (ab) precede their respective nouns (AB): "EGRESSI **optata** potiuntur TROES **harena**" (EMERGING **welcome** occupy TROJANS **sand**; the emerging Trojans occupy the welcome sand, *Aen.* 1.172).[50] Bede's example is similarly ordered. He explains that the penultimate word agrees with the first word, and the last with one in the middle. His example is not from Virgil, but from Sedulius: "PERVIA **divisi** patuerunt C[A]ERULA **ponti**" (UNOBSTRUCTED [**of the**] **divided** lay open WATERS **sea**; unobstructed waters lay open the divided sea). Four more examples from Sedulius's *CP* follow, although Bede warns not to do this sort of thing very often, as it cheapens the

---

48. "fastidium . . . ac tedium"; *DAM*; Kendall, *Libri II*, p. 103.
49. Robinson, "Syntactical Glosses in Latin Manuscripts." See also the dissertation of his student, Gretchen Brunk, "Syntactic Glosses in Latin Manuscripts of Anglo-Saxon Origin."
50. Example from Young, "Schematized Word Order in Vergil," p. 516; for qualifications, see Wilkinson, *GLA*, pp. 215–20.

device. The golden line is sometimes used to recapitulate a passage and lend it a sense of finality.⁵¹

Bede then casually turns to other pleasing forms of a hexameter. "Sometimes," he writes, "it is pleasing [*gratum est*] to compose a line with nouns alone." A list of flowers from Fortunatus follows, then a list of famous women, then a list of verbs—all from Fortunatus. (A correlation between flowers and women will appear in the Aethelthryth hymn, as well.) Next Bede turns to another stylistic item, the position of adjectives and nouns. Adjectives should come before their nouns, he writes, but at a distance. The example is from Prosper: "**Mitis** in **inmitem** virga est animata **draconem**" (HARMLESS into **fierce** ROD is changed **dragon**; a harmless rod is changed into a fierce dragon). Bede calls the intertwined syntax decorous ("decori"). Similarly decorous are verses from Prosper and a description of the battles of Caesar and Pompey by Lucan. Why Lucan should figure in this chapter while Virgil does not is a question we shall unfortunately pass over, although I suspect it has something to do with differentiating imagined matter in Virgil from historical matter in Lucan. Bede is recommending stylistic variation and a mosaic of syntactic patterns. We shall return to these stylistic particulars in a moment.

Sedulius, Fortunatus, and Prosper provide the bulk of examples for Bede's *DAM*. When we look at Bede's prose works, we find that these same poets seem always to be lurking somewhere in Bede's mind. Fortunatus's *Carmina* 8, also called *De virginitate*, comes up again in Bede's *Commentary on Revelation*, when Bede notes that Matthew 5:3 is beautifully expressed by Fortunatus.⁵² He mentions Fortunatus by name in his *Historia ecclesiastica*, I.vii, during the story of St. Alban. In the *HE* Bede also names Sedulius (V.xviii). Sedulius is quoted extensively in Bede's *Commentary on the Book of Kings*.⁵³ So are Juvencus, Victorinus, and Virgil. Bede cites four lines

---

51. Roberts, *The Jeweled Style*, p. 37.
52. *Bede: Commentary on Revelation*, trans. Wallis, p. 118, on Revelation 2:9.
53. *Bede: A Biblical Miscellany*, trans. Foley and Holder, p. 134, from Sedulius, *CP*, ed. Heumer, 1.183–86.

from Sedulius in his commentary on 4 Kings 28:11.⁵⁴ This citation concerns the name Heliae 'Elijah' and its similarity to the Greek word for sun, *helios*. Obviously, the difficulty in assessing the depths of Bede's reading and stylistic devotion is that modern editors (and translators) of these works cannot list the vast number of allusions that Bede makes, and most are a matter of conjecture. When we turn to Bede's *Hymn to Aethelthryth*, we will see some of these allusions, but we await Michael Lapidge's edition of Bede's poems for a fuller list. As an example, some of the significance of Sedulius's *CP* lies in its relation to Virgil. Roger Green demonstrates how Sedulius opens his poem with an allusion to Virgil, contrasting the Christian "via namque salutis" (indeed the path of safety, 1.35) with the alluded-to phrase from Virgil, "via prima salutis" (first [your] path of safety, *Aen*. 6.96). Sedulius uses Virgilian language throughout his introduction to call readers out of the Virgilian world and into a life of Christ.⁵⁵ Bede himself uses the phrase "via salutis" twice, once in his commentary on the Canticle of Canticles while describing the path to salvation through Christ, and again in similar circumstances in his commentary on the Acts of the Apostles.⁵⁶ Understandably, none of these instances fired the synapses of modern editors. After all, Bede learned his Latin from books, so it is not surprising that he should echo those books; the question is whether those echoes are intentional markers for readers.⁵⁷ Green implies in his study of Sedulius that allusions, however faint, are often part of a poem's importance. (Our nun of Barking would not have known whether an allusion was intentional or not; nor can we.) Sedulius manages to allude simultaneously to Virgil and to Isaiah, which is equally important. This particular simultaneous allusion would be apparent to our nun of Barking, only because these works would have comprised a portion of her likely reading. As mentioned earlier, patterns

---

54. *In Regum librum xxx quaestiones*, p. 319, citing *CP* 1.184–87.
55. Green, *Latin Epics of the New Testament*, p. 164.
56. Bede, *Cantica canticorum Libri VI*, 1.1.25; Bede, *Expositio actuum apostolorum*, 16.16.
57. Ray, "Bede and Cicero," p. 13.

of meaningful allusion constitute another stylistic device in Bede's repertoire, one that he would have seen as essential to his models. We shall see it in Bede's allusions to Ovid, Horace, and Virgil in his *Hymn to Aethelthryth*.

Besides Sedulius, Fortunatus, and Prosper, Bede cites a dozen other poets in *DAM*. Classical pagan poets are Horace, Lucan, Lucretius, and Virgil. Christian poets are Ambrose, Arator, Cyprianus Gallus, Hilary of Poitiers, Juvencus, Paulinus of Nola, and Prudentius. Additionally, Bede cites three anonymous hymns, Sergius on Virgil, five verses from Scripture, and a contemporary of Ovid named Cornelius Severus, who left only a fragment of his epic poetry.[58] Each of these poets in some way has *auctoritas* 'authority', as Bede writes in chapter 15. Bede not only uses them as examples, but also points out peculiarities in their verse that authorize poetic license. But what of their reception in Anglo-Saxon England? Why were they valued?

Consider Prudentius, a Spanish poet possibly from Saragossa and born in 348. Prudentius is considered "the greatest Christian poet of the Late Antique period."[59] He is thought to have been central to the literary inheritance of Carolingian and Ottonian poets and regarded as "the most Christian of authors"; Sinead O'Sullivan calls him "by all accounts the most important Latin Christian poet of Late Antiquity."[60] Her opinion is shared by E. K. Rand, who wrote in 1920 that Prudentius was "the finest expression of Christian humanism that has appeared in poetry."[61] Aldhelm certainly knew him, as did Bede, and he was relatively popular in Anglo-Saxon England. But aside from syntax and vocabulary, which elements of his style might have

---

58. A similar list is given by Alcuin, who describes the library holdings of York. See Godman, *Alcuin*, p. 124. Theodulf of Orléans (b. 760), a Visigoth and one of the great Carolingian poets, will cite a similar list of authors; Theodulf of Orléans, Poem 45, "De Libris quos legere," MGH, PLAC 1, p. 543.
59. Palmer, *Prudentius on the Martyrs*, p. 1.
60. O'Sullivan, *Early Medieval Glosses*, pp. 3 and 5.
61. Quoted in Orchard, *PAA*, p. 171. See Orchard for a fuller description of Prudentius in ASE, pp. 171–78.

been valued by Bede? Lavarenne, an early editor and translator of Prudentius, considers some of his qualities to be a capacity for picturesque expression, with gracious and colorful descriptions, as well as his realism and eloquence.[62] Ruotger, a tenth-century Ottonian writer, indicated that Prudentius was valued for his orthodox Catholicism and that he was "most elegant in the variety of his meters and writings," which instilled Catholic teaching with "great sweetness."[63] Peter Godman, using a doublet well over a thousand years old, says that Prudentius's writing "equals anything written during the Latin Middle Ages in elegance and variety."[64] O'Sullivan, too, remarks on the "elegance and vividness of his style."[65] We should note that Orthodox Catholicism might well recommend a poet to Christians, but religious orthodoxy is not a technical element of style.[66] A good Christian can be a bad poet. But there is more to style than technical elements—Marouzeau reminds us that a primary factor is the quality of thought and the finesse of its expression.[67] We can surmise that Prudentius's command of balance and allusion, of vocabulary and rhetorical tropes of parallelism, and his descriptive ability comprise a good portion of what critics call his elegance.

Along with Sedulius, Prudentius, and Fortunatus, another author common in the schools that appears in Bede is Juvencus (fl. 329). Juvencus is described by Jerome as "nobilissimi generis Hispanus, presbyter" (a Spaniard of noble family, a priest).[68] Raby judges his work "clear and unadorned, but thoroughly Virgilian even to the

---

62. Prudentius, *Cath.*, pp. ix–xi. For a thorough overview of criticism and commentary regarding Prudentius, see Threade, *Studien*, chap. 1. See also Witke, *Numen Litterarum*, pp. 102–44.
63. Cited and trans. by O'Sullivan, *Early Medieval Glosses*, p. 11.
64. Godman, *Poetry of the Carolingian Renaissance*, p. 1.
65. O'Sullivan, *Early Medieval Glosses*, p. 17.
66. The point is made implicitly by Threade, *Studien*, p. 15: "Die Originalität des Dichters kann daher nur in seiner poetischen Technik liegen" (The originality of the poet can therefore lie only in his poetic technique).
67. Marouzeau, *Traité*, p. 341.
68. Cited in Green, *Latin Epics of the New Testament*, p. 1.

imitation of the great poet's characteristic archaisms."[69] Carolinne White call his famous work, *Evangeliorum Libri IV* (*EL*), a hexametrical version of the Gospels, "very restrained." She points out that Juvencus was interested in prophecy and that he was known for his neologisms, one of which—*altithronus* 'enthroned on high'—is used prominently by Bede.[70] Helen Waddell notes that Juvencus was especially esteemed in Ireland.[71] Juvencus provides the first illustration in Bede's next chapter, which concerns caesurae and correct scansion of the hexameter. A caesura is a break or pause in a verse (marked with ||). It might occur at the end of a phrase or clause, or between words. When a caesura corresponds with the end of a metrical foot (which is marked with |), it is called dieresis. Strong caesurae follow long syllables; weak caesurae follow short. David Califf writes, "The Greeks and Romans believed that the variation of caesura and dieresis was central to the poet's rhythmic artistry."[72] In this respect, the best sort of dactylic verse according to Bede is conjunctive, when "the end of a word never coincides with a foot division."[73] Bede's example of the best sort is taken from the opening to Juvencus's *EL*: "Īnmōr|tālĕ nĭ|hīl mūn|dī cōn|pāgĕ tĕ|nētur" (Naught in the world keeps an immortal stay); note also the fifth-foot dactyl.[74] In a rhythmical parallel, Wordsworth initially conceals then reveals his iambic tetrameter: "I wán|dered lóne|ly ás | a clóud," then reveals it fully, "That flóats | on hígh | o'er váles | and hílls." We see Wordsworth's initially conjunctive verse dissolve into one where caesurae correspond to word divisions. Conjunctive caesurae characterize the *Hymn to Aethelthryth*. The first line reads, "Ālmă Dĕ|ūs Trĭnĭ|tās, quæ| sæcŭlă || cūnctă gŭb|ērnăs."

---

69. Raby, *CLP*, p. 17. Brunhölzl, *LLMA*, and Manitius, *Geschichte*, begin their narratives after Juvencus; they do not include him except incidentally.
70. White, *CLP*, pp. 34–35. The term is found in the *Hymn to Aethelthryth*. Note that Aethelthryth was thought to have the power of prophecy, Bede, *HE*, 4.19, pp. 392–93.
71. Waddell, *More Latin Lyrics*, p. 64.
72. Califf, *A Guide to Latin Meter*, p. 14.
73. *DAM*, XII; Kendall, *Libri II*, p. 109.
74. Trans. Waddell, *More Latin Lyrics*, p. 67.

Apart from the fourth foot, it scans as a perfectly conjunctive verse—Bede places a caesura after the fourth foot in imitation of Bucolic verse, which differs from the hexameter in strictness of meter, caesura, and dieresis. Like the Golden Line, the art of the caesura lies in using it appropriately and decorously.

In enjambment and hyperbaton, and in the play of caesura and dieresis, we see some of the elements that Bede prized in poetry. Other elements include elision and the judicious modification of syllable length. Again, an appropriate and decorous use of these elements makes the art. What remains to be done in the final pages of this chapter is a brief review of the received reputations of the remainder of Bede's poets. To make those summaries more readable, there follows a series of excerpts from the more influential of Bede's poets.

SEDULIUS. We have seen something of Caelius Sedulius above. He was a priest and a poet who wrote during an age consumed with a "debate on Christian *rusticitas*, which constituted a great obstacle to cultivated persons embracing Christianity."[75] Sedulius is author of the *Carmen Paschale*, a prose version of the same work called the *Opus*, an epanaleptic elegy (the same form as Bede's *Hymn to Aethelthryth*), and an alphabetic hymn ("A solis ortus cardine").[76] Aldhelm says he was from Italy, which is likely. He was popular well into the nineteenth century; Martin Luther thought him one of the most Christian of poets.[77] Manitius finds twenty-eight citations of Sedulius in Bede's poems.[78] Huemer notes that Bede often cited him in prose and verse.[79] Here is the opening of the first book of his famous *CP* (the first sixteen lines of the poem are a preface in a different meter):

---

75. Di Berardino, *Patrology*, p. 323—this is volume four of Johannes Quasten's essential reference, *Patrology*.
76. These summaries mirror those of Orchard, *PAA*, chap. 4. For Sedulius, see the introduction to Springer's Sedulius, *CP*.
77. Di Berardino, *Patrology*, p. 324.
78. Manitius, *Zu Aldhelm und Beda*, pp. 621–22.
79. Huemer, *De Sedulii poetae*, p. 53; and Huemer's introduction to *Sedulius, CP*.

Cūm **sŭă** *gēntīlēs* STŬDĔĀNT **figmēntă** *pŏētāe*   17
Grandisonis pompare modis, tragicoque boatu
Ridiculoue Geta seu qualibet arte canendi
Saeua *nefandarum* RENOUENT **contagia** *rerum*   20
Et scelerum monumenta CANANT, rituque magistro
Plurima *Niliacis* TRADANT **mendacia** *biblis*,
Cūr ĕgŏ, Dāuĭtĭcīs | āssuētūs cāntĭbŭs ōdas   23
Chordarum RESONARE decem santoque uerenter
STARE choro et placidis caelestia PSALLERE uerbis,   25
Clara *salutiferi* TACEAM **miracula** *Christi*
Cum POSSIM manifesta LOQUI, dominumque tonantem
Sensibus et toto DELECTET corde FATERI?[80]

(Since pagan poets try to trick out their fictions   17
With pompous phraseology, and use tragic bombast,
Or the comic Geta, or any other style of singing
To recreate the cruel contagions of wicked deeds   20
And memorialize criminals in song, in the traditional way,
Passing on multiple lies in books of papyrus from the Nile,
Why should I, who am used to sound out in the songs of David
The psalms for the ten-stringed lyre, standing in awe
In the holy choir and singing with gentle words of heavenly
    things,   25
Keep silent about the famous miracles of Christ the Savior
When I can speak the plain truth, and it is my wholehearted
    delight
To confess the thundering Lord with all my senses?)

Springer comments on this passage: Sedulius poses a rhetorical question that "attacks pagan poetry and defends his own poetic project."[81] Bede does precisely the same thing at the beginning of his

---

80. Sedulius, *CP*, p. 17; modified by Springer, p. 2; trans. Springer. Length markers and other typographical features relate to the ensuing discussion.
81. Springer, in Sedulius, CP, p. 25. The rest of this paragraph recites Springer's comments.

Sources   109

Hymn to Aethelthryth, although he does not pose a question. Springer notes that Sedulius also establishes an antithesis between the fictional, violent poetry of the Greeks and the salvific, true poetry of Christianity. With respect to specifics, Geta (l. 19) was a slave in a comedy by Terence. "The traditional way" refers to writing on scrolls of Nile papyrus, again implying an antithesis between the old way and the new. The harp with ten strings (l. 24) refers to Psalm 144:9, indicating Christianity's equally antique lyre. "Tonantem" (l. 27) is a common epithet for Jupiter, an importation from pagan verse that correlates to Scripture (e.g., Job 38).

Turning to Bede's *DAM* and his recommendation of enjambment, we see that the passage is composed of two long periods. In fact, the complete sentence continues on until line 35. Classical authorities recommended that a period not exceed nine lines (we should think of these lengths temporally rather than spatially since a line was delimited by time, not by the width of a page). The passage is arranged in successively shorter clauses beginning with "cum" and "cur." Line 27 begins a longer Christian antithesis to line 17's gentile poets. In our passage, the first long clause runs through six lines, the syntax overrunning their ends. Similarly, lines 23 to 26 are syntactically enjambed. A reader experiences the meaning of the lines not in equivalent chunks (isocolon), but unfolding in disproportionate temporal succession over several lines. The particular textures and nuances of that unfolding are part of the art of a Latin poem. For example, we finish line 18 with a sense of the tragic, "tragico," which is upturned after a pause at the beginning of line 19 with a reference to the comic, "ridiculoue." Similarly, the sense of orderly modulation and song in "arte canendi" at the end of line 19 is immediately juxtaposed to line 20's immoderate "saeva" (fierce, vehement). This antithesis is mirrored in the Christian portion with "placidis verbis" (gentle words, l. 25) juxtaposed to the "dominum tonantem" (thundering Lord, l. 27). Other juxtaposed antitheses obvious here are the written poems of the gentiles (l. 22) versus the Christian's sung psalms (l. 23). Grammatical antitheses are many. The first clause begins "Cum sua," a dactyl, while the second begins "cur ego," also a dactyl, setting a plural "sua" against a singular "ego." *Cantare* and its participial and nominal forms play a structural role, as do "choro" and "chordarum." There is almost too much to notice! For example, the hyperbaton is extremely artful: note the generally central position in a line of the verbs (in small caps), sparingly disposed throughout the passage. Golden lines cluster around line 20, as if to mock their overuse in pagan verse. In the second clause, only line 26 is golden. In that line the reader serially experiences an idea of fame and then an idea of salvation, "clara salutiferi," as she moves toward the name of Christ. The verb of this line, "taceam," reaches back to "ego" in line 23, and fulfills the syntax of *cur*, the backwards movement of grammatical memory perhaps alluding to the name of Christ reaching back through the line of David. There are no instances of elision or hiatus. Metrically, we see a caesura after the first syllable of the third foot, which is typical of good hexameter verse, in both lines 17 and 23. These are the first lines of our two major clauses, and they are metrically similar but for the second and third feet. Line 17 is *ddss* and line 23 is *dsds*. The major difference concerns Bede's preferred conjunctive style: in line 17, a caesura corresponds to the end of a foot only once, while in line 23, there are three instances of such dieresis. Perhaps Sedulius is implying that the artful verse of pagans is transformed metrically by the model of David's psalms.

VIRGIL. If ever a poet prompted an anxiety of influence, it was Virgil. All of our poets, Bede included, contended with this greatest of Latin poets, as every English poet must contend with Shakespeare. There is far too much to say about Virgil, so I will confine myself to a brief summary. Publius Virgilius Maro was born October 15, 70 BC.[82] He moved from Mantua probably to Naples, and thence to Rome. His oeuvre begins with the pastoral *Bucolics*, also called the *Eclogues*, comprising 829 hexameters; then the didactic *Georgics*, containing 2,188 hexameters; and finally the epic *Aeneid* of about ten

---

82. For Virgil and all major Latin poets, see first Conte, *Latin Literature*. The literature on the influence of Virgil in ASE is too vast to note here.

thousand hexameters. In *Eclogue* 1, which introduces the pastoral genre to Latin poetry, Virgil writes,

> impius haec tam culta noualia miles habebit,
> barbarus has segetes?
>
> (Shall a wicked soldier have these fallow lands so beautifully
>   tilled,
> A barbarian these crops?)[83]

At this point in the poem, Meliboeus, a farmer, is lamenting the loss of his confiscated farm. An Irish commentator who knew or knew of Adamnán of Iona (d. 704 AD) commented on Virgil's verse.[84] Following closely a much earlier commentary by the so-called Junius Philagurius, this Irish commentator explains that the "impius miles" is the soldier who took Meliboeus's land. He also says that Meliboeus is angry, and that the soldier carried arms for Anthony, who brought the civil war. "Novalia" means new, that is, a field left for a year without seeds. "Habebit" refers to planting seeds in hope of a crop. The commentary is straightforward and explanatory. It reads much like the notes of today's college literary anthologies. It seeks to inform rather than to direct interpretation. For example, like the commentary on this poem, much early medieval commentary on the *Aeneid* concerned the relation of the poem to Virgil's life.[85]

William Fitzgerald comments on the style of these lines. He begins by saying that this is "one of the most melodious and fluid passages of Latin poetry in the whole canon."[86] It is dactylic but for the second foot, "hāec tām." The quantity of the verse (syllable length) is consonant with its rhythm (emphasis or accent). The adjective "impius" connects by half-rhyme to its noun, "miles." The half-line

---

83. Lines 70–71; trans. Fitzgerald, *How to Read a Latin Poem*, p. 145. The analysis of these lines is entirely from Fitzgerald, pp. 145–52.
84. See Lapidge, "The Career of Aldhelm," pp. 29–30. The text is edited by Hagen, *Appendix Serviana* in volume 3, fascicle 2 of Servius, *Commentarii*.
85. Starr, "Vergil's *Seventh Eclogue* and its Readers," p. 131.
86. Fitzgerald, *How to Read a Latin Poem*, p. 145.

contains an adjective, "barbarus," which reaches back for its antecedent, "miles," while the accusative object "has segetes" reaches back for its verb, "habebit." The grammar inhibits a quick forward movement by the reader, but it encourages looking backwards, as Meliboeus does. Fitzgerald continues:

> The first two words of the half line echo the first two words of the previous line: an adjective in the nominative and a demonstrative pronoun in the accusative. It is an answering phrase, a dying cadence that completes a glorious bel canto melody, but one that pivots on the words *impius* and *barbarus*, which one would expect to be spat out rather than sung. There is an alarming disjunction between the sound of these words and their meaning.[87]

The symmetries of the verse include the qualities of land and the qualities of their owners: fallow land and uncultivated soldier set in antithesis to cultivated land and civilized Meliboeus. Other antitheses are those absent versus those present, the heroic versus the pastoral, and so forth. One can glimpse in this brief passage some stylistic habits echoed by Sedulius. Although it is unlikely that Bede would have recognized Virgil's many allusions to Theocritus, he would have found much to admire about this verse.[88] We shall see an extensive use of antithesis in Bede's *Hymn to Aethelthryth*.

PROSPER. Prosper of Aquitaine (d. AD 455) was a school author. Well educated, he moved to Marseilles, and although in contact with the monasteries of Lérins and St. Victor, he remained a layman his entire life. He was a correspondent with and staunch defender of Augustine, as well as a contemporary of Hilary of Poitiers. Around 430 he moved to Rome, where he wrote a commentary on the Psalms, an epitome of Jerome's chronicle, poetic epigrams (*Epigrammata*), a long hexameter

---

87. Ibid., p. 147.
88. Bede may have known these allusions from Servius's life of Virgil. For the text, see Ziolkowski and Putnam, *The Virgilian Tradition*, pp. 181–89, §66. On the importance of allusions to Theocritus in this Eclogue, see Breed, *Pastoral Inscriptions*, chap. 5.

poem (*Carmen de ingratis*), and other works. The works best known in Anglo-Saxon England were his *Epigrammata*. The *Carmen de ingratis* is a 2,000-line hexameter poem in defense of Augustine. Orchard calls it "lengthy and influential"; it may have been known to Aldhelm.[89] Bede thought that a poem known as *Poema conjugis* was by Prosper. It includes 53 elegiac distichs—which is the form of Bede's *Hymn to Aethelthryth*. Adalbert Hamman comments, "Prosper excels especially in his precision of thought, flexibility of expression, capacity of judgment, and in the clarity of his exposition and the force of his argumentation."[90] Pope Celestine I said that Prosper had a "religious spirit"; Hilary of Poitiers called him a "vir tum moribus, tum eloquio, et studio clarus" (a man not only moral, but also eloquent and illustrious in devotion); Cassiodorus thought him holy and venerable.[91]

In *DAM*, Bede cites Epigram 53 twice (lines 5–6 and then lines 7–8):

Sōlūs | pēccātōr sērvīt mălĕ; | quī lĭcĕt | āmplō   5
Ūtātūr rēgnō, || sāt mĭsĕr | ēst fămŭlūs;
Cūm mēns | cārnālīs, nĭmĭūm dŏmĭnāntĕ tȳrānnō,
Tōt sērvīt scēptrīs || dēdĭtă | quōt vĭtĭīs.

(The sinner serves evil alone; although he may possess a great kingdom, he is a wretched enough slave. / [7] When the tyrant sin excessively dominates the flesh, the mind serves as many masters as the number of vices to which it is given.)[92]

Here, the distichs are elegiac: comprising a hexameter followed by a pentameter. The central division in the pentameter is marked ||. Prosper's closest reader, Abbott L. Valentin, notes that Prosper took

---

89. Orchard, *PAA*, pp. 183–85. The *Epigrammata* are found in *PL* 51:497–531; the excerpt here is at col. 514B.
90. Adalbert Hamman, "Prosper of Aquitaine," in di Berardino, *Patrology*, pp. 551–58, p. 552.
91. Cited in *Prosperi Aquitani*, p. 3. On Prosper's life and theology, see Hwang, *Intrepid Lover of Perfect Grace*. Hwang lists seventeen works confidently attributed to Prosper, p. 29.
92. Kendall, *Libri II*, pp. 98–101; trans. Kendall. Only diaresis is marked.

care to find precisely the correct word; he thought it a duty.[93] As an example, Valentin writes, "What is the soul before the arrival of grace? A field which is not yet sown (*novalis*)."[94] There in Prosper is Virgil's famous word. Prosper repeats words that are important to his theme (epanalepsis); he employs a good deal of alliteration[95]; he enjoys rhyme; and he uses adjectives soberly. He is nevertheless appropriately emotive, recalling Augustine's example of reading tearfully. Valentin writes, "The sight of the ideal excites in the soul that contemplates it a gentle and powerful feeling which makes the voice of the orator vibrate delicately."[96] Valentin, who like Raby relishes emotion and pathos, notes that Prosper's epigrams contain a "solemn and pathetic lyricism," while simultaneously borrowing Augustine's realism.[97] Technical mastery is paramount. Prosper's meter "is always correct," although he sometimes takes license to shorten final –o, which we also find in Ovid.[98] His caesurae are carefully placed—his hexameters appropriately have a strong caesura after the first syllable of the third foot, called a penthemimer break. In line 5 above, as Valentin explains, Prosper has typically set off a distinct idea with a fourth-foot caesura.[99] The same couplet has a chiastic rhyme: "solus" and "famulus," and "amplo" and "regno." The hexameters of his distichs are overwhelmingly spondaic, even showing a fifth-foot spondee in line 7.[100] The lines show dieresis (marked), and the heavily spondaic character of Prosper's lines is on display here. The first two-and-a-half feet of these pentameters are wholly spondaic.

---

93. Valentin, *Saint Prosper d'Aquitaine*, p. 526.
94. Ibid.: "Qu'est-ce que l'âme avant l'arrivée de la grâce? Une terre qui n'a pas encore été ensemencée (*noualis*)."
95. Ibid., p. 547.
96. Ibid., p. 538: "Le spectacle de l'idéal excite dans l'âme qui le contemple un sentiment doux et puissant qui fait vibrer légèrement la voix de l'orateur."
97. Ibid., pp. 540–41.
98. Ibid., p. 565.
99. Ibid., p. 593. Aldhelm will use the fourth-foot caesura similarly.
100. Ibid., p. 594.

They are balanced by the second two-and-a-half feet, which are more dactylic.

Bede uses these two couplets in the *DAM* as examples of enjambment. Note the enjambment of "amplo regno" (great kingdom) between lines 5 and 6. The first half of line 6 reaches back to "licet." Line 7 waits for its verb to appear in line 8, "servit." As we have seen, the best elegiac couplet lets its sense overflow its internal bounds. But, as Bede warns, the pentameter should never flow into the following hexameter. The second couplet of lines, Bede writes, "although they are subjoined to [lines 5 and 6] . . . are nevertheless linked to each other in their turn, and the second completes the sense of the first."[101] We see that Prosper has joined his two couplets by rhyming "amplo" and "tyranno," both of which have two spondees. The chiastic rhyme with "regno" has barely faded as the reader approaches "tyranno," leaving traces of kingdoms and tyrants in her mind. Katherine O'Brien O'Keeffe recently put these epigrams into their monastic contexts, describing how they were used to teach both the rudiments of grammar and correct conduct.[102] Thus, in *DAM*, Bede uses them to teach the rudiments of verse. Bede cites Prosper nineteen times in his *DAM*. There, Prosper's *Epigrams* offer examples of elision (*Praef.* 7–8, p. 53 and 8.7, p. 115), variable syllable length (of *ne*, 5.5–6, p. 85), and more.[103]

Looking a little more closely at what O'Brien O'Keeffe notes, we can see that not only is there an obvious call for obedience in these couplets, but also a careful definition of monastic service implied in the phrase "servit male." Prosper repeats the word "servit" in these couplets, indicating its importance. Augustine opposes a *servus bonus*

---

101. Kendall, *Libri II*, p. 101.
102. O'Brien O'Keeffe, *Stealing Obedience*.
103. The remainder are from *Epigrammata* 8.7 (Kendall, *Libri II*, p. 115); 15.4 (p. 125); 19.1 (p. 115); 29.1 (p. 107); 31.2–4 (p. 55); 40.3 (p. 121); 41.1–2 (p. 107); 43.3–4 (p. 115); 53.5–6 (p. 101); 53.7–8 (p. 101); 64.3 (p. 127); 67.3–4 (p. 61); 72.1–2 (p. 117); 91.9 (p. 85); 92.1–2 (p. 57); 102.17–18 (p. 119); and 104.5 (p. 111).

to a *servus malus* in his Commentary on John.[104] Service is admirable, but its moral worth derives from the object of one's service. *Famulus* 'servant', in line 6, is what Bede famously styled himself in his dedication of the *HE*, "Beda famulus Christi et presbyter" (Bede a servant and priest of Christ); Augustine would do the same. Prosper is using a vocabulary of service, but in a context of serving corrupt power. The implicit moral dilemma lies in the potential disloyalty of a servant who is called to abandon a corrupt lord. Great wealth, "amplo regno," is sinful only in its single-minded pursuit, while the tyranny of excess causes widespread imbalance. Bede saw this as a problem in his own day, as he points out vividly in his *Commentary on Ezra and Nehemiah*.[105] Here, Prosper subtly recommends control of excess by illustrating his grammatical and metrical control of the subject.

In the service of brevity, we shall skip over Paulinus of Nola, Fortunatus, Juvencus, Prudentius, and Arator. Although something of their influence can be seen in the style of both Bede's elegy and his hexameter *Life of Cuthbert*, the greatest number of Bede's extant poems are hymns. Along with Prudentius, the two great writers of hymns whom Bede cites are Hilary of Poitiers and Ambrose of Milan, both of whom I provide examples of below. The subject of hymns and liturgical song is vast; it will be touched upon sporadically as we read through the *Hymn to Aethelthryth*.

HILARY. Hilary of Poitiers (c. 310–367) was Bishop of Poitiers and "one of the most important fathers of the fourth century," according to Raby (Augustine thought so, too).[106] He wrote five important commentaries, including one on the Psalms.[107] We shall see the influence of his commentary on Psalm 118 on Bede's *Hymn to Aethelthryth*.

---

104. *In Iohannis euangelium tractatus*, PL 35:1379, v. 8.
105. Bede speaks there of the poverty, *miser*, of the overtaxed Northumbrian people. DeGregorio, *Bede: On Ezra and Nehemiah*, p. 184.
106. Raby, *CLP*, p. 42. Raby thinks Hilary's hymns "tedious and prosaic," p. 43.
107. *CPL*, 427 et seq.

De Trinitate was Hilary's best known doctrinal work, but he also wrote dozens of letters and tractates, and dedicated one (*De synodis*) to the bishops of Britain. Hilary introduced his hymns into the local liturgy, reports Isidore of Seville. He wrote thirty to forty years before Ambrose, whose influence on Christian hymnody is unparalleled, but his hymns were not as attractive to Christians as were those of Ambrose. Hilary modified Eastern lyric forms to Latin and mimicked the idiom of praise and supplication of the Psalter.[108]

Although medieval sources attribute a large number of hymns to Hilary, only three fragments are confidently assigned to him.[109] They are thought to have originated in his lost book of hymns, *Liber Hymnorum*. One hymn, which Bede thought genuine, begins "Hymnum dicat turba fratrum" (see below). It was likely a morning hymn. Bede cites it as an especially beautiful ("pulcherrimus") example of the septenarius, or trochaic tetrameter catalectic.[110] Bede thought the meter took either a trochee or spondee in every foot but the third, which had to be a trochee. It was an error that had great influence, although Bede clearly allows for a spondaic third foot.[111] The meter requires eight feet, the last of which is docked half a foot, thus making it catalectic. There is an obligatory break halfway through each line (marked || below), and a secondary break recommended after the first two feet, or dipody (marked |). Hilary makes that secondary break obligatory. Like most others using this form, he avoids disyllabic words at the end of his line. A last point to mention is that in

---

108. See Palmer, *Prudentius*, p. 59.
109. Szövérffy, *Latin Hymns*, p. 79, and "Latin Hymns," p. 381. See also his *Annalen*, 2:69–73. Summary of works in *CPL*, 463. Editions in CSEL 65, pp. 209–16. "Hymnum dicat" can be found along with its gloss in *The Irish Liber Hymnorum*, 1:36–42; modified after Bede's manuscripts by Kendall, *Libri II*, p. 157. Its editors, Bernard and Atkinson, see no reason to refute Hilary's authorship, 2:126. Meyer and Raby did, though, as Szövérffy points out, *Annalen*, 1:69. The hymn is also found in the *Antiphonary of Bangor*. See the introduction to the hymn in Walpole, *Hymns*, pp. 1–15; and *AH* 51, pp. 259–63.
110. Kendall, *Libri II*, p. 159. See Brunhölzl, *LLMA*, 1:163.
111. Norberg, *Introduction* (English), pp. 70–71. Kendall, *Libri II*, pp. 158–59: "you will find here and there a spondee even in the third foot. . . ."

this form, syllable length very often corresponds to rhythm.¹¹² (To demonstrate the rhythm and caesurae, the following lines can be sung to the tune of Beethoven's "Ode to Joy.") We see these characteristics in the first two (often rendered as four) lines of the hymn:

Hỹmnūm dīcāt | tūrbā frātrūm, || hỹmnūm cāntūs pērsŏnĕt,
Crīstō rēgī | cōncīnnēntēs || lāudēs dēmūs dēbĭtās.

(Let the congregation sing a hymn,
let the music swell the hymn,
singing in chorus to Christ the King,
let us offer his merited praises.)¹¹³

In another hymn, Szövérffy points out that antitheses lie at the heart of Hilary's style. An example here is that of the many and the one. We see it in "turba fratrum" (crowd of brothers) who sing a single hymn, and in the plurality governing the verb "demus" praising the one "Cristus." Hilary is also known for repetition—here we see it in "hymnum" and its synonyms, "cantus" and "dicat" (*dicere*). Hilary was also responsible for a large number of neologisms as he tried to express the complexities of Christian theology in Latin, and he used existing words in new ways; for example, in another work he used "altissimus," a superlative adjective, as a substantive for "The Most High."¹¹⁴

Glosses to the hymn in the *Irish Liber Hymnorum* are fairly straightforward and include grammatical information. One notes that *cantus* is a nominative, another that "concin[n]entes" is from the verb *concinere*. Others indicate allusions. In line 3 is the phrase "tu via tu veritas," and the glossator has written, "ut dicitur, Ego sum via et veritas et vita . . ." (that is to say, I am the way, the truth, and the life.).¹¹⁵ And another is semantic: "fratrum," which reads, "means brothers in

---

112. Norberg, *Introduction* (English), p. 68.
113. Kendall, *Libri II*, pp. 158–59: his trans.
114. Kinnavey, *The Vocabulary of St. Hilary of Poitiers*, pp. 1 and 33. See *TLL*, 1.1782 ff. Virgil famously used *altus* as a substantive in the third line of the *Aeneid*, "in alto."
115. Bernard and Atkinson, *The Irish Liber Hymnorum*, 1:36.

Christ." We might continue where the glosses leave off. The hymn's vocabulary ensures that the piece is to be classed as a hymn: Augustine had famously defined hymns as those songs that refer "to song, praise, and God" (Hymnus ergo tria ista habet, et canticum, et laudem, et Dei).[116] With "Cristo," "laudes," and "cantus," therefore, we are assured that the hymn's self-definition as a hymn is authorized. Bede will use similar vocabulary in his hymn, "Adesto Christe vocibus." Indeed, the vocabulary ultimately may have been allusive: Hilary may have had Horace and Propertius in mind, whose first odes include the phrase "dicere carmen."[117] Note also that the few adjectives here carry no metaphors; the "literary" quality is left to the verbs and nouns. Yet within this seemingly plainer form, a good number of theological niceties are being explored. For one, notice that the hymn acts out its own claim: it fulfills a desire to praise Christ with the sung praise that the hymn itself offers. Perhaps Hilary has in mind a distinction drawn by Ambrosiaster between the spirit that prays and the mind that may or may not understand the prayer, as suggested in 1 Corinthians 14:4.[118] The mood is subjunctive, not imperative. It invites rather than commands. Consider the difference between "Let the congregation sing" and Caedmon's "Nu sculon herigean" (Now we must praise). But, like *Caedmon's Hymn*, a sense of Christian community is built into Hilary's vocabulary, especially the first-person plural subjunctive "demus" (*dare*). While the focal point is a singular Christ, and the means a singular hymn, the actors join in concert. The verb "personet" alludes perhaps to Cassiodorus, who writes about singing a new song ("novum canticum personabant"), recalling the famous strophe of the Psalms, for example 32:3, "Cantate ei canticum novum."[119] Hymns were a new song introduced into the long tradition of Latin lyric. Like the septenarii on which this

---

116. In his *Enn.*, PL 37:1947; cited by Szövérffy, *Latin Hymns*, p. 29. See also den Boeft, "Ambrosius lyricus," p. 77.
117. Walpole, *Hymns*, p. 5, n. 1.
118. Mohrmann, *Liturgical Latin*, p. 55.
119. Cassiodorus, *Complexiones in Apocalypsin*, p. 118.

hymn is based, they were written to be recited by crowds or troops. Bede will speak of the new song ("nova carmina") sung by Christians in the penultimate strophe of his Hymn.

AMBROSE. Ambrose, Bishop of Milan (339–397), was one of the most important Fathers of the Church.[120] Szövérffy writes that Ambrose is rightly called the father of church hymnody,[121] while Jacques Fontaine says that his hymns comprise "one of the most original and perfect poetic creations of Latin Christianity."[122] Certainly, they were highly esteemed both for their form and their orthodoxy. His focus in his hymns was on Trinitarian theology. Like Hilary, Ambrose was ascribed dozens of hymns that are probably not his. His authentic hymns number fourteen, but may number between four and sixteen, depending on his editor; Szövérffy and Fontaine list fourteen. One is cited by Bede, who calls it "a hymn of great beauty ['pulcherrimo'] and dignity ['decore']." Walpole calls it the oldest martyr-hymn, noting a citation by Maximus of Turin.[123] Commonly known as Hymn 14, these are the opening lines cited by Bede:

Āetērnā Crīstī mūnĕrā
Ĕt mārtўrūm vīctōrĭās,
Lāudēs fĕrēntēs dēbĭtās,
Lĕtīs cānāmūs mēntĭbŭs.

(The eternal gifts of Christ
And the victories of the martyrs,

---

120. *CPL*, p. 123 et seq. Bede is the first to name him as one of four most important fathers; see Ray, "Who Did Bede Think He Was?," p. 12. Alcuin numbered Bede among the most important five, see ibid., p. 13. The best introduction to Ambrose's hymnody that I have found is Jacques Fontaine in his edition of Ambrose, *Hymnes*, pp. 11–123.
121. Szövérffy, *Annalen*, 1:48.
122. Ambrose, *Hymnes*, p. 11. See also Ramsey, *Ambrose*, p. 65.
123. Walpole, *Hymns*, p. 104. Bulst doubts its authenticity; see Ambrose, *Hymnes*, p. 586.

Which bring about merited praises
Let us sing with joyful hearts.)[124]

Bede cites this hymn in his chapter on the iambic tetrameter. He explains that the form can take an "iamb in every foot, and the spondee only in the odd feet." One can also use a tribrach (three shorts) in the first three feet, and replace the spondees with a dactyl or a tribrach. There are four feet in the iambic dimeter, but one counts only two metrons (also called a dipody), which is why it's called a dimeter and not a tetrameter. One dipody equals two iambic feet. The form was popular in classical Rome and used by Horace, Seneca, and Ausonius, among others. It sometimes appeared in Roman comedy, where the line could be legally resolved with a tribrach.[125] Disyllabic words at the end of a line were also common in Roman comedy, although there was a general tendency to avoid such endings, as we see here.[126] And, moreover, it is the most common meter of Latin hymns.[127] (One will recognize in its modified rhythmic form the meter typical of Emily Dickinson's poems.) Ambrose wrote lines in iambic tetrameter to be sung by choirs and congregations, who traded verses back and forth. The lines had to be carefully crafted so that the sense didn't cross the chancel with the tune. Bede follows Ambrose's model closely, although Ambrose sometimes compromised meter in order to cite a Biblical verse (e.g., 6:19–20, noted by Bede). Along with the Bible, Ambrose used theological key phrases, symbols, and poetic and rhetorical formulae.[128] We will see a number of these elements in Bede's *Hymn to Aethelthryth*.

Anne-Marie Palmer points out that due to Ambrose's focus on performance, the form of the hymns "imposed a certain economy and simplicity on the actual content of the hymns." The result was

---

124. Kendall, *Libri II*, p. 155; his trans. Walpole, *Hymns*, reads "Lāetīs" rather than "Lĕtīs" in line 4.
125. Raven, *Latin Meter*, pp. 58–59.
126. Marouzeau, *Traité*, p. 316.
127. Norberg, *Introduction* (English), p. 63.
128. Szövérffy, *Annalen*, pp. 52–53.

"a rich synthesis which 'converts' the features of classical hymnody and the language and spirit of Latin lyric to Christian purposes, combining them with the lyric element necessarily involved in the individualistic self-expression of Christian prayer."[129] "Canamus," the first-person plural form, captures that self-expression while simultaneously articulating a common body of believers, a "we." Den Boeft notices a similar antithesis between the one and the many in Ambrose's *Aeterne rerum conditor*. He remarks on a polyptoton "which by the twofold use of the plural *tempus* emphasizes the multiple temporariness of creation, in contrast to the uniform eternity of the Creator."[130] Ambrose's images are clear, his word order "never contorted or strained." Moreover, "Ideas develop in a series of readily grasped concrete images . . ." and "[a] clear image is presented in a single line, with a wide use of parallel phraseology, and antithesis within this . . ."[131]

Indeed, we notice simple language in the hymn above. There are no extended metaphors, no catalogues of synonyms, no rhetorical flourishes more appropriate to the hexameter. The second and third lines are connected by end-rhyme. That connection plays against any semantic break between lines two and three. Syntactically, the lines are very similar, and they read literally, "Eternal *of Christ* gifts / And *of martyrs* the victories / Praises *producing* appropriate / With glad *let us sing* hearts." The italics indicate the second word of each line; in each case, the second word separates a semantic cluster. The unfolding sense of the lines moves backwards and forwards, a syntactic microcosm of the voices trading verses across a chancel. Because of metrical restraints, certain inflectional endings provided convenient syllables—much like Virgil placing third-conjugation infinitives in his fifth foot.[132] We can also see shifts in syntax that Jan den Boeft describe as "an elegant alternation of symmetry and chiasmus in the

---

129. Palmer, *Prudentius on the Martyrs*, p. 65.
130. Den Boeft, "Ambrosius Lyricus," p. 81.
131. Palmer, *Prudentius on the Martyrs*, p. 65.
132. Marouzeau, *Traité*, p. 317. Some examples include "euertere gentem," "conuellere silvam," and "excedere terra."

arrangement of subject, predicate, and object."[133] With the repetitive meter, typical coincidence of syllable length and accent, and a fairly repetitive syntax, these hymns promoted habits of composition that we shall see in Bede.

Bede's style is a plainer form of the jeweled style. His readers have long praised the clarity of his Latin, his *sermo simplex*.[134] But many of his most powerful influences were not as direct as Ambrose or Gregory the Great. By the fifth century, the regnant style was virtually Baroque. Roberts says of Juvencus, Sidonius, Cyprianus, Ausonius, Prudentius, Avitus, and Dracontius:

> Fundamental to the examples we have cited is a combination of synonymy, enumeration, and antithesis, which endows the texts with their characteristic regularity and density, the sense that every word counts.... Enumeration regularly coexists with synonymy; typically the items enumerated are related as species belonging to a common genus. Antithesis, as well as often establishing a basic regularity within a passage, also by contrast with schemes of parallelism (synonymy or enumeration) introduces an element of variation and can itself be varied by shifts in the ground of comparison or semantic categories. Synonymic parallelism may also operate at the level of clause rather than vocabulary, the figure of *interpretatio*.[135]

Rhetorical figures that grow out of antithesis, enumeration, and synonymy are found to be essential to the structure and art of these early Christian poets. For example, parallelism is invoked by alliteration, while the meanings of alliterated words might be either synonymous, giving us enumeration, or antonymous, giving us antithesis. Chiasmus describes antithetical sets of words, sounds, grammatical cases, and so forth. Bede constructs his elegiac *Hymn to Aethelthryth* so that in each stanza the clauses run chiastically A1-B1

---

133. Den Boeft, "Ambrosius Lyricus," p. 80.
134. For example, Wetherbee, "Some Implications of Bede's Latin Style."
135. Roberts, *The Jeweled Style*, p. 36.

/ B2-A2, where A1 is repeated verbatim in A2, and B2 varies a theme from B1. He breaks this regularity in some stanzas by making B2 a syntactic extension of B1. The art of many of his poems and those of his antecedents lies in "a play of tension and continuity that contradicts the static effect such passages often communicate at first."[136]

The poets with whom Bede was most familiar are steeped in this jeweled style. Their individual variations on the style constitute the wider scope of Bede's literary ambit. Bede's hymns, as we shall see, look to other models. But his elegiac *Hymn to Aethelthryth* and hexameter *Life of Cuthbert* are written in the variegated light and shadow of the jeweled style. Finally, his poems both vary and oppose pagan classical tradition. As a Christian priest and monk, his business is not to sustain pagan religion, but to enlarge the meditative and liturgical capacity of his co-religionists. The higher registers of literary Latin could offer that to him. But classical or liturgical Latinity was not simply a superficial matter of decoration. Bede's poems are sung in response to the pagan and Christian past while simultaneously harmonizing with the literary world of his own modernity. Bede's style illustrates how he fit himself into the world of Christian Latin literature. In the next chapter, we will see how Bede used the form of pagan and Christian elegy to shape the story of Queen Aethelthryth.

---

136. Ibid., p. 37.

Chapter Five

St. Aethelthryth in the *HE*

Having looked at some elements of style in Bede and at some of his sources, let us turn to his *Hymn to Aethelthryth*. Before commenting closely on the *Hymn* in the remaining chapters, I would first like to look at its immediate context in the *HE*. The *Hymn* is placed in book four, which also contains the famous account of the poet Caedmon. Like the story of Caedmon, Bede's *Hymn to Aethelthryth* picks up a centuries-old trope of reforming traditional poetry to a Christian purpose. Employing this trope, Bede addresses the fleeting pleasures of pagan Latin poetry, and the necessary role of female saints and martyrs in the birth of the English Church. As a monk versed in Scripture and in the liturgy, Bede is interested in the role of narrative and poetry in directing the spiritual life. His *Hymn* is especially ingenious in its control of allusion and form. Bede, a master of styles, is attuned to the effect form has on a reader. My proposition is that with this *Hymn*, Bede is doing something deeply and spiritually significant. Book four, according to Scott DeGregorio, is about reform.[1] So it is no surprise that the *Hymn to Aethelthryth* speaks to *form*, which seems to me to be the meaningful element of *reform*—that is, the kind of order expected in the speech and writing of an ordered life. In a very general way, Caedmon's *Hymn* seeks to reform pagan poetry in Old English, while Aethelthryth's *Hymn* seeks to reform pagan poetry in Latin. The *Hymn* does not appear in any

---

1. DeGregorio, "Monasticism and Reform."

Old English translation of the *HE*. That omission suggests that the hymn's capacity to reform a well-trained reader of Latin is of little use to a reader of Old English. My use of "reformation" to denote the formal elements of a poem is not idle; in keeping with a view that distinguishes poetry from prose solely on a formal level, Isidore in his *Etymologiae* (8.7) writes about the transformation and reformation of historical matter by poets. Writing poetry is all about reformation, and from a wider perspective, reformation of poetic form is of a kind with reformation of liturgical forms, as well as a reformation of historical memory through the Roman genre of written history. In short, my aim here is to bring the forms of the Aethelthryth narrative into conversation with the rest of book four.

In chapter nineteen of book four, Bede crafts a story of Aethelthryth, consort to King Ecgfrith of Northumbria, and daughter of King Anna of the East Angles.[2] Bede was about six years old when Aethelthryth died, five years after the King had granted lands to Benedict Biscop for the foundation of Wearmouth.[3] At the time, Aethelthryth was serving as Abbess of the minster at Ely, which she had founded. Her life has been celebrated since her death in 679, most famously and much later in the Book of Ely.[4] After telling her story in prose, Bede inserts a poem to Aethelthryth.[5] Giving the same story in prose and verse yields an *opus geminatum*, also known as *geminus stilus*, a phrase famously used by Hraban Maur.[6] This was not Bede's first *geminus stilus*. Earlier in his career, Bede had adapted

---

2. Bede, *HE*, pp. 390–91; Thacker, "Æthelthryth (*d*. 679)." Bede is not so much telling a story (in the etymological sense of reciting facts) as he is crafting a narrative in partial imitation of a *vita*.
3. Bede, *HA*, pp. 22–33 and 32–33.
4. *Liber Eliensis*, ed. Blake. All later retellings rely on Bede.
5. The *Hymn* is found in every complete manuscript of the *HE*. See Szarmach, "Æðeldreda in the *Old English Bede*." Singly, it is found in four manuscripts, including St. Gall 265, an edition of which is found in this volume (see pp. 163–64 below). See Lapidge, "Beda Venerabilis," p. 129. Lapidge has the current, authoritative edition.
6. Wieland, "Geminus stilus," p. 127, n. 1. See also Wallace-Hadrill, *Bede's Ecclesiastical History*, p. 161. Friesen, "Opus geminatum," p. 127: the verse,

a verse *Life of St. Felix* by Paulinus of Nola into prose and praised Cuthbert in both prose and poetry.[7] The *Hymn to Aethelthryth* is not strictly a retelling of her life, but a meditation on literary and spiritual transformation, and, like Bede's *DST*, it substitutes Christian for classical content. Jean-Yves Tilliette notes, with respect to an *opus geminatum* by Alcuin, that "the prose version is intended for public recitation, while the verse is to serve as a focus for meditation and as an intellectual stimulus for *scolastici*."[8] So at a very basic level, prose and verse tell one how to read appropriately. The style of each of Bede's works is distinct, as Tom Mackay pointed out in his edition of Bede's *Life of St. Felix*. Not only do prose and verse indicate how to read a work appropriately, but so do the various styles of prose and the various forms of verse. Each prompts a particular kind of *lectio divina*. Heroic hexameters are meditated upon differently than are Sapphics—there are different aspects of the form to account for, different patterns by which the sense unfolds in time. It seems obvious, but a consequence of this correlation between verse form and meditation is that once you translate a poem into English, you lose the Latin cues for spiritual meditation. What might Bede have been suggesting by placing an elegy at this point in the narrative?

The fourth book of the *HE* speaks to the *Hymn* in a number of ways. One concerns Bede's manner of narration. Bede pauses his narration of history to explain that he composed this elegy many years before writing the *HE*, and that he will intercalate it here. In other words, he stops telling a story in order to describe how he tells a story. (The *Hymn* is filled with similar apostrophes.) The simplicity of Bede's editorial comment, as it were, is belied by Bede's

---

vs. the prose, has "better claim to the meaning of its subject," according to Quintilian.

7. *Vita S. Felicis (Beati Felicis Confessoris Vita)*, PL 94:789–98; the most current edition is Mackay, "A Critical Edition of Bede's Vita Felicis." Among other examples of similar transformation, Paulinus of Périgeaux, a poet known to Bede, adapted Sulpicius Severus's prose *Vita Sancti Martini* into 3,500 hexameters; see Orchard, *PAA*, p. 181.

8. Tilliette, "Verse Style," p. 120.

terminology. Bede calls the poem a "hymnum uirginitatis . . . in laudem ac praeconium euisdem reginae ac sponsa Christi" (hymn concerning virginity . . . in praise and celebration of this queen and bride of Christ).[9] Since Bede has earlier designated the poem an elegy, one wonders whether his designation of the poem here as a "hymn" is formal or material, a question I discuss below. Moreover, Bede's lexical doublets signal that the poem does double duty, in praise of virginity generally and in praise of Aethelthryth specifically. In another editorial comment, Bede explains that he inserts his hymn here "imitari morem sacrae scripturae, cuius historiae, carmina plurima indita et haec metro ac versibus constat esse conposita" (imitating the manner of sacred Scripture into whose account many songs are introduced and these arranged by means of meter and verses, as is well-known).[10] Bede's explanation has been understood by scholars as a straightforward claim that he imitates the structure of Scripture. Yet earlier in the HE, he inserted a series of epistolary exchanges between Pope Gregory and Augustine known as the *Libellus Responsiorium*; in doing so, Bede also followed the structure of Scripture (for example, the letter of Artaxerxes inserted into Ezra 4), but without similar editorial comment.[11] If Bede's motive is to imitate the structure of Scripture, then the obvious question is why

---

9. Bede, *HE*, 4.20, p. 396.
10. Bede, *HE*, 4.20, p. 396; my translation. This sentence is quite mannered in its syntax—consider the placement of the two participles and of "et"—which suggests something more is going on than relaying of fact. Bede is speaking of the *mores* 'habits, practices' of Scripture, and he may be imitating them as he writes about them. "Indita" 'introduced' and "conposita" 'arranged' bracket the phrase that claims poetry stands alongside prose; that is, the syntax seems to imply that poetry is (literally) integral to prose, not distinct from it. The sentence ends with a form of *conpositus*, which is the same word Bede uses to describe Caedmon's poetic talent (4.14, p. 414)— that is, Caedmon is a poet not because he invents material (he doesn't), but because he can arrange that material into verse. The words "cuius historiae carmina plurima" also echo the account of Caedmon, "cuius carminibus multorum . . ."
11. See DeGregorio, *Bede: On Ezra and Nehemiah*, pp. 73–77.

Bede should feel a need here to step out of the narrative mode, assert his voice as compiler, and justify at some length his method.[12]

J. M. Wallace-Hadrill—who was writing as a historian—observes merely that no new information about Aethelthryth is introduced in Bede's poem.[13] Consequently, as a historical source, very little has been said about it. That is in keeping with *geminus stilus*, which promises no new information, only a poetic counterpart to prose.[14] This point is unlikely to have escaped Bede's notice, although it has prompted modern readers to treat the poem as an unnecessary diversion from Bede's narrative. It seems to me that by shifting voice, Bede more clearly signals an important change in narrative form. At this point, one hears the voice of Bede the Commentator, asking his reader to switch modes of reading—to put away her technique of reading history and to cast a more devotional eye on the text. Cuthbert speaks of "ruminating" over a poem, employing Scriptural language that indicates deep spiritual meditation.[15] Bede implicitly invites our nun of Barking to examine the *Hymn* with the ruminative judgment necessary for a poem.[16] Specifically, Bede is reminding

---

12. Malaspina, "Tre meditazioni salmiche," p. 975. Bede combines his prose and verse versions here, perhaps thereby stressing their unity, whereas Aldhelm's prose and verse *De virginitate* likely circulated separately. We might also make hay of Bede's claim to have written the poem first, rather than the prose. As noted above, Bede's first paraphrase was the *Life of St. Felix*, taken from a poem by Paulinus of Nola, which Bede then rendered into prose. In doing so, he expressly followed the example of Cassian, who turned Prudentius's poems into prose. Bede may be authorizing his own hymn by placing himself in the footsteps of Cassian. See Friesen, "Opus geminatum," p. 137.
13. Wallace-Hadrill, *Bede's Ecclesiastical History*, p. 161. Compare Plummer, 2:240–242.
14. The point is made by Wallace-Hadrill, *Bede's Ecclesiastical History*, pp. 160–61.
15. Malaspina, "Tre meditazione salmiche," p. 973.
16. Compare Hosea 7:14, "et non clamaverunt ad me in corde suo sed ululabant in cubilibus suis super triticum et vinum **ruminabant** recesserunt a me" (And they have not cried to me with their heart, but they howled in

his reader of the generic expectations of Deuteronomy or Psalms. If Bede's shift in voice from narrator to commentator is a gesture to his reader to read as a Christian, then what might that entail?

Bede introduces the *Hymn* with a generic distinction. Immediately prior to his shift from history to elegy, he differentiates the words *historia* and *carmina*: "cuius HISTORIAE, CARMINA plurima indita."[17] Note that the words are positioned here cheek by jowl, physically juxtaposed just like his history and elegy, a syntactic pattern that mirrors the generic one. *Carmina* are arranged in "metro ac versibus" (meter and verses). And one ought not to forget that lyric poems were often sung.[18] *Historiae*, meanwhile, are accounts or stories that can be told in verse or in prose. Grammatical handbooks of the period do not distinguish between poetry and prose on the basis of content (*historia*), but rather on the basis of form. Bede nevertheless

---

their beds: they have **thought** upon wheat and wine, they are departed from me; my emphasis). Ululation and rumination are important elements of the Caedmon story, as is Caedmon's departure from the hall. Caedmon is a lay brother, assigned various tasks. The evening of the feast, he had been assigned to the cattle stalls (his vision could have taken place in a kitchen had his assignment been otherwise). That is fortuitous and significant because he physically exited (*recesserat*) the main building; Bede notes another passage of Hosea (11:19), regarding physical houses and cities, that "those who estrange themselves from participation in the worldly city become more worthy of this indwelling of their Creator"; Kendall, *Bede: On Genesis*, p. 154. (One wonders whether Caedmon's cattle stall is also an implicit invitation to ruminate.) There are more theological associations in these stories than are dreamed of in our philology.

17. The comma between the words is a modern addition. See, on *historia*, Ray, "Bede's *Vera Lex Historiae*." Irvine, *The Making of Textual Culture*, p. 86: *historia* is "the narrative content of the classical canon." The matter is taken up at book length by Gunn, *Bede's Historiae*. On Bede's juxtaposition as a stylistic device with political implications, see Higham, *(Re-)Reading Bede*, p. 11.

18. Not only religious hymns were sung, but also, for example, *susceptaculum* or greeting chants, sequences, the *caritas* or drinking song, the Modena song, and so forth. See Szövérffy, *Secular Latin Lyrics*, 1:17–27.

recognizes that in previous centuries, content determined form.[19] By form is meant the rhythm or meter of the words, not the shape of the text on the page. (Readers of all Old English verse manuscripts will recognize that rhythmical language can be laid out on the page like prose.) From particular rhythmical and metrical forms of speaking arise decorousness, a pleasing propriety of diction. We can recall that the *HE* begins with a dactyl, "Brĭttănĭ(a)," lending the opening heroic dignity. These metrical forms, because they depend on phonic context, are artificial, even though they might seem natural. Bede writes, "Solet aliquoties in Scripturis ordo verborum causa decoris aliter quam vulgaris via dicendi habet figuratus inveniri" (Sometimes, the order of the words in the Scriptures, for the sake of decorousness, is different than the way vulgar speech is found to be fashioned).[20] Decorousness implies a meaningful propriety, not mere ornament. The opening words of the *HE* are decorous not only in their invocation of heroic meter, but also in their imitation of the order of creation in Genesis: water literally appears before earth, "oceani insula."[21] Also suggestive of Genesis, Bede's first word is "Brittania" with a *b* rather than "Albion" with an *a* (the sixth word of the sentence), perhaps in imitation of the Hebrew *Beresheit*, which begins Scripture—something Bede knew from Jerome's *Hebrew Questions on Genesis*.

Whether prose or poetry, all storytelling employs artifice. The distinction for Bede (as perhaps for all writers) is not between natural and artificial storytelling, but between types and degrees of artificiality.[22] Less artificial types are more likely to invoke literal inter-

---

19. Bede, *DAM*, pp. 96–97: the dactylic hexameter "heroicum vocatur, eo quod hoc maxime heroum, hoc est, virorum fortium."
20. *DAM*, pp. 168–69. The distinctions involved here are not simple dichotomies: one must distinguish the *vulgus*, those who speak in dialect, from a speaking style called *sermo simplex*, simple speech, and from the *populus*, the common people.
21. A comparison of Book I to Genesis was made in vague terms by Greenfield, "The Architectonics of Bede's *Historia Ecclesiastica*."
22. Norden, *AK*, 1:12, cited in Hays, "Prose Style," p. 217. Artificiality was

pretations by readers. Bede's prose, in other words, may seem to us more realistic and less figurative because its form mimics common speech more so than poetry. Of course, mimetic fidelity is complicated by the consideration that written texts constitute a dialect unto themselves.[23] That fidelity is further complicated by realism's studied conflation of sense and meaning, the antagonism of which, according to Auerbach, "permeates the early, and indeed the whole, Christian view of reality."[24] Yet the Christian reader is challenged by Bede's generic break at the *Hymn to Aethelthryth* to disentangle sense and meaning, as her embodied intellect pursues an elusive comprehension of impression and thought. As a devotional reader, a Christian reader may allow the poem to suggest the means of comprehension by reforming her earlier impressions gained from the prose. To put it another way, she allows the highly allusive *carmina* to reform the prosaic *historia*.

The monastic ideal of an ordered life extends beyond consuetudes, and includes ordered language (for example, authorized prayer, a Roman liturgy, correctly sung hymnody, and properly made meters) as well as ordered thought (for example, the properly executed devotions of the offices). Correct form, or formality, seems to me a more comprehensive, if more abstracted, theme of book four. The highly wrought form of the *Hymn to Aethelthryth* suggests that the devotion it prompts is to be equally directed, patterned, ordered,

---

prized: "Ein Kunstwerk war ein *opus artificiale*" (An artwork was an artificial work), writes Assunto, *Die Theorie des Schönen*, p. 27.

23. "Il y a une langue écrite, qui doit se distinguer nettement de la langue parlée" (There is a written language, which one ought to distinguish clearly from a spoken language); Marouzeau, *Traité*, p. xx. Marouzeau also notes that "la langue écrite est une langue parlée deux fois … par celui qui écrit et par celui qui lira" (written language is a language spoken twice … by he who writes and by he who reads), p. 1.

24. Auerbach, *Mimesis* p. 43. On the artificiality of written Latin, see Auerbach, *Literary Language*, p. 121. We should recognize that the representation of abstraction was equally "realistic," insofar as the intelligible, unseen world was as much a reality to orthodox Christians as were mountains and rocks.

and formed. The metrical and strophic form, derived from Scripture, gives Christian shape to its English matter. Correlatively, this reformative relation between Christian form and English matter appears throughout book four. Bede narrates episodes illustrating the way in which various external, physical forms aid or hinder the expression of internal, intellectual, and spiritual matters. For example, we see Aethelthryth's life change dramatically as she becomes subject to various forms of community: to marriage, the court, and the minster. In expressing those dramatic changes in Aethelthryth's life, Bede explores form at a very abstract level. He asks after the consequences of particular forms of church government, monastic government, and self-government. We see these three forms explored, among other places, in the royal and ecclesiastical ritual displayed in Ecgfrith's court, the rituals of feasting in Hild's abbey, and the pagan verse form that sends Caedmon fleeing to a cattle stall. Like DeGregorio, I see these rituals as subjects of Bede's reformist impulses. But perhaps too capaciously, and imagining as well an audience beyond Britain, I see them also as part of any Christian's desire for perpetual reform and self-reflection. The court of Ecgfrith seems to me a metonymy for political and ecclesiastical reform; Hild's abbey, a metonymy for monastic reform; and the hymns of Aethelthryth and Caedmon, a metonymy for liturgical and devotional reform.[25] These sites of reform are set alongside Aethelthryth's marriage to Christ, her charitable and saintly acts in the monastery, and the divinely oriented content of both Aethelthryth's and Caedmon's hymns. I think that Bede's is not some hidden epistemological game, but a deeply Christian inquiry into the combinatory mystery of divine form and (inherently compromised) human substance.

Bede pursues these more abstract thematic relations between form

---

25. Cf. Theodoric's letter to Emperor Anastasius, collected by Cassiodorus, in which Theodoric compliments Anastasius: "Regnum nostrum imitatio vestra est, *forma boni propositi*, unici exemplar imperii" (My kingdom is an imitation of yours, *the form of good order* and the unique exemplar of an empire; my emphasis); translated by Noble and Head in *Soldiers of Christ*, p. xiii; text in MGH AA 12, p. 10.

and content grammatically as well. Those relations are most obvious in liturgy, where the forms of prayer were undergoing much revision in the late seventh century. (It is not the depth of devotion that needs liturgical order, but its temporal disposition in language.) The form of a prayer, its syntactic and lexical arrangement, prompts a particular series of emotions and thoughts as one moves through the prayer. I see this syntactic arrangement as a formal control of devotion: a prayer's management of a reader's serial responses. Observing this process as it is encoded in grammar demonstrates the many but limited possibilities of interpretation that arise from meditative reading.

The Apostles' Creed offers an example of how syntax orders the seriated responses of one praying. It begins, "Credo" 'I believe,' immediately setting the one praying into the role of one confessing faith. (Compare this role with the public and communal one implicit in speaking the word "credimus" 'we believe.') Note that the prayer begins not with pronominal reference to the self, *ego* 'I', but with a first-person verb, indicating a personal act, an internal motion of the self. Grammatically, that act of inner credulity moves toward its credal objects, which appear in a series of rhymed accusatives—*deum, patrem, creatorem, Iesum Christum, filium,* and *dominum*. The distinction is subtle, but "credo" does not reify the self as much as it reifies an act, specifically an act that depends on objects external to the self. The rhymes provide a feeling of contiguity and thereby of equality, as each Person is inflected equally in direct relation to the act of belief. That same pattern of a first-person verb followed by a series of rhymed accusatives both opens and ends the prayer. So the one praying is invited to relate her believing self twice to a series of coordinated objects. Those objects appear in a particular order in the prayer: first the creating Godhead, then the life of Christ, and finally the apostolic works of the Holy Spirit. In the portion dedicated to the life of Christ are a series of past participles (*conceptus est, natus, passus, crucifixus, mortuus, sepultus*) followed by active verbs (*descendit, resurrexit, ascendit, sedet*). The first series describes non-recurring historical events, the second, spiritual events that recur every year at Easter. The verbals at the poem's center suggest Christ's twofold activity at the center of one's faith, once historically, and then spiritually. That implies, among other things, the importance of first putting one's faith in the historical reality of Christ, and then in the spiritual gifts of the Resurrection. Looking again at the three portions, we see the Trinity: first the Father, then the Son, then the Holy Spirit. The order of these Persons is not accidental; it corresponds to historical revelation. The Father is the Person revealed in the Old Testament; the Son is revealed in the Gospels; and the Holy Spirit is revealed in Acts and in the Church. Thus we see how the form of the prayer might invite particular topics of contemplation in a particular order.

In Bede's narrative, Aethelthryth also moves temporally through a series of sites and stages. Her journey resembles that of Scripture itself, and its order invites contemplation. She begins in a court such as we might see in the Books of Kings or Samuel. (Recall that Bede compared King Aethelfrith to Saul in *HE* 1.34.) She then moves to a minster, an apostolic community wed to Christ such as we might see in the Gospels, and within that community to sanctity in the universal Church, as we see exhibited in the Epistles. Aethelthryth's life develops decorously, mimicking Scripture. Moreover, her journey toward Catholic sanctity is homologous to the narrative of book four. Book four portrays seventh-century Britain's formation into a Christian nation—from intrigues in court, through submission to ecclesiastical direction, to the indwelling of the Spirit. While Britain's geography submits to ecclesiastical demarcation, its faith submits to orthodox expression.[26] Thus in Bede's telling, the ordered (orthodox) faith of King Ecgfrith brings form and order to Christian government, just as the ordered (orthodox) faith of Aethelthryth brings form and order to her self-government.[27] In the Apostles' Creed,

---

26. R. A. Markus describes an "emergence of the English churches as a unified English Church" as "the central thread" of the *HE*. Jarrow Lecture, 1975, 1:396.
27. And perhaps also to monastic life. The extent of organization at Ely and the putative success of the house is discussed by Fell, "Saint Æðelþryð." Hers is an astute introduction to the sources of and questions concerning Aethelthryth's life. See also Thompson, "St Æthelthryth."

faith shapes terrestrial order. And orthodox Christian faith, Bede's narrative suggests, shapes good government, lay and religious.

The form of faith is essential to the point: Bede makes his priority not mere Christianity but *Roman* Christianity. That distinction is explicit in his Preface to the *HE*, where he reminds King Ceolwulf that a king reigns only by appointment of God and with the counsel of orthodox ecclesiastics. The *HE* is filled with examples of kings—even Christian kings—who are capable of ruling but who reject the primacy of the Church, thereby dooming their rule. Bede narrates Aethelthryth's life to emphasize this non-exclusive distinction between content and form. We see that her sanctification begins with her oath of virginity, a submission that does not sublimate desire but that formalizes and orders it. Her sanctity results, too, from submission to a monastic order and thereby to a reform of the self-government of her own life. Like her oath of virginity, her extraordinarily difficult submission to monastic order is not a diminishment of her will, but an exercise of will to reform her appetites in the service of right order. As if to mimic the Christianization of Aethelthryth's life through her submission to form, the *Hymn to Aethelthryth* is set in the heart of this reformation narrative. Bede's interpolation of a poem into his prose narrative at this point is not idle, nor is it a sign of his vanity.[28] Instead, Bede is formalizing Aethelthryth's spiritual achievement by translating it into the meter and structure—the Scriptural order—of Psalm 118. To put it another way, as Aethelthryth's worldly life achieves its apogee in Christian holy orders, so does the prosaic account of her life achieve its apogee in formal Christian verse.

By virtue of this larger thematic resonance, the *Hymn* functions as a meditative guide to this section of book four. Bede selects matters for his *Hymn* that will allow reflection on the historical narrative, and readers can return to the prose with a view to what Bede considers of primary value. At a very basic level, one assumes that Bede wants to offer a practical lesson: "de bonis bona referat" (to recall that good

---

28. Wallace-Hadrill wrote, "It is not vanity that moves Bede . . ." Wallace-Hadrill, *Bede's Ecclesiastical History*, p. 160.

things come to good people), as Bede puts it in his preface.[29] But the salient points of the *Hymn* are not overtly moral. Its most obvious focus is on female sanctity, a focus that invites us to reconsider the importance of otherwise prosaic facts. For example, the word *familia* 'family' occurs in the *Hymn*. Because it occurs in a poem, a reader is invited to consider its ambiguity. But does that ambiguity carry over to the prose? Can we read the prose as equally ambiguous and multivalent? In the prose, Hild is said to be an aunt and a sister; Aethelthryth, a sister and a wife. Literally, both women have family connections. But having read the verse, and having contemplated female sanctity, *familia* takes on two contemporaneous meanings: the literal family into which one is born, and the more expansive spiritual family of men and women religious, the family of Christ. With the poem's *familia* in mind, we may return to the prose to consider the religious *familiae* of book four: Hild and Aethelthryth, Aethelthryth and her literal and spiritual sister Seaxburh, Ethelburg (founder of Barking Abbey) and Hildelith, and many others.

Indeed, book four is filled with women, some related literally, some spiritually. We see that Aethelthryth, like the apostles, leaves her biological family to join the spiritual family of Christ. She does not cease to be a daughter or a sister or a niece, but she begins to operate within a world of multivalent meanings and relationships.

---

29. *lit.* "recall good things from out of good people." Colgrave and Mynors translate, "tell of good men and their good estate." *Referat* is not strictly 'to tell', for which Bede uses other vocabulary. Nevertheless, one cannot be pedantic: the phrase is elastic. It can also mean "tell of the prosperity of the upper classes." But I don't see how either would urge a listener to do good, as Bede claims. The phrase is used by Augustine and Jerome in the collocation *bona bonis, mala malis*—good things for the good, bad things for the bad. See Augustine, *Enarrationes*, 39:5, CCSL 38; and 148:1, CCSL 40. Also his *Contra Iulianum* (*CPL* 351) where he speaks of the Last Judgment, "quo bona bonis et mala malis retribuuntur," *PL* 5:805. Jerome speaks in his commentary on Ezechiel of Paradise, "dum uident et mala malis et bona bonis restitui," *Commentarii in Ezechielem* (*CPL* 587), *PL* 10:31. The phrase is found in Jerome's Vulgate, Sirach (Ecclesiasticus) 39:30, "bona bonis creata sunt ab initio." Each of these cases offers far more compelling reasons to do good.

Her physically unconsummated marriage on earth may or may not imply a literal virginity, but it is clearly a sign of a spiritual virginity, or chastity. Conversely, her spiritually consummated marriage in Heaven is an invisible reality that is manifested on earth as physical signs—in her dress, her prayers, her acts of charity, and so forth.[30] So we come to see that Bede's narrative is simultaneously prosaic history and spiritual guide. In the manner of Scripture, Bede has correlated facts on the ground with spiritual realities. The royal women of the *gentis Anglorum* (that is, the extended families of the English) are both literal realities and symbolic of an invisible reality, an essential portion of a people forged by God for salvation.

Female religious, especially virgins, are foundational to the Christian mission in Britain and to a shared vision of ecclesiastical integrity. In Bede's narrative, Hild and Aethelthryth both act simultaneously on terrestrial and spiritual levels. As Bede writes concerning Jacob's ladder, "The ladder which he saw is the Church, which has its birth from the earth but its way of life in heaven."[31] The Church rests on Peter as Jacob's ladder rests on a rock. *Ecclesia* in Latin is a feminine noun, and is often portrayed as female in the iconography—thus, holy Mother Church. We will see her portrayed as the Strong Woman (*mulier fortis*) of Proverbs 31 in relation to Bede's *Hymn*; there she is a bride (*sponsa*) of Christ. Elsewhere the Church is born from Christ as Christ is born from the Virgin. Virgins and the foundation of the Church are closely connected in Bede's mind. Aldhelm

---

30. Discussed by Fell, "Saint Æðelþryð." See also Weston, "The Saint-Maker and the Saint," esp. pp. 61–65, where she explores the scope of spiritual motherhood and family derived from Aldhelm's prose *De virginitate*. Weston also notes the lost Barking *Libellus*, which Bede describes as telling the story of the church of the East Saxons (p. 57).

31. Bede, *Opera Homiletica,* I, 17, ed. Hurst (CCSL 122: p. 126); Lawrence and Hurst, *Bede the Venerable*, I, p. 176. Aldhelm also speaks of virgin nuns as stones in the edifice of the Church; prose *De virginitate*, 39:2–3; cited in Weston, "The Saint-Maker and the Saint," p. 65. In a similar image, Jacob's ladder was compared to the Cross in hymns of the period. See Szövérffy, *Annalen*, 1:174.

held that every "virgin, male or female, of whatever earthly lineage, is the child of Ecclesia by the Logos."[32] It seems to me no surprise, therefore, that Bede records the testimony of women's lives so extensively in the narrative of the Christianization of Britain. He notes the multitude of religious female witnesses to the death of Hild, some at great geographical remove. He observes religious women bringing the native, secular customs of the island into closer accord with the Christian faith—exemplified by Caedmon's secular poetic form infused with Hild's religious content, for example.

Bede's focus in these chapters on female sanctity seems to me emblematized by Benedict Biscop's portrait of the Virgin Mary, which was the focal point of Bede's daily liturgical experience. A portrait of the Virgin stood at the center of Jarrow's church iconography. As Éamonn Ó Carragáin points out, Wearmouth "was the chief center in England of liturgical devotion to the Mother of God."[33] In 682, when Bede was a novice, a chapel to Mary was built and five years later decorated with Roman icons. At Wearmouth, Bede composed a hymn to Mary and a sermon on the Feast of the Purification of the Virgin in which he speaks of the equal, if differentiated, role of both sexes in the Christian church.[34] Also important witnesses to Bede's celebration of female sanctity and his devotion to Mary are his major contributions to Marian theology, especially in explaining her preservation from original sin.[35] We must suspect, then, that the cult of Mary and Marian theology were very much in Bede's mind as he composed his hymn to the virgin queen Aethelthryth. Bede

---

32. Weston, "The Saint-Maker and the Saint," p. 61; Aldhelm writes, "[T]he Church . . . fertilizes through the chaste seed of the Word the offspring who are the lawful heirs of eternity," *De virginitate* (prose), ed. Lapidge, *APrW*, 5.6–9.
33. Ó Carragáin, "The Wearmouth Icon of the Virgin," p. 35. See also Darby, "Bede's Eschatological Thought," for the scope of Bede's reading and for imagery of the end times prevalent in seventh-century Northumbria, some of which will concern us in the *Hymn*.
34. Bede, Hymn 11; Bede, *Homilia* I, 18, p. 131.
35. Clayton, *The Cult of the Virgin Mary*, p. 16.

invites his readers to consider not only the political and ecclesiastical power, but also the spiritual significance, of these female Anglo-Saxons in Christian life and salvation.

Another obvious area of focus in the poem is the sanctity of Aethelthryth. Bede puts her in communion with some of the most influential female saints and virgins of the Church. A number of commentators suggest that Bede's evident interest in Aethelthryth arose as much from her participation in the community of virgin martyrs as it did from her nationality. She was a contemporary English virgin martyr.[36] That may be so, but Bede's interest in Aethelthryth need not be exclusively nationalistic. Whatever the case, Aethelthryth's sanctity required a particular form of announcement. We return again to the preoccupation with form in this fourth book. A *vita* was a necessary, formal declaration of sanctity, and a poem was a worthy addition to it. As one reexamines the surrounding prose, the outlines of a saint's *vita* become clearer. Aethelthryth's unconsummated marriage, for example, distinguishes her from a wife, as described in 1 Corinthians 7:33. In this state, she joins Perpetua, Felicity of Carthage, Felicity of Rome, Agnes of Rome (about whom Bede also wrote a hymn), Agatha of Catania, Lucy, Thecla, Euphemia, Cecilia, Genevieve of Paris, Radegund of Poitiers, Eulalia, and others. Six of these are mentioned in this *Hymn*. As a virgin queen, Aethelthryth joins, among others, Helena, mother of Constantine, whom Rufinus calls "foemina incomparabilis" (an incomparable woman), "regina venerabilis" (venerable/saintly queen), and "famularum Christi" (of the handmaidens of Christ).[37] Some of these terms appear in Bede's account, for obvious

---

36. Especially Higham, *(Re-)Reading Bede*. Higham argues that the verse on Aethelthryth is intended "to leave the audience uplifted" (p. 163), something he earlier calls the "'feel good' factor" that Christian readers experience (p. 21), as opposed to, one imagines, Bede's political wiles, sublimated desire for authority, and cunning self-interest. The opposing camps in the study of Bede are described by Gunn, *Bede's Historiae*, pp. 10–11.

37. Rufinus, *Historia monarchum*, PL 21, p. 475. Incidentally, England's most famous Virgin Queen, Elizabeth I, seems to have had little interest in the London church dedicated to Aethelthryth, controlled by the bishops of

reasons. As a virgin devoted to the study of Scripture, she joins Martha and Mary (Luke 10.41). Aethelthryth's story also parallels contemporary *vitae* in a number of very complex ways. Tomb miracles, contact miracles (her shroud and coffin), holy suffering, patron of a lineage, prophecy, an incorruptible corpse—all are elements recognizable in sixth- and seventh-century saints' cults. But to be precise, Aethelthryth is not the focus of the hymn. To give a sense of content, Bede's *Hymn* praises virginity in twenty couplets (excluding the codicil), and Aethelthryth in only eight. In other words, the poem is not a compact version of Bede's prose narrative, but a meditation on virginity more generally, and on Aethelthryth's place within the Catholic tradition.

As a poem set within a kind of *vita*, the *Hymn to Aethelthryth* demonstrates a transformation, or rather a reformation, of classical elegy to Christian use. That reformation, if not the broader subject of the poem, is its informing context. Bede writes that he is inserting a *hymnus* 'hymn' that concerns virginity and is also "in laudem" (in praise of) Aethelthryth. It is a *praeconium* 'celebration, laudation'. If these terms tell us what the poem does, then what did Bede mean by calling the poem a hymn? English-speaking Christians today have a sense of hymnody that develops from the Great Awakening and is reflected in the poetry of Emily Dickinson—sung, simple, and sincere. But medieval hymns were written in various meters, some quantitative, some rhythmic, some even in prose.[38] Clearly, Bede cannot be referring to the Ambrosian form of hymnody in iambic dimeter. And the hymn does not praise God directly, as Augustine had insisted hymns should. Yet Anglo-Saxon England and Ireland during the seventh century were the sites of innovation in hymnody. Sechnall (Secundius) wrote perhaps the first, to St. Patrick, in an alphabetic form, and so Bede's readers may well have seen his *Hymn to Aethelthryth* as a parallel to the dominant saint of the Irish

---

Ely. King James allowed the Spanish ambassador Gondomar to use it as a private Catholic chapel. My thanks to Professor Joseph Black of Massachusetts for this information.

38. Szövérffy, "Latin Hymns," 6:379–85.

landscape.[39] We find, in the end, that the terms "hymn" and "elegy" are not exclusive. The poem is both. By using the elegiac form, Bede invites readers to contemplate the relation of form to genre. More precisely, readers are invited to attend to their own generic expectations with regard to matter and form—as readers had done for Sedulius, Fortunatus, Prudentius, Juvencus, Arator, and others. The elegy is defined by its meter, which Ovid erotically sends up as the rising hexameter and the flaccid pentameter (*Amores* 1.1). Fitzgerald calls this the cycle of both love and the elegy.[40] Bede knew Ovid, and the critical demands of his poems; but Bede transforms—or reforms—those erotic demands. As the marital love of Aethelthryth for her martial husbands is transformed into spiritual love for Christ, so the amorous classical elegy is repurposed for spiritually amatory Christian devotion. The same reformation is offered in the meter of the poem.

The classical elegy is described by Bede in his *DAM*. As we have seen, he explains that a hexameter line can have a spondee in every foot except the fifth. The final, sixth foot has a spondee, but because poets treat the last syllable as common, some allow a trochee (which displeased Bede). Each long vowel lasts two morae; each short vowel lasts one. The total morae are twenty-four, or twelve long vowels, which, Bede explains, is the number of ounces in a *libra*, a Roman pound. Thus, the hexameter line is balanced (like a *libra* 'scale') in weight and measure. Here is the hymn's first line:

Ālmă Dĕ|ūs Trĭnĭ|tās, quæ |sæcŭlă |cūnctă gŭ|bērnas

Bede follows classical grammarians (and Aldhelm) by employing a sixth-foot spondee. A distinguishing mark of Bede here is the word *deus*, which can scan as either an iamb or a pyrrhic, depending on the onset of the following word. In the line above, due to the <t> of "Trinitas," "deus" is an iamb. When Aldhelm uses *deus*, it is virtually always the second word of a verse, following a monosyllable with a long

---

39. The connection to Ireland is made by Raby, *CLP*, 144, and by Szövérffy, *Annalen*, 1:167.
40. Fitzgerald, *How to Read a Latin Poem*, pp. 57–58.

vowel. In these cases, his third word rarely starts with a consonant (only 8.4 percent of the time), thereby giving him an opening dactyl.[41]

Another practice that Bede employed also echoes Aldhelm. The final feet of a hexameter offer a kind of repeating metrical motif.[42] *Gubernas* and *gubernans* derive from *gŭbērnārĕ* 'to govern'. A word like *gŭbērnārĕ* offers a convenient medial spondee; *gŭbērnās*, a bacchius, offers a final spondee and could span the fifth and sixth feet, a span that is valued aesthetically. Bede uses it to span the fifth and sixth feet in this first line, perhaps following Aldhelm, who opens his *Carmen de virginitate* with a metrically similar line.[43] Both *gubernās* and *gubernāns* have a long final syllable, which helps to explain the variants in the manuscripts—*cuncta gubernas* and *cuncta gubernans* are identical metrically. Because first-conjugation verbs and deverbals are well suited to this position, similar phrases can be used where a poet needs an infinitive, a singular verb, or a participle. Such phrases are treasured, stored, and reused. Adamnan used "cuncta gubernans" in his *Life of Columban*; the phrase is also used by Paul the Deacon and by Virgil. As this reuse of a phrase shows, poets sometimes borrow for meter, so it is not always clear that in borrowing a phrase, Bede intends to allude.[44] In this case, we cannot be sure whether Bede is alluding to Aldhelm or whether he is merely using a convenient, well-made phrase (or formula).[45]

---

41. Orchard, *PAA*, pp. 98–99. The statistic is Orchard's. The only instance where *deus* is the second word preceded by a disyllabic word is in Aldhelm's verse *Carmen de virginitate*, line 686, "Quanta Deus dederit devoto dona clienti."

42. Following Lapidge, cited by Orchard, *PAA*, p. 93.

43. *Carmen de virginitate*, line 1, "Omnipotens genitor mundum dicione gubernans." See Orchard, *PAA*, p. 92.

44. Orchard distinguishes three levels of borrowing, one of which is "borrowings of diction," in which a poet "has simply fitted lexical elements from . . . [a source's] verse into recognizable patterns of his own, without attempting to assimilate any of the thought or context of . . . [the source's] words"; *PAA*, p. 169.

45. See Hays, "Prose Style," pp. 220–21; and Tilliette, "Verse Style," pp. 248–49. Orchard makes this point in *PAA*, pp. 102–3.

In a classical elegy, a pentameter follows the hexameter. Ideally, the two lines in the elegiac couplet should be independent clauses, but syntactically connected. The third and fifth feet of a pentameter are catalectic, and it has a caesura separating the two halves of the verse. The scribe of St. Gall 265 places a *punctus medius* at that precise point of metrical division. The first half takes a dactyl or spondee in either foot. The second half takes only dactyls in both full feet. Again, each half ends with a catalectic foot, which leaves a spondee. Although there are many exceptions, it is inadvisable to use a one-syllable word to fill the catalectic foot.[46] Here is the second verse:

ādnŭĕ | iām coē|ptīs || ālmă Dĕ|ūs Trĭnĭ|tās

Bede is not risking elision between the first and second feet, since the <i> of "iam" is acting as a consonant. "Adnue" is a dactyl, used in initial position by Paulinus of Nola and others, and in penultimate position by Virgil, who uses the phrase "adnue coeptis" in his *Aeneid*. Raby says of this hymn that Bede "uses the *Aeneid* as the type of that secular poetry which he contrasts unfavorably with the matter of his poem."[47] The hymn reshapes Virgil to praise virginity, and so the reformation enacted by the poem is captured in the delicious ambiguity of this simple opening phrase.

When one considers the metrical demands of an elegy, especially as Bede has put it together with its repeating onset and end, one cannot but be impressed with his technical virtuosity. The third foot of his hexameter must be divisible into two or more words, one of which will serve in his pentameter's final catalectic foot. This means that he cannot bridge the second and third feet with a three-syllable dactylic word. He must begin his hexameter with a two-and-a-half foot phrase, consisting of two dactyls and a final long syllable.[48] Consider his opening phrase, which ends with *Trīnĭtās*, a third-

---

46. See Raven, *Latin Metre*, pp. 103–9.
47. Cited in Szövérffy, *Annalen*, 1:172.
48. One is reminded that Lapidge observes Aldhelm's tendency to treat the fifth and sixth feet of a hexameter as "detachable units"; in *APW*, p. 21.

declension feminine noun and an amphimacrus (long-short-long). Its first <i> is long by nature, its second short, and its <a> long. Bede says that the word cannot be put into hexameter poetry because of its metrical shape.[49] As described earlier, a similarly difficult word is *veritas*; others common to Christian poetry and illicit in hexameters are listed by Aldhelm in his *Letter to Arcircum*.[50] Perhaps more circumspect than Bede, Aldhelm does not use *trinitas* in his hexameters, although he uses "alma Trinitas" in his prose *De virginitate*. The word is licit in other meters, of course. Ambrose of Milan, in his famous hymn "Aeterne rerum conditor," writes "fove precantes, trinitas" (strophe 8, line 29). There, *trinitas* accords with his iambic dimeter (four iambs) both quantitatively and qualitatively. But unlike an iambic dimeter hymn, a hexameter does not admit amphimacri.[51] *Trinitas* won't fit in or between any possible hexametrical feet. Yet Bede allows, on the authority of Jerome (who is describing Hebrew poetry), that in such cases one can count morae rather than syllables. Christian Latin poets can thereby substitute a foot of equal syllables but unequal morae. Another authority behind this use of *trinitas* is a hexameter by Fortunatus in his double acrostic *Carmina* 5, line 5: "ēxclū|sōr cūl|pāe, trĭnĭ|tās ēf|fūsă, crĕ|ātor" (SSDSDC).[52] The final

---

49. Bede, *DAM*, X, p. 132. But a molossus can open a hexameter line: Virgil, *Aen*, 1.37, "Hāec sēcūm"; 9.445, "Cōnfōssūs"; and many others. See Winbolt, *Latin Hexameter Verse*, p. 21. Winbolt writes, "Lucretius makes this a favorite pause [after 1 1/2 feet] . . . and he has such a decided preference for the form – – – that it becomes almost a mannerism," p. 23.

50. MGH AA 15, pp. 168–69. Aldhelm notes other examples: *unitas, caritas, orbitas, sanctitas, claritas, dignitas, quantitas, civitas, falsitas, vanitas*, and *pontifex*. Aldhelm nevertheless allows them in a hexameter on the authority of Virgil and Ovid.

51. *Trinitas* fits well into a trochaic septenarius, as in "Arbor alta, crux beata, uirtus orbis unica," attributed to Carus Scotus, MGH AA 5.3, p. 660; *AH* 43.

52. Fortunatus, MGH 4.1, p. 32; see this volume's *Index rei metricae*, p. 427, for examples of variation by Fortunatus in the length of vowels in *trinitas*. Compare Bede's use of *spiritus* in the genitive as a dactyl in his verse *Cuthbert*; see Neil Wright, "The Metrical Art(s) of Bede," p. 158. My thanks to Professor Kendall for clarifying Bede's understanding of poetic license with

<a> of "effusa" is short because it precedes a mute-liquid combination, <cr>, thus achieving a dactyl in the fifth foot. And *Trīnĭtās* has been turned into an anapest, *Trĭnĭtās*. Bede knew the poem. So in his hexameter and pentameter, Bede has by poetic license and by Christian authority shortened the first <i> of *Trinitas*.[53] By placing the metrically irregular *Trinitas* at the top of his poem and at the center of his line, Bede is loudly declaring not just his Christianity, but a reformation in faith of pagan, classical verse. This metrical declaration does not seem accidental, as the reformation of pagan, classical verse is a prominent theme in the opening of Bede's poem.

The reformation suggested by the meter is also suggested by the strophic form. The hymn is an acrostic, again invoking a company of poems including all the lyric poems of Commodian, an African poet contemporary with Ambrose.[54] As well as being an acrostic, the hymn is also alphabetic, placing it in a line that reaches back to Psalm 118, to Proverbs, to Deuteronomy, and especially to the Book of Lamentations, four of five chapters of which are alphabetics. Aside from Biblical models, the earliest alphabetic Christian poems include an anonymous north African psalm called the *Psalmus responsorius* (c. 350) of 23 verses[55]; Sedulius, "A solis ortus cardine"[56]; Augustine,

---

respect to morae. Note again that I do not mark vowel length in the final syllable of a hexameter.

53. Another consideration is that Bede's faith trumps metrical rules. Such is the case with Milo of Saint Amand. Milo writes "... salva virtute fidei / Posthabui leges, ferulas et munia metri / Non puto grande scelus, si syllaba longa brevisque / Altera in alterius dubia statione locetur" (in the saving virtue of faith I have neglected the rules, tenets, guidelines of meter. I have not considered it a great crime if one syllable (long or short) is placed in a doubtful position instead of another; trans. Orchard); cited by Alistair Campbell, in turn cited by Orchard, *PAA*, p. 75.
54. Di Berardino, *Patrology*, pp. 259–65. Commodian may have been from Gaul or Spain or Palestine, and his dates much later, but a majority of scholars put him in the third century in northern Africa.
55. Ibid., pp. 340–41. Alphabetic hymns are listed in *AH* 29, pp. 10–11.
56. Walpole, *Hymns*, pp. 151–58. Bede cites this hymn in his *DAM*; Kendall, *Libri II*, pp. 154–55.

Psalmus contra partem Donati[57]; Fortunatus, Hymn 8[58]; and a hymn of Hilary of Poitiers, "Ante saecula qui manes."[59] In the British Isles, an early if not the earliest alphabetic is the anonymous hymn to St. Patrick, "Audite omnes amantes."[60] The earliest extant manuscript in which it appears is the Antiphonary of Bangor, written during Bede's lifetime. There are reasons to suspect the influence of this hymn to St. Patrick on Bede's *Hymn to St. Aethelthryth*. Other possible influences may include hymns to St. Brigit and to St. Comgall. But rather than seeing direct or indirect influence, it is likely that all these alphabetic hymns resulted from a confluence of models and regnant styles, all tracing ultimately back to Scripture.

And here we return to the issue of the alphabet described in *DAM* and raised in a previous chapter. What role did the various Latin alphabets play in hymnody? It may seem commonsensical to reply that the alphabet helped in memorization. Isidore had implied as much. But a monk who could memorize the entire Psalter didn't need help with twenty-two short stanzas. If Bede's Biblical models all had twenty-two letters, then why did Bede choose a twenty-three-letter alphabet for this hymn? Recall that Isidore numbers the Latin letters at twenty-three, Donatus at seventeen. Aldhelm wrote a riddle on the alphabet, which relies on Isidore, distinguishing an original seventeen Latin letters from six Christian newcomers, giving us twenty-three.[61] Bede in *DAM* notes that Christians use twenty-seven letters. Bede's *Hymn* has twenty-three letters and four trailing stanzas with the acrostic "amen," for a total of twenty-seven. Whether twenty-

---

57. Caillau, *Collectio selecta ss. ecclesiae patrum*, pp. 107–17. Wilhelm Meyer suggested that Augustine's psalm might be the first such poem in which quantity was ignored in favor of word accent. Meyer, *Anfang und Ursprung*, p. 3. Meyer's proposal is thought unlikely by Beare, "The Origin of Rhythmic Latin Verse," esp. p. 15.
58. Cited by Bede, Kendall, *Libri II*, p. 178.
59. *Hilarii Pictaviensis Opera*, pp. 209–14.
60. See Orchard, "'Audite omnes amantes,'" pp. 153–73.
61. Aldhelm, "Enigma XXX," MGH AA 15, p. 112. See O'Brien O'Keeffe, *Visible Song*, pp. 52–53.

three or twenty-seven, Bede has arranged his poem to suggest that the Christian Latin alphabet has extended the Hebrew alphabet.

Psalm 118 is likely Bede's ultimate model. Jerome wrote in his *Commentarioli in Psalmos* that Psalm 118 is divided into thematic sections. He cites Josephus as confirmation that the psalm is written in elegiac meter, which consists, he says, of a hexameter completed by a pentameter.[62] In an exposition of Psalm 119, he refers back to 118 and notes that it's not possible to read Psalm 119 without first knowing the letters of the alphabet (in 118); thus we learn that it is impossible to understand Scripture without first knowing our letters.[63] Ambrose will repeat that claim in his commentary on the psalm. Knowledge comes in stages; therefore, Jerome continues, 118 is a moral psalm, a *gradus* or ladder that we climb up. Each rung corresponds to stages in understanding and moral improvement. Recalling the notion of unity in diversity that we saw earlier, Jerome writes, "In diversis quidem stant gradibus, sed unum psalmum in laudes Domini canunt" (Indeed the rungs stand separately, but they sing one psalm in praise of the Lord).[64] Martyrs earn the right to move to the top of the ladder. Jerome then relates these stages of spiritual and moral improvement to Jacob's ladder in Genesis 28, especially verse 11, which describes Jacob going into Bethel and resting his head on a stone. The stone on which we lay our heads is Christ, Jerome writes, a help to those who suffer persecution. Jacob fled an extremely cruel-hearted man ("hominem crudelissimum") and his brother Esau; that is the kind of thing one ought to do in order to get one's foot on the ladder.

Still, to ascend the ladder is difficult. The first rung, Jerome believes, is fasting (*ieiunium*), hunger, Lent—Ash Wednesday is "caput ieiunius"—in short, abstention ("abstentia primum gradum est"). We withdraw from the world, from corporality and concupiscence,[65] and we purify our souls for the Lord. The second rung is a rejection

---

62. Jerome, *Commentarioli in psalmos*, p. 235.
63. Jerome, *In librum psalmorum*, p. 246.
64. Ibid., p. 248.
65. Ibid., p. 249.

of profane and worldly things.[66] The arduous climb requires one to be an "athleta Christi," an athlete of Christ. Concluding his tractate on 119, Jerome writes to men and women religious: forsake your mothers, parents, brothers, sisters, wives, sons, homelands, homes, and the rooms in which you were born and nurtured, and come into the monastery.[67] In short, Psalm 118 is in part a lesson in the orderly, arduous development of a spiritual life. The psalm is ultimately about happiness, Jerome says, and about spurning false pleasure. Similarly, Bede's *Hymn* begins with a rejection of the pleasures of pagan poetry and proceeds step-by-step through a litany of female saints and martyrs who enjoy the happiness of a blessed afterlife.

Augustine calls the psalm profound. Few can fathom it; moreover, he says, "I cannot even demonstrate how profound it is."[68] He dedicates an extraordinary thirty-two sermons to its exposition.[69] Augustine, like Jerome, sees the psalm as organized in stages. First, the reader sees how honorable are the ways of righteousness, then longs for those ways, and finally takes delight in practicing them.[70] Martyrdom, too, is to be celebrated and revered.[71] Augustine also notes that at verse 45 the psalm switches from petition to narrative.[72] Bede also switches narrative form in his *Hymn*, but from narrative to petition, and then back again: whereas after verse 45 the psalm presents "the words of one who recounts facts, not those of a suppliant,"[73] Bede's life of Aethelthryth in book four switches from a narrative that recounts facts to a meditation, that is, to the *Hymn*

---

66. Ibid., p. 250.
67. Ibid., p. 259.
68. Augustine, *Exposition*, 5:342.
69. In a passage that might have struck a teacher and scholar, Augustine warns concerning the wicked: "They do not aspire to be wise for the glory of God; they only want to appear wise in order to be glorified by other people." Ibid., 5:345.
70. Ibid., 5:277.
71. Ibid., 5:379.
72. Ibid., 5:403.
73. Ibid., 5:403.

itself. With respect to the alphabet, Augustine admits that "I found nothing in the psalm that seemed to be affected by the letters."[74] Hilary of Poitiers, in contrast, did have something to say about the letters, and Ambrose thought them significant as well. In each letter, Hilary writes in his extensive commentary on the psalm, different distinctions are made (*discrepare*). In the order of the alphabet is "to be taught the plan and distinctions of doctrine regarding faith, life, and instruction in God" ("credendi et vivendi et erudiendi in Deum doctrinae ratio et distincto doceretur").[75] Hilary also points out the significance of the psalm's eight verses per stanza, each of which begins with the theme letter. Eight, he explains, is the first perfect number (*perfectus est*) by reason of all the equalities that are found in it (2+2+2+2, 2+2 twice, and 4+4). The number is also sacred in the Law ("in lege sanctus est"), since the sign of circumcision was received by Christ on the eighth day. Christ was presented at the Temple, the place of prayer and sacrifice, and the physical sign that was there inscribed indicates the frailty of the human body.[76] Cassiodorus in his commentary on this psalm also relates the eight verses per strophe to circumcision, symbolically the circumcision of the heart.[77] Hilary adds that eight indicates sacrifice and the dignity of martyrs. Heinrich Müller examined other traditions dating back to Origen and Eusebius, and suggested that each of the eight strophes corresponds to a theme: (1) Proverbs, (2) Speech, (3) Law, (4) Commandments, (5) Justice, (6) Testimony, (7) Orders, (8) Doctrine.[78]

Cassiodorus notes that letters are not arbitrary, nor their meanings incidental: "each of these letters has its peculiar significance, since blessed Jerome attests this."[79] Because Hebrew was largely unknown

---

74. Ibid., 5:496.
75. Hilary, *Commentaire*, 1:96–97.
76. Hilary, *Commentaire*, 1:98–99. On numerical symbolism in strophic structure, see Szövérffy, "Hymnologische Streifzüge," esp. pp. 12–18 on Bede.
77. Cassiodorus, *Explanation*, 3:174.
78. Müller, *Die Deutungen der hebräischen Buchstaben*, §2, p. 2. My thanks to Damien Fleming for this reference.
79. Cassiodorus, *Explanation*, 3:174.

to Latin speakers of the Empire, Jerome is an essential guide to the language and alphabet of the Old Testament. In Epistle 30, Jerome explains Psalm 118. He notes other alphabetic psalms in other meters—iambic trimeter and iambic tetrameter. He also mentions Lamentations, the first two chapters of which he says are in Sapphic meter, the third in trimeter. Lamentations 1 is an alphabetic and figures in Ambrose's commentary on Psalm 118. Some Proverbs are also alphabetic, and rendered in tetrameter[80]; Proverbs 31 contains an alphabetic. Jerome writes that each of the letters means something, as follows:

ALEPH is interpreted as *doctrina* 'teaching',
BETH *domus* 'home',
GIMEL *plenitudo* 'abundance, fullness',
DELETH *tabularum* 'documents, archives',
HE *ista* 'that',
VAV *et* 'and',
ZAI *haec* 'this' (feminine),
HETH *vita* 'life',
TETH *bonum* 'good',
IOD *principium* 'beginning',
CAPH *manus* 'hand',
LAMED *disciplinae* sive *cordis* 'instruction or heart',
MEM *ex ipsis* 'themselves',
NUN *sempiternum* 'everlasting',
SAMECH *adiutorium* 'support',
AIN *fons* sive *oculus* 'fountain or eye',
PHE *os* 'mouth' ... ,

---

80. Jerome, Epistle 30, p. 245. All further mention of Jerome and the alphabet in the following chapters is to this epistle. For more on the letters and their relation to the order of Scripture, see Fleming, "'The Most Exalted Language,'" pp. 34–36. Fleming points out that Jerome's letter was available in ASE, p. 42. He also provides lists of the Hebrew letters and their interpretations in various glossed Psalters; e.g., the Vespasian Psalter gives *filius* for *Beit* (p. 85), and Exeter Cathedral 3507 gives *confusio* (p. 106). A table comparing the meanings according to Ambrose, Eusebius, and two lists by Jerome can be found in Müller, *Die Deutungen der hebräischen Buchstaben*, p. 7.

SADE *iustitiae* 'justice',
COPH *vocatio* 'calling',
RES *capitis* 'leader',
SEN *dentium* 'teeth',
TAU *signa* 'signs'.[81]

Müller notes that in Hebrew and Aramaic, *'lf* as in *Aleph* means "to teach."[82] *Beit* means "house," and so on. Jerome is fairly accurate. The order of the alphabet, says Jerome, is also significant, an idea Jerome takes from Eusebius.[83] The first five letters, "doctrina domus plenitudo tabularum ista," indicate the teaching of the Church ("doctrina ecclesiae"), which is the home ("domus") of God; and this all is discovered in the fullness of divine books ("in librorum repperiatur plenitudine divinorum").[84] The next three letters ("et haec vita") indicate the life one has through a knowledge of Scripture. *Principium* is to be understood in light of 1 Corinthians 13:9–12—now we see through a glass darkly, but we will come to understand in the presence of Christ. By *manus* is to be understood works, and by *cor* and *disciplina* our experience through which knowledge is had.[85] The remainder of Jerome's interpretation of the Hebrew alphabet will be addressed as we read through the strophes of Bede's *Hymn*.

There are also important analogues to the alphabetic hymn and the power of letters in local lore and traditions. Five sentences after closing his *Hymn*, Bede presents a story that describes a Christian analogue to a runic loosing spell. It is one that he recommends "to the salvation of many."[86] It concerns two brothers named Imma and Tunna. Imma is captured after a battle, but his captors are unable

---

81. Jerome, Epistle 30, p. 246.
82. Müller, *Die Deutungen der hebräischen Buchstaben*, p. 12.
83. Ibid., p. 8. According to Müller, another source, now lost, is a tract by Philo of Alexandria on the symbolism of the Hebrew letters.
84. Jerome, Epistle 30, p. 246. My thanks to Paul Early for his help with Jerome.
85. Ibid., p. 247.
86. Bede, *HE*, 4.22, pp. 400–401. All translations regarding this story are by Colgrave and Mynors.

to keep him bound. As soon as they leave his presence, "his fetters were loosed" ("solveretur," see Matthew 18:18 below). His brother is abbot of a monastery and a priest. Tunna, thinking Imma dead, says masses for the absolution of Imma's soul. And "on account of these celebrations" Imma could not be bound. His captor asks if he possesses any "loosing spells" ("litteras solutorias"), something Colgrave notes literally means "loosing letters."[87] Imma explains that he knows nothing of such things, but that his brother is a priest who offers masses on his behalf. "So," Imma says, "if I had now been in another world, my soul would have been loosed from its punishment by his intercessions." Importantly, Imma is freed not by runic magic, but by the effect that his brother's prayers have on his soul. The story depends on the formula spoken by Jesus to his disciples in Matthew 18:18, "quaecumque SOLVERITIS super terram erunt soluta in caelo" (whatsoever YOU SHALL LOOSE upon earth shall be loosed also in heaven). After reuniting with his brother, Bede explains, Imma understood that his loosened fetters and other comforts "had been bestowed by heaven, through the intercession of his brother and the offering up of the saving Victim ['hostiae salutaris']." That Victim, of course, is the Host. Bede adds that Imma had been one of Aethelthryth's thanes. We see in this story a confluence of service (thane), sacrifice (the Victim), and prayer (the Mass), which all lead to a liberation of the soul, through which the body becomes liberated from the chains of earthly servitude.

Bede is not advocating charms, however. His narrative and his *Hymn* speak to the intercessory power of the Church in bringing Christians to salvation. There are, nonetheless, insular traditions that ascribed magic power to letters. Invocations and charms required uttering sounds in the correct order, thereby invoking supernatural power. Runes cut into sticks in the correct order could serve as charms. The Old English *Nine Herbs Charm* requires cutting a rune into a piece of wood after which it is named (*asc* in ash

---

87. Ibid., p. 402. Wallace-Hadrill notes some analogues in Gregory of Tours and Gregory the Great; see his *Bede's Ecclesiastical History*, p. 162.

wood, e.g.), and casting nine of them.[88] There is also a tradition of "mantic alphabets," which are divinatory alphabets found in medieval manuscripts.[89] One in BL Royal 7 D.xxv (f. 75), of the twelfth century, requires one to open a Psalter before randomly choosing a letter from which to divine one's future. But in Christian poets, the power of letters is over the spirit, which through the will has power over the body. Katherine O'Brien O'Keeffe has written masterfully on the relation of speech to writing in Old English, describing at one point the Devil of *Solomon and Saturn I*, who writes "the letters of death."[90] Opposed to these letters are those of the Pater Noster. Each letter is a weapon. <S>, for example, is the "letter of glory." This figurative association might explain the profusion of <s> in the fires that glorify Agatha and Eulalia in Bede's *Hymn*. There is an earlier parallel in the battle of letters in Prudentius's *Psychomachia*, as E. J. Christie has demonstrated. Christie has described this manner of viewing letters as "a semiotic whereby all letters are divinatory signs and symbols that (to paraphrase Jerome) conceal profound secrets."[91] The secrets are revealed by understanding letters as signs of profound truths. Following Jerome, Augustine, and Cassiodorus, Bede conceived of letters as possessing deeper meaning. In his *Commentary on Samuel*, he writes, "If we make it our business to bring out from the treasury of Scripture only the old, that is to follow the shapes of the letters in the Jewish manner, what edification among the daily sins, what consolation among the increasing cares of the age, what spiritual instruction among the manifold errors of this life will we gain by reading or listening?"[92] Alphabetic organization of strophes signals a spiritual lesson, an orderly ascent to a spiritual truth.

---

88. See Elliot, "Runes, Yews, and Magic," p. 258.
89. Chardonnens, "Mantic Alphabets."
90. O'Brien O'Keeffe, *Visible Song*, p. 57.
91. Christie, "By Means of a Secret Alphabet," p. 146. On Prudentius, see ibid., pp. 158–59.
92. Regarding Mark 13:52; trans. Wansbrough, *The Use and Abuse of the Bible*, p. 72, n. 41. The Latin text is from *PL* 91:499–500.

There are dozens of alphabetic hymns. Clemens Blume, who collated them in a volume of his *Analecta Hymnica*,[93] writes that they tended to be found as Nocturn antiphons. Many are dedicated to female saints; the acrostics spell out their names.[94] Given that Bede's *Hymn* is a celebration of Christian women, an important model is Proverbs 31:10–31, on the strong woman or *mulier fortis*. Proverbs walks through each of the Hebrew letters, associating each with a quality of the strong woman. In traditional Jewish households, the poem is recited on the eve of the Sabbath. The phrase "aperi os tuum" (open your mouth, 31:9) is repeated twice before the alphabetic commences, and it echoes Psalm 50:17, which is the first Psalm sung by a monk on awaking—"Domine labia mea aperies et os meum adnuntiabit laudem tuam" (O Lord, thou wilt open my lips: and my mouth shall declare thy praise). The phrase indicates to men and women religious that God does not have one plan of salvation for men and another for women; all Christians should be like the Strong Woman. In his commentary on Proverbs, Bede writes that the Catholic Church is called the Strong Woman: "Mulier fortis ecclesia catholica vocatur."[95] He explains that the poem follows the letters of the Hebrew, with one verse assigned to each letter. Bede then explains further that the alphabetic form indicates plenitude, which in turn can be ascribed to faith or the Church, to the elect or all catholic virtues.[96]

---

93. *AH* 29; subtitled *Pia Dictamina: Reimgebete und Leselieder der Mittelalters* (Leipzig, 1898).

94. Some are 4.115, Agnes; 4.171 and 4.172, Barbara; 4.234, Elisabeth; 4.312, Katherine; 4.343, Ludmilla; 4.364, Margaret; 4.365, Melania; 4.381, Martha; 4.408, Odilia; 12.109 and 12.110, Gaudia Maria; 22.138, Domitilla; 22.283–285, Lucia; 23.169, Agatha; and 23.412, Margareta.

95. Bede, *In proverbia Salomonis*, 3.31. Albert the Great also wrote a commentary on the *mulier fortis*. On authorship see del Barrio, "'Non est in aliquot opera modus nobilior.'"

96. "Cuius ordine perfectissimo alphabeti typice innuitur quam plenissime hic uel animae cuiusque fidelis uel totius sanctae ecclesiae quae ex omnibus electis animabus una perficitur catholica uirtutes ac praemia describantur."

By *mulier* we are to understand sons and daughters of the Spirit of God, born out of water and the Spirit (that is, baptism), who suffer for their faith yet nevertheless show fortitude. Ambrose writes in his commentary on Luke, "mens, quae credidisti deo, esto fortis mulier, qualis illa uel anima ecclesiastica uel ecclesia, de qua dicit Salomon: mulierem fortem quis inueniet?" (a mind believing in God will be the Strong Woman, which is like the spirit of the Church or the Church, of which said Solomon, Who shall find a Strong Woman?)[97] The *mulier fortis*, writes Augustine, should inspire all Christians to have patience in tribulation.[98] In his Institutes for Monks, John Cassian (c.360–435) alludes to Proverbs 31: "mulier illa sapiens, quae fortitudine et decore induta est" (that wise woman who is clothed in strength and beauty).[99] He uses the image to admonish monks to better behavior. It is essential to Bede's *Hymn* that we understand that female virgins, martyrs, and saints are inspirations and guides to male Christians, too.[100] Lisa Weston reports on Aldhelm's *De virginitate*, like the perfect virginity of St. John, "[Mary] embodies the Church's spiritual fertility which results, through prayer and (more significantly) the reading and imitation of texts, in the (re)production of virginity in other bodies."[101] Bede was one of many who recognized the centrality of women to a fuller understanding of the means of salvation. Most importantly, it does not seem to me accidental that Bede should write a hymn in praise of virginity and the *mulier fortis* at a point in his narrative when the burgeoning *ecclesia Anglorum* (grammatically feminine) is producing its first female virgin saint. With all this in mind, let us finally turn to an exposition of Bede's *Hymn to Aethelthryth*.

---

97. Ambrose, *Lucam*, p. 56.
98. Augustine, *Sermones* 37 (CCSL 41), line 211.
99. Cassian, *De institutis coenobiorum*, 10.21, p. 91.
100. The point is made by Yorke, *Nunneries and the Anglo-Saxon Royal Houses*, p. 5.
101. Weston, "The Saint-Maker and the Saint," p. 61.

(ENGLISH)

Hymn to Aethelthryth

In my translation that follows, I have not attempted to rhyme or to recapture the meter of Bede's hymn. It is more word-for-word than sense-for-sense. The words in small caps indicate the first word of the Latin strophe. A is for "alma" (nourishing); B is for "bella" (wars); and so forth. I have not placed the corresponding word in the pentameter in small caps unless its English translation differs from that in the hexameter.

A God, NOURISHING Trinity, you who governs all the ages,
   grant now this undertaking, God, nourishing Trinity.

B Let Virgil echo WARS, let us sing the gifts of peace;
   let us sing the rewards of Christ, let Virgil echo wars.

C Chaste SONGS for me, not the abduction of shameful Helen;
   sumptuousness suits the inconstant, chaste songs for me.

D I will speak of heavenly GIFTS, not of wretched Troy's battles;
   I will speak of heavenly gifts by which the earth rejoices.

E SEE! The High God approaches the womb of the honorable Virgin;
   in order to free men, see, the High God approaches.

F The pious virgin WOMAN bears the parent of the world;
   The virgin woman Mary, Gate of God, begets.

G The devoted retinue REJOICES over the Virgin Mother of the Thunderer,
   over virginity the gleaming, devoted retinue rejoices.

H Honor OF HER begat many from the Sacred Seed;
   [many] virginal flowers honor of her begat.

I The burnt virgin Agatha did not yield to the savage FLAMES;
   and Eulalia endures, the burnt one to the savage flames.

K CHASTE Thecla by the eminence of her mind overcomes beasts;
   chaste Euphemia overcomes accursed beasts.

L JOYFUL Agnes, stronger than iron, laughs at swords;
   joyful Cecilia laughs at hostile swords.

M MANY a victory flourishes in the world by means of sober hearts;
   MUCH love of sobriety flourishes in the world.

N Likewise now, an exceptional virgin blessed OUR times;
   likewise, our exceptional Aethelthryth shines.

O Having been BORN to a distinguished father, to a royal and illustrious family
   She was born nobler to God the distinguished Father.

P Thence her beauty SEIZES the scepters of a queen under the stars
   Thence her enduring beauty seizes more over the stars.

Q WHICH man do you court, gracious one, devoted now to the highest groom
   Christ the Groom is with you, which man, gracious one, do you court?

R I believe that now you follow the mother of the ethereal KING
   that you likewise are a mother of the ethereal king.

S The devoted BETROTHED of God had reigned for twice six years
   and in a monastery was consecrated betrothed of God,

Hymn to Aethelthryth

T   Where she, WHOLLY devoted to Heaven, blossomed by her lofty deeds,
    and [whence] she returned her soul, wholly devoted, to Heaven.

V   The nourishing flesh of the VIRGIN is entombed on twice eight November
    nor rots in a tomb the nourishing flesh of the virgin.

X   CHRIST, it is through your doing that the robe itself in the tomb
    inviolate shines, Christ, it is through your doing.

Y   And the deadly SERPENT departs in honor of your sacred robe
    Diseases disperse and the deadly serpent departs.

Z   JEALOUSY rages in the enemy who once had defeated Eve
    the rejoicing Virgin triumphs, jealousy rages in the enemy.

A   SEE what glory is yours among the nations having married God
    you who abide in the heavens, see, having married God.

M   You receive joyful GIFTS gleaming with festive torches
    behold the bridegroom arrives, you receive joyful gifts.

E   AND new songs you play with sweet-sounding plectrum
    and you, the new bride, exult with a sweet-sounding hymn.

N   No ONE separates her from the retinue of the high-throned Lamb
    she whom no one bore away through passion from the high-throned One.

(English)

(Latin)

Hymn to Aethelthryth

What follows is the edition by Colgrave and Mynors. For a key to the orthography of scansion, see the Note on Orthography at the beginning of this volume. Since I have followed the edition by Colgrave, I observe his use of <u> for both <u> and <v>. But I have removed all punctuation since it dissuades readers from entertaining syntactic possibilities that Bede may have intended. The meter alone should suggest syntactic clusters to readers.

A Ālmă Dĕ|ūs Trĭnĭ|tās quae | saēcŭlă | cūnctă gŭ|bērnas
    ādnŭĕ | iām cōe|ptīs || ālmă Dĕ|ūs Trĭnĭ|tās

B Bēllă Mă|rō rĕsŏ|nēt nōs | pācīs | dōnă că|nāmus
    mūnĕră | nōs Chrī|stī || bēllă Mă|rō rĕsŏ|nēt

C Cārmĭnă | cāstă mĭ|hī fē|dāe nōn | rāptŭs Hĕ|lēnae
    lūxŭs ĕ|rīt lŭbrĭ|cīs || cārmĭnă | cāstă mĭ|hī

D Dōnă sŭ|pērnă lŏ|quār mĭsĕ|rāe nōn | prōelĭă | Trōiae
    tērră quĭ|būs gāu|dēt || dōnă sŭ|pērnă lŏ|quār

E Ēn Dĕŭs | āltŭs ă|dīt uĕnĕ|rāndāe | uīrgĭnĭs | ālvum
    lībĕrĕt | ūt hŏmĭ|nēs || ēn Dĕŭs | āltŭs ă|dīt

F Fēmĭnă | uīrgŏ pă|rīt mūn|dī dē|uōtă pă|rēntem
    pōrtă Mă|rĭă Dĕ|ī || fēmĭnă | uīrgŏ pă|rīt

G Gāudĕt ă|mīcă cŏ|hōrs dē | uīrgĭnĕ | mātrĕ tŏ|nāntis
uīrgĭnĭ|tātĕ mĭ|cāns || gāudĕt ă|mīcă cŏ|hōrs

H Hūiŭs hŏ|nōr gĕnŭ|īt cā|stō dē | gērmĭnĕ | plūres
uīrgĭnĕ|ōs flō|rēs || hūiŭs hŏ|nōr gĕnŭ|īt

I Ĭgnĭbŭs | ūstă fĕ|rīs uī|rgō nōn | cēssĭt Ă|gāthe
Ēulălĭ(ă) | ēt pēr|fērt || īgnĭbŭs | ūstă fĕ|rīs

K Kāstă fĕ|rās sŭpĕ|rāt mē|ntīs prō | cūlmĭnĕ | Tēcla
Ēufĕmĭ|ā sā|crās || kāstă fĕ|rās sŭpĕ|rāt

L Lāetă rĭ|dēt glădĭ|ōs fēr|rō rō|būstĭŏr | Āgnes
Cāecĭlĭ(ă) | īnfē|stōs || lāetă rĭ|dēt glădĭ|ōs

M Mūltŭs ĭn | ōrbĕ uī|gēt pēr | sōbrĭă | cōrdă trĭ|ūmphus
sōbrĭĕ|tātĭs ă|mōr || mūltŭs ĭn | ōrbĕ uī|gēt

N Nōstră quŏ|qu(e) ēgrĕgĭ|ā iām | tēmpŏră | uīrgŏ bĕ|āuit
Āedīl|thrȳdă nĭ|tēt || nōstră quŏ|qu(e) ēgrĕgĭ|ā

O Ōrtă pă|tr(e) ēxĭmĭ|ō rē|gāl(i) ēt | stēmmătĕ | clāra
nōbĭlĭ|ōr Dŏmĭn(o) | ēst || ōrtă pă|tr(e) ēxĭmĭ|ō

P Pērcĭpĭt | īndĕ dĕ|cūs rē|gīn(ae) ēt | scēptră sŭb | āstris
plūs sŭpĕr | āstră mă|nēns || pērcĭpĭt | īndĕ dĕ|cūs

Q Quīd pĕtĭs | ālmă uī|rūm spōn|sō iām | dēdĭtă | sūmmo
spōnsŭs ă|dēst Chrī|stūs || quīd pĕtĭs | ālmă uī|rūm

R Rēgĭs ŭt | āethĕrĕ|ī mā|trēm iām | crēdŏ sĕ|quāris
tū quŏquĕ | sīs mā|tēr || rēgĭs ŭt | āethĕrĕ|ī

S Spōnsă dĭ|cātă Dĕ|ō bĭs | sēx rē|gnāuĕrăt | ānnis
īnquĕ mŏ|nāstĕrĭ(o) | ēst || spōnsă dĭ|cātă Dĕ|ō

T Tōtă să|crātă pŏ|lō cēl|sīs ŭbĭ | flōrŭĭt | āctis
rēddĭdĭt | ātqu(e) ănĭ|mām || tōtă | să|crātă pŏ|lō

V Vīrgĭnĭs | ālmă că|r(ō) ēst tŭmŭ|lātă bĭs | ōctŏ Nŏ|uēmbres
nēc pŭtĕt | īn tŭmŭ|lō || uīrgĭnĭs | ālmă că|rō

162 (Latin)

X   Xrīstĕ tŭ|(i) ēst ŏpĕ|rīs quĭă | uēstĭs ĕt | īpsă sĕ|pūlchro
    īnuĭŏ|lātă nĭ|tēt || Xrīstĕ tŭ|(i) ēst ŏpĕ|rīs

Y   Ȳdrŏs ĕt | ātĕr ă|bīt sā|crāe prō | uēstĭs hŏ|nōre
    mōrbī | dīffŭgĭ|ūnt || ȳdrŏs ĕt | ātĕr ă|bīt

Z   Zēlŭs ĭn | hōstĕ fŭ|rīt quōn|dām quī | uīcĕrăt | Ēuam
    uīrgŏ trĭ|ūmphăt ŏ|uāns || zēlŭs ĭn | hōstĕ fŭ|rīt

A   Āspĭcĕ | nūptă Dĕ|ō quāe | sīt tĭbĭ | glōrĭă | tērris
    quāe mănĕ|āt cāe|līs || āspĭcĕ | nūptă Dĕ|ō

M   Mūnĕră | lāetă că|pīs fē|stīuīs | fūlgĭdă | tāedis
    ēccĕ uĕ|nīt spōn|sūs || mūnĕră | lāetă că|pīs

E   Ēt nŏuă | dūlcĭsŏ|nō mŏdŭ|lārīs | cārmĭnă | plēctro
    spōns(a) hȳmn(o) | ēxūl|tās || ēt nŏuă | dūlcĭsŏ|nō

N   Nūllŭs ăb | āltĭthrŏ|nī cō|mītătŭ | sēgrĕgăt | Āgni
    qu(am) āffē|ctū tŭlĕ|rāt || nūllŭs ăb | āltĭthrŏ|nī

Hymn to Aethelthryth   163

(Edition)

Hymn to Aethelthryth

This diplomatic edition is presented for comparison with the edition above, and is based on St. Gall Ms. 265, pp. 122–23. The scribe has pointed the verses to indicate metrical clusters.

Incip[it] carmen eiusde[m] de uirginitate Edildrudae reginae ·

Alma d[eu]s trinitas quae secula cuncta gubernas · Adnue iam coepti[s] alm[a] d[eu]s trinitas ·
Bella maro resonet nos pacis dona canamus · Munera nos [Ch]r[ist]i bella maro reson[et] ·
Carmina casta mihi fed[a]e non raptus helenae · Luxus erit lubricis carmina casta mihi ·
Dona superna loquar miserae non proelia troiae · Quaemundum exhilarant[1] dona superna loquar ·
En d[eus] altus adit uenerandae uirginis aluum · Liberet ut homines · En d[eus] altus adit ·
Femina uirgo parit mundi deuota parentem · Porta maria d[e]i · Femina uirgo parit ·
Gaudet amica cohors de uirgine matre tonantis · Virginitate micans · gaudet amica cohors ·
Huius honor genuit casto de germine plures · Virgineos flores · Huius honor genuit ·

---

1. Colgrave, *HE* (hereafter Ed.), reads *terra quibus gaudet*.

Ignib[us] usta feris uirgo non cessit agathae · Eulalia et perfert · ignib[us] usta feris ·

Kasta feras superat mentis prolumine[2] tecla · Eufemia sacras · casta feras superat ·

Laeta ridet gladios ferro robustior agnes · Cecilia inferros · Laeta ridet gladios ·

Multos[3] in orbe uiget p[er] sobria corda triumphus · Sobrietatis amor · multos inorbe uiget ·

Nostra aliis sacrior sed[4] tempora uirgo beauit Aedildruda nitet · N[ost]ra aliis sacrior ·

Orta patre eximio regali et stem[m]ate clara · Nobilior d[omi]no est orta patre eximio · [p. 123]

Percipit inde decus reginae et sceptra sub astris · Plus [supe]r astra manens · percipit inde decus ·

Quid petis alma uirum sponsa iam dedita summo · Sponsus ade[st] [Ch]r[istus] · quid petis alma uirum ·

Regis ut aetherei matrem iam credo sequaris · Tu quoq[ue] sis mater regis ut aetherei ·

Sponsa dicta d[e]o bis sex regnauerat annis · In q[ue] monasterio e[st] sponsa dicata d[e]o ·

Tota sacrata polo celsis ubi floruit actis · Reddidit atq[ue] anima[m] · tota sacrata polo ·

Uirginis alma caro e[st] [t]umulata bis octo nouembres · Nec pu[t]et in tumulo · uirginis alma caro e[st] ·

X[rist]e tui e[st] operis quia uestis [et] ipsa sepulchro · Inuiolate nitet · X[rist]e tui e[st] operis ·

Ẏdros et ater abit sacrae pro uestis honore · Morbi diffugiunt · ẏdros et ater abit ·

Zelus in hoste furit quonda[m] qui uicerat eua[m] · Uirgo triumphat ouans · Zelus in hoste furit ·

Aspice nupta d[e]o quae sit tibi Gloria terris · Quae maneat caelis · Aspice nupta d[e]o ·

---

2. Ed. *pro culmine.*
3. Ed. *multus.*
4. Ed. *Nostra quoque egregria iam tempora.*

Munera laeta capis festiuis fulgida tedis[5] · Ecce uenit sponsus · munera laeta capis ·

Et noua dulcisono modularis carmina plectro · Sponsa ȳmno exultas et noua dulcisono ·

Nullus ab altithroni comitatu segregat almi · Quam affectu tulerat · nullus ab altithroni ·

---

5. Ed. *taedis*.

CHAPTER SIX

Hymn to Aethelthryth, A–G

Bede's ultimate source for his *Hymn to Aethelthryth*, as we have seen, is Scripture. Two alphabetic poems in Scripture will concern us here: Psalm 118 and Proverbs 31. Recall that each letter of the Hebrew alphabet was thought to have held a peculiar significance. In commenting on Bede's *Hymn*, I shall coordinate the commentaries of Bede, Hilary, Jerome, Augustine, Ambrose, and Cassiodorus with each alphabetic strophe of Bede's *Hymn*. We may be able to determine to what extent Bede arranged his *Hymn* so as to recapture the thematic particulars of each strophe of the Scriptural alphabetics. Bede learned from Jerome that Aleph means *doctrina* 'teaching, doctrine'. Do the Aleph strophes of all Bede's alphabetics speak to the themes of doctrine or teaching? Indeed, do all the Aleph strophes of every Scriptural alphabetic speak to teaching? Doubtful. Nevertheless, there may have been a desire on the part of Christian exegetes to find in Aleph strophes some relation to Jerome's governing theme, *doctrina*. The meanings of the Hebrew letters may have exerted some influence on interpretation. Those meanings are, after all, part of the Patristic tradition of commentaries on alphabetics.

The Aleph strophe of Psalm 118 declares that happy are those who follow the teaching of the Lord, those who "walk in the law of the Lord."[1] The Aleph strophe of Proverbs 31, which is verse 10, is not

---

1. The correspondence between letters and verses is made by Müller, *Die Deutungen der hebräischen Buchstaben*, §2. *Aleph* means 'teaching' according

so clearly connected to *doctrina*. It asks about the *mulier fortis*, the Strong Woman: "Mulierem fortem quis inveniet procul et de ultimis finibus pretium eius" (Who shall find a valiant woman? Far and from the uttermost coasts is the price of her).[2] Bede writes that the Strong Woman is a figure of the Catholic Church. Moreover, we are to read *mulier* spiritually, indicating all children of God born of baptism and the Holy Spirit. These children must be strong, *fortis*. That strength is spiritual, not physical. Bede writes "quia cuncta saeculi, adversa simul et prospere, pro Conditoris sui fide contemnit" (because of faith in his Creator, man scorns everything of the world, equally in adversity and prosperity). Our only hope in this life lies in the mediation of God and his grace. For the congregation of the elect, hope lies in the end of time with the Second Coming, with the Lord whose passion unto death redeemed us.[3] The Church, like the Virgin, brings the incarnate Word of God, the Son, into our daily lives. In the Aleph strophe of Proverbs we see figured the nourishing Church under the orderly government of the Creator of time and the world. The Church *docet*, teaches or leads; she nourishes and fosters faith like a mother. Jerome makes explicit a connection between doctrine and the Church: he combines the first five letters of the Hebrew alphabet into a *conexio* 'union' that reads "the doctrine of the Church, which is the home of God, can be found in the fullness of divine books." *Doctrina* connects to the Church and to Scripture. If we rely on Jerome, the thematic connection of Bede's hymn to the

---

to Eusebius, Jerome, and Ambrose. Rabbi Akiva says the same thing, illustrating his point with an acrostic from the Torah; see pp. 12–13. Bede's *Hymn on the Feast of Ss. Peter and Paul* (Hymn 9) is also an alphabetic; but for the name of Christ, *Xriste*, Bede uses different vocabulary to begin those strophes.

2. Bede is not using the Old Latin Bible here; 31:10 in that version reads, "Mulierem fortem quis inveniet? pretiosior est lapidibus pretiosis, quae eius modi est" (Who shall find the strong woman? She is more precious than the precious stone, which is the measure of her). See *Bibliorum sacrorum*, 2:343–345. The image of a precious stone is commonplace in hymns celebrating virgins.

3. Bede, *PL* 91:1041.

Aleph strophes is less tenuous; nevertheless, Bede seems to have had Proverbs 31:10 in mind when he wrote his own Aleph strophe.

1. Bede's *Hymn to Aethelthryth* begins, "Ălmă Dĕ|ūs Trĭnĭ|tās quæ | sæcŭlă | cūnctă gŭ|bērnas" (God, nourishing Trinity, you who governs all the ages). Bede uses the same terms in his commentary on the *mulier fortis*. A phrase in his commentary, *cuncta saeculi*, has become the *Hymn*'s *saecula cuncta*, and the commentary's *conditor* has become the *Hymn*'s *gubernator*. (Bede uses *condere* in the opening strophe of his first hymn, "Primo Deus.") Aldhelm began his hexameter praise of virgins by invoking the heavenly *gubernator*.[4] By comparing Bede's opening verse with his own commentary on Proverbs 31, we see that with *saecula* Bede refers not only to temporal ages, but also to the physical world. The government of time, one might note, is also the province of the poet attuned to meter. By setting *Deus* in the first half and *saecula* in the second half of this verse, Bede sets up an opposition between the divine and the earthly.[5] Also in this verse, he has juxtaposed the image of a *gubernator* 'governor, steersman, navigator', a masculine form when a noun, to that of nourishing mother. The first word, *alma* 'nourishing', is a feminine form; it also can mean 'bountiful, sweet, gracious' or indicate a mother's breast. The form *alma* is not used in the Vulgate. It appears in classical authors, and in the *Aeneid* it sometimes indicates the nourishment or fostering by parents or a goddess: "alma parens" (2.591, 2.664, 10.252) and "alma Venus" (1.618, 10.332). Virgil uses *alma* to describe not only Venus, divine mother of Aeneas and therefore of all Romans, but also Ceres, goddess of agriculture and growth (*Geor.* 1.7), as does Ovid (*Fasti*, 4.547). Throughout the *Metamorphoses*, Ovid uses the epithet *alma* for Venus. As an epithet, it can be translated 'gracious

---

4. Aldhelm, *CDV*, p. 352, line 1; trans. Rosier, *APW*.
5. Aldhelm places *mundum* in the middle of his line, surrounding it with God: "Omnipotens genitor mundum dicione gubernans" (Almighty Progenitor, guiding the world by your rule; trans. Rosier). His line alludes to Virgil and Sedulius; see *CDV*, p. 352, note. Bede will use *genitor* in the <H> strophe of the *Hymn* to imply spiritual birth.

one'. The term belongs to pagan poetry as well as to Scriptural commentary and the traditions of the Church. It is fairly common in medieval authors, notably Arator, Aldhelm, Cassiodorus, and Gregory of Tours.[6] It appears in the hymn, "O Stella maris, ave alma mater dei atque virgo semper et felix porta cęli" (O Star of the sea, Hail Holy Mother of God, ever virgin and joyful gate of Heaven). Mary is the *alma mater*. Jerome in his commentary on Isaiah explains that *alma* is Hebrew for holy, in Latin, *sancta*. A gloss edited by Lindsey notes that *alma* means *virgo* 'maiden' or *sancta* 'holy'.[7] We see Bede setting both meanings in apposition to one another in his *Hymn to St Agnes*, "Illuxit alma saeculis / Dies beata virginis." In keeping with the Marian devotion of Jarrow, Bede's term connotes maternal nourishment—perhaps we might infer that it is the nourishment of true doctrine.

With the feminine "alma" as the first element in his poem, Bede echoes the Christian trope of reforming the classical poet's invocation of the Muses—all of whom, incidentally, are female.[8] The nourishing, (grammatically) feminine Trinity is his muse. Importantly, Bede is not calling directly upon the Holy Spirit to be his nourishing, gracious muse. Aldhelm, too, in the Preface to his *Carmen de virginitate*, calls on "Trinus in arce Deus" (Triune God in the citadel of heaven), a grammatically masculine construction.[9] Aldhelm also rejects the "ruricolas versus et commata Musas" (verses and poetic

---

6. In his *CDV*, Aldhelm tends to use the word to confer the idea of 'graceful'. See line 481, "alma membra" (graceful limbs, a phrase Bede uses elsewhere); line 612, "alma species" (graceful appearance); line 970, "alma praeconia" (graceful praise); line 1405, "alma virtute" (graceful virtue); line 1612, "alma palma" (holy/grace-filled hand); and so forth.
7. *TLL*, 1:1702, s.v. Old English glosses translate *alma* as *halig* 'holy'; Gneuss, ed. *Hymnar und Hymnen im Englischen Mittelalter*, no. 66.1, p. 349. And *Alme Gregori*, in Milfull, *Hymns*, no. 116.1, p. 386.
8. For the trope, see Fontaine, "Le Poète latin," p. 10; in Fontaine, *Études*, p. 140.
9. Aldhelm, *CDV*, p. 350, line 3. In line 4, the Trinity is the "regnator mundi," which compares to Bede's *gubernator*. Aldhelm also calls God "mundi formator et auctor" (l. 11).

measures from the rustic Muses).[10] Alcuin invokes the Holy Spirit when, in the dedicatory poem of his *De fide sanctae*,[11] he describes the Holy Spirit as "almus," also grammatically masculine. Elsewhere, Bede speaks of the nourishing life of Cuthbert. The first book of his metrical *Life of St. Cuthbert* begins, "Alma Deo cari primo coelestis ab aevo / Vita micat famuli" (The nourishing life of the dear servant of Heaven glitters/trembles from the first age before God). We will see *micare* in the <G> strophe of the *Hymn*. Bede's use of "alma" is therefore not unusual. The image of nourishment appears to be important to early medieval notions of Christian grace acting in the world. Bede calls the hermit monk Felgeldus a "largitor muneris almi" (giver of kind service).[12] In a poem attributed to Bede, May is the gentle, nourishing month ("alma Nones").[13] In Bede's hymn on the beheading of John the Baptist, John is "praecessor almus gratiae" (holy herald of grace),[14] and St. Peter is "doctor almus gentium" (nourishing doctor to the gentiles) in Bede's *Hymn on the Feast of Ss. Peter and Paul*.[15]

Among other authors, the phrase "alma Trinitas" is found in Aldhelm's prose *De virginitate*, during a doxological invocation of the Trinity.[16] As in Bede, Aldhelm is describing the government of the universe. One can see in both Aldhelm and Bede a Bartheian

---

10. Aldhelm, *CDV*, p. 353, line 23.
11. *PL* 101:14B.
12. Bede, VSC, line 944.
13. *Martyrologium poeticum*, Giles, I:51. Giles and later editors doubt the attribution to Bede. The edition by Giles comes chiefly from BL Sloane 263. It is an eleventh-century manuscript in Caroline minuscule, possibly from Lyons. For a detailed study of the poem in its various forms, see John Hennig, "Studies in the Literary Tradition of the 'Martyrologium poeticum,'" *Proceedings of the Royal Irish Academy* C-2 (1954): 197–227. Hennig discusses the medieval attribution of the poem to Bede on pp. 212–13, and at 216, n. 64.
14. Hymn *10*, line 1.
15. Hymn *9*, line 6.
16. *PDV*, line 58: "orantem pro nobis beatitudinem uestram *alma Trinitas*, una deitatis substantia et trina personarum subsistentia, *totius mundi*

syntagme, a confluence of signs: NOURISHMENT, TRINITY, and GOVERNANCE. Alcuin, like many Christian poets before him, joins *alma* with virginity. An image of a nourishing God corresponds to an image of the Virgin nourishing the baby Jesus, *alma virgo* in the poetic imagination of early Christian writers. God also acts as a mother. Bede uses this image of God's maternal power throughout his prose life of Aethelthryth found in chapter nineteen of book four, and returns to it in other works. In his *De die iudicii*, he writes "candida uirgineo simul inter agmina flore, / quae trahit ALMA DEI genitrix, pia uirgo maria" (likewise a virginal flower among spotless troops, whom the NOURISHING Mother OF GOD leads, the pious Virgin Mary).[17] Again in a hymn on St. Andrew, a nourishing city (the Heavenly Jerusalem) is mother of all: "Excepit ALMA CIUITAS / nostrumque mater omnium . . ." (The NOURISHING CITY received / and mother of us all . . .),[18] she receives Christ. Bede finds the same nourishment in the wine of the Mass, which is figured by a nourishing chalice: Christ "aquas in ALMA transtulit / vini rubentis POCULA" (transformed waters / into NOURISHING CUPS of red wine).[19] And, of course, he will later describe Aethelthryth as "alma" 'gracious' (l. 31).

Perhaps in anticipation of the explicit theme of the poem in the next strophe, *alma* alludes obliquely to the most famous hexameter of all, Virgil's "Arma virumque cano," the opening of the *Aeneid*, which Bede will later invoke explicitly. Ovid made a similar allusion, but turned it to the theme of love, joking in his elegy's third line that Cupid had stolen a foot from the second line (thus making a pentameter), turning his heroic meter into elegiac.[20] Perhaps also alluding to Ovid, Bede makes the point that he is singing of Christian love, not pagan. If his allusion is to Virgil's arms and the man, Bede is declaring his topic to be *alma* (*almus*) 'nourishment' and *deus* 'God'.

---

monarchiam *gubernans* ab alto caeli culmine iugiter tueri dignetur!" Alcuin uses similar vocabulary as Bede.

17. *DDI*, 5:139.
18. Hymn 12, lines 41–42.
19. Hymn 11, lines 39–40.
20. Ovid, *Amores*, 1.1.

The comparison here is a medieval trope, one that Curtius describes as a distinction between Christian freedom and pagan war-lust.[21] This reforming theme seems to carry into the sound and syntax of the strophe. Note the profusion of <a>, which invites a comparison to the joyful *Alleluia* of the Mass—in the following centuries it will become the site of troping and sequences. Almost every word of this hexameter ends with an <a>.[22] There is no elision, which means that each word is sonically independent. Elongated terminal vowels are cut crisply short by consonants. Singers will recognize this disposition of sounds as optimal for choirs. The meter which Bede opposed to Virgil's *dsss* was Fortunatus's *ddds*; here the meter is *ddsd*, its three dactyls closer to Fortunatus than to Virgil. Bede describes this pattern favorably in his *DAM*, citing Fortunatus.[23]

The grammar also contributes to the theme, perhaps a little more impressionistically. Notice that the verb is the last word of the hexameter, so that one's intellection of the content proceeds by first taking in a sequence of nouns, adjectives, and pronouns, and second, structuring their relationship and activity with reference to a verb. "Alma," "cuncta," and "saecula" hang in grammatical suspension until the verb clarifies them. The reader is invited to appreciate the uncertainty of the cluster of nouns and adjectives and their subsequent resolution, not only as a sensation, but as possibly symbolic of the poet's larger point. Analogically, the verb (*Verbum*, the Word) governs and gives order to the words as God governs and gives order to the world. A similar observation might be made of the *Credo*, described above, in which nominal and adjectival forms bracket the verbal activity at the center of the prayer. The connection between verbs and the activity of Christ is a commonplace, following John 1:1. Aldhelm says God created the world "verbo," through His word,

---

21. Cited in Szövérffy, *Annalen*, 1:172.
22. Aldhelm, by contrast, litters his line with alliteration—the first four lines of his *CDV* contain alliteration. And the *PDV* reads in places like an exercise in alliteration. For a remarkable example, see *PDV*, p. 234, lines 19–20.
23. *DAM*, pp. 96–7, citing *De Virginitate*, line 1.

and through the Word—the Son.[24] (*CDV*, line 3). Where "alma" carries the metaphor in the first hemistich, in the second hemistich the metaphor is carried by the verb: the Trinity *governs*. That is, time does not pass as much as it is mediated and ordered through God, in whom we live and move and have our being. Besides the metaphorical value of parts of speech and inflectional categories, there is also the semantic potential of grammatical gender. The poem begins with an adjective, "alma." An adjective can be inflected in any of the three genders. In this case it is feminine, in a first-declension inflection. The second word, "Deus," is a second-declension noun and is masculine. And the third word, "Trinitas," is a third-declension noun, and is feminine. Recall that Virgil's *Aeneid* begins with "arma," neuter, and "virum," masculine; the next substantive is "Troiae," feminine. Bede the schoolmaster may have deepened his allusion to Virgil by employing a variety of grammatical genders in his opening hemistich. He has also given us three consecutive words in the first, second, and third declensions. Given the topic of this hymn, however, it is suggestive that two of the three opening words are feminine.

The second line of the strophe is a pentameter: "ādnŭĕ | iām cōe|ptīs ‖ ālmă Dĕ|ūs Trĭnĭ|tās" (grant now this undertaking, God, nourishing Trinity). Repeating the opening phrase at the last position, something that is common to all the strophes in the *Hymn*, makes this elegy epanaleptic. *Adnue* is relatively rare in the Patristic period, but it is used with *coeptis* by Virgil, *Aen.* 9:622, "Iuppiter omnipotens, audacibus *adnue coeptis*." (Bede will allude to Jupiter the Thunderer in the <G> strophe.) If "alma Deus" was an echo of Virgil's opening foot, then perhaps the pentameter echoes Virgil, too. Servius comments on 9:622 that Jupiter's epithet, *omnipotens*, sometimes depicts the glory of divine will, sometimes the motivation for speaking, and so forth.[25] In the mind of our ideal reader, Bede's allusion may juxtapose the absent pagan Jupiter to the omnipresent

---

24. Aldhelm, *CDV*, line 3.
25. Servius, *Commentarii*, 2:364. *Omnipotens* is Aldhelm's first word in his *CDV*.

Christian Trinity. Here, as in Virgil, Bede's imperative "adnue" 'acknowledge, grant' directed at God echoes the traditional Christian practice of invoking the Son or the Spirit. Paulinus of Nola in his twenty-third poem writes, "adnue, fons verbi, verbum deus . . ." (acknowledge, fountain of words, Word of God . . .).[26] The Preface of Juvencus to his hexameter paraphrase of the Gospels makes a similar move: after invoking the poetry of Rome, he writes, "Nam mihi carmen erit Christi vitalia gesta . . ." (But my song will be the life-giving deeds of Christ).[27] In the <C> strophe, Bede will also use the phrase "carmina mihi." Juvencus calls these works a gift (*donum*), a word Bede will use in the <B> strophe. Juvencus then invokes the Holy Spirit (lines 33–34), using an image of the Jordan River, the site of Christ's baptism, as well. With these allusions at the outset of his *Hymn*, Bede suggests his theme of replacing pagan literature with Christian literature.

Turning to grammar, verbs sit in the middle of Bede's couplet, but not in the middle of each verse. That creates a chiasmus across the lines. The middle of the strophe is active (verbs), the outer limits are static (nouns and adjectives). To put it another way, if more speculatively, there is a cross made of verbs at the center of this couplet. The syntax is classical, but following on my earlier speculation, one might see it baptized into a Christian context. Furthermore, in the stasis of the outer nouns and the activity of the inner verbs we might see a relation to the Christian Platonism of Augustine, in which the outer limits of divine creation are static and unmoving, free from time, and the inner reaches (which we inhabit) are in constant motion, seeking the divine. In that active middle of the Ptolemaic universe, the Word (*Verbum*) became man (John 1:1) and died on a cross. This larger syntactic structure recollects the Credo, discussed above. Here, the center of each verse is taken by the Trinity and by Nourishment,

---

26. Paulinus of Nola, *Carmina*, p. 195, line 27.
27. Juvencus, *PL* 19:60; see also line 10 and note, and lines 23–28. Bede cites Juvencus's *Preface* in his *DAM*. It may also be the source of the word *altithronus* (Juvencus, l. 32), which Bede uses here in the final strophe.

thereby reinforcing stylistically the theme of both the couplet and the poem. Finally, in the progression of the verse, we find that the repeated phrase has a slightly different meaning when we reach it a second time. Christine Fell says that in cases like this, the modified meaning sometimes turns on paradoxes. We might note that in the case of the <A> strophe, *alma* is used to describe the person of the Trinity who governs the world (the Son), and then to describe an intercessor in the activity of Christian poets (the Holy Spirit).[28]

2. The second strophe begins with the second letter, <B> in Latin, *Beit* in Hebrew. According to Jerome, *Beit* means 'house' or 'temple', although Ambrose says it means *confusio* 'blending, confusion' (on the example of Babel or Babylon).[29] Bede's hexameter reads, "Bēllă Mă|rō rěsŏ|nēt nōs | pācīs | dōnă că|nāmus" (Let Virgil echo wars, let us sing the gifts of peace). We see a caesura in the third foot between –*et* and *nos*. This caesura is extremely common in Latin elegy, and so is known as *the* caesura.[30] The epanaleptic form contributes to the third-foot caesura because the first two-and-a-half feet will be repeated at the end of the pentameter. Thus, the third foot of the hexameter must begin with a terminal or independent syllable, which in turn will serve as the last, long syllable of the pentameter. Unusual here (and in the first strophe) is a trisyllabic ending to the pentameter; disyllabic endings are far more usual.[31] We saw in the first strophe a possible allusion to Virgil, but here it is not "arma," but the echoes of "bella" 'wars', the absent signifier in the *Aeneid*'s opening synecdoche "arma." The Christian sings plainly, without synecdoche, songs of peace. The parallel opposition of the nouns "bella" and "dona" continues with the verbs: the reception of resonance (*resonare*)—of an echo—is opposed to active singing (*canere*). Note

---

28. On the Son as governor, see Ambrose, "Aeterne rerum conditor" Hymn 1, ed. Fontaine in *Hymnes*; and a note by Walpole, *Hymns*, p. 30.
29. Müller, *Die Deutungen der hebräischen Buchstaben*, p. 13.
30. Platnauer, *Latin Elegiac Verse*, p. 6; on caesurae in elegies, see chap. 2(a).
31. Ibid., p. 17.

that Bede places verbs in the center of his hexameter and in the middle of his couplet, a slight contrast with the <A> strophe. Moreover, the two verbs sit in syntactic parallel, immediately preceding caesurae, and at positions used in hexameters for leonine rhyme—all characteristics that invite the reader to make a close comparison. The first verb is singular, the second plural, introducing an antithesis we saw earlier in Fortunatus.[32] In these carefully balanced antitheses lies the beauty of Bede's art.

Turning to a more speculative and impressionistic response, we can read the antitheses figuratively, as well. They are the fundamental divisions of creation introduced in Genesis: many and One, light and dark, water and sky, land and water, death and life, woman and man, law-keeper and law-breaker, war and peace, and so on. The antitheses inherent in this verse are also reflected in the vocabulary. *Resonare* is relatively common in poetry, but it famously appears with respect to a house (recall Jerome's *Beit*) in a satire of Horace. In the first book of his satires, Horace recommends prostitutes, rather than married women, to the philanderer, lest on a husband's return, "pulsa domus strepitu resonet, vepallida lecto" (the house, shaken, should resound on all sides with a great noise).[33] If "arma" (and the elegiac form) suggests Ovid, "resonet" may suggest Horace's satirical review of categories of sexual partners. Another suggestion that might offer itself to the mind of our ideal reader is Book 7 of the *Aeneid*, which begins with a description of Circe's land, where her song resonates ("resonat cantu") in the wild woods. Songs resonate throughout Virgil's *Georgics*, too. Resonant songs sound throughout Ovid. In Ambrose and in later Christian writers, *resonare* comes to mean 'denote' or 'signify'.[34] Bede may be playing with both meanings,

---

32. Notably, this opposition is lost in Colgrave's translation, which uses the first person singular; Bede, *HE*, p. 399. Colgrave translates, "Battle be Maro's theme, sweet peace be mine; / Christ's gifts for me, battle be Maro's theme."
33. Satire 2, line 129; trans. Smart, *The Works of Horace*, p. 147.
34. Stotz, *HLSM*, 2:149 = V, 75.6. Aldhelm seems to allude to Virgil's Circe in *CDV*, line 15.

suggesting both the empty echoes of pagan verse and their later significance as precursors of Christian verse.

Bede comments on the *Beit* of Proverbs 31, which Jerome had noted means 'house' or 'temple'. Here, says Bede, it refers to the Catholic Church. Verse 11 reads, "Confidit in ea cor viri sui, quia spoliis non indigebit" (The heart of her husband trusteth in her: and he shall have no need of spoils). The *vir* 'husband' of the Church is Christ. Bede cites 2 Corinthians 11:2, "For I have espoused you to one husband, that I may present you as a chaste virgin to Christ." Christ is drawn to humanity; those who are strong in their faith ("fortem fidelem") and those who are espoused to Christ in purity desire His love. Thus, "Dominus et Redemptor noster in Ecclesia confidit" (The Lord and our Redeemer trusts in the Church).[35] *Spolium* 'spoils' are the temptations of demons, yet the Church never ceases to free us from diabolical deceit. The strength and purity of faith necessary to this freedom are also described by Hilary in his commentary on the *Beit* stanza of Psalm 118. Moreover, the letters of the alphabet figuratively indicate the true rules and perfection of faith in God: he who learns the elements of faith during his youth, and reforms himself continually, will not grow into the habit of sin.[36] Psalm 118:10 reads "in toto corde meo exquisivi te non repellas me a mandatis tuis" (With my whole heart have I sought after thee: let me not stray from thy commandments). Also, *Beit* of both Proverbs 31 and Psalm 118:10 makes reference to a heart ("cor viri" and "corde meo"). Both strophes concern a relationship between two ideas or people. And finally, both conclude by contrasting a good state with the negation of a bad one—do *x* and do not do *y*. Yet, the subjunctives imply a coexistence: let Virgil sing his songs, let us sing ours. This (Biblical) manner of articulating a contrast is a feature of Bede's style and characteristic of the epanaleptic form in these early strophes. For example, Bede does not ignore Virgil in his advocacy of Christian song, but names him. To name rather than to elide that which ought

---

35. Bede, *PL* 91:1041–42.
36. Hilary, *Commentaire*, 1:126–29.

not to be done is a way of acknowledging the variety of creation, the good and the bad together.

The pentameter reads, "mūnĕră | nōs Chrī|stī || bēllă Mă|rō rĕsŏ|nēt" ([let] us [sing] the rewards of Christ, let Virgil echo wars). A complex relation with Virgil was part of the allusive nature of Latin poetry. But as we have seen, that relation is fraught with potential idolatry or vanity. In his commentary on the *Beit* strophe of 118, Augustine notes that those who do not walk in the way of God's law, his doctrine, are those who want only to appear wise to others. Therein lies the schoolmaster's weakness, his propensity to intellectual vanity. Bede has set the gifts of Christ against these literary vanities. His opposition is built from allusion, and thereby recalls the *cento*, which comprises pieces of other poets. It was a popular genre, and the most celebrated, as we have seen, is by Faltonia Betitia Proba, who rearranged hemistichs from Virgil to retell the story of the Bible. Like Bede, she acknowledges the awkward place of Virgil in Christian letters. She describes a consequence of her aim: "Vergilium cecinisse loquar pia munera Christi" (I will imply that Virgil sang the pious gifts of Christ).[37] To our sagacious nun of Barking, it may seem that Bede indirectly takes up Proba's ambivalent relation to Virgil, with "munera Christi" in this context alluding both to Virgil and to Proba's Christian reconfiguration of Virgil. The phrase "munera Christi" appears in the first line of Ambrose's famous hymn on Christian martyrs (no. 14), which is especially germane to Bede's *Hymn*: "Aeterna Christi munera / et martyrum victorias / laudes ferentes debitas / laetis canamus mentibus" (Eternal gifts of Christ / and martyrs' victories, / paying our debts of praise / we sing of them with joyful mind).[38] Ambrose provides the chief allusive background to Bede's pentameter, but the allusions run deep. Not only is the topic of martyrdom relevant, but so are some of the images

---

37. Line 23, trans. Green, "Proba's Introduction to her Cento," p. 556. Bede shares much vocabulary with Proba's dedication to Christ and her invocation of the Holy Spirit; Green shows that her introduction mirrors sentiments in Paulinus of Nola, especially poem 10, at p. 554.

38. Hymn 14, ed. Alain Goulon in Ambrose, *Hymnes*, p. 597.

that Ambrose employs to speak of martyrs. Martyrs, sings Ambrose, are "Ecclesiarum principes, / belli triumphales duces" (princes of the Church / triumphant leaders in war). This image of the "bella" waged by "milites Christi" (soldiers of Christ) sits in antithesis to the "bella" of Virgil's epic song. Bede has even rhymed this antithesis: "bella" and "munera." Ambrose then calls martyrs the "vera mundi lumina" (true lights of the world), which Bede will echo in the <P> strophe with an image of stars. Syntactically, Bede has placed his terms of antithesis at the outermost edges of this verse, simultaneously putting "munera" and "canamus" in the all-important center of his strophe, indicating the centrality of a song of thanksgiving. As in the first strophe, a chiasmus is established simply by nature of the form of the poem—although, as we will see, Bede modifies the form's inherent chiasmus in later strophes. Here, the strophe builds on the obvious parallel between "nos pacis" and "nos Christi," and sets the peace of Christ in chiastic antithesis to the battle of Virgil's heroic poem. Finally, this light, dactylic line is divided by the heavy, regal rhythm of the second foot, a spondee. Into that regal spondee Bede has placed the name of Christ.

3. The third strophe begins with <C> in Latin, *Gimel* in Hebrew. We should note that Bede does not coordinate the remainder of the Latin letters with Hebrew letters—the coincidence of *Alpha-Aleph* and *Beta-Beit* is not coordination. To a Latin speaker, *Gimel* might seem to coordinate with *gamma*. To her, the third letter of each holy alphabet sounds similar. Latin <g> is pronounced /k/ and spelled either <c> or <k>, as Isidore and Bede point out in their grammatical works. The third strophe of 118 in the Septuagint is numbered 3, which in Greek is the letter *gamma*, and there named *gimal*.[39] All that

---

39. *Septuaginta*, ed. Hanhart. Coordinating Greek letters with Hebrew ones is not unusual in Anglo-Saxon manuscripts. See Fleming, "'The Most Exalted Language.'" In one, *gimel* is called *camel*, illustrating the unvoiced velar stop. The importance of the order of the letters within each alphabet as opposed to their cross-alphabet coordination is suggested by Cassiodorus, *Explanation*, 3:174.

aside, as we shall see, Bede is not coordinating the alphabets phonologically, but viewing them as homologous entities, comprised of a series of steps—thus, the Christian alphabet has more steps than the Hebrew alphabet. Bede did not need to coordinate Hebrew strophes with the order of the Latin alphabet. After all, it is the Hebrew letters, not the Latin ones, that have semantic force. So Bede follows the serial order of the (Hebrew) strophes in Scripture while using the Latin alphabet—just as the Septuagint followed the order of the Hebrew strophes using the Greek alphabet. The spiritual *gradus* is demonstrated in the Hebrew, strophe by strophe, and cannot be rearranged by a phonological correlation of Hebrew and Latin letters. That *gradus* is demonstrated in Psalm 118 and in Proverbs 31. Thus, the third strophe should resonate with the meaning of *Gimel*, regardless of the Latin alphabet.

According to Jerome, *Gimel* means *plenitudo* 'abundance, fullness' and in his commentary on Hebrew names adds *retributio* 'return, give back', which is what Ambrose says it means. The *Gimel* strophe in Psalms 118, according to Hilary, indicates that reward is the measure of our works and our sins.[40] He tells his readers to remember that the Lord is merciful, and the body is his dwelling place. Christians earn reward by service to God, while the sinner serves sin. Hilary alludes to Paul's first epistle to Timothy 5:5–6, concerning the widow who serves the Lord. The same epistle warns Christians to avoid "the profane novelties of words and oppositions of knowledge falsely so called" (6:20). The "ordo intellegentiae" (order of intelligence) contained in the first verse is the aim of the Law, an aim a Christian aspires to, as he desires the revealed Lamb.[41] Hilary writes of eyes and hands, sight of the present and sight of the future, and seeing through a glass darkly. The Christian, Hilary continues, knows that the Law is spiritual. Some of the distinctions that Hilary draws are between the physical and spiritual, the worldly and the transcendent. And in this context, the Christian is a servant who keeps the

---

40. Hilary, *Commentaire*, 1:146–47.
41. Ibid., 1:154–55.

law in anticipation of a just reward. The *Gimel* strophe of Proverbs is 31:12, and it declares that the *mulier fortis* "will render him good, and not evil, all the days of her life." That is, the soul (*anima*, a feminine noun) doing service (*munus*) and living rightly returns good to Christ. Those who accept good from the Lord repudiate evil, especially heresy. Their speech is not corrupted by evil (cf. 118:17 "I shall keep thy words"). Those who receive good from the Lord and return it to the Lord shall be rewarded. A contrast in this strophe and in the *Gimel* strophe of Psalm 118 seems to be between good and evil and their just rewards.

Bede's third strophe is about Helen of Troy. Helen is decidedly not the *mulier fortis*. Bede writes, "Cārmĭnă | cāstă mĭ|hī fē|dāe nōn | rāptŭs Hĕ|lēnae" (Chaste songs for me, not the abduction of shameful Helen). *Castitas* 'chastity' is a state of virginity; Aldhelm speaks of it as more laudable than the state of widowhood. It refers to "the state attained by someone who has once been married but who has rejected this marriage for the religious life."[42] Aldhelm's acrostic preface to *CDV* speaks of his "carmina castos" (line 1). Some women who rejected or dissolved their marriages were royal: Hildelith of Barking, Hild of Whitby, Eanflaed of Whitby, Cuthberg of Wimborne, and Aethelthryth. Perhaps a portion of Bede's audience was similarly composed.

Bede is singing a *carmen* to the Lord, not meditating on the *carmina* of Virgil. As one who works in the field of words, Bede is reiterating his commitment to Scripture.[43] He reinforces that distinction metrically, singing chaste songs in iambic feet and alluding to the *Aeneid* in spondees (except for the necessary dactyl of the fifth foot). The pentameter reads, "lūxŭs ĕ|rīt lŭbrĭ|cīs || cārmĭnă | cāstă mĭ|hī" (sumptuousness suits the inconstant, chaste songs for me).[44]

---

42. Lapidge, *APrW*, p. 56.
43. A similar phrase occurs in Bede's hymn on the birth of Mary (Hymn 11), verse 17, "Hymnos sacrae quos virgini / Matrique castae dicimus . . ."
44. *Mihi* can be scanned as a pyrrhic or as an iamb; Quicherat, *Thesaurus poeticus*, s.v. *Lubricis* should be scanned lūbrīcīs, but Bede has shortened the first two syllables by poetic license. My thanks to Seppo Heikkinen for his

Augustine equates *lubricis* with scurrilous words, while Prudentius uses it in a verse that echoes these Scriptural *Gimel* strophes:

> Sic tota decurrat dies,
> ne lingua mendax, ne manus
> oculiue peccent lubrici,
> ne noxa corpus inquinet.

(May the whole day pass without sin of tongue, nor of hand nor eye, weak to temptation, nor any fault defile the body.)[45]

Lubricis also has the sense of 'slippery', as in an ambiguous meaning, unsure footing, or inconstancy. *Luxus* is related to *luxuriosus* 'luxurious, prodigious, voracious, lascivious'.[46] Lucan, for instance, describes Cleopatra as *luxus*.[47] Bede uses it for Helen's beauty, and as a figure of ornate and slippery language. *Luxus* also suggests the ornate, high style of classical verse, opposed to the plainer style of Bede's and other Christian hymns. Ausonius of Bordeaux in his *Cento nuptialis* used Helen as an illustration of ornate dress—"ornatus Argivae Helenae" (adornment [worthy of] Grecian Helen).[48] Similarly,

---

help on the meter of this line. Furthermore, *erit* should be a pyrrhic, given that the t-l combination constitutes a mute + liquid, but Bede reads *erit* here as an iamb, perhaps following Fortunatus's "albă smaragdus," *DAM*, pp. 48–9. On the license to change syllable length, see *DAM*, chapter 15, and chapter 3, section 9.

45. Hymn 2, lines 101–4; Prudentius, *Cath.*, p. 11. I have tried to distinguish between <u> and <v> throughout, except when editors insist on <u>, as Lavarenne does here for the enclitic –*ve* 'or'.

46. *TLL*, 7.2.1930. Aldhelm, *CDV*, uses the phrase "lubrica gaudia" (false joys; trans. Lapidge and Rosier, *APV*), lines 946 and 1145; as well as "lubrica oscula" (dangerous kisses; trans. Lapidge and Rosier, *APV*) to describe the temptations of seductresses set on Chrysanthus.

47. Lucan, *Pharsalia*, 10.109–10.

48. Ziolkowski and Putnam, *The Virgilian Tradition*, p. 473. We might compare the much more florid Aldhelm, who opens his *CDV* with the interlocked phrases "Metrica tirones . . . carmina castos" (metrical songs . . . chaste novices), juxtaposing chastity to songs but avoiding the claim of chaste song.

Prudentius in the preface to his *Psychomachia* speaks of the "foedae libidini" (shameful passion) to which the body (*corpus*) can become enslaved (l. 54). To counteract this passion, he asks that Christ enter into the chaste heart of the believer. Bede uses the word *foedus* elsewhere in reference to fornicators.[49] In Prudentius's *Psychomachia*, virtues and vices appear as female warriors who engage in battle; Chastity battles Lust. Likewise, Bede has set a similar pair of ideas to battle each other in this pentameter. In the hexameter, Chastity is set against "raptus"; in the pentameter, chastity is set against "luxus." In Bede's couplet, Chastity appears twice, each time with a different opponent. Perhaps in the hexameter we are to infer an opposition between physical chastity and sexual excess, and in the pentameter an opposition between spiritual chastity and rhetorical excess.

Bede's *sermo simplex*, like the Latin *sermo purus*, represents a chaste style. But perhaps Bede also wants us to know that a chaste style need not be Spartan. He decorates this strophe with alliteration on both <c> and <l>. Alliteration, remarks Marouzeau, was considered a mark of Roman verse as opposed to Greek, so perhaps our ideal reader can sense the *Romanitas* of this strophe. Indeed, alliteration was an essential element of early Latin *carmina*; it is found throughout Plautus, Ennius, and Naevius.[50] But its abuse was always chastised. The abundance of alliteration in this strophe may be intended to refer to that chastisement. In his description of paromoeon (alliteration over two or more lines), Bede cites two psalms: 117:26–27, which alliterates on <d>, and 57:5, concerning serpents, which alliterates on <s>. The sound /s/ was avoided in Latin poetry, as we saw above, although it could be expressive of wind, gliding, or whispering, or indeed the "whistling of a serpent."[51] The liquidity of the <l>, its lubricious glistening, is suggestive perhaps of the Trojan prince's

---

49. Bede, *In epistulas septem catholicas*, 3.2, line 155.
50. Marouzeau, *Traité*, pp. 46 and 47.
51. Ibid., p. 28. Marouzeau writes alliteratively, "le sifflement du serpent." Aldhelm, *CDV*, line 2405, writes "ulterius serpens," bridging the words with the hissing of a serpent. On paromoeon in ASE, see Knappe, "Classical Rhetoric," pp. 21–22.

self-destructive lust.⁵² Similarly, St. Columba's alphabetic hymn "Altus Prosator" in its <C> strophe alliterates on <l> to describe the *lapsu lugubri* (melancholy fall) of Satan.⁵³

One should note also Bede's term *raptus*, which I have here translated as 'abduction'. The term has been carefully studied in regard to Chaucer, who was released from the charge of *raptus* by Cecily Chaumpaigne in 1380.⁵⁴ Scholars cannot agree on its meaning. Its use by Bede is equally ambiguous, perhaps more so, since Bede allows a figurative interpretation. Augustine uses the phrase in his discussion of Psalm 90:4 to describe how a hawk snatches away its prey.⁵⁵ And Gregory the Great in his *Moralia in Job* speaks of the rapture (*raptus*) in Heaven when we are newly recreated after this bitter life.⁵⁶ In the prose version of Aethelthryth's life that precedes the poem, Bede writes of Aethelthryth, "Rapta est autem ad Dominum in medio suorum . . ." (She was TAKEN AWAY however to the Lord in the midst of her own), which is to say amid her own family in Christ.⁵⁷ Here we see a connection between the *raptus* of Helen and the *raptus* of Aethelthryth. Both married women are taken away from their own families and set among others. Bede is explicit on this point:

---

52. Aldhelm in his *PDV* asks to be protected against "the rocks of labdacism," which Lapidge explains is "the intrusion of l-sounds into correct speech"; Lapidge, *APrW*, p. 130.
53. *One Hundred Latin Hymns*, pp. 208–9; trans. Walsh.
54. Cannon, "*Raptus* in the Chaumpaigne Release."
55. Augustine, *Enarationes in Psalmos*, ed. Dekkers, 90.1, §5.
56. Gregory the Great, *Moralia in Job*, 24.6, §11, p. 1195.
57. Bede, *HE*, 4.19, p. 392. The same term is used for Abbess Aethelburh of Barking, *HE*, 4.9, p. 360. Aldhelm, *CDV*, writes of a "raptu angelico" (grasp of an angel; trans. Lapidge), line 1476. Bede may be indicating to the reader the moral bivalence of language (and the things of the world), which may prompt a reader to purify her mind. In his hymn on the birth of Mary (Hymn 11), Bede asks Christ, "Da membra casta corporis" (verse 2); the "casta membra corporis" are chaste limbs of the body, recalling Aldhelm, but *membrum* is typically used to indicate the male reproductive organ. Again, by placing this term in a hymn to virginity, Bede prompts his reader to purify her mind.

Aethelthryth is buried "in medio suorum" (in the midst of them, that is, the nuns). Bede may be suggesting to his ideal reader that she contemplate these two famous queens, how each was removed from her family, and the consequences for those among whom she rests.

There is only one verb in this strophe. But for a pronoun and a particle, the remainder of the words are nouns and adjectives. This is not a strophe of action, but of two opposed states that the reader is invited to compare. Moreover, once a reader discerns the four phrases of the strophe and compares them, she might also compare the syntax. She will find that the syntax is more prosaic when speaking of chaste songs than it is when speaking of the matter of Troy. For example, "chaste songs" is syntactically congruent—physically juxtaposed—while "filthy Helen" is not. Instead, it is rendered into scattered grammatical pieces by the intercalated phrase "non raptus." The next strophe (<D>) is similar: "heavenly gifts" ("dona superna") is physically congruent on the line, but "wretched Troy" ("miserae ... Troiae") is not. Another comparison is metrical. "Carmina" and "casta mi-" are both dactyls, while "fedae" and "(He)lenae" are spondees. Each set of words is connected by rhyme. Again, Bede ensures a strong distinction between the hemistichs and thereby illustrates a difference between the plain style (of Christianity) and the ornate, high style (of Troy). The reader should be enraptured (that is rapt, *raptus*, snatched away from this world) by the spiritual meaning of the words, and not by the rhetorically ornate Helen.

4. The fourth strophe begins with <D> in Latin, *Daleth* in Hebrew. According to Jerome, *Daleth* means *tabulae* 'documents, archives'; Ambrose says it means *timor* 'fear' or *nativitas* 'birth'. Psalm 118:25, the opening verse of the *Daleth* strophe, reads, "Adhesit pavimento anima mea vivifica me secundum verbum tuum" (My soul hath cleaved to the pavement: quicken thou me according to thy word). *Pavimento* 'pavement, hard floor' indicates the world, according to Augustine.[58] The adhesion, Augustine explains, is not of the soul to the body, but

---

58. Augustine, *Exposition*, 5:382.

of the soul to the concupiscence of the flesh. The Psalmist asks to be released from concupiscence, and to increase the longing of the spirit. Psalm 118:27 reminds its reader, "The law of faith is this: that we believe and pray to be empowered through grace to accomplish what we cannot do by ourselves, lest being ignorant of God's justice and attempting to set up our own, we fail to submit to the justice of God."[59] Cassiodorus says similarly that the speakers—a chorus that includes apostles, martyrs, and all who serve the Church—once cleaved to the world, but now they cleave to testimony in the Lord.[60] He also points to the importance of grace, God's gift (*munus*), to growth in Christ. Also focusing on gifts, this strophe of Bede's *Hymn* contrasts the "dona superna" (heavenly gifts) with the battles of Troy—contrasting as well the terrestrial and the heavenly. To the general discussion, Hilary adds that the adhesion of the soul to the *pavimento* is an indication to prostrate oneself toward the earth, to show humility.[61] That humility is suggested in Bede's adjective *miser* 'wretched', connected to the formula found throughout the Psalms, "miserere mei" (have mercy on me, Psalms 4:1, 6:2, 25:16, 26:11, 118:58, and so forth).

Bede's strophe also addresses the theme of separation from concupiscence. This theme is found in Bede's commentary on Proverbs 31:13, the *Daleth* strophe. It reads, "Quaesivit lanam et linum et operata est consilio manuum suarum" (She hath sought wool and flax, and hath wrought by the counsel of her hands). The images here are of weaving and of labor that yields counsel. Bede reminds his reader that the *mulier fortis* is the Church. He cites Isaiah 58:7, "when thou shalt see one naked, cover him, and despise not thy own flesh." Bede writes that the verse suggests that one should work, doing not empty and blind labor, but instead giving counsel and alms to the poor. Thus in Matthew 25:42–45, after Christ's parable of the wise and foolish virgins, we read of the last judgment, when the Lord says to men unworthy for Heaven, "I was naked, and you covered

---

59. Ibid., 5:385.
60. Cassiodorus, *Expositio*, PL 70:847; Walsh, 3:189.
61. Hilary, *Commentaire*, 1:178–79.

me not." *Lana* 'wool' indicates sheep, from which we infer simple labor and piety in all things. Flax originally has color, but after long and careful work becomes brilliant white (*candor*). By that image we are to be castigated to work at the filth of our inborn sin, so that we may be worthy of clothing ourselves for Christ—following Galatians 3:27, "Christum induistis" (have put on Christ). The Church solicitously asks if we have cleansed ourselves of the allure of carnality ("a carnalibus emundet illecebris"). Bede's prose life of Aethelthryth distinguishes between the wool garments (*lana*) that Aethelthryth wears in life and the linen garment (*linum*) that she wears in death.

Like the *mulier fortis*, Bede offers counsel. In the preceding strophe, he set one idea next to another, and this strophe is similarly constructed. It has two verbs; one indicates the poet's act of counsel: *loquor* 'to speak'. Bede's strophe reads, "Dōnă sŭ|pērnă lŏ|quar mĭsĕ|rāe nōn | prōelĭă | Trōiae" (I will speak of heavenly gifts, not of wretched Troy's battles).[62] The syntax derives from the Psalms, as we saw above: *x* but not *y*. As Aethelthryth put off the robes of secular royalty and put on the humble, woolen robes of Christ, Bede again counsels his reader to put off the ornate clothing of Troy and put on the plain clothing of grace ("dona superna"). Bede seems to have modified a dactyl and spondee of Aldhelm's, "sceptra superna" (scepters of Heaven, *CDV*, line 7) by speaking not metonymically of the royalty of Heaven, as Aldhelm had, but plainly of its gifts. Bede has also foregone the alliteration but not the rhyme of Aldhelm's phrase. The conflict (*proelium*) is literal—the battle at Troy—and also figurative. *Proelium* is how Tertullian describes the many battles of the soul with temptation, or the internal battle of the Christian during confession. Ambrose uses the word similarly, while Aldhelm uses it in his description of the battle between the Virtues and Vices.[63] The word can be used to indicate virtually any conflict.[64]

---

62. *Troiae* is usually disyllabic. The <a> of *proelia* is short by nature and remains so because it is followed by a mute + liquid <tr>.
63. Aldhelm, *CDV*, line 2465, "proelia mundi" (battle[s] for the world; trans. Lapidge); used for the last two feet.
64. *TLL*, 10.2.1649–57, s.v.

Proelium serves as a figure of antonomasia, substituting a characteristic for a name. Bede explains antonomasia in *DST* by using examples that avoid naming the Devil (1 Kings 17:14), Judas (Matthew 26:14), but also David (1 Kings 22:7), the disciple John (John 21:7), and even Christ (Matthew 21:9). Antonomasia is also a way of indicating an absent or invisible reality by means of its physical manifestations. In the first hemistich, the phrase "dona superna" refers to the manifest gifts of the Holy Spirit, and the phrase "proelia miserae Troiae" refers to the literary patrimony of Virgil or Homer. In the second strophe, Bede spoke of the "munera Christi" (blessings/gifts of Christ), recalling Cassiodorus's reading of 118's *Daleth* strophe. These gifts are manifest in the world. As Bede writes in his pentameter, "tĕrră quĭ|būs gaū|dēt, || dōnă sŭ|pērnă lŏ|quăr" (I will speak of heavenly gifts by which the earth rejoices). In keeping with his commentary on Proverbs 31:13, Bede shows how the physical world ("terra") is redeemed by the gifts of the Spirit ("dona superna"), how works can be made blessed through grace. Bede expresses this idea through songs (*carmina*) and speaking (*locutus*)—the manifest labor of a monk. This strophe is tied to the last by a similar rhyme scheme and by meter. The first hemistich of both hexameters runs *dd*, metrically associating songs with speech. The second hemistich of both ends *sds*, metrically associating Helen with Troy. The pentameters are identical: *ds + dd*, again associating songs with speech. What distinguishes this strophe most from the earlier ones is that the first hemistich of the pentameter is grammatically congruent with the second hemistich of the pentameter, rather than with the second hemistich of the hexameter. In other words, unlike the previous strophes, this one does not form a grammatical chiasmus; the pentameter stands fully on its own. We have two severed thoughts: the matter of Troy is dispensed with in the hexameter in an ornate, rhyming hyperbaton, and will not appear again in the poem; the matter of Christ appears in the humbler, plainer pentameter.

The first four strophes of the *Hymn* establish an antithesis between the poetry of the pagan past and Christian poetry. From invoking a muse to rejecting the matter of Troy, Bede has portrayed a Christian reformation of the literary arts. His method has been to establish oppositions within oppositions, a mosaic of contraries, each of which invites his reader to contemplate dissonance and concinnity within a Latin literary inheritance. Moreover, the matter of Troy serves as a synecdoche for a nation's establishing narrative. As the *Iliad* was for Greece and as the *Aeneid* was for Rome, so will Christian songs be for Britain. One cannot help but think of Milton, whose *Lycidas* is similar thematically to Bede's *Hymn*, and whose *Paradise Lost* became the great Christian epic of Britain. In the opening line of *Lycidas*, Milton writes, "yet once more," alluding to Paul.[65] Paul explains that with this phrase, "he signifieth the translation of the moveable things as made, that those things may remain which are immoveable." Milton shakes off the pastoral constraints of the lyric tradition of Theocritus and leaves that which is immovable: the Kingdom of God.[66] Bede, too, rejects the transitory appeal of classical matter (as suggested by the verse of Proverbs, "My soul hath cleaved to the pavement") in order to concentrate on the Kingdom of God (as suggested by "quicken thou me according to thy word").

Yet neither poet fully rejects the classical tradition. Both Bede and Milton write within the received, learned tradition, but both use it to speak of "dona superna" and "the Pilot of the Galilean lake."[67] Like Milton at the end of *Lycidas*, Bede in his fifth strophe moves on "to Fresh Woods, and Pastures new."[68] Bede began his poem by invoking the nourishing Trinity; then, he rejected that portion of the tradition that provoked admiration of violence and lust. Now, at this point in the temporal unfolding of the *Hymn*, Bede and his reader are prepared to accept the presence of Christ within a classical literary form. The remainder of the poem will develop the theme of virginity, beginning with the Incarnation (strophe <E>, lines 9–10), turning next to the birth of Christ (strophe <F>, lines 11–12) and choirs of

---

65. Milton, *Lycidas*, line 1; Hebrews 12:27.
66. My thanks to William Kerrigan for his insight into Milton's allusion.
67. Milton, *Lycidas*, line 109.
68. Ibid., line 193.

rejoicing angels (strophe <G>, lines 13–14). Next we will encounter the Blessed Virgin Mary (strophe <H>, lines 15–16). She is described after we read of the Incarnation. Then comes a litany of female saints, virgins, and martyrs (strophes <I–M>, lines 17–24); the birth, life, cloistering, and death of Aethelthryth (strophes <N–V>, lines 25–40); and her Heavenly reward (strophes <X–N>, lines 41–54). In this hymn, a reader encounters not historical time, but successive stages of the revelation of Christ in Britain. Each new strophe builds spiritually upon preceding ones. For example, the chaste songs of Christians (<C> strophe) contrast with the resonating songs of Virgil (<B> strophe) and compares to the choirs of angels (<G> strophe). The <E> strophe, which we shall encounter in a moment, picks up on the "dona pacis" (gifts of peace, line 3) and the "munera Christi" (blessings/presents of Christ, line 4) of the <B> strophe by showing again the descent (that is, the gracious humility) of God and His gifts as they become manifest in the physical realm. Bede now alerts his reader to the approach of God in the present tense.

5. The fifth strophe begins with <E> in Latin, *He* in Hebrew. According to Jerome, the word means *ista* 'that'; Ambrose says it means *est* 'is' or *vivo* 'I live'. Bede seems to have treated this fifth stage in the *gradus* (or rather, the Hebrew letter itself) as semantically suggestive of *this life* and *that life*, that is the life of this world and the life of the next. Hilary comments on Psalm 118:35, noting that the speaker asks for a law. But Moses had already established a law, so the speaker seeks not a law, but the end of the Law ("finem legis").[69] What is the end of the Law? Hilary cites Paul, "For the end of the law is Christ, unto justice to every one that believeth" (Romans 10:4). Cassiodorus also reads this strophe as announcing Christ:[70] "The Lord's justice is the Word made flesh."[71] And as if providing a template for Bede's second, third, and fourth strophes, Cassiodorus writes concerning

---

69. Hilary, *Commentaire*, 1:202.
70. Cassiodorus, *Explanation*, 3:190.
71. Ibid., 3:193.

118:37 that "the blessed crowd begs the Lord to divert the eyes of their hearts . . . so that they may not become enmeshed in worldly delights . . ."[72] He points out especially "spectacles" and "foul love for women" ("mulierum foedo amore").[73] This phrasing makes sense of Bede's "f[o]edae" (filthy, line 5) as applied to Helen in the previous strophe. Aldhelm often uses extreme language in his prolix descriptions of foul, filthy, excremental vice in opposition to virginity.[74] Such language inspires a desire for freedom from worldly delights. Thus Bede's "liberet" in the pentameter: liberty is a central theme in narratives of virginity.

Moreover, of 118:37, Augustine writes, "To covet this world is vanity; but Christ, who frees us from this world ['qui ex hoc mundo liberat'], is truth."[75] Bede connects liberty to the *He* strophe of Proverbs 31 by noting there the soul's desire to be free of this present life. Proverbs 31:14 reads, "facta est quasi navis institoris de longe portat panem suum" (She is like the merchant's ship, she bringeth her bread from afar). In his commentary on the verse, Bede remarks that the Church—of whom the wife is a figure—is laden with gifts of divine grace ("divinae gratiae dona"), which the soul seeks.[76] And like a ship, the soul desires to cross over from this present life, carrying with it its burdens. Thus we read, says Bede, "Come to me, all you that labor, and are burdened, and I will refresh you."[77] The mercantile language of the *He* strophe in Proverbs concludes Bede's explanation; he cites Matthew 6:5, "amen dico vobis receperunt

---

72. Ibid., 3:191.
73. Ibid.; *PL* 70:848D.
74. James Rosier, "Introduction to the *Carmen de Virginitate*," in Lapidge and Rosier, *APW*, p. 98. A common image in the *PDV* is the foul stench of human waste in a dungeon where a virgin sits awaiting martyrdom.
75. Augustine, *Exposition*, 5:393; *PL* 36:1531.
76. Bede, *PL* 91:1043B. Aldhelm is very fond of the image of a ship at sea, using it widely in *PDV* and *CDV*.
77. Matthew 11:28, mislabeled in *PL* 91:1043C as 11:5. The KJV offers a closer parallel to the heavy-laden ship: "Come unto me, all ye that labour and are heavy laden, and I will give you rest."

MERCEDEM suam" (Amen I say to you, they have received their RE-
WARD). Here we see another antithesis: the free gift of grace and the
earned reward of Heaven. Bede concentrates on the gift of grace
brought into the world and human freedom gained through the Son.

The hexameter of Bede's fifth strophe reads, "Ēn Dĕŭs | āltŭs ă|dīt
uĕnĕ|rāndāe | uīrgĭnĭs | ālvum" (See! The High God approaches the
womb of the honorable Virgin); the pentameter reads, "lībĕrĕt | ūt
hŏmĭ|nēs || ēn Dĕŭs | āltŭs ă|dīt" (in order to free men, see, the High
God approaches). The metrical arrangement of the hexameter recalls Fortunatus: *ddds*. As we saw, Fortunatus used it to speak of divinities and battles. The implicit lightness of the dactylic line might
be intended to refer to the celebration (*gaudere*) of line 8, thankful
joy for liberation from sin. And perhaps the implicit speed of Bede's
verse reminds us of the parable of the foolish virgins, referenced
above, instructing Christians to be ready *now* (Caedmon's opening
word), for the Bridegroom might arrive at any minute. (The Bridegroom, *sponsus*, arrives in line 50 of the *Hymn*.) Certainly that is the
sentiment of the first hemistich. In previous strophes, the hemistichs
had been divided thematically, metrically, and sonically. But in this
strophe, Bede reduces any sense of division. The hexameter is sewn
together with alliteration: "venerandae virginis" is surrounded by
"altus adit . . . alvum." Bede uses another device to sew together the
pentameter: assonance. The first hemistich –*es* ends with the same
vowel as the next word *en*, thereby sonically bridging the caesura.
Additionally, the pentameter is framed by homoeoptoton, "liberet"
and "adit." We will see that the next strophe ends each line with similar half-rhymes, which themselves rhyme with those of the following
strophe: "alvum/parentem" and "adit/parit." Those rhymes tie together strophes five and six, both of which concern the Virgin birth.

It is appropriate that Bede uses "altus" in the verse that introduces
this section on the Incarnation (strophes 5–7); Ambrose also used it
in his third hymn to describe the Incarnation. As a result, "altus"
has a hymnic association to the Incarnation. Because it means 'high',
the word "evokes the extremity of that which concerns divinity," as

Jean-Louis Charlet notes.[78] To put it another way, this strophe concerns matters well beyond the reach of men. Authors used *altus* also to suggest a moral or social distance between a reader and the subject matter. Augustine speaks often in his commentary on the Psalms of *altus deus* to remind a Christian of his own humble station. Besides the use of "altus," there may be another echo of Ambrose. Charlet notes that Ambrose used an active participle, "docens" (showing), to indicate the active will of Christ in His own incarnation.[79] Bede also uses an active verb, *adire* 'to approach'. In this strophe, Bede portrays God actively approaching and freeing mankind. (Similar is Christ's active approach to the Cross in *The Dream of the Rood*, partially inscribed in a stone cross at Ruthwell during this period.) These acts are portrayed as things given (i.e, *dona* < *donare* 'to give', line 7), rather than portrayed as things received. And perhaps Bede echoes Ambrose a third time. Ambrose writes that Mary's honor and the high mystery ("alto mysterio," line 22) of the virgin birth were preserved when Mary was formally married to Joseph.[80] Bede, too, points out that honor (*veneratus* 'adoration, reverence, honor' > English *venerable*) was done to the Virgin. From the exalted, active gift of the Incarnation, Bede next turns his reader's focus to the Blessed Virgin Mary.

6. The sixth strophe begins with <F> in Latin, *Vav* in Hebrew. According to Jerome, the word means *et* 'and'; Ambrose says it means "ille est" (that is) or an exclusive *and*. Jerome combines the sixth, seventh, and eighth letters of the Hebrew alphabet into a second *conexio* 'union' that reads "and this life," that is the life of Christians in this world. Where the last strophe focused on the approach of Christ, whose dual nature bridges the natural and supernatural, this strophe focuses on Mary as a gateway to Christ in this world. The

---

78. Hymn 3, ed. Jean-Louis Charlet in Ambrose, *Hymnes*, p. 224. Aldhelm uses it in his *CDV*, line 3 to describe God's "high throne."
79. Charlet, "Hymne 3," p. 223.
80. Ambrose, *Lucam*, pp. 44–45. Ambrose also points out "virgo, qui est ecclesiasticae typus," p. 45.

perspective of the reader is shifted from looking up (*altus*) to looking directly at the *parens mundi* (parent of the world). This shift in perspective is magnificently artful. The perspective of this strophe is similar to the perspective of a congregant in St. Paul's Jarrow. Earlier, we noted that Wearmouth and Jarrow were sites of Marian devotion, and that a portrait of Mary hung at the center of Monkwearmouth's iconography. During the Mass, congregants in the church would have viewed the Host through the door of what amounted to a rood screen.[81] So the Real Presence of Christ in the Eucharist would be visible through its *porta* 'gate, door' above which hung a picture of Mary. The association is obvious. The figure of Mary as *porta Dei* was traditional in Christian writing. Ambrose uses the figure a great deal in his treatise on virginity, *De institutione virginis*.[82] Arator used the phrase "Porta Maria Dei" in his hexameter *Historia apostolica* (I, 52).

Along with the *porta Dei*, other images we have seen resonate with Scripture's *Vav* strophes. Of Psalm 118:41–48, the *Vav* strophe, Hilary notes that they are foolish (*stultus*) who imagine that their learned and polished words are true, and that erudite and learned truth is of their own making.[83] Instead, the Christian understands that wisdom derives from the perfection of the heavenly realm, from the Wisdom of God (who is the Son). Our *salus* 'health, salvation' comes from the mercy of God and the gift (*munus*) of his bounty. (These, ultimately, are the "dona superna" of Bede's <D> strophe.) Awareness

---

81. On the early Northumbrian precursor to the Rood Screen at Monkwearmouth, see Radford, "Saint Peter's Church, Monkwearmouth."
82. Ambrose, *De institutione virginis*, *PL* 16:316–47. Ambrose is considering Ezekiel 40 and 44. Mary is the "porta clausa" (closed gate) of 44:1, and the "bona porta" (good gate) by which mankind crosses over into the Heavenly City, and through which Christ comes into the world; *PL* 16:234B–C, §52–53. See also Ambrose, *De virginitate*, *PL* 16:279–316, at 302B: Ambrose is considering the Heavenly City and Apocalypse 21:10. He writes in this passage of the "lapis pretiosissima" (most precious stone), which we have seen is a comparandum for the Strong Woman of Proverbs 31 in the Old Latin version. Bede considers *porta* in his discussion of the gates of Jerusalem in DeGregorio, *Bede: On Ezra and Nehemiah*, pp. 166–67.
83. Hilary, *Commentaire*, 1:224–25.

of our own sins without the necessary humility narrows our souls so that we become unworthy of the habitation of the Word of God.[84] The term "altus" reminds us of this necessary humility. Through the gift of the Spirit, salvation comes to us—"adit" in this strophe. The Holy Spirit, Augustine writes, dwells in us. Augustine also writes that "Christ himself is the salvation of God."[85] Cassiodorus adds that *Vav* asks that the "salutarem Dominum" (the Lord of salvation) be granted to the speakers, that is, "Dominus Salvator" (the Lord Savior).[86] Both the coming of the divine into the world and God's indwelling in each of us is illustrated figuratively in the virgin birth. The commentaries on *Vav* broach a complex relationship between the indwelling of Christ and the salvation of Christians. Is that relationship one-way, conveyed by God to mankind? Or is it two-way, returned to God? The complicated multiplicity of God's relationship to human salvation is captured by Bede's "porta." The term means both 'gate' (a site of two-way traffic) and 'conveyor' (one-way motion). Mary, as "porta Dei" (conveyor of God), brings Christ, the Means of Salvation, physically into the world. As a subject of veneration, she returns it as "porta" (gate). In both ways, she feeds the faithful with the incarnate Host, like the *mulier fortis*: Proverbs 31:15 reads, "et de nocte surrexit deditque praedam domesticis suis et cibaria ancillis suis" (And she hath risen in the night, and given a prey to her household, and victuals to her maidens).

The hexameter of Bede's strophe reads, "Fēmĭnă | uīrgŏ pă|rīt mūn|dī dē|uōtă pă|rēntem" (The pious virgin woman bears the parent of the world); the pentameter reads, "pōrtă Mă|rīă Dĕ|ī || fēmĭnă | uīrgŏ pă|rīt" (The virgin woman Mary, Gate of God, begets). In the hexameter, Bede uses the verb with an object—"bears the parent." But in the pentameter, there is no object, perhaps implying that the

---

84. Ibid., 1:236–37.
85. Augustine, *Exposition*, 5:399.
86. Cassiodorus, *Expositio*, PL 70:849D–850A; Walsh, 3:192–93. Compare the Communion prayer of the Ordinary of the Mass, "Domine, non sum dignus ut *intres* sub tectum meum . . ." (Lord I am not worthy that you should enter under my roof . . .), my italics.

Virgin continues to beget offspring (such as Aethelthryth and our nun of Barking). Moreover, Bede names Mary only in the pentameter, perhaps implying the typological order of Scripture: like the virgin of the hexameter are the unnamed virgins of the Old Testament (e.g., Gen 24:43). They typify Mary, the Virgin mother of God, as Matthew explains in his gospel (1:22). Turning to form, Bede is artful with his meter here. His pentameter is entirely dactylic. Like a Strauss waltz, the meter lifts the reader with its light touch. The promise of freedom and salvation thereby comes to the reader in Fortunatus's preferred meter for dignified Christian subjects. Bede's hexameter is also largely dactylic, but for two spondees, "pă|rīt mūn|dī dē|uōtă." Their metrical weight is a perfect metaphor for the descent of the anointed ("dēuōtă") Christ into the world ("mūndī"), like a weight sinking through the ether. Phonically, the strophe picks up on earlier lines whose terminal vowels suggested hymns. The <C> stophe gave us "carmina casta mihi" (chaste songs for me), and here, but for the verb "parit," every word ends in a continuant. "Femina," "devota," "porta," and "Maria" not only rhyme, but also phonically suggest the *Alleluia* of the Mass. Bede has introduced variation into this strophe not through meter, but through syllabification. Throughout the poem so far, Bede has varied the length of his words to ensure a pleasing variety. Only two hemistichs so far contain three sequential disyllables: line 8 ("terra quibus gaudet") and the repeated hemistich of strophe 5 ("Deus altus adit"). Bede also limits his use of tetrasyllables: so far in the *Hymn*, there is only one, "venerandae" (venerating). In this strophe, Bede varies trisyllables and disyllables. Hymns were places for *sermo simplex*, not for grandiloquent virtuosic syllabicity. Bede does display virtuosity, but gently.

Like the previous strophe, this one is sewn together by alliteration. In the hexameter, the caesura in the second foot precedes a /p/, "parit," while the caesura in the fifth foot also precedes a /p/, "parentem." Alliteration binds the hexameter to the pentameter, too. "Parentem," the last word of the hexameter, alliterates with "porta," the first word of the pentameter. And "porta" alliterates with "parit," the last word of the strophe. They are also homophonous insofar as they share the same consonants and a vowel. These alliterations bind the whole, reinforcing a contrast with the bifurcated hemistichs of earlier strophes. "Mundi," which reaches back to "terra" in line 8 (and contrasts with "saecula" in line 1), alliterates with "Maria," connecting Mary closely to the world. But perhaps most artful, if our ideal reader wishes to allow it, is the visual grammar of line 12. Here, "Maria . . . femina virgo" surrounds "Dei," as the mother surrounds the unborn child. And surrounding her is "porta . . . parit," the more capacious, abstract designation—the gate who bears, conveys, carries the Christ child. Such a designation contains and defines Mary, and Mary contains the anointed child. We can compare this visual grammar to that of line 9, where "altus Deus" (the high God) sits at the opposite end of the line from "alvum virginis" (the womb of the virgin). So, in line 9, God approaches from on high the womb of the Virgin who must be honored. By line 12, God sits within the Virgin's womb.

7. The seventh strophe begins with <G> in Latin, *Zain* in Hebrew. According to Jerome, *Zain* means *haec* 'this' (feminine); Ambrose says it means *huc* 'hither, to here'. *Zain* strophes seem to contemplate what is *here* on earth as opposed to *there* in Heaven. Commenting on Psalm 118:49, Hilary remarks that all of Scripture calls for hope in heavenly good. We are consoled in the face of menacing secular powers by the hope of eternal promises ("spe aeternorum promissorum consolemur"); the verse in Psalms reminds the servant of God to remember these promises.[87] We are consoled *here, haec* (118:50), a word that refers to the hope God has placed here in *this* world.[88] Verse 52 suggests that the judgments of God that concern us have been established in *this* time (*hoc saeculum*) and in *this* world.[89] Verse 54 indicates that a hymn confessing one's faith should be sung. And, like the Psalms, the hymn should be heard once in the ear, again

---

87. Hilary, *Commentaire*, 1:244–45.
88. Ibid., 1:246–47.
89. Ibid., 1:248.

in the heart, and repeated by the mouth. Divine eloquence should be sung as a song without interruption ("sine intermissione cantatae").[90] Not a moment should pass in which one is turned away from these celestial sacraments ("illo caelestium sacramentorum").[91] Cassiodorus says much the same thing, adding that a Christian would spare little thought for the death of family or friends whom he knew to be joining the chorus of angels ("choris . . . angelorum").[92] Sedulius says in the <G> strophe of his alphabetic hymn, "A solis ortus cardine": "Gaudet chorus coelestium, / Et angeli canunt Deo" (The chorus sings of the heavens / And angels sing of God), using vocabulary similar to Bede's.[93] Bede uses micans 'gleaming, flashing' perhaps thinking of stars and lightening as suggested by Augustine's commentary on 118:55–56, as we shall see in a moment. In contrast, Augustine comments on the image of night. He says, "Our humbled state of mortality can reasonably be called a night, for the hearts of men and women are hidden from each other . . ."[94] Flashing light indicates the opposite of that state, as we shall see below.

Many of these Patristic themes recur in Bede's commentary on Proverbs 31:16. The verse reads, "consideravit agrum et emit eum de fructu manuum suarum plantavit vineam" (She hath considered a field, and bought it: with the fruit of her hands she hath planted a vineyard). Bede comments that "agrum" (field) indicates heavenly inheritance, the blessings on the son by the father (referring to Genesis 27). The field of the Church which has been bought

---

90. Ibid., 1:250.
91. Ibid., 1:252.
92. Cassiodorus, *Expositio*, PL 70:852C.
93. *AH* 2, 23, pp. 36–37, verse 6. Another <G> strophe that contains both "gaudens" and praise of the Virgin is "Amicus sponsi, magno gaudens gaudio," *AH* 12, no. 236, pp. 133–34: "Gaudens in sua parentis visceribus / Mariae sanctae salutantis vocibus." An alphabetic hymn on the Epiphany has a <G> strophe that reads, "Gaudebunt sancti et gaudebunt angeli, / Gaudent prophetae, martyres et virgines / Propter Jesum, qui natus fuit de virgine"; *AH* 19, no. 7, p. 14. See also *AH* 23, no. 10, pp. 13–16.
94. Augustine, *Exposition*, 5:411. Augustine devotes an entire paragraph to explaining the use of *haec*.

represents the joys of eternal life ("gaudia vitae perennis"); we see *gaudia* 'joy' again in Bede's opening verb "gaudet." The Church (*mulier fortis*) plants the vine by sewing the seeds of faith. The field may also be interpreted as the world in which joyful faith is planted, as well as the words of the apostles and the Fathers; we will see the image of vines and flowers in the next strophe.

Bede's seventh strophe reads, "Gāudĕt ă|mīcă cŏ|hōrs dē | uīrgĭnĕ | mātrĕ tŏ|nāntis" (The devoted retinue rejoices over the Virgin Mother of the Thunderer); "uīrgĭnĭ|tātĕ mĭ|cāns || gāudĕt ă|mīcă cŏ|hōrs" (over virginity the gleaming, devoted retinue rejoices). The sentiment of this strophe seems to be fairly commonplace in Scripture; we see it in Jeremiah 31:13, "tunc laetabitur virgo in choro iuvenes et senes simul et convertam luctum eorum in gaudium et consolabor eos et laetificabo a dolore suo" (Then shall the virgin rejoice in the dance, the young men and old men together: and I will turn their mourning into joy, and will comfort them, and make them joyful after their sorrow).

The celestial imagery is especially interesting—thunder and the glittering heavens. "Micans" is used to indicate the glittering or flashing of the heavenly retinue; or perhaps by association, flashing eyes, a common image in Catullus and Ovid ("igne micant oculi," *Met.* 3.33). Virgil likewise uses it several times to describe the lights of the skies. Like Ovid, Ambrose in his *Exameron*, 1.6.20, explains that the flash of the stars is from fire, which derives from Lucretius, *De rerum natura*, 5.514. Similar phrasing is found throughout Cicero's *Arateus*. Bede has used this image from love poetry to speak of virginity. "Micans" also serves to contrast the brightness of Mary with the implied darkness around her, thereby recalling the night and darkness of the *He* strophe of Psalm 118, described by Augustine. Aldhelm continually distinguishes virginity from cupidity using a contrast between dark and light. Further, he distinguishes the "dusky shadow" of the Old Testament from "the clear beauty of the Gospel flashing ['coruscante'] forth."[95]

---

95. Aldhelm, *PDV*, p. 236; Lapidge, *APrW*, p. 65. See also Job 38:31,

The word "tonantis" (*tonans*) seems out of place here, although it does have semantic associations with "micans" (a trembling of sound and a trembling of light). It is a classical epithet for Jupiter. But as we saw earlier, it had been baptized into Christian use. After invoking the Virgin, Arator placed the epithet in a similar passage to describe the resounding heavens.[96] H. J. Arnetzius notes that Arator's line is in imitation of Lucan (I, 35), "Coelumque suo servire Tonanti" (and if heaven could serve its Thunderer).[97] Bede uses a form of *tonans* elsewhere in his *Song on Psalm 112*: "Laudate Altithronum, pueri, laudate tonantem" (praise the High-throned One, children, praise the Thunderer).[98] Bede's immediate source seems to be Aldhelm, *CDV*, line 10, who writes that the saints "with unceasing praise duly glorify the Thunderer ['Tonantem'] ruling his kingdom."[99] Aldhelm uses the phrase again to close a hexameter, as Bede's modified phrase does. In line 86, Aldhelm calls Heaven "rēgnă Tŏ|nāntĭs" (the kingdom of the Thunderer).

Bede was able to achieve a dactyl + trochee by substituting *mātrĕ* for *rēgnă*. This strophe of Bede's is another that relies on Aldhelm for vocabulary, presumably vocabulary that had become common to the discussion of virginity among Anglo-Latin authors. We shall see more of this vocabulary in the following chapters. For now, we can glance at the prose *De virginitate*, in which Aldhelm describes the apostle Thomas. Thomas is said to have preached on virginity in eastern India. Aldhelm writes, "EN, apostolicae clangor bucinae velut TONITRUALI fragore concrepans DEVOTAS VIRGINUM MENTES ad integritatis cultum COHORTATUR" (SEE how the blast of apostolic trumpet, blaring as if with the roar of THUNDER, URGES the DEVOUT MINDS of VIRGINS to

---

"micantes stellas," cited by Aldhelm, *De metris*, p. 72; he describes stars as *micans*, in his letter 5, p. 492.
96. Arator, *De actibus apostolorum*, 1.49.
97. Arnetzius is the editor of Arator, *De actibus apostolorum*; his note is found at PL 68:93D.
98. Hymn 18, line 1.
99. Aldhelm, *CDV*, trans. Lapidge and Rosier. p. 102.

the veneration of integrity).[100] Note the highlighted vocabulary, which we have seen resurface so far in Bede's *Hymn*. Bede is not parroting Aldhelm but rather refashioning Aldhelm's garrulous eloquence into his hymn's simpler style. Like Aldhelm, Bede makes the point that Aethelthryth inspired many women to become virgin nuns.[101] Along with recognizable vocabulary and careful allusion, Bede is employing techniques from Sedulius, Virgil, Ambrose, and others to create a hymn whose meter and syntax contribute artfully to its messages. In the next chapter, we leave antiquity and come to the portion of Bede's *Hymn* that contemplates the Virgin Mary and her acolytes.

---

100. Aldhelm, *PDV*, MGH AA 15, p. 255; Lapidge, *APrW*, p. 81; his trans.
101. Aethelthryth becomes a "mater virgo" ("virgin mother") of "virginum ... devotarum perplurium" ("very many devoted virgins"), Bede, *HE*, 4.19, pp. 392–93.

Chapter Seven

Hymn to Aethelthryth, H–R

We now come to the section of Bede's *Hymn* that concerns female virgin martyrs and saints. Bede's catalogue is limited to women, which is not an obvious choice: recall that John the Baptist is a virgin martyr. Aethelthryth's feast day is the sixteenth Kalends of November (October 17); in line 39, Bede writes "bis octo Novembres" (twice November 8). He does so for metrical reasons, but perhaps also to imply a relation between Aethelthryth and John the Baptist. The Baptist's conception is celebrated on the eighth Kalends of October (September 24) and his birth on the eighth Kalends of July (June 24)—twice eight.[1] Also, Aethelthryth lies in her tomb for sixteen years, or twice eight. Aldhelm writes extensively of male virgins in both his prose and verse *De virginitate*. Ten other works on virginity that circulated in Britain during the seventh century also treat of male virgins.[2] But Bede decided to limit himself to female virgins, even to the extent

---

1. Because the Baptist was thought to have preceded Christ by six months, Christ, too, is celebrated on "twice eight"—the eighth Kalends of April (March 25) and the eighth Kalends of January (December 25). See Ó Carragáin, *Ritual and Rood*, p. 83.
2. See Lapidge and Rosier, *APW*, p. 191, n. 8. They are, following Lapidge's list, Cyprian, *De habitu virginum* (*PL* 4:440–64); Augustine, *De sancta virginitate* (*PL* 40:397–427); Ambrose, *De virginibus ad Marcellinam* (*PL* 16:187–232); Ambrose, *De virginitate* (*PL* 16:265–302); Ambrose, *De institutione virginis* (*PL* 16:305–34); Ambrose, *Exhortatio virginitatis* (*PL* 16:335–64); Tertullian, *De velandis virginibus* (*CCSL* 2, pp. 1209–26); Jerome, *Epistola* 22

of omitting reference to male suitors, torturers, fathers, brothers, betrothed, husbands, priests, or popes. Except for a reference to Virgil, the only *vir* 'man' in the poem is Christ (l. 31), although Christ is elsewhere figured as feminine. Bede's rationale for the litany of virgins and martyrs he names is unknown. Perhaps they relate to cults current in Bede's day, or to patrons of select Anglo-Saxon minsters. My sense is that each shares a different characteristic with Aethelthryth. For example, Agnes and Aethelthryth both share a connection to necklaces and clothing—more generally, to earthly adornment. Another possibility derives from Cassiodorus's discussion of love (*caritas*) in his commentary on Psalm 118:167. He writes of love "tormentis omnibus fortiorem quae flammas vincit, gladios susperat, et coelesti virtute cuncta transcendit" (which is stronger than all tortures, which conquers flames, overcomes swords, and rises above all things with its heavenly power).[3] The parallel is uncanny: in four consecutive strophes of Bede's *Hymn* (9–12), we see death by torture (Thecla, Euphemia), by flame (Agatha and Eulalia), by swords (Agnes and Cecilia), and transcendent triumph over worldly things.

Whatever direct connection to Bede's world those saints may have had, there is also a figurative aspect to naming only women. The *mulier fortis*, who informs this *Hymn*, provides imagery in Catholic tradition used for Christian saints. The *mulier fortis* weaves and makes linen, for example. She represents the universal Church, who is espoused to Christ.[4] Nuns, too, are espoused to Christ. Wives, weaving, wool, linen, virginity, bridal chambers, decoration, beauty—this is not the place to investigate the extremely complex ramifications of imagery of the Church and female martyrs and saints, but we will see much of it in the following strophes. Up to this point, the *Hymn* has rejected the matter of Troy, specifically Helen; that rejection allowed

---

(Loeb, pp. 152–59); Avitus, *De virginitate* (MGH AA 6.2, pp. 274–94); and Fortunatus, *De virginitate* (MGH AA 4.1, pp. 181–91).

3. Cassiodorus, *Explanation*, *PL* 70:896C; Walsh, 3:253–54.

4. Augustine, *De sancta virginitate*, cap. 2, *PL* 40:397. Some of the imagery is explored by Williamson, "Bede's Hymn to St. Agnes of Rome."

a new view of the role of married women (the <F>strophe, "femina parit") to be introduced without prejudice. Bede reminded his reader of the intimate relation between God, Mary, and the unborn Savior. In the <G> strophe, he correlated virginity with celestial joy ("gaudet"). So far in the poem the perspective of the speaking voice has been from the ground looking up. With the <H> strophe, perspective shifts entirely to the terrestrial; we are looking at the world directly. Bede emphasizes this shift to an earthly perspective with an extended metaphor involving seeds and flowers.

8. The eighth strophe begins with <H> in Latin, *Heth* in Hebrew. According to Jerome, the word means *vita* 'life'. Hilary notes of this eighth letter in Psalm 118:57 that the speaker says that the Lord lives in a portion of him ("Portio mea Dominus"), in those places where the cares and vices of this world have been rejected. Prompted by the word "portion," Hilary adduces the examples of a portion of the twelve tribes and a portion of Christians who attain the Promised Land. He cites Matthew 19:28–29, saying that those who leave everything and everyone behind to follow Christ shall receive a hundredfold in this other life (*vita*). Speaking of one of the central paradoxes of Christianity, Hilary says that we must die to the world in order to live in Him.[5] Few will. Cassiodorus, too, describes self-selection, noting that those who acknowledge their own faults (making a place for the Lord to live) and turn their feet to the paths of the Lord "have decided to endure any dangers whatsoever in favor of the Lord's commandments."[6] Such people include the holy chorus singing the psalm, "people of proved devotion, whose fear is most chaste ['castissimo'] and whose love invites respect."[7] Bede will use *castus* in the <K> strophe. Augustine adds that Christ shared in this lot: "Thus the grain of wheat fell into the earth, to die and bear

---

5. Hilary, *Commentaire*, 1:262–63.
6. Cassiodorus, *Explanation*, 3:200–201.
7. Ibid., 3:202. *PL* 70:857A.

a rich yield." The Psalmist contemplates "that abundant harvest."[8] Augustine also introduces an image of a flowering field. Bede's strophe also concerns the crop of the Sacred Seed: the crop, the harvest—these represent the life (*vita, heth*) that proceeds from faith. The *Heth* strophe of Proverbs is 31:17 and reads, "accinxit fortitudine lumbos suos et roboravit brachium suum" (She hath girded her loins with strength, and hath strengthened her arm). Bede writes that "she" is the Church showing contempt for carnal allure and being ardent for the true light.[9] Herein lies a distinction between regeneration of the flesh and regeneration of the spirit, which Bede will employ. The *mulier fortis* has children, but she inspires an increase of virtue. Bede's strophe reads, "Hūiŭs hŏ|nōr gĕnŭ|īt cā|stō dē | gērmĭnĕ | plūres" (Honor of her begat many from the Sacred Seed); "uīrgĭnĕ|ōs flō|rēs || hūiŭs hŏ|nōr gĕnŭ|īt" ([many] virginal flowers honor of her begat). In honoring Mary, women come to emulate her and to follow Christ. Bede's strophe and the *Heth* strophes of Scripture concern a contempt for worldly delights and spiritual regeneration through Christ.

Metrically, we notice immediately the conjunction of word-endings with the last two feet of the hexameter, which has happened only twice before (line 7 and line 9). It is one of the most common endings and has the metrical feel of "búrrowing hédgehóg." Also common is the caesura in the third foot, the twin dactyls opening the verse, and the variation achieved with two spondees. After several strophes of metrical play, Bede has returned to a fairly standard metrical arrangement. One might note that spondees mark out "plūrēs" and "flōrēs," both things of the world. If things of the world are marked with the associative weight of spondees, we see that "cāstō ... gērmĭnĕ" comprises a spondee and a dactyl—perhaps implying that the Sacred Seed is part of this world and part of the other. The abstractions HONOR and SPIRITUAL BEGETTING are dactylic. An admixture

---

8. Augustine, *Exposition*, 5:416–17: "granum cecidit in terram, ut mortificatum multum fructum faceret; de ipso fructu secutus adiunxit..."

9. Bede, *PL* 91:1045A. The true light, *vera lux*, is Christ. See below.

of abstract, spiritual things and concrete, terrestrial things is thus expressed in a robust admixture of feet. The relation of the flowers to spiritual life is suggested at the outset of Bede's *De die iudici*. Of course, a flower is a traditional image for a virgin; Aldhelm uses it throughout his prose and verse works on virginity. In the passage in which he spoke of the flashing light of the New Testament and of the Thunderer, Aldhelm speaks of "virginitatis flores."

As well as meter, syntax and sound send a reader's mind in multiple directions. The alliteration of the first two words, "huius honor," recalls "carmina casta" of strophe 3, the only other strophe in the poem with initial alliteration. The same strophe is recalled through the adjective "casto" 'chaste, pure, sacred', which we hear in both strophes. Alliteration on <h> calls attention to a second alliteration, on <g> ("genuit . . . germine"), that ties the first hemistich of the hexameter to the second. No such alliteration ties the hexameter to the pentameter, though, thus serving to isolate the pentameter. That isolation allows the reader to see two distinct statements—one in the hexameter, one in the pentameter. Thus, "virgineos flores" is read as an independent object of the repeated epanaleptic hemistich, "huius honor genuit." When the reader completes the hexameter in isolation, the adjective "plures" (many) must act as a substantive. But once the reader reaches the end of the pentameter, that "plures" suddenly becomes either an appositive to "virgineos flores" (i.e., begat many, / begat the virginal flowers) or an adjective that modifies them (i.e., begat many virginal flowers), thereby enjambing the verses. The separation between the two statements (of the hexameter and the pentameter), which had seemed so clear is now unclear. A sense of continuity and a sense of separation are both at play.

One rhetorical figure here is therefore antithesis. Another is prolepsis, where "plures" anticipates "virgineos flores." A reader might see similar anticipation in the term "germine" (seed), which perhaps anticipates "flores" (flowers). Increasing a sense of continuity is the parallelism of "casto germine" and "virgineos flores." Note also the underlying sonic continuity provided by /r/, a sound Bede calls naturally harsh (durum).[10] That lexical parallelism gives us an image of the chaste Christ bringing forth chaste virgins. As we saw earlier in the chapter on Aethelthryth, the image is paradoxical if not read spiritually. Paradox is seeing continuity in discontinuity, something Bede achieves in this strophe sonically, rhetorically, and syntactically. He has built an opposition in this strophe between chastity ("casto," "virgineos," and the apostrophe to Mary, "huius") and fecundity ("genuit," "germine," and "flores"). A similar chaste fecundity is described in 1 John 5:1, a passage cited by Hilary in his exposition of the *Heth* strophe of Psalm 118: "Whosoever believeth that Jesus is the Christ, is born of God. And every one that loveth him who begot ['genuit'], loveth him also who is born of him." Within these overlaid paradoxes of sound and sense, Aethelthryth is portrayed as the chaste spiritual mother of many children—a portrait that Bede will pick up again later in the *Hymn*.

9. At this point the Hebrew and Latin alphabets are most clearly out of alignment. Although it might be tempting to skip a Hebrew letter and coordinate *Iod* with <I>, *Kaph* with <K>, and *Lamed* with <L>, the point of the alphabetic poem is to move through the letters of a particular alphabet like rungs on a ladder. Again, we are not coordinating alphabets phonically, but ascending a spiritual ladder described in the order of Hebrew letters. The next rung in Latin is <I>, and the next rung in Hebrew is *Teth*. So Bede's ninth strophe begins with <I> in Latin, but its sense derives from *Teth* in Hebrew. According to Jerome, the word means *bonum* 'good'. Jerome combines *Teth* and *Iod* into a third *conexio* that reads "good beginning," setting this earthly life in conjunction with a heavenly reward. This is precisely what Bede is doing in strophes 9 through 12: the earthly life of six virgin martyrs is lauded, along with their spiritual reward.[11] Hilary

---

10. *DAM*, chapter 14, pp. 126–9. My thanks to an anonymous reader from West Virginia University Press for this observation.

11. All but one of these virgin martyrs (Euphemia) are treated by Aldhelm. The following list gives pages in the translations by Lapidge (prose, *APrW*)

precedes his exposition of the *Teth* strophe of Psalm 118 (vv. 65–72) with a review. The psalm, he writes, contains nothing but instruction for human life ("doctrinam humanae vitae").[12] The psalm forms us like the letters of the Hebrew alphabet, thanks to the lessons in doctrine that we receive in their proper order. This ninth letter indicates that joy has arrived. Now joy is not the same thing as constant happiness, like that enjoyed by a Lotus-eater. Joy includes suffering, for even in suffering and tribulation ("passione ac tribulatione") the affection of the Father is recalled. Temptations test patience and in adversity God's grace comes.[13] Recalling Jerome's *bonum*, Hilary notes that "Bona ergo est severitatis disciplina" (Good therefore is the discipline of severity) so that it may correct vice.[14] Cassiodorus writes similarly that in the ninth letter the "blessed folk . . . give thanks that they have been made humble so that they might with total devotion attain the Lord's justifications."[15] And again, that they are thankful "for the affliction which wins salvation."[16] This strophe concerns the joy of suffering and martyrdom.

The *Teth* strophe of Proverbs 31, verse 18, reads, "gustavit quia bona est negotiatio eius non extinguetur in nocte lucerna illius" (She hath tasted and seen that her traffic is good: her lamp shall not be put out in the night). "Negotiatio," writes Bede, refers to *agri*, which is the field of endeavor seen earlier. Holy Mother Church desires what is good ("bona"), that is, whatever in this life earns heavenly reward. With regard to the lamp, we have already seen the moral valences of light and dark. If the lamp is filled with the "oil of charity" ("oleum charitatis") then the light of the Holy Church will not be extinguished. Bede uses this image of fire (*ignis*) to illuminate the spiritual achievements of Agatha and Eulalia. Because of the epanaleptic

---

and Rosier (verse, *APW*): Cecilia (p. 107, p. 141), Agatha (p. 107, p. 141), Agnes (p. 112, p. 145), Thecla (p. 113, p. 146), and Eulalia (p. 113, p. 147).
12. Hilary, *Commentaire*, 2:10.
13. Ibid., 2:12.
14. Ibid., 2:14.
15. Cassiodorus, *Explanation*, 3:202.
16. Ibid., 3:203.

form and the demands of meter, Bede had to choose two virgin martyrs with metrical names who suffered fire. But that ought not to dissuade us from pursuing their figurative implications. Bede's ninth strophe reads, "Īgnĭbŭs | ūstă fĕ|rīs uī|rgō nōn | cēssĭt Ă|gāthe" (The burnt virgin Agatha did not yield to the savage flames); "Ēulălĭ(ă) | ēt pēr|fērt || īgnĭbŭs | ūstă fĕ|rīs" (And Eulalia endures, the burnt one to savage flames).

My English translation unfortunately masks the syntax of the Latin. Bede has placed Agatha (d. February 5) physically next to Eulalia (d. February 12) in the middle of the strophe, connecting them spatially as well as phonically with the same long vowel (AgathĒ Ēulalia), motivating hiatus. At each end of the strophe sits fire. Again, if our reader will allow the visual grammar, we see both virgins cheek by jowl amid the flames. The serial experience of our reader as she processes the words of the strophe reveals the nature of the fire. First comes "ignibus," a dative (or ablative) plural; it awaits a verb and subject. A reader anticipates that this fire is inflected as an instrumental dative. But what sort of fire? Is it a purifying fire as seen in the burning bush, a sign of God's presence? Is it a sacrificial fire of a Temple holocaust? Is it the inspiring fire of Pentecost? Or is it one of the four figurative fires of Fursa's vision?[17] "Usta" 'burnt' answers the question. The stubble of a field is burnt (*ustus*), for example.[18] An *ustor* is "one employed to burn dead bodies."[19] The reader now knows it to be a consuming fire. But the word

---

17. *HE*, 3.19. See also Bede, *De tabernaculo*, 3.1, p. 107: "Let Aaron and his sons offer not some illicit fire, but rather the fire that was sent from above to kindle the lamp, and also to consume the holocausts and to diffuse the fragrance of the incense . . . This fire they use to enlighten the hearts of their hearers with the knowledge of faith, to complete the holocausts of their good works and consecrate them to God, and to burn the incense of holy prayers." Bede uses the image of the kindled lamp again in his *Hymn on Pentecost* (Hymn 7), p. 424, verses 6 and 7. The flames fill the spirit with charity and the mind with ardor (verse 10).
18. Isidore, *Etym.*, 17.3.18; Barney, p. 338.
19. *OLD*, s.v.

is a feminine participle, an adjective describing corporeal suffering waiting for its noun. Next, the image is made even more unpleasant with "feris," which connotes wild animals, savage barbarians, or uncultivated land. Isidore says that animals "are termed wild (*ferus*) because they enjoy a natural freedom and are driven (*ferre*) by their own desires . . ."[20] We shall see that association with desire again in the Hymn's last strophe ("tulerat," line 54). That implicit desire will contrast with the virgins at the heart of the flames. The unfolding sense of the line is of increasing ferocity.

A reader next comes to "virgo," a nominative, which therefore stops the developing flow of the sentence. The dative plural phrase is now concluded, and the adjective and noun connected. Here in the third foot is found the subject to govern the flames. ("Virgo" rhymes with "casto" of the previous strophe, has the same metrical weight, is related semantically, and is also experienced in the third foot of the hexameter.) Also, the hissing *s*'s of the flames—"ignibus usta feris"— cease with "virgo," as do the running dactyls. Dare our reader imagine that the r of "virgo" growls back at the r of "feris"? With "virgo" comes a series of spondees, stating slowly and dramatically that "the virgin did not yield." Then another dactyl and two hissing s's before the spondees return to pronounce the saint's name, "Agāthē." After a light dactyl to name the saint, Ēulălĭă, the pentameter continues with spondaic dignity. Bede dramatically states that "she endures" ("ēt pērfērt"), also changing from the perfect to the present tense (*–ert*), presumably to gain a spondee, but also for emphasis and to indicate the continuing relevance of the story to his reader.[21] Then the reader once again encounters hissing, dactylic flames. As the whole experience of the strophe is digested, a reader feels the hissing, fiery, outer dactyls and the dignified, spondaic saints in their midst.

---

20. Isidore, *Etym.*, 12.2.2; Barney, p. 251. Prudentius described the office in his *Peristephanon* (or *Book of Martyrs*) 10.847, concerning St. Romanus of Caesarea in a particularly gruesome passage describing torture and corpses torn by dogs.

21. On Bede's use of the vivid historic present, see Grocock and Wood in Bede, *HA*, pp. lxxiii–lxxiv.

The nominatives—Agatha and Eulalia—sit still in the middle of the strophe, bracketed by verbs governed by the saints' names ("cessit" and "perfert"), which are themselves bracketed by grammatically inflected fire. Their cool stillness contrasts with the burning activity of the flames, appropriate for winter saints of the Mediterranean.

10. The tenth strophe begins with <K> in Latin, *Iod* (or *Yodh*) in Hebrew. According to Jerome, the word means *principium* 'beginning'. Hilary opens his comments on *Iod* by noting that the beauty and decoration of the world tell us of God. The beauty of the world—its look, decoration, and use—is for our benefit. The creatures of the water and the earth and the air all offer us knowledge from which we can profit.[22] But the faculties of the mind must be prepared to receive the benefit of this knowledge. If one falls into sin ("in vitia deciderit"), one loses the ability to gain that knowledge. This correlation between knowledge and acting in the image of God was established "in creatione mundi," at the beginning of the world—in *principium*, as Jerome translated *Iod*.[23] A similar relationship between knowledge and good works is established in the *Iod* strophe of Proverbs, 31:19. It reads, "manum suam misit ad fortia et digiti eius adprehenderunt fusum" (She hath put out her hand to strong things, and her fingers have taken hold of the spindle). According to Bede, "fortia" signifies charitable works. Bede writes that heavenly reward comes from loving one's enemies, doing good to them (Matthew 5:43–44), and guarding one's virginity ("de virginitate servanda").[24] The Church patiently suffers the world's hardships and is strong in the face of violence (citing Matthew 9:12).

The image in this verse of spinning—with the distaff in the left hand and the spindle in the right—signifies the present life (left) and eternal life (right). We must gather goods widely, as the unspun wool is gathered in the left hand, but do so for the love of God, as the spun

---

22. Hilary, *Commentaire*, 2:24.
23. Ibid., 2:28.
24. Bede, *PL* 91:1046A.

wool of the Lamb is gathered around the spindle of intelligence in the right hand.[25] That is, one must always keep in mind the higher law of God. Bede elsewhere speaks of a need for higher faculties to ensure a better presbytery. He writes, "For all those who are to be advanced to a higher rank in the Holy Church must apply their minds to the law of God with greater industriousness . . . with a mind that is more astute than the rest."[26] Leaders of the Church must possess an "exceptional eminence ['mentis culmine'] of their minds."[27] (Bede will use that same phrase in this strophe.) Cuthbert says that his teacher Boisil is such a person.[28] When that eminence of mind is corrupted, as happened to the British bishops in the *HE* (1.14), God's wrath arrives. In Britain, the luxury that accompanied victory over the Picts brought on the fierce (*fera*) Saxons. The *Iod* strophes of Proverbs and the *Hymn* set the higher faculties of the mind ("culmen mentis") against the ferocity ("feras") of suffering and divine retribution. Bede's strophe reads, "Kāstă fĕ|rās sŭpĕ|rāt mēn|tīs prō | cūlmĭnĕ | Tēcla" (Chaste Thecla by the eminence of her mind overcomes beasts); "Ēufĕmĭ|ā sā|crās || kāstă fĕ|rās sŭpĕ|rāt" (chaste Euphemia overcomes accursed beasts). Thecla was a disciple of St. Paul who vowed perpetual virginity; Bede puts her martyrdom on September 23.[29] Euphemia (d. September 23) was martyred by a lion. Like Agatha and Eulalia, these virgin martyrs are celebrated a week apart in the same month.

We see "feris" from the previous strophe ("feris ignibus," fierce flames) reappear in this one, "feras." Both evoke the barbaric, fierce

---

25. Bede expounds the image of left and right hands in DeGregorio, *Bede: On Ezra and Nehemiah*, pp. 162–63. Note again the figurative relation of wool to Aethelthryth's clothing.
26. Bede, *De tabernaculo*, 3.2, p. 109. Compare Bede, "Homily I.13 on Benedict Biscop," in *HA*, pp. 1–19, pp. 4–5, §2.
27. Bede, *De tabernaculo*, p. 110.
28. Bede, *Vita sancti Cuthberti*, c. 22, p. 230; ed. Colgrave.
29. Bede describes Thecla "quae a Paulo Apostolo instructa in confessione Christi, ignes et bestias devicit" (who was trained in the confession of Christ by the Apostle Paul and was overcome by fire and beasts); Quentin, *Martyrologes*, p. 93.

tortures undergone by those who live calm, wholly ordered lives. An opposition between a disordered, bestial savagery and the civilized behavior of martyrs is essential to the point. As described in earlier chapters, the Christian aspires to live in the image of God with an ordered, moderate, properly disposed life. Sin is an irrational imbalance or disordered excess of something otherwise natural—desire, hunger, sleep, and so on. But the opening words of the hexameter seem to confuse this essential distinction between order and disorder. "Kasta" is a variant of *casta* 'chaste', which appeared earlier as the second word in the <C> strophe. There it modified Bede's songs ("carmina casta"). A reader bearing in mind the third strophe in which the saints were contained by outer fires might now be alarmed by the adjective "kasta," since it is so closely juxtaposed to beasts at the outer edges of the strophe. Not for another five feet of the hexameter will a reader encounter the name Thecla, which is the noun attached to "kasta," eventually giving us "chaste Thecla." Bede's use of "kasta" plays masterfully with semantic suspension, perhaps in order to make a subtle point about the time necessary for discernment. As with the rhetorical figure of zeugma, a reader must patiently read the entire phrase before coming to a sound judgment. Bede suggests the same thing with "sacras" in the pentameter. The word usually means "holy," although it can sometimes mean "accursed." Because "sacras" sits next to "kasta," the meaning "holy" is obviously inferred. But a reader then encounters "feras," immediately pairing it with "sacras," flipping the meaning of "sacras" from "holy" to "accursed" in her mind. Over time and through a fog of grammatical ambiguity, she soon discerns a chaste Euphemia among the accursed beasts.

Ambiguities are clarified in a particular order as the reader plows through the verse. The position of words is not only important to the order in which the meaning of the strophe unfolds, and to the specific play of ambiguities, but it also serves as a figure. As in the previous strophe, these two virgin martyrs sit calmly in the middle of the strophe, cheek by jowl between the beasts at either end. Increasing a reader's sense of chiasmus, Thecla and Euphemia are joined by rhyme and euphony (requiring hiatus) across the line break. The primary difference between this pentameter and the previous one is its intertwining syntax. The accursed beasts and chaste Euphemia are physically intertwined in the line, much like Aeneas and Dido in the famous verse of the *Aeneid* (discussed above). But where Dido had to reach around the leader for the conjunction ("Dido duc et"), Euphemia and the beasts are separated by their juxtaposed and intertwined adjectives—literally, "Euphemia *accursed* chaste *beasts*." This syntactic pattern contributes to the simultaneous synonymy and antonymy of *casta* and *sacra*. Bede's discerning reader gathers the unspun wool of the words and weaves out their meaning "pro culmine mentis" (by the eminence of her mind), which makes order out of apparent disorder. Thus is illustrated the role of her orderly, educated, God-centered mind in discerning meaning. She will next encounter ideals of joy ("laeta") and a sober heart ("sobria corda") in the next two strophes.

11. We have reached the center of the Hebrew alphabet (22 letters), but not of the Latin one (23 letters). This strophe marks the last of Bede's brief litany. The eleventh strophe begins with <L> in Latin, *Kaph* in Hebrew. According to Jerome, the word means *manus* 'hand'. Jerome combines *Kaph* and *Lamed* into a fourth *conexio* that reads "hands of the heart," signifying the faith necessary to good deeds. The literal meaning of *Kaph* is clear in Proverbs 31:20, which reads, "manum suam aperuit inopi et palmas suas extendit ad pauperem" (She hath opened her hand [*Kaph*] to the needy, and stretched out her hands to the poor). Bede writes very briefly about this verse. The verse is to be understood as signifying both works of charity and the word of God, which is bestowed on the soul like a garment of salvation. Bede associates the figure of a garment with both Agnes and Aethelthryth. Cassiodorus, speaking of the *Kaph* strophe in Psalm 118 (vv. 81–88), says that the singers now "relate their great sufferings from the persecutions of the proud."[30] He notes that the word

---

30. Cassiodorus, *Explanation*, 3:209.

defectus, found in verse 81, indicates an end, as in Psalm 9:7, "The swords of the enemy have failed ['defecerunt'] unto the end." It is an example appropriate to Bede's strophe, which concerns the failure of swords in the ultimate victory of these virgin martyrs. Agnes was killed with a sword because fire would not consume her. Some say she was lanced in the neck; so was Aethelthryth—a doctor lanced her tumor. In his hymn on Agnes, Ambrose relates the executioner's fire to paganism, and light to Christianity. Flames also suggest erotic passion, which Agnes's chastity conquered.[31] But Ambrose does not mention a sword except to say that Agnes was pierced ("percussa," line 25). Prudentius describes the sword, *ferrum* 'iron', and as it is thrust, Agnes says that she is more joyful ("laetior") and exults ("exulto"). She willingly accepts the sword into her breast ("ferrum in papillas omne recepero"), as it will quench the burning (*calentia*) desire of her suitor.[32] In his *Martyrology*, Bede noted that Cecilia, too, was killed by iron—a synecdoche for a sword, and therefore an intriguing euphemism that serves to connect these saints in Bede's mind.[33] The relation between Agnes (< Lat. *agnus* or *agna* 'lamb') and swords may trigger in a reader the verse of Isaiah (34:6) concerning the sword of the Lord ("gladius Domini") thickened by the blood of lambs ("sanguine agnorum").[34]

---

31. Hymn 8, ed. Gérard Nauroy in Ambrose, *Hymnes*, pp. 363–403, at p. 297. Ambrose's distinction and phrasing are echoed by Sedulius, *CP* 1:205, noted by Nauroy.

32. Prudentius, Hymn 16, lines 68–69 and 77. Compare Aelfric's life of Agnes in Skeat, *Aelfric's Lives of the Saints*, 1:184, line 244. Rhonda L. McDaniel makes sense of all these sources in "Agnes among the Anglo-Saxons."

33. Quentin, *Martyrologes*, p. 60, "ignem quidem superans, sed ferro occisa."

34. For variant spellings of the saint's name (Agnes, Agne, Agna), see *Acta Sanctorum* 2 (21 January), p. 714. The name in Greek means 'purity' or 'chastity'. Her name figured in the litany of the Roman mass. For an overview of Anglo-Saxon knowledge of Agnes, see E. Gordon Whatley, "Acta Sanctorum," in Biggs et al., *Sources of Anglo-Saxon Literary Culture*, 1:57–9. St. Ambrose wrote her *acta*; *De virginibus ad Marcellinam* (see above), lib. 2. He says she was decapitated, not burned. Prudentius wrote a poem about her (Hymn 14 of his *Peristephanon*). It was used in the Mozarabic breviary

Also important in the psalm's *Koph* strophe is a distinction between "bodily eyes" ("carnalibus oculis") and "eyes [or light] of faith" ("fidei lumine"); that is, discerning worldly significance from spiritual significance.[35] That Cassiodorus should use *lumen* 'light' here correlates to Ambrose's spiritual distinction between fire and light. The psalm strophe also distinguishes between this life and eternal life: the singers "asked to be given life through a glorious death, so that by losing this life for the faith they might purchase eternal rest . . ."[36] Bede's strophe reads, "Lāetă rĭ|dēt glădĭ|ōs fēr|rō rō|būstĭŏr | Āgnes" (Joyful Agnes, stronger than iron, laughs at swords); "Cāecĭlĭ(ă)| īnfē|stōs || lāetă rĭ|dēt glădĭ|ōs" (joyful Cecilia laughs at hostile swords). "Ferro" picks up on Prudentius as well as a detail in a *vita* in which her blood is said to have been powerful enough to extinguish fire. Moreover, it is the third instance of a phonically similar term in these three recent strophes: "feris," "feras," and "ferro." The phonic shape of these three words is perhaps intended to set them subtly against "flores" in the <H> strophe. That phonic distinction and variation between the martyr strophes is continued by the vowels: the vowels of the pentameter of the <K> strophe are dominated by /a/ (especially "sacras kasta feras"), while a major role in the following hexameter of the <L> strophe is played by /o/ (especially "gladios ferro robustior"). We can imagine Bede alert to the sound of these strophes in anticipation of their performance by choirs.

Bede wrote a hymn to St. Agnes.[37] There he describes her receiv-

---

during her feast day. See Prudentius, *Peri.*, pp. 190–95. Bede commented on portions of this chapter of Isaiah; see Bede, *On What Isaiah Says*, p. 47.

35. Cassiodorus, *Explanation*, 3:211; *PL* 70:863B. Similarly, Hilary, *Commentaire*, 2:5–55.

36. Cassiodorus, *Explanation*, 3:213; *PL* 70:865A. Similarly, Bede, *Vita Felicis*, p. 141; and in his commentary on Genesis, citing Psalm 118; Kendall, *Bede: On Genesis*, p. 154.

37. "Illuxit alma saeculis," (Hymn 3), pp. 414–15. Kendall and Wallis consider this hymn to be genuine. See also Williamson, "Bede's Hymn to St. Agnes of Rome." Bede, *Martyrology*, writes, "gladio percussa est"; cited by Williamson, p. 43. Prudentius also wrote a hymn to Agnes; Hymn 14, "Passio Agnetis," in *Peri.*, 4.196–200.

ing "gaudia vitae" (joys of [eternal] life). Although a commonplace in *vitae*, Bede's prominent use of *gaudia* in his Agnes hymn resonates with his adjective *laeta* 'joyful, delighted'. Bede also associates another important virgin martyr, John the Baptist, with rejoicing (*laetare*) and joy (*gaudia*).[38] These characteristics appear in Prudentius, as well; he writes that having ascended to Heaven, Agnes looks down on the world and laughs ("ridet," line 96)—like Troilus at the end of Chaucer's *Troilus and Criseyde*. Agnes is relevant to Aethelthryth in a number of ways, but they both share a relation to necklaces. In a passion of Agnes known to Bede, Agnes is reported to have said of Christ, "Dextram meam et collum meum cinxit lapidibus pretiosis" (My right hand and my neck he has cinched with precious stones).[39] We have seen those precious stones before in descriptions of Christian virgins. Aethelthryth famously wore resplendent necklaces as queen, and she was struck with a tumor on her neck in apparent retribution. When she was disinterred, the tumor was found to have dissolved, leaving only a thin, red line. The dual significance of necklaces is paralleled by a dual significance of clothing. As described above, in verses 6 and 7 of his hymn to Agnes, Bede describes the difference between Agnes's terrestrial dress and her spiritual dress, a difference also described in his Aethelthryth story. These differences are figuratively related to the Church and the trials that beset her.[40] Cecilia is said to have been clothed with a hair shirt, while Aethelthryth, Bede writes, was known to have refused linen garments and worn only woolen ones.[41]

Correlating with the two keys of St. Peter, Bede writes that Agnes left the iron gates ("ferreas portas") of the world to enter the golden

---

38. Hymn 8, verse 1, p. 426. Fortunatus calls Agnes "virgo felix," Hymn 14, line 124.
39. In Williamson, "Bede's Hymn to St. Agnes of Rome," p. 53. Aldhelm draws the same distinction between married women and virgins in his *PDV*, p. 246; Lapidge, *APrW*, p. 73.
40. Williamson, "Bede's Hymn to St. Agnes of Rome," p. 65; she discusses the spiritual significance of these garments, pp. 60–64.
41. Bede, *HE*, 4.19, p. 391, "solum laneis vestimentis."

palace ("auream regiam") of Heaven.[42] She is therefore figuratively "robustior ferro," stronger than iron. Bede describes the ascent into Heaven in another hymn as a mockery of mortality, "Derisus a mortalibus."[43] Bede seems to imply Agnes laughing at mortality as well. Consider the repetition highlighted in the juxtaposed words, "ferRO ROBustior." In a review of classical poetry, Herescu observes, "Même les noms contentant des syllables redoublées sont généralement ressentis comme expressifs, le plus souvent teints d'une nuance de ridicule ou d'obscénité" (Similarly, nouns that contain redoubled syllables are generally felt to be expressive, most often tainted by a nuance of ridicule or obscenity).[44] With "ro ro" we hear Agnes laughing. The preceding dactyls contribute to the lightness of her laugh, set off from the images of hostility and iron rendered in heavy spondees. The swords of this strophe are also significant. In a homily, Bede writes that by *gladium* is signified "the Lord's passion and death on the cross, and this sword will pierce Mary's soul, for she could not without painful sorrow see him crucified and dying."[45] The swords that surround the two virgin martyrs in the middle of the strophe imply that eternal salvation is achieved through, or perhaps despite, earthly suffering. One might also note that as in the preceding strophe, in which "kasta" was separated from "Tecla," so is "laeta" separated from "Agnes." In both cases, the means of execution are interposed between the attribute (adjective) and the saint (noun). Similar, too, is the close juxtaposition of the saints at the break in the strophe, their names bracketing a suspension in syntax, a moment of quiet as the completed hexameter gives way to the pentameter. Finally, Bede closes the strophe with an /s/, lending a sense of completion to the couplet, whose verse-final "Agnes" and

---

42. Bede distinguishes the spiritual meanings of gold and iron in his commentary on the Tabernacle; *De tabernaculo*, book 1, c. line 1368. Williamson, "Bede's Hymn to St. Agnes of Rome," has a very nice translation of Bede's *Hymn to Agnes*, pp. 55–56.
43. "In Ascensione Domini," Hymn 6, stanza 2, line 8, p. 419.
44. Herescu, *La Poésie latine*, p. 59.
45. Bede, Homily, 18, trans. Martin and Hurst, *Bede the Venerable*, p. 184.

"gladios" will resonate with the upcoming <M> strophe's "Multus . . . triumphus."

12. Narrative perspective shifts again in the twelfth strophe. Like the narrator of *Beowulf* who occasionally steps back to offer proverbial wisdom, the speaker of the *Hymn* steps back to describe the wider world. This shift in perspective serves to set off earlier strophes, and by implication to anticipate a new section of the poem—we are at the middle of the Latin alphabet. A reader is thereby invited to compare upcoming strophes to earlier ones. For example, the shift in this strophe from particular saints to a global perspective is mirrored later by a shift from a particular saint, Aethelthryth, to a wide view of salvation history in the <Z> strophe. The twelfth strophe begins with <M> in Latin, *Lamed* in Hebrew. According to Jerome, the word *Lamed* means "disciplinae sive cordis" (of instruction or of the heart).[46] *Lamed* concludes the fourth *conexio* of Jerome, which has focused on the hand and the heart, representing works and charity. As the <M> strophe shifts perspective, so does the *Lamed* strophe of Psalm 118. Its first verse reads, "For ever, O Lord, thy word standeth firm in heaven" (118:89). Hilary comments that the psalm's speaker is not limited to speaking of humble or ordinary ("pervulgatis") topics, but will treat of elevated and dignified topics concerning God ("excelsa et Deo digna tractare").[47] This new perspective serves to improve our knowledge of invisible realities, and seems to inform Bede's narrative move. Hilary then develops a distinction between permanent things in Heaven and transitory things on earth ("in terris," while Bede uses "in orbe"). Hilary also notes Matthew 24:45, "Heaven and earth shall pass, but my words shall not pass." Ambrose notes that *cor* recalls Mary, who kept Christ in her heart both in words and deeds.[48] The notion of the permanence of the words of

---

46. Ambrose agrees, but adds it may also mean "servo"; *Expositio*, §1, p. 252.
47. Hilary, *Commentaire*, 2:72.
48. Ambrose, *Expositio*, §1, p. 252. Ambrose writes, "vel dicta vel gesta," and *gesta* is also used to refer to accounts of deeds, history, or stories. Ambrose

God and the impermanence of the world was not lost on Bede. The consequent importance of Scripture and of Christian literature may explain why Bede begins this poem neither with Aethelthryth nor with the birth of Christ, but with reference to the poems that record history and inspire action.

Also suggestive of the importance of Christian literature is that five sentences after concluding his *Hymn*, Bede writes that he will record another story "since the story may lead to the salvation of many."[49] Such stories are part of the evangelical and pastoral mandate of confessed Christians. Bede may have thought while he was writing chapters 19 and 20 that his own story of Aethelthryth would help to establish her as a major English saint and help to inspire others.[50] The inspiration that virgin martyrs provide is the topic of this strophe (as the inspiration of the Virgin Mary was the topic of the <H> strophe). That inspiration affects the heart, *cor*, which Jerome said was the meaning of *Lamed*. Bede speaks of hearts in his commentary on Proverbs 31:21, the *Lamed* strophe. The verse reads, "non timebit domui suae a frigoribus nivis omnes enim domestici eius vestiti duplicibus" (She shall not fear for her house in the cold of snow: for all her domestics are clothed with double garments). Commenting on that verse, Bede writes that frost and snow "CORDA sunt reproborum, perfidiae suae torpore rigentia" (are blameworthy HEARTS, made rigid their perfidy by numbness).[51] He cites Matthew 24:12,

---

also writes of heavenly permanence and the need to serve the Word of God in one's heart, §5, p. 254; and that the Word remains in Heaven, "quod secundum verbi dispositionem regitur et gubernatur," recalling Bede's first verse, "quae saecula gubernans" (§11, p. 257).
49. Bede, *HE*, 4.22, p. 401, trans. Colgrave.
50. On Bede's view of his place in Patristic tradition, see Roger Ray, "Who Did Bede Think He Was?"
51. Compare Ambrose, *Expositio*, §§12.13–14, p. 258–59, on the *Lamed* strophe. In his discussion of a heart attuned to Christ, Ambrose cites Psalm 23(24):7, "Tollite portas, principes vestri, et elevamini, portae aeternales, et introibit rex gloriae" (Lift up your gates, O ye princes, and be ye lifted up, O eternal gates: and the King of Glory shall enter in), which resonates with Bede's sixth strophe.

"And because iniquity hath abounded, the charity of many shall grow cold ['refrigescet caritas multorum']." At the same time, the whiteness of snow indicates the angelic condition and the spotless clothing of the saved. It is likely no accident that in his prose Bede writes that Aethelthryth's body was moved from a simple wooden coffin to a tomb of very beautiful white marble ("marmore albo pulcherrime").[52] Returning yet again to Aethelthryth's clothing, a woolen garment and a linen one, the double garments of Proverbs indicate works and a faithful mind ("mentis fidei"); which in turn recalls Bede's description of Thecla's "culmine mentis."[53] Bede's strophe reads, "Mūltŭs ĭn | ōrbĕ uĭ|gēt pēr | sōbrĭă | cōrdă trĭ|ūmphus" (Many a victory flourishes in the world by means of sober hearts); "sōbrĭĕ|tātĭs ă|mōr || mūltŭs ĭn | ōrbĕ uĭ|gēt" (much love of sobriety flourishes in the world).

Bede's focus in this strophe is on Christian triumph in the world ("in orbe"), which reflects Ambrose's discussion of the endurance of the divine Word "in saeculum" and "in aeternum."[54] Elsewhere, Ambrose speaks of the necessity of a temperate heart ("cor temperans"), and sobriety ("sobrietas") as medicine to the mind and body.[55] In one of his most famous hymns, Ambrose writes,

> Te cordis ima concinant,
> te vox canora concrepet,
> te diligat castus amor,
> te mens adoret sobria.
>
> (Let inmost parts of hearts chant of you / The singing voice acclaim you / A chaste passion love you / A sober mind adore you)[56]

---

52. Bede, *HE,* 4.19, p. 394.
53. Bede, *PL* 91:1047B. Ambrose speaks of the treasure of a precious intellect; *Expositio,* §12.4, p. 253.
54. Ambrose, *Expositio,* §12.7, p. 255.
55. Ambrose, *De noe,* cap. 11, p. 437: "si . . . cordi sit temperantia, nulla flamma inardescit libidinis . . . ; sobrietas enim mentis medicina est corporis." Similarly, in his commentary on Psalm 61:31; *Explanatio psalmorum xii,* ed. Petschenig, p. 396.
56. Ambrose, "Deus creator omnium," Hymn 4, lines 13–16, ed. Michel

"Concinant" (*concinere* 'chant, harmonize') also relates to artful symmetry and literary elegance. It is used in Christian poetry to signify unanimity, as in choral singing.[57] Sobriety (that is, moderation) requires spiritual vigilance and is a major theme of Ambrose's spirituality.[58] This complex of related ideas may explain Bede's vocabulary in this *Lamed* strophe. While Ambrose reaches back to Virgil and Catullus for some of his imagery, so Bede might be reaching back (directly or indirectly) to Horace. Book 1, Ode 12 is a famous song by Horace in praise of Augustus and his nephew Marcellus. Horace begins by invoking the muse Clio. He names Orpheus and calls his ability to sing a "maternal art" ("arte materna"), in reference to the Muse Calliope. Echoing this classical inheritance, Bede, too, has invoked a feminine muse ("alma Trinitas"), and his art draws from both the Blessed Virgin Mary and St. Aethelthryth. Bede revises these many inherited images into one of a great Christian victory flourishing through sober hearts.

As in previous strophes, he employs symmetrical (*concinna*) oppositions to create the tension and movement of the strophe. The explosive word "triumphus" is set against sobriety, and sits at the innermost heart of the strophe. The inner heart itself, *cor*, is juxtaposed to "triumphus" and set against the outer world, *orbis*. Chaste love of God, implied by the paradoxical "sobrietatis amor" (love of sobriety), is set alongside thriving and flourishing, *vigere* 'to be vigorous, to thrive'.[59] This last pair seems to me very important for our reader: chastity is reproduced by means of examples in stories and

---

Perrin, in Ambrose, *Hymnes*, pp. 231–61, at p. 237. Perrin notes that the quadruple anaphora on *te* sets God at the front of each verse and recalls Ambrose's "Te Deum," p. 249. The phrase "cor imum" derives from, among others, Virgil and Catullus, p. 249. In his exposition of the *Lamed* strophe, Ambrose writes that the *anima* is the gateway or door to Christ; *Expositio*, §12.15, p. 259.
57. Ambrose, "Deus creator omnium," p. 249.
58. Ibid., p. 251.
59. In an equally floral image, Ambrose writes that the soul/spirit (*anima*) surges forth and opens for the Word of God; *Expositio*, §12.17, p. 260.

poems. Those stories excite a passion for moderation, one we shall see again in the Hymn's last strophe. I should also mention the two prepositional phrases in the hexameter, which exceed all previous uses of prepositions—one in line 13/15, and one in line 19. These prepositions help to give the line a rhythmical and syntactical symmetry. This line is not golden, but the nominal cluster ("multus triumphus") straddles the hexameter, just as "kasta Tecla" and "laeta Agnes" did in the previous two strophes. Within the span of the great triumph a verb ("viget") sits between two imbalanced prepositional phrases. Bede gives us balanced imbalance. The resulting sensation of order governing disorder is important because it does not occur in the pentameter. That difference serves to separate the two verses. But just as the hexameter conveys disorder within order, the strophe conveys continuity within discontinuity. Continuity derives from a chiasmus created by the repetition of *sobria-sobrietatis* (a similar chiasmus occurs in the <V> strophe). Discontinuity derives from the pentameter's syntax and the unusually long word "sobrietatis." It is one of four five-syllable words, all of which are found in the first hemistich of a pentameter—suggesting something about Bede's compositional habits.[60] Given the *sermo simplex* of the majority of the hymn, such words stand out. An alert reader may notice that triumph and sobriety are at the precise center of the hymn. They are surrounded by "corda" and "amor," words expressing the gospel message of love, themselves surrounded by images of flourishing in the world.[61] Having read three strophes in which saints' names take the central position of the strophe, a reader has been conditioned to see that central point as the site of Christian triumph. Where Agnes stood now stands victory. Where Cecilia stood now stands sobriety. Also, as "kasta" and "laeta" had been separated from their nouns, so too is "multus" separated from "triumphus"; and just as the means of earthly death were interposed

---

60. The four are *virginitate* (line 14), *sobrietatis* (line 24), *monasterio* (line 36), and *inviolata* (line 42).
61. My thanks to an anonymous reader from West Virginia University Press for these suggestions.

between the saints' attributes and their names, so too is the world now interposed between "many" and "victories." Where stood fire, beast, and sword now stands the world. Finally, a reader may notice the extraordinary dactylic lightness of the strophe. It may convey to a reader a sense of speed or joy, make of it what she will.

13. Bede now turns to Aethelthryth. Having set his hymn within the tradition of Christian literature, and having invoked the Blessed Virgin Mary and a number of important virgin saints, Bede has prepared his reader to see Aethelthryth within the universal history of salvation. Two saints are from Rome (Agnes and Cecilia), two from Byzantium (Euphemia and Thecla), one from a Roman province (Eulalia, from Spain), and another from a Byzantine province (Agatha, from Sicily). Each of the virgin martyrs shares something in common with Aethelthryth, be it her nobility (Agatha), marriage (Cecilia), clothing (Agnes and Eulalia), austerity and learning (Thecla), or a tomb miracle (Euphemia).[62] Into the geographical expanse of Christian Europe, Bede introduces a saint from the Roman province of Britain. The <M> strophe shifted physical perspective; now the <N> strophe shifts temporal perspective. Our reader is now ("iam") in "nostra tempora" (our time). And by using "quoque" (likewise), Bede invites her to extend the Christian past into "our time."

The thirteenth strophe begins with <N> in Latin, *Mem* in Hebrew. According to Jerome, the word means "ex ipsis" (from themselves).[63]

---

62. Bede notes that a dove (a symbol of the Holy Spirit) was seen flying from St. Eulalia's decapitated head. Bede, *Martyrology*, p. 71. Aethelthryth's scar may link to this image, as well. Another characteristic that Aethelthryth shares with the *passio* of Eulalia is that both are associated with modesty—Aethelthryth wore modest clothes and was buried in a white garment, and to preserve her modesty Eulalia's naked body was miraculously covered with fresh, falling snow. Finally, many people are said to have sung joyfully to Eulalia; Bede's hymn is intended to prompt joyful song to Aethelthryth. See *BHL* 1:405, s.v. "Eulalia."
63. Ambrose adds "ex intimis" and "ignis ex ultimis"; *Commentario*, 13 §1, p. 281

Perhaps coincidentally, Bede's strophe concerns Aethelthryth, who came out of the Anglo-Saxons themselves. Jerome combines *Mem*, *Nun*, and *Samech* into a fifth *conexio* that reads "out of these comes eternal help," by which is meant out of the books of Scripture. It might also be read as announcing the power of divine mediation of an English saint. Proverbs 31:22, the *Mem* strophe, reads, "stragulam vestem fecit sibi byssus et purpura indumentum eius" (She hath made for herself clothing of tapestry: fine linen, and purple is her covering). Bede writes that her clothing of tapestry indicates the strength of the Church, as well as the diversity of her virtues.[64] He cites Psalm 44:10, "The queen stood on thy right hand in gilded clothing; surrounded with variety." Linen represents chastity, and purple, the effusion of precious blood (martyrs) as well as the beautiful flowers of the Church (virgins). He continues, "purpura autem regalia est habitus" (however purple is [or indicates] royal garments); linen clothes the Church, the example of which chastens the bodies of the elect, those worthy of Heaven. Aethelthryth is described as having been buried in fine (white) linen. Bede cites Apocalypse 19:7–8, in which the bride of the Lamb "should clothe herself with fine linen ['byssine'], glittering and white ['splendens candidum']. For the fine linen are the justifications of saints." The regalia marks the bride of Christ, and its splendor, too. Another word for glittering is *nitere*, and for splendor, *clara*. We shall see *clara* and *regalia* in the next strophe.

Bede's strophe reads, "Nōstră quŏ|qu(e) ēgrĕgĭ|ā iām | tēmpŏră | uīrgŏ bĕ|āuit" (Likewise now, an exceptional virgin blessed our times); "Āedīl|thrȳdă nĭ|tēt || nōstră quŏ|qu(e) ēgrĕgĭ|ā" (likewise, our exceptional Aethelthryth shines). Bede allows a multiple ambiguity of accord in his first verse. *Nostra* and *egregia* are two adjectives that can be either feminine (nom. sg.) or neuter (nom. or acc. pl.). As a reader processes the words serially, she may suppose that the two words accord: "our extraordinary." This temporary accord fills a reader's mind with a sense of her participation in the wider Catholic community. She is part of the exceptional Us. Grammatical

---

64. PL 91:1047D.

ambiguity and its resolution characterize this strophe. As the sentence plays out, the adjectives and nouns coalesce, providing a sense of delayed resolution—appropriate to readers anticipating a Heavenly life. By the time a reader reaches the hexameter's closing verb, the line clearly yields "our times" and an "extraordinary virgin." In the interim, "nostra" can agree with both "tempora" and "virgo"—"our time" and "our virgin."[65] Yet the verb requires an accusative object, so "egregia" is most likely to agree with "virgo," "exceptional virgin," as in an early Spanish hymn.[66] The same sense of resolution and ambiguity pervades the pentameter. There, the same two adjectives are not divided but coordinated, "our exceptional Aethelthryth." What had been a momentary possibility of grammar in the hexameter is now asserted in the pentameter.

Nevertheless, the grammar of the pentameter yields two slightly different arrangements of adjectives and therefore of sensations. In other words, exceptional Aethelthryth is ours; and our Aethelthryth is exceptional. The first inspires a reader to confirm local possession of an extraordinary saint, while the second inspires a reader to emulate one of her own people. In both cases, the local English church is simultaneously set against and within the universal Church. Similarly, the singularity of Aethelthryth is set against and within the community of saints. Readers of the *HE* will recall Bede's use of *egregria* to describe the hair of the Anglian boys whom Pope Gregory saw in the market place. There, the term also plays on the name of Gregory, *Gregorius*. Anglians were soon to come into the flock (*grex*,

---

65. For example, Ovid, *Tristia*, 2.471, "perdere rem caram, tempora nostra, solent"; Eusebius (in Rufinus's translation), *Historia Ecclesiastica*, 3.36, §1, "in nostra quoque tempora" (and 4.7, §14); Paulinus of Nola, *Carmina*, 10.125, p. 29; and Augustine, in a phrase attributed to skeptics that resonates with this strophe, "nec miracula illa in nostra tempora durare permissa sunt," *Retractationum libri duo*, 1.13.89. Bede elsewhere speaks of "nostra tempora" and "orbis nostri"; *De tabernaculo*, 3.772. Ambrose, *De virginibus*, 2.6.41, speaks of "virgo nostra."
66. "Inter quos igitur uirgo egregia," Hymn 115, line 89, in *Hymnodia hispanica*, p. 427.

gregis > congre*gation*) of this papal shepherd. Also, the Anglians are described as physically distinct, suggesting the independent identity of the English within the Church. Similarly, the story of Aethelthryth is intended to demonstrate identifiably English participation in the heavenly community. A reader may notice that distinct adjectives become coordinate and that independent verses become a single thought (aided by the homoeoteleuton of the first words of the verses). Athelthryth, too, is described in terms widely used for Christian virgins. Aethelthryth shines or glitters ("nitet"). Eugenius of Toledo, whose poems range from dolorous meditations on aging to dedications for cathedrals, writes an epitaph for a bishop, in which he speaks of the bishop's "virginitate nitens" (shining with virginity). He also speaks of a "corde pius" (pious heart), which recalls the "corda sobria" of the previous strophe.[67] Finally, we see only the third instance of elision in the poem so far. Metrically, spondees characterize the current era (they include "iam" and "tempora") as well as Aethelthryth, both within an otherwise dactylic strophe. Those dactyls carry ideas of an EXTRAORDINARY VIRGIN, BLESSINGS, and SHINING. Once again, Bede seems to have set the worldly and temporal in spondees against the otherworldly and eternal in dactyls.

14. The fourteenth strophe begins with <O> in Latin, *Nun* in Hebrew. According to Jerome, the word means *sempiternum* 'everlasting'; Ambrose says it means *unicus* 'only, sole', specifically in relation to the Son and his Passion. Hilary begins his comments on the *Nun* strophe of Psalm 118 (vv. 105–12) by noting the ignorance of men concerning their own nature. Man cannot know by himself the cause

---

67. Eugenius of Toledo, *Carmina* 20, p. 248, lines 6–7. Christ asks for those who are "humilis corde" (humble of heart, Matthew 11:29). As an example of common vocabulary among Christian poets of the seventh century, consider terms that Bede shares with this poem: "Hic *raptus* recubat felici sorte sacerdos, / quem *laetum caelis* intulit *alma* fides, / nomine baptistam referens et *mente* Iohannem, / doctrina pollens, *uirginitate nitens*, / *corde pius*, uultu placidus et *mente* benignus, / prudenter simplex, simpliciter sapiens" (lines 3–8).

and reason of his origin ("causam et rationem originis suae"); he is born of the bounty of God.[68] Similarly, Bede's *Nun* strophe concerns birth from the Father. Hilary writes that man seeks the light of knowledge ("lucem scientiae"), which derives from God, "qui VERA LUX est et qui OMNEM HOMINEM lucificat" (who is the TRUE LIGHT and who illuminates ALL MEN, where the highlighted text indicates John 1:9). Bede will imply that same light with "clara" (bright, clear, shining). (*Claritas* is one of the key features of beauty, as Aquinas reports.[69]) Hilary focuses on the obligations of a Christian to the less fortunate, and compares earthly wealth to heavenly bounty. He says that others are puffed up by the vanity of worldly glory ("Alii gloriae saeculi tument") and forget the beatitudes.[70] He cites Matthew 25:34, "Come, ye blessed of my Father, possess you the kingdom prepared for you from the foundation of the world."

Likewise, Bede will focus in this strophe on the distinction between earthly royalty and heavenly royalty, especially on the role of a father. A similar focus characterizes the *Nun* strophe in Proverbs 31:23, which reads, "nobilis in portis vir eius quando sederit cum senatoribus terrae" (Her husband is honourable in the gates, when he sitteth among the senators of the land). Bede explains that the *vir* is the husband, who is the Lord of Life ("animae Dominus").[71] "Nobilis ergo," writes Bede, "Dominus in portis civitatis" (Noble therefore is the Lord in the gates of the city). Bede will use *dominus* in this strophe of the *Hymn*. Concerning Proverbs, Bede also speaks of the ingress of the elect into the "patriae coelestis" (fatherland of Heaven), emphasizing the home of the *pater*, the Father. *Pater* is another important term in this strophe of the *Hymn*. About Proverbs, Bede also says that those who are seen as ignoble (*ignobilis*), who are tortured and spit upon and whipped, will be found

---

68. "ex bonitate Dei . . . quod natus est"; Hilary, *Commentaire*, 2:120.
69. De Bruyne, *Études d'esthétique médiévale*, 2:280.
70. Hilary, *Commentaire*, 2:132. *Tumere* (Hilary's "tument") is the verbal form of the word that Bede uses to describe the swelling on Aethelthryth's neck. Aethelthryth attributes her tumor to earthly vanity.
71. Bede, *PL* 91:1048B.

noble (*nobilis*) and judged worthy with all the angels.⁷² He will use *nobilior* in this strophe. The *Nun* strophe of Proverbs thus concerns the Father, judgment, spiritual paternity, and nobility. Bede's strophe uses the same vocabulary as his commentary and reads, "Ōrtă pă|tr(e) ēxĭmĭ|ō rē|gāl(i) ēt | stēmmătĕ | clāra" (Having been born to a distinguished father, to a royal and illustrious family); "nōbĭlĭ|ōr Dŏmĭn(o) | ēst || ōrtă pă|tr(e) ēxĭmĭ|ō" (she was born nobler to God the distinguished Father).

"Orta" picks up on "nitet" in the previous strophe, since both can be used of heavenly bodies—for example, a rising sun and shining stars. As opposed to *natus* 'birth', the term *ortus* means birth or generation "in relation to its source, origin, derivation."⁷³ With it Bede implies that Aethelthryth's terrestrial father is the source of her terrestrial life, while her heavenly father is the source of her spiritual life. This dual paternity is expressed in the phrase "patre eximio," which is both dative and ablative. In the hexameter, it seems to be used as a dative—to this royal father and family she was born.⁷⁴ Notice that Bede uses "stemma" here, not *familia* or a variant of it. *Stemma* refers to a genealogical tree like the one in Matthew 1. It contrasts with the spiritual paternity described in the pentameter. In the pentameter, "patre eximio" seems to be used in the instrumental dative—by means of the heavenly Father she was born. The presence of *est* may momentarily suggest to our reader the dative of the possessor, implying only fleetingly that Aethelthryth is closer to God than to her father.⁷⁵ Before our reader processes the entire strophe, she may imagine something like, "born of the Lord, she has (*est* + dat.) a nobler, distinguished father." But I have read *est* with "orta,"

---

72. Ibid.
73. *OLD*, s.v. *ortus*. Catullus (66.8) writes of "nitens clarius astris."
74. The phrase may equally be an ablative of origin; see Gildersleeve and Lodge, *Latin Grammar*, p. 254. Used with *orti*, see Caesar, *Bello Gallica*, 2.4.1 (their example 1). Compare Horace, whose Hymn to Apollo (4.6) addresses "virginum primae puerique claris / patribus orti" (lines 31–32).
75. This dative "denotes an inner connection between its subject and the Dative"; Gildersleeve and Lodge, *Latin Grammar*, p. 223.

which sets the claim of the strophe firmly in historical time. However she settles the matter, the reader is invited by the mix of datives and ablatives to contemplate origins. Aethelthryth's birth as a chaste bride of Christ did not erase her terrestrial father, nor divorce her from her husband.

This sense of a mishmash of terrestrial and heavenly relationships is extended by elision throughout the strophe. Elision dissolves the boundaries between words. (Elision and hiatus are permitted by Latin rhetoricians if the poet intends a special effect, "suauitatis causa" 'because of smoothness', for example.[76]) *Pater* 'father' elides with *eximius* 'distinguished, unique' (recall that Ambrose says *Nun* means 'unique'); *regalis* 'regal' elides with *et* 'and'; and *Dominus* 'Lord' elides with *est* 'is'. All the fathers of this strophe lose their phonic distinction and blend into the surroundings. Yet the phonic blending is not limited to elision. The flow of sound stops only four times between words, with *pater, et, clara,* and *est.* Otherwise, vowels, continuants, and spirants maintain a fairly steady flow of sound.[77] Other harmonies of sound include repeated and transposed syllables: "patRE . . . REgali," "ET stemmaTE," and "ORta . . . obilioR."[78] Our reader may also contrive to see a playful elision that yields "rex . . . regalia" (king . . . royal): "patR(E) EXimio REGALIA." A contrast between earthly and terrestrial genealogy is also suggested by the arrangement of words. At the center of the strophe are "clara" and "nobilior," two adjectives that create a chiasmus, reaching forward and backward to their immediate neighbors, "stemmate" and "Domino." Those two clusters (adj. + n.) sit at the center of the strophe, bracketed by two homophonic monosyllables, *et* and *est.* If we listen to the strophe rather than look at it we hear an illustrious genealogy and a nobler Lord at its center. On either side sit identical

---

76. Cicero, cited by Herescu, *La Poésie latine*, p. 60.
77. I have tried to mimic the flow of sound in the phrase, "a fairly steady flow of sound."
78. Classical examples that include *-et* and *-te*, *-or* and *-ar*, and the repetition of *-ur* and *-ur* are offered by Herescu, *La Poésie latine*, pp. 55–59. The previous strophe included "egregIA IAM" (l. 25).

claims of distinguished paternity. Yet those claims appear to be inflected differently. The contrast that we imagine between two kinds of paternity as a result of possibly different inflections is undercut by the cross-verse chiasmus, prevalent elision, homoeoteleuton, and repetition and variation on syllables. One might also see prolepsis across the verses in the pair *pater* and *Dominus*. A reader is thereby invited to imagine that the strophe both distinguishes between earthly and heavenly royalty and connects them.

15. The fifthteenth strophe begins with <P> in Latin, *Samech* in Hebrew. According to Jerome, the word means *adiutorium* 'support'; Ambrose says it means *audi* 'you listen' (imperative) or *firmamentum* 'support, authority, the sky', by which is meant in part that we ought to listen to nature and natural law as well as to our bodies and minds.[79] We hear physically, but we must also hear spiritually—"audi ergo spiritualiter" (therefore listen spiritually)—and understand.[80] Firmament (*firmamentum*) indicates mystical or spiritual meaning. Ambrose cites the *Samech* strophe of Lamentations to contrast terrestrial captivity with salvation in Christ.[81] Bede will allude to the firmament in this strophe with his image of stars. Patristic commentaries on the *Samech* strophe focus on a distinction between worldly and heavenly. Bede renders that distinction with the images "below the stars" and "above the stars." Earthly things are odious, but not irrelevant. Hilary in his commentary on the *Samech* strophe of Psalm 118 (vv. 113–20) notes that a Christian disciple is enjoined to reject her family (citing Luke 14:26).[82] But this precept seems contrary to Christ's commandment to love. Nothing, says Hilary, is difficult in God, and nothing contradicts earlier precepts.[83] The family relations

---

79. Ambrose, *Expositio*, §1, p. 330.
80. Ibid., §2, p. 330.
81. Ibid., §4, p. 331.
82. Hilary, *Commentaire*, 2:154. Luke 14:26 reads, "If any man come to me, and hate ['oderit'] not his father, and mother, and wife, and children, and brethren, and sisters, yea and his own life also, he cannot be my disciple."
83. Hilary, *Commentaire*, 2:156. It is likely only a coincidence, but Hilary's

of Luke 14 are to be understood associatively. Hate for one's son is not to be taken literally; instead, it means that many ("plus," a word Bede will use in this strophe) parents love their children so recklessly ("inconsulti") that they would have them cease from pursuing martyrdom. Reciprocally, hate for one's mother and father means that parents press a child to obey them rather than allow a child to pursue the glory of Christian martyrdom. Hate of the world ("odium saeculi") assists in the love of Christ.[84]

Bede's <O> strophe compared Aethelthryth's terrestrial father to her heavenly one; this <P> strophe places heavenly glory over worldly glory while simultaneously praising worldly virtue. Hilary writes that death has equal power over all ("mors aequaliter dominator universorum"), but Christians have hope of the true life ("vitae verae").[85] And continuing his distinction between the earthly and the heavenly, Hilary distinguishes between "peccatores terrae" (sinners of the earth) and "peccatores caeli" (sinners of heaven), that is, those who sin against natural law and those who sin directly against God.[86] The heavenly is also signified in the fine linen of the *Samech* strophe of Proverbs 31. There, verse 24 reads, "sindonem fecit et vendidit et cingulum tradidit Chananeo" (She made fine linen, and sold it, and delivered a girdle to the Chanaanite). Bede explains that Canaan indicates the gentile who converts to Christianity, indicting figuratively a desire for spiritual change.[87] Bede's strophe reads, "Pērcĭpĭt | īndĕ dĕ|cūs rē|gīn(ae) ēt | scēptră sŭb | āstris" (Thence her beauty seizes the scepters of a queen under the stars); "plūs sŭpĕr | āstră mă|nēns || pērcĭpĭt | īndĕ dĕ|cūs" (thence her enduring beauty seizes more over the stars). "Decus" refers to outward beauty, grace, decorousness, and so forth, and by extension to inner virtue, honor,

---

commentary on the *Samech* strophe begins with "praecepti," which is related to Bede's first word "percipit."
84. Ibid., 2:158.
85. Ibid., 2:164.
86. Ibid., 2:170–72. Augustine draws a similar distinction, citing Psalm 118:115 in the Old Latin; *PL* 36:1570.
87. Bede, *PL* 91:1048–49B.

or distinction. In light of "inde" (thence), I have added "her" to tie this strophe to the previous one. But the claim in this strophe is not only about Aethelthryth; it is also more abstract and general: beauty/virtue seizes such things.

The contrast and connection between earth and heaven invoked in the previous strophe is continued in this one. Aethelthryth's virtue and beauty brought her to the throne of the East Angles, and her virginity and Christian virtue brought her to the throne of Christ. Bede makes the same point in his prose introduction to the *Hymn*, when he describes Aethelthryth as "reginae ac sponsae Christi" (a queen and more, a bride of Christ).[88] *Ac* is an emphatic connective ("and . . . too" or "and what is more"), suggesting that in the case of Aethelthryth, Bede prized her virginity over her royalty.[89] Moreover, Aethelthryth was a virgin *uxor* 'wife' of Ealdorman Tohdbehrt, a virgin *conjunx* 'spouse' of King Anna, and a *sponsa* 'fiancée, betrothed' of Christ.[90] Bede is careful to distinguish her terrestrial from her spiritual relationships: he is very explicit in his introduction to this *Hymn* about "eiusdem reginae ac sponsae Christi, et ideo veraciter reginae quia sponsa Christi" (this queen and bride of Christ, and therefore truly a queen because the bride of Christ).[91] Aethelthryth did not lose her royalty when she took up the veil.[92] But her understanding (or grasp, *percipere*) of the precepts (*percepti*) of Christian service permit her terrestrial and heavenly dominance. Thus she seizes (*percipit*) a queen's scepter.

---

88. Bede, *HE*, 4.20, p. 396.
89. *OLD*, s.v. *atque, ac*.
90. Bede, *HE*, 4.19, pp. 390 and 394.
91. Ibid., 4.20, pp. 296–397, trans. Colgrave. Bede notes that Cecilia was a *sponsa* on earth before becoming a virgin martyr; Bede, *Martyrology*, p. 64.
92. There remains the important question of heavenly queens. Idelfonsus of Toledo, writing just before Bede, prays, "O Domina mea, dominatrix mea, dominans mihi, mater Domini mei"; Idelfonsus of Toledo, *De virginitate perpetua sanctae Mariae*. He speaks of Mary as Queen. Aethelthryth is portrayed here as a heavenly queen over queens. How did queens figure into the imagined landscape of Heaven?

Her beauty is not *pulcher*, but "decus," which is sometimes translated "glory," as in "thine is the glory," referring to both earthly and heavenly glory. Bede uses it as in Jeremiah 10:7 ("Who shall fear thee, O king of nations? for thine is the glory [*decus*]"), referring to heavenly glory, and 10:25 ("they have eaten up Jacob, and devoured him, and consumed him, and have destroyed his glory [*decus*]"), referring to earthly glory. Bede differentiates Aethelthryth's heavenly virtue by modifying it, such that "decus" in the hexameter is markedly different from the word in the pentameter. In the latter, it is "manens" (abiding, remaining, enduring). This distinction is not an opposition, but an extension. In other words, heavenly *decus* is not the opposite of earthly *decus*, but an extension of it, a magnification. Similarly, an earthly father is not the opposite of a heavenly father. Where earlier strophes artfully managed oppositions and contraries (such as pagans and Christians), Bede is now exploring the connection between earthly signs and heavenly realities. Stars are such a sign; the heavenly is signified by light. Aethelthryth's sanctity is revealed when her body is brought into the light ("in lucem").[93] In the strophe, the stars indicate that same light—what is called "Deus lumen verum" (God the true light).[94] The admixture of terrestrial and heavenly in the sign is further implied by chiasmus. "Sub astris" and "super astra" reach across the verses to create continuity in their opposition. Continuity is also suggested phonically by sibilants: "sceptra sub astris / plus super astra manens." We earlier saw /s/ represent the sound of consuming, earthly fire ("ignibus usta feris," lines 17–18); now the fire is celestial. Also indicative of continuity is the repetition of the hexameter's opening letter, <P>, as the opening letter of the pentameter, something that only happens twice in the poem—here and in the first strophe. And as befits the balance in this strophe between the earthly and the heavenly, the hexameter is

---

93. Bede, *HE*, 4.19, p. 394.
94. Idelfonsus, *De virginitate*, 96:53. He prays, "da mihi lumen, per quod te videam," which illuminates Bede's image of Aethelthryth's body being brought into light that reveals Christ's miracles. The image of God as light is conventional, as we saw in earlier chapters.

metrically balanced (*ddss*), with a dactylic pentameter and its two heavy syllables.

16. Bede dedicates a third strophe to a distinction between earthly and heavenly. In the <Q> strophe he returns to the topic of marriage, but he shifts perspective again. This time, the poetic voice addresses Aethelthryth directly in an extended rhetorical question.[95] Now she has become more than Aethelthryth (<N> strophe), more than a daughter (<O> strophe), and more than a queen (<P> strophe); she is a bride of Christ. We are in the middle of a progression of characteristics in these strophes from individual to saint. Another way to describe the same progression is as an expansion of her relationships: first to her family, then to her nation, and then to the universal Church. By the <X> strophe, Aethelthryth will become a saint through whom the power of Christ can be invoked. Her heavenly home is also suggested by the epithet "alma," which we heard in the first strophe as a characteristic of the Trinity. Her spiritual presence before the reader is announced by "iam" (now), which in the <N> strophe seemed to refer historically to the seventh century. Here, it seems to refer to the present-time of the reader as she annunciates the words. Bede will use "iam" again in the next strophe with a slightly different temporal sense. Just as temporal perspective changes in the poem, so does the speaking voice. The poet spoke authoritatively in the <C> and <D> strophes, and now becomes a petitioner asking about heavenly mysteries.

The sixteenth strophe begins with <Q> in Latin, *Ain* in Hebrew. According to Jerome, the word means "fons sive oculus" (fountain or eye); Ambrose explains that we use the eye to see the gift of life. A discussion of physical sight, through which we are often tempted, develops into one on baptism and penance. Eyes lead to generation: with them one sees the beauty of women ("mulieris pulchritudinem"), artistic works, and the beauty of nature ("venustatem

---

95. A similar shift in perspective and a change to apostrophe characterizes the last strophe of Prudentius's hymn to St. Agnes, *Peri.*, 14.124–33.

naturae"). Spiritual generation is had by casting one's reverent eye on a consecrated maiden ("sacram puellam") and respect for chastity ("reverentia castitatis").[96] Jerome combines *Ain*, *Phe*, and *Sade* into a sixth *conexio* that reads "the eye of the face of justice," which he says signifies the same as the third *conexio*, that is, we see now as through a glass darkly and we will need no doctrine when we are with Christ. In general, Patristic commentary on the *Ain* strophe focuses on knowledge of heavenly mysteries. Hilary writes that by reading one letter after another of the alphabet, we receive a lesson of piety, intelligence, and faith just as children gain a knowledge of speech.[97] The voice of the *Hymn* now asks for such knowledge. Moreover, adds Hilary, by loving frugality and sobriety we do not lose the nobility of our celestial soul ("nobilitatem animae caelestis").[98] That difference between earthly nobility and heavenly nobility, inner and outer, is invoked by Bede in the <O> strophe ("nobilior"). Aethelthryth's beauty ("decus" from the previous strophe) is similar. We see the same beauty in the *Ain* strophe of Proverbs 31:25, which reads, "fortitudo et DECOR indumentum eius et ridebit in die novissimo" (Strength and BEAUTY are her clothing, and she shall laugh in the latter day). Aethelthryth has put on this beauty. Bede's strophe reads, "Quīd pĕtĭs | ālmă uĭ|rūm spōn|sō iām | dēdĭtă | sūmmo" (Whom do you court, gracious one, devoted now to the highest groom); "spōnsŭs ă|dĕst Chrī|stūs || quĭd pĕtĭs | ālmă uĭ|rūm?" (Christ the Groom is with you, which man, gracious one, do you court?).

At this point, Aethelthryth is above the stars, in the celestial light of Heaven. The light of the previous strophe brings us to Ambrose, who explains in his commentary on Psalm 118's *Zain* strophe that "'in lumine dei' est cui adest Christus" ('in the light of God' is someone

---

96. Ambrose, *Expositio*, §16.6, p.354. This terrific passage also describes eyes as a spring of good, of grace, and of justice (cf. Psalm 118:18). Ambrose quotes the Bride (*Sponsa*) in Canticles (Song of Songs) 7:4. Bede will employ the figurative meanings of the image in his last four, acrostic strophes. The *Ain* strophe of Lamentations (4:17) also mentions eyes.
97. Hilary, *Commentaire*, 2:174.
98. Ibid., 2:176.

who is close to Christ), a phrase Bede uses in this very strophe.[99] Bede knows it from Paulinus of Nola ("Christus adest nobis," Christ is with us), whom he cited in his own Life of St. Felix.[100] The phrase "quid virum" (which man) can be translated as "whom," but *vir* is essential to the allusion Bede makes here to the husband of the *mulier fortis*, that is, to Christ. The word stands out. "Virum" is one of very few nouns in the *Hymn* inflected with an –*m*. This may have something to do with Bede's disdain for elision. But considering that all accusative singulars of the first and second nominal declensions (and the masculine and feminine singular of the third, fourth, and fifth) as well as the genitive plural of every nominal declension end in –*m*, the feat is remarkable. Its rarity in this *Hymn* marks it as especially important. I think that Bede is not establishing a distinction between an earthly man/husband and Christ, but instead asking the *mulier fortis* about her *vir*.[101] Aethelthryth is among the 144,000 virgins who attend the Bridegroom in Heaven, a point Bede makes again in his twenty-fourth strophe ("nupta Deo").

The centrality of Christ-*vir* to this strophe is suggested twice. First, "virum" and "sponso" sit cheek by jowl in the center of the hexameter. They meet together in the third foot. Further, "sponso" is surrounded by the rhyming pair "virum/iam," themselves surrounded by the rhyming pair "alma/dedita." As the line unfolds, "sponso" is shown to be phonically isolated and central. That is, until the last word. "Summo" grammatically completes "sponso," instantly giving a reader an image of the "highest groom." That image in the center of the hexameter is reinforced, although not precisely repeated, in the center of the strophe. We read "summo / sponsus." The juxtaposed words are grammatically distinct, but connected phonically and semantically by an association with "sponso." They are also connected by alliteration, rhythm, meter, and sibilance. "Sponsus" is further

---

99. Ambrose, *Expositio*, §7.33, p. 146.
100. Bede, *Vita Felicis*, PL 94:793; Paulinus of Nola, *Carmen* 6, line 147.
101. Aethelthryth had two husbands, although she consummated neither marriage; if Bede intended to refer to one of them with *vir*, then which one? My point is that as a nun, she seeks only one *vir*, Christ.

connected to "Christus" by homoeoteleuton. As in earlier strophes, /s/ serves to fasten terms together. The Highest Groom sits at the center of the hexameter and at the center of the strophe. Aethelthryth, who seeks this groom, is grammatically absent from the strophe but for adjectives describing her as "alma" and "dedita," and the second-person "petis." Both those words are physically distant from *Christus*, surrounding Him like petitioners in the strophe's outer margins.

17. The seventeenth strophe marks the close of the speaker's apostrophe to Aethelthryth. In the next strophe, the speaker will turn to narrate a very brief history,[102] and the <X> strophe will be spoken as an apostrophe to Christ. Then an enraptured voice in the final strophes will describe the heavenly life. Strophe 17 begins with <R> in Latin, *Phe* in Hebrew. According to Jerome, the word means *os* 'mouth'; Ambrose also says it means *os*, but includes "erravi" (I have erred) and "aperui" (I have revealed). These combine, says Ambrose, in the *Phe* strophe of Psalm 118 (vv. 129–36), especially v. 131 ("os meum aperui") to indicate the celestial light of mercy that draws those who live in the shadow of death.[103] Likewise ("quoque"), says Ambrose, citing Jerome, the *Phe* strophe of Lamentations (1:17) speaks of the lack of consolation for Jerusalem, which suffers—this is captive Israel ultimately freed by Christ.[104] He writes, "Sequi noluerunt, audire noluerunt" (Those unwilling to follow are those unwilling to hear).[105] Bede will use that image in this strophe, portraying Aethelthryth as following (*sequi*) Christ. Hearing is very important, as is speaking, since faith also enters through the ears (recall that many alphabetics begin with "Audite"), and through the sight of miracles and wonders. Hilary notes that after giving the law to Moses, God said to Moses, "Say to the people of

---

102. I use *turn* conscious of the Greek roots of *apostrophe*. The narrative voice turns (Gk. *strephein*) away from (Gk. *apo*) one perspective to another. As I discuss below, these multiple perspectives/voices imbue a reader with a sense of the universal scope of Aethelthryth's achievement.
103. Ambrose, *Expositio*, §17.1, p. 377.
104. Ibid., §17.2, p. 378.
105. Ibid., §17.4, p. 379.

Israel" (Exodus 3:14). The law was written in stone; it needed to be written into flesh. Through the intermediary of a mouth, human ears must hear the word of God.[106] The term *os* is used in Proverbs 31:8 and 31:9, which both begin, "Aperi os tuum . . ." The *Phe* strophe of Proverbs is 31:26; it reads, "os suum aperuit sapientiae et lex clementiae in lingua eius" (She hath opened her mouth to wisdom, and the law of clemency is on her tongue). Similar phrasing is found in Psalm 125(126):2. Bede writes that there is an inner knowledge of truth spoken by the mouth of the heart ("os cordis"), invoking Luke 6:45 and Matthew 12:34. Commenting on Psalm 118:103, Augustine says that wisdom is as sweet as honey to the mouth of the heart.[107] Bede's advocacy for Aethelthryth's sanctity in these chapters of the *HE* includes the oral testimony of witnesses; but his advocacy follows from his inner conviction rather than from a line of argument. Bede hears and then speaks from the mouth of his heart. Furthermore, the *Phe* strophe in Proverbs calls for penance and God's mercy. Christ is an example of God's clemency.[108] In short, the *Phe* strophe involves speaking one's faith (Bede's "credo"), God's mercy (Ps 118:132), and the revelation of God's presence such as happened at Aethelthryth's tomb.

---

106. Hilary, *Commentaire*, 2:204. See Psalm 17:1. Bede's role as a poet and the testament of Aethelthryth's miracles all fulfill this need to speak the word of God. In support, Hilary cites Isaiah 29:12–14, "And the book shall be given to one that knoweth no letters, and it shall be said to him: Read: and he shall answer: I know no letters. [13] And the Lord said: Forasmuch as this people draw near me with their mouth, and with their lips glorify me, but their heart is far from me, and they have feared me with the commandment and doctrines of men: [14] Therefore behold I will proceed to cause an admiration in this people, by a great and wonderful miracle: for wisdom shall perish from their wise men, and the understanding of their prudent men shall be hid."
107. Augustine, *Enn.*, *PL* 36:1565–66; *Exposition*, 5:448.
108. Bede, *PL* 91:1049D–1050A. Also, Cassiodorus, *Explanation*, 3:235. Hilary also notes the mouth of the heart, *Commentaire*, 2:208. Cf. 2 Corinthians 3:3. An early example of the phrase is in Cyprian of Carthage, *Epistulae*, 59.3, §3. Cyprian's phrase is cited by Paulinus of Nola a number of times. On the need for oral penance and confession, see Hilary, *Commentaire*, 2:222.

Bede's strophe reads, "Rēgĭs ŭt | āethĕrĕ|ī mā|trēm iām| crēdŏ sĕ|quāris" (I believe that now you follow the mother of the ethereal king); "tū quŏquĕ | sīs mā|tēr || rēgĭs ŭt | āethĕrĕ|ī" (that you likewise are a mother of the ethereal king). "Credo" is not a casual word in Christian Latin; as we have seen, it is the first word of the Nicene Creed.[109] It sets the speaking voice at the grammatical forefront of the strophe, although that voice does not announce itself until the close of the hexameter. In other words, the sentence is first and foremost about the speaker and what he believes—"credo ut." The speaker is addressing Aethelthryth, but also confessing faith: "I believe that . . ." Like someone praying the Nicene Creed, the reader merges her own voice with that of the text's speaker. As she does so, she may notice that the indicative mood of earlier strophes has become subjunctive. Our reader's experience of the poem has now prepared her to confess her faith in the sanctity of Aethelthryth. Bede's "iam" (now) is in her eternal present; a reader today might speak *iam* and it would refer to the twenty-first century, bridging the temporal gap by reference to an ever-present spiritual reality. Moreover, she is prepared to confess her faith in this English member of the communion of saints because her eyes have read one line after another, moving like a plow across the page, tilling ground for the seed of faith. That seed is planted when Bede indicates the cumulative force of his many comparisons by using the word "quoque" (likewise). We heard it earlier in the <N> strophe to compare Aethelthryth to other virgin martyrs. Our alert reader took in the arguments implied by characteristics that Aethelthryth shared with the communion of virgin saints (clothing, necklaces, pierced neck, white linen, etc.). By that <N> strophe, Bede's "quoque" set Aethelthryth firmly into that community. The next three strophes testified to her earthly and celestial queenship; they portrayed her heavenly life as an extension (or type) of her earthly one.

---

109. In order to achieve a smooth English translation, Colgrave must omit *credo*. He writes, "Royal Mother of Heaven's King your leader now; / You too, maybe, a mother of Heaven's King." His choice illustrates—as do mine—what can be lost in translation.

By the <Q> strophe, Aethelthryth is so well established in Heaven that the speaker can address her there directly. And now, at this point in the poem, Bede's "quoque" sets Aethelthryth firmly within the virginal, celestial company of Christ. (He will later call that company the "comitatus Agni," company of the Lamb). And as befits that distinguished company, the order of address must follow decorum. So, in the hexameter, the ethereal king comes first ("regis . . . aetherei"), then the Blessed Virgin mother ("matrem"), and following (*sequens*, "sequaris") at the very end; humbly hiding in a tiny inflection (*–is*) is Aethelthryth. Once we come to hear the poet's voice directly ("credo"), the narrative perspective shifts and with it, Aethelthryth's position. She is at once the humble supplicant to the Lord and the higher focus of the poet's attention. Thus, the order of words is visually interesting, as well. At the center of the strophe sits Aethelthryth. The second-person inflection of "sequarɪs" sits next to "tu" (you) and the second-person "sis" (may be, are). Note that the royal center of this central cluster of words is "tu," a word spoken by the poet and the reader, around which the verbs "sequaris" and "sis" are connected by homoeoteleuton, alliteration, and verbal mood. The reader and her immediate historical moment surround that center. Outside the cluster indicating Aethelthryth sit "credo," "iam," and "quoque." The adverbs bring Aethelthryth into present company with the speaker and the reader by declaring Aethelthryth's eternal presence in Heaven ("iam"), and her likeness to Mary ("quoque"). That cluster in turn is bracketed by "matrem/mater," which indicates the mediation of the Virgin Mary in the figuration of Aethelthryth's life and sanctity. Simultaneously, the Virgin Mary brackets the historical present of the reader. That larger cluster in turn is bracketed by the ethereal King, by whom all things exist. As if in the middle of a chart of the Ptolomaic universe, Bede's sublunary reader experiences a series of increasingly distant, concentric heavens, each more perfect and timeless than the last. In the next chapter, we will take up Aethelthryth's abbacy and death and the concluding strophes of this *Hymn*.

Chapter Eight

Hymn to Aethelthryth, S–end

Bede begins the final section of the alphabet with a historical narrative. The narrative runs for four strophes (lines 35–42) and concludes with an apostrophe to Christ. All the verses of these four strophes (<S> through <X>) are connected together by rhyme: *abababba*; they rhyme on *–is* and *–o* (lines 37 and 39 are connected by homoeoptoton, *–is* and *–es*). The subsequent two strophes (<Y> and <Z>) extend the rhyme scheme with modification, *cada*. The rhyme scheme is clearest visually in St. Gall ms. 265, pp. 122–23 (see above). There, the scribe has written each strophe from margin to margin across the page. He or she has placed a *punctus medius* (medial period) between the hexameter and the pentameter, and another at the end of the pentameter. The alphabet is visible along the left margin, and any terminal rhyme schemes along the right. We can see, for example, that the <E>, <F>, and <H> strophes are connected by homoeoteleuton and homoeoptoton. The structuring role of rhyme is inherent in the form that Bede has chosen. The epanaleptic elegy has four major points of rhyme: at the end of each verse (cola that I'll call *b* and *d*) and just before the medial caesurae (cola that I'll call *a* and *c*). Because it repeats the first colon in the fourth, the form has a built-in rhyme at *a* and *d*. If its hexameter is leonine (rhyming *a* and *b*), the rhyme heightens a sense of structural interweaving. Such is the case in the concluding acrostic strophes (spelling "amen"). The hexameters of strophes 25 (second <M> strophe) and 27 (second <N> strophe) are leonine. The twenty-sixth strophe (second <E> strophe) is also leonine in the hexameter, but the rhyme extends into the pentameter, as well (*a*, *b* and *d*, with a rhyme in the middle of *c*):

26. Et noua dulcisono [*a*] || modularis carmina plectro [*b*]
 sponsa hymno exultas [*c*] || et noua dulcisono [*d*].

Note how the remainder of the content words of the strophe rhyme on −*a* (except for "modularis," which picks up on the major rhymes of strophes 18–27, that is <S> through to the final strophe).

The artistic achievement of the strophe would be most evident in its articulation. In strophe 26, the vowels would resonate off the walls of St. Paul's: /o/ (five times in each verse) and /u/ (twice in each verse), regularly interspersed with /a/ (four times in the hexameter, twice in the pentameter) and /i/ (three times in the hexameter and once in the pentameter). The terminal vowels of the four cola of the strophe comprise the following pattern: *o-o-a-o*. Its theme vowel, as it were, is /o/. It is part of a longer phonic composition. The theme vowels of the last three strophes of the poem (25–27), when heard this way, resonate in the following pattern: *i-o-i*. Strophe 24, which begins the acrostic, is a combination of the two: *o-i-i-o*. And strophe 18, which begins the narrative, has a similar pattern: *o-i-o-o*. When our nun of Barking thinks about the sound that Bede's *Hymn* makes, she may imagine strophes 18 (<S>) through 27 (second <N>) resonating with similar phonic patterns. Running one's finger down the right margin of St. Gall 265 (along the rhyme at *d*), one can almost hear the resonating vowels: *o-o-o-i-i-i*. The hexameters (*b*) run counterpoint: *i-i-e-o-e-a*. As the poem begins to treat of Aethelthryth's *vita* and afterlife, it takes on more obvious characteristics of a sung hymn. Within this beautifully woven phonic setting Bede places his concluding, jeweled strophes.

18. Although Bede has turned to historical matter, this strophe reaches back to the topic of Heaven. *Sponsus*, *sponsa* 'betrothed' was used in the <Q> strophe (line 32, "sponsus") to speak of Christ. A *sponsus* is one who has vowed himself, pledged his troth, a fiancé,

a betrothed. By the current strophe, our reader sees Aethelthryth replying with her own offer of marriage. She is now a *sponsa*, a betrothed of Christ. Our reader begins the strophe with this word and with its spiritual resonance. Since our reader is a nun, she may well empathize with the identification. She will then consider the historical matter of Aethelthryth's life, carrying with her a reminder of its spiritual figuration. This strophe begins with <S> in Latin, *Sade* in Hebrew. According to Jerome, the word means *iustitia* 'justice'; Ambrose adds *consolatio* 'consolation'. Psalms 118:137, the opening verse of the *Sade* strophe, reads, "Thou art just, O Lord: and thy judgment is right." In his commentary on this strophe, Ambrose writes that the letter *Sade* indicates the consolation desired by those who suffer, distinguishing justice that repays criminal punishment from justice that forgives and consoles.[1] He adduces verses from Scripture that, among other things, distinguish those who effect earthly justice (such as kings and magistrates) from Christ, who effects merciful, heavenly justice. Aethelthryth's role as queen places her in two roles: a sovereign who effects earthly justice and a subject of divine mercy. Hilary notes the profound justice of the divine order and of earthly suffering, however difficult it might be for us to understand. We are proved by suffering, and the force of our patience defeats the Devil.[2]

Hilary, like Cassiodorus, spends time on the significance and ambivalence of the word *zelus* 'zealous', which begins Bede's <Z> strophe. Cassiodorus also speaks of the need for suffering so that one recognizes that salvation does not come through one's own deeds.[3] He notes that by this point in Psalm 118, the speaking voices have triumphed over the flesh and desire eternal life. Similarly, Bede's reader recognizes by this point in the *Hymn* that Aethelthryth has achieved eternal life. Finally, Cassiodorus notes that devotion to

---

1. Ambrose, *Expositio*, §§1–2, pp. 396–97.
2. "Vinci diabolum patientiae nostrae virtutibus delectatur," that is, the Lord desires it; Hilary, *Commentaire*, 2:224–26. Bede makes precisely the same point in his commentary on Nehemiah 2:2; see DeGregorio, *Bede: On Ezra and Nehemiah*, pp. 158–59.
3. Cassiodorus, *Explanation*, 3:239; *PL* 70:885A–B.

the law is shown by the whole Church, by the "people of grace, the new people who are later in time but prior in distinction of faith."[4] Aethelthryth's monastic devotion in the seventh century ("dicata est," line 36) places her clearly in this modern company.[5] Bede makes a similar distinction between earthly and divine justice in his commentary on the *Sade* strophe of Proverbs 31. Verse 27 reads, "considerat semitas domus suae et panem otiosa non comedet" (She hath looked well to the paths of her house, and hath not eaten her bread idle). Echoing Ambrose and Hilary on *Sade*, Bede writes that the second phrase signifies that which is known through sacred eloquence ("sacro eloquio") and the works that will be exhibited before the eyes of eternal judgment.[6] The first phrase signifies the justice by which eternal life in the house of the Lord is gained. Bede relates *domus* 'house' to the heavenly *patria* 'homeland'.

Bede's strophe reads, "Spōnsă dĭ|cātă Dĕ|ō bīs | sēx rē|gnāuĕrăt | ānnis" (The devoted betrothed of God had reigned for twice six years); "ĭnquĕ mŏ|nāstĕrĭ(o) | ēst || spōnsă dĭ|cātă Dĕ|ō" (and in a monastery was consecrated betrothed of God). Let us take the words in order, following the unfolding sense of the strophe. "Sponsa," as we saw, inspired our reader to consider the historical particulars of Aethelthryth in a spiritual manner. "Dicata" (pledged, dedicated) can be used of citizens or men and women religious. Having experienced strophe after strophe containing an antithesis between literal and spiritual, terrestrial and heavenly, our reader immediately recognizes the dual valence of "dicata," and perhaps more. Aethelthryth is a chaste queen and a devout Catholic. But when she takes her vows in a monastery, she will become a consecrated virgin. Augustine writes in *De sancta virginitate* that physical chastity is not the same as devotion, but exists for a female religious "quia *deo dicata*

---

4. "populus gratiae, populus novus, qui aetate sequitur, sed fidei dignitate praecedit," trans. Walsh; Cassiodorus, *Explanation*, 3:241; *PL* 70:886D.
5. Augustine writes that a virgin is "deo dicata est"; *De sancta virginitate*, §8, para. 8, p. 241.
6. Bede, *PL* 91:1050A. Cf. Bede's commentary on Nehemiah 3:16, the House of the Strong; DeGregorio, *Bede: On Ezra and Nehemiah*, pp. 173–74.

est" (because she is dedicated to God; my italics).[7] And, Bede writes, Aethelthryth is "dicata deo." This strophe maintains an antithesis between these two meanings of *dicata*—therefore, I have translated the first "devoted" and the second "consecrated." "Deo" then confirms Aethelthryth's devotion to God, completing the colon and the image.

Our reader is sustaining two levels of meaning by this point, which is reinforced by the next word, "bis" (twice). Reading "bis" according to what is being held in memory ("Sponsa dicata Deo"), Aethelthryth is a "sponsa dicata" twice: once as a virgin queen and once as a consecrated nun. "Sex" (six) is a number filled with spiritual significance. It can suggest worldliness. In his *Commentary on Genesis*, Bede notes that it is the number of days during which God worked and perfected the world.[8] There are six ages of the world; the seventh is the world to come.[9] It can also suggest that which is close to God. In his *Commentary on the Tabernacle*, Bede writes that Moses ascended the mountain and was in God's presence for six days.[10] Six has both a terrestrial and a heavenly significance; thus, the reign of Aethelthryth was twice six. She reigned once as a queen and once as an abbess, once on earth and once in heaven. Twice six, of course, is twelve. The significance of twelve would fill volumes.[11]

---

7. Augustine, *De sancta virginitate*, 8.8, p. 241. This is the only place I have identified the phrase used in reference to virginity. Augustine uses the phrase throughout his sermons on the Psalms. It is ubiquitous in Patristic writing. Ambrose uses it twice in his *Expositio* concerning *Lamed* (12th strophe) at §37, p. 272, and at §41, p. 275. Bede describes those who profess a more perfect life ("vitae perfectoris") as "deo dicati sunt"; *In Ezram et Neemiam libri iii*, Book 3, line 561; trans. DeGregorio, *Bede: On Ezra and Nehemiah*, p. 175.
8. Kendall, *Bede: On Genesis*, p. 96. The interpretation is found throughout Bede's work.
9. Bede's Hymn 1 (*Primo Deus caeli*) reads "Et sex in huius saeculi / Aetatibus nos praecipit" (strophe 24). The seventh age is perpetual life (strophe 25).
10. *De tabernaculo*, 1, lines 114, 125–28.
11. A portion is explored by Michell and Rhone, *Twelve-Tribe Nations*. My thanks to Michael Moynihan for putting this delightful book in my hands. Bede notes twelve signs of the zodiac, twelve months of the year, twelve

Twelve tribes of Israel and twelve apostles are typologically related. Again, our reader contrasts the Old Law with the New, the physical with the spiritual.

A correlative contrast is between the past and the present. "Regnaverat" in the pluperfect tense contrasts with the "iam" (now) of the previous strophe. A distinction in time also invites an antithesis between Aethelthryth's earthly and heavenly queenship. The former is historical, the latter omnipresent. We also see a distinction between earthly status and heavenly status: Athelthryth's reward in Heaven proceeds not from her earthly royalty, but from her earthly humility. That distinction is buttressed by meter. Note that weighty spondees record the length of her terrestrial reign ("bīs sēx . . . ānnīs"). The reign itself is both terrestrial and heavenly (as we saw in the previous strophe); perhaps then our reader sees a light, heavenly dactyl overlaid on a heavy, earthly spondee ("**rēg**nāuĕrăt"). "Annis" concludes the colon and the hexameter, and rhymes with *bis*, the line's central word (literally and figuratively). The duality that pervades the line, the bivalence of meanings, the earthly and heavenly significances—all are mirrored structurally in the hexameter by rhyme and meter (two dactyls + one spondee is mirrored by two spondees + one dactyl). In the interest of brevity, I shall note of the pentameter only that it is in the pluperfect and perfect tenses, indicating the historical fact of Aethelthryth's consecration. That pervading sense of temporal coherence will prepare our reader for the next strophe, whose topic and rhyme scheme tie it closely to this one.

19. The nineteenth strophe continues the historical narrative, indicated most clearly through the perfect tense of the verbs. The scene is the monastery of the previous strophe. Here Aethelthryth flourishes, and here she dies. The strophe begins with <T> in Latin, *Koph*

---

hours in a day, twelve loaves of bread in the Tabernacle, twelve stones in the High Priest's breast-plate (i.e., the number of precious stones ["lapidibus pretiosis," Bede, *In primam partem Samuhelis* 4.23, line 121]), twelve cubits in the columns of the Temple, and so on.

in Hebrew. According to Jerome, the word means *vocatio* 'calling'; Ambrose says it means *conclusio* 'conclusion, blockage' or *aspice* 'you consider, behold' (imperative). Jerome combines the last four Hebrew letters into a seventh and final *conexio* that means, "By means of the teeth the articulated voice is expressed and in these signs one reaches the head of all, which is Christ."[12] The *conexio* combines speaking voices and signs, indicating their mediation between reader and divinity. At this point in the poem, we are at the heart of beauty, where order and number and weight resonate with the divine order. The *Koph* strophe of Psalm 118 (v. 145) invokes the speaking voice, the words of God, and the relation between understanding and salvation. The strophe begins, "Clamavi toto corde meo" (I cried with my whole heart); Bede's strophe begins with "tota." Hilary explains that the sound of the voice ("vocis sonus") is not elevated, nor of the physical word, but the cry of faith and of the spirit ("clamor fidei, clamor mentis"). It is raised to the heavens ("caelestia").[13] Similarly, Aethelthryth devotes herself to high heaven ("polo celsis").

The influence on Bede of these *Koph* strophes is even clearer when we consider Cassiodorus's commentary: the chorus of speakers promises "to seek the Lord's justifications, and to take joy in His word with a confession preceding that promise."[14] That confession of faith devotes one to the Lord as Aethelthryth is devoted. Verse 148 of the psalm speaks of the life to come. Ambrose writes of the feverish desire of the soul (*anima*, a word Bede will use here) for the afterlife.[15] That same eternal life is signified in Proverbs 31:28, the *Koph* strophe, which reads, "surrexerunt filii eius et beatissimam praedicaverunt vir eius et laudavit eam" (Her children rose up, and called her blessed: her husband, and he praised her). Bede comments that

---

12. My thanks to Paul Early of Lowell, Massachusetts, for his insights into this line.
13. Hilary, *Commentaire*, 2:244–46. Bede uses similar phrasing in his commentary on Proverbs 31:28, "coelestibus bonis"; Bede, *PL* 91:1051A.
14. Cassiodorus, *Explanation*, 3:243.
15. Ambrose, *Expositio*, §1, p. 422. See also §39, p. 442, "Penetrat ergo animam et quasi candor aeternae lucis inlustrat," etc.

the children of Holy Mother Church, all the elect in the new dispensation, those who transcend the hardships of daily life, will be granted immortality of the body.[16] Bede writes at length about the reward that comes to those who devote themselves to Christ in this life.

Bede's strophe reads, "Tōtă să|crātă pŏ|lō cēl|sīs ŭbĭ | flōrŭĭt | āctis" (Where she, wholly devoted to Heaven, blossomed by her lofty deeds); "rēddĭdĭt | ātqu(e) ănĭ|mām || tōtă | să|crātă pŏ|lō" (and [whence] she returned her soul, wholly devoted, to Heaven). Bede repeats the fact of Aethelthryth's devotion, reminding his readers of the rewards that come to those who are similarly devoted. But in the pentameter, "celsis" (lofty, high) drops out, suggesting that Aethelthryth is no longer in a position inferior to Heaven. By the fourth colon of the strophe, Aethelthryth is in Heaven. Moreover, the verb *reddere* 'return, deliver', which opens the pentameter, takes a dative object as well as an accusative one. That dative object will be found in the pentameter's "polo" (Heaven). In other words, as the sense of the pentameter unfolds, she returned her soul to the minster and thence to Heaven. "Reddidit" is an active indicative form, implying Aethelthryth's activity in her own salvation. That activity is expressed in "actis" (acts, deeds). Bede explains in a number of his commentaries that good deeds do not merit salvation, but they are a necessary component of the life of a faithful Christian. They arise from faith—Bede uses the image of flowering ("floruit"). This flower results from the sacred seed ("casto germine," line 15) planted in good earth. Flowering acts correlate to the virgin flowers (line 16), or nuns whom Aethelthryth tended at Ely. Our reader might recall Bede's earlier report that St. Alban was martyred on a high hill covered in flowers, a place dignified by Nature to receive his blood.[17]

The grammar of the epanaleptic colon (*a* and *d*) connects this strophe to the previous one and prepares the reader for the next. "Ubi" 'where' reaches back to "monasterio" (l. 36), where

---

16. Bede, *PL* 91:1050C–D.
17. *HE*, 1.7, pp. 32–33. See also Bede's poem *DDI*, 14.146–48. A good deal of imagery and vocabulary from this *Hymn* can be seen in those lines.

Aethelthryth's deeds flowered. But the strophe also sets Ely in apposition to Heaven, two sites to which Aethelthryth is wholly devoted and in which her deeds flower. The duality of the preceding strophe ("bis") is replicated in this doubling of sites, one earthly, one heavenly. Moreover, Bede suggests an image of singularity in plurality, a thematic correlation to Aethelthryth's distinctive sanctity among a community of women religious. "Tota," the first word of the strophe, can be singular or plural; a reader awaits clarification as the strophe unfolds. "Sacrata," the second word of the strophe, clearly refers back to Aethelthryth and is a singular feminine nominative, "she, wholly devoted." Thus, in this very brief opening moment, the strophe unfolds by offering a reader a momentary choice between a plurality and a singularity, then clarifying the matter. A reader perhaps infers through this momentary coincidence of singularity and plurality Aethelthryth's harmony with her community. But praise of Aethelthryth's singular devotion is not an opportunity for pride. Instead, her humility is suggested by "polo celsis," which places her far under the heavens.[18] Ironically, "celsis" (lofty, high) is a spondee, which readers are trained to consider weighty. Apart from "celsis" and "actis," the strophe is entirely dactylic, as befits its light, joyful topic. The strophe has distinguished between Aethelthryth's participation in a community and Aethelthryth's singularity. Her individual self is indicated with the singular, feminine word "animam" (soul). Her soul is further individuated by sitting outside the rhyme scheme established in the previous strophe—thus, *o-i-o-o* versus *o-i-a-o*. What is at first an individuated portion of Aethelthryth, her soul, will gain its reward through her participation in the community of the faithful and in the body of Christ. At this point in the poem, Aethelthryth's soul goes out from a monastic community and joins the communion of saints; her individual achievement is thereby framed in terms of her participation in a community. Perhaps to celebrate her

---

18. Humility plays an important role in Ambrose's exposition of the *Resh* strophe of Psalm 118, which begins "Vide humilitatem meum"; see Ambrose, *Expositio*, §§ 3–4, p. 446–47.

achievement, one can almost hear "Alleluia" sung in the homophony and rhymes of the pentameter "Atque animam tota sacrata."

20. The twentieth strophe describes the two graves of Aethelthryth and her physical incorruption. There is a distinct shift in tense when Bede places her incorruption into the present day. This shift again suggests Aethelthryth's continuing presence among the faithful. Strophe 20 begins with <V> in Latin, *Resh* in Hebrew. According to Jerome, the word means *caput* 'leader'; Ambrose says it means *caput* 'head' or *primatus* 'the supreme one'. In his commentary on the *Resh* strophe of Psalm 118, Ambrose comments on the senses and wisdom in our heads, how it informs the spirit and the blood. He writes that the body is entombed without beauty, but in the head lie the vigor of life and the grace of beauty.[19] Mystically, Christ is the head, and in acknowledging that, we accept our own concomitant humility. Hilary cites Luke 22:26 and Matthew 23:12, that it is better to serve and to abase oneself. That is why kings, prophets, saints, and Christ himself all trace their lineage according to the flesh ("secundum carnem," Romans 1:3). In this fleshly state, they cry out with the Psalmist, "See my humiliation and deliver me: for I have not forgotten the law" (118:153). Hilary explains in terms that apply equally well to Aethelthryth, "He asks that one see in him not the force of royal power, nor the spirit of prophecy, nor other titles of human ostentation, but humility."[20] (Recall that Aethelthryth was ascribed powers of prophecy.)[21] Each one of us, says Hilary, is responsible to know God; ignorance is no excuse. He is evident in the things around us and in the knowledge of eternal truths found in Scripture. An example, Hilary writes, is the six years of servitude given a Hebrew servant (Exodus 21:2), which relates back to Bede's <S> strophe

---

19. Ambrose, *Expositio*, §1, p. 445: "sepelitur igitur sine decore suo corpus; in capite etenim uigor uitae, in capite est gratia uenustatis."
20. Hilary, *Commentaire*, 2:268: "Non regni opes, non spiritum prophetiae, non alia aliqua humanae iactantiae nomina conspici in se, sed humilitatem precatur."
21. Bede, *HE*, 4.19, pp. 492–93.

("bis sex"). Those who refuse to understand are not part of the body of Christ.

Likewise, Bede concentrates on heretics in his commentary on the *Resh* strophe of Proverbs. Verse 31:29 reads, "multae filiae congregaverunt divitias tu supergressa es universas" (Many daughters have gathered together riches: thou hast surpassed them all). These daughters are heretics.[22] But even these can be reborn through the sacraments. The treasures are good works (cf. Aethelthryth's "actis"), prayers, fasting, alms, and the suffering and chastity of the flesh ("carnis," used in its nominative form in this strophe of the *Hymn*). But these treasures are useless unless done in the name of God (citing Matthew 7:22–23). Thus, the Catholic Church will surpass these daughters; for the Church, in her chaste faith and perfect works, follows in the footsteps ("vestigia") of her Redeemer.[23] Again we see an antithesis between carnality and spirit, between the corruptible flesh (of concupiscent men) and the incorruptible body (of the faithful). Bede's strophe reads, "Vīrgĭnĭs | ālmă că|r(ō) ēst tŭmŭ|lātă bĭs | ōctŏ Nŏ|uēmbres" (The nourishing flesh of the virgin is entombed on twice eight November); "nēc pŭtĕt | īn tŭmŭ|lō || uīrgĭnĭs | ālmă că|rō" (nor rots in a tomb the nourishing flesh of the virgin).

"Alma" was the leading word of the first strophe, where it modified the Trinity. Now it modifies the entombed flesh of Aethelthryth. Aethelthryth's flesh is literally "alma" because it will restore the eyesight of the faithful, expel devils, and heal disease. The origin of its healing power is the Trinity; thus does "alma" connect Aethelthryth to the Trinity in the *Hymn* and in the world. Moreover, the physical, fleshly aspect of virginity recalls the <F> strophe, in which the "femina virgo" begets the parent of the world. That harmony of themes suggests the importance of physical chastity; in other words, the spiritual

---

22. Bede, *PL* 91:1051B–C. Bede was much concerned with heresy. See Wallis, "Introduction," *Bede: Commentary on Revelation*, pp. 56–57. Her notes will lead a reader to relevant sources.

23. Bede, *PL* 91:1051D, "Sed omnes istiusmodi filias Ecclesia catholica supergreditur, quae fide casta, et opere perfecta, Redemptoris sui vestigia sectatur."

mandates of Christian faith cannot be fulfilled except through the body. Bede reminds his readers in a citation that Christ delivered his message "incarnatus" (in the flesh).[24] Putrefying flesh signifies sin, and it is a component of images of Hell.[25] Aethelthryth's flesh does not rot ("nec putet") in the present tense. Also of interest in this strophe is the repetition of *tumulus* 'tomb, hill'. Tombs are at the center of each verse and so are likely significant. In Mark 6:29, the apostles lay John the Baptist's body in a *monumentum*, the same word used for Christ's tomb (16:2). Luke uses *monumentum* (24:2), as does John (20:1). Matthew uses *sepulchrum* (28:1). A Spanish hymn speaks of the "Xristus tumulo," as does Ambrose.[26] Bede notes that all these words are synonyms.[27]

Although it is not clear whether Bede is making a theological point with *tumulus*, a reader may imagine that he is referring to Aethelthryth's wooden coffin, not to her white marble one. Bede may be indicating a typological connection through the wooden coffin and the incorruptible flesh (*caro, carnis*). Noah's ark, made of wood, is interpreted as the Church; 1 Peter 3:20 explains that eight souls were saved, indicating that baptism (the waters of the flood) helps to wash away the filth of the flesh ("carnis depositio sordium").[28] Thus, "octo" (eight) is also significant in the figure of the ark. Like "sex" in the <S> strophe, eight seems to carry two meanings. Literally, Aethelthryth died on the 16th Kalends of November (October 17). She also lay in her tomb for sixteen years. Figuratively, the number eight signifies the saved: eight also signifies the day of the Lord's resurrection, which "is the eighth

---

24. Bede, *HE,* 4.17, p. 384.
25. Bede, *DDI,* 14.103.
26. *Hymnodia Hispanica,* no. 36, line 21: "Cum surgit Xristus tumulo"; p. 210.
27. Bede, *DO,* p. 55, line 1191. Ambrose also uses them as synonyms, *Lucam,* lib. 6, p. 250: "nec inmerito etiam sanctus Matthaeus in monumentis illos habitasse signauit, siquidem talium animae in quibusdam uideantur habitare tumulis sepulchrorum."
28. Bede, *In Genesim,* p. 104; notes and trans., Kendall, *Bede: On Genesis,* p. 174.

day from the first day of creation."[29] The wooden timbers of the ark, writes Bede, signify the faithful. Aethelthryth's second tomb, indicated in the pentameter by a second *tumulus*, recalls that of King Sebbi of the East Saxons, like Aethelthryth a royal turned monastic, who was buried in a miraculous stone sarcophagus. Where Aethelthryth's tomb seems to have been bought randomly and fit her perfectly, so Sebbi's tomb lengthened to fit the monk-king. He was buried in St. Paul's in the diocese of Eorcenwold (Erkenwald), Bishop of London, who founded Barking Abbey and whose sister Aethelburh was its abbess. Perhaps it is too frivolous to imagine, but "virginis" (three syllables) does not match the length of the wooden "tumulata" (four syllables, five morae) of the first verse; yet by the arrival of the second, marble tomb, "virginis" and "tumulo" are equal in size (three syllables, four morae). Nevertheless, read figuratively, the wooden *tumulus* tells us that Aethelthryth is one of the elect saved from the flood. When her body comes to rest, it does so in a white, marble *tumulus*, perhaps indicative of the petrine stone of the Church. This second tomb may also refer to the bride of Christ (Apocalypse 21:2, 21:9), whom Bede says is "white and ruddy."[30] The coffin is white, and Aethelthryth's body is marked by a thin, red line around the neck. This came about, as we saw above, because Aethelthryth had a large tumor ("tumulo") on her neck.[31] The colors signify those, as Bede explains concerning the sardonyx, who are "ruddy in the passion of their body, white in the purity of their spirit."[32]

21. The twenty-first strophe is the third so far that sustains an overwhelmingly dactylic meter. Its light meter interacts with the sustained

---

29. Trans. Kendall, *Bede: On Genesis*, p. 174. My thanks to Professor Kendall for pointing out the coincidence between the date of Aethelthryth's death and the length of time she spent in her tomb. Note also the play on "*octo Novem*bres"—eight, nine.
30. Wallis, *Commentary on Revelation*, p. 268, citing the Song of Solomon 5:10.
31. *HE*, 4.19, p. 394.
32. Ibid., p. 271. Red also signifies martyrdom.

rhymes of strophes 18–27 and suggests joyful hymns or psalms. The speaker now turns from narrating facts about Aethelthryth's tomb to an apostrophe. Addressing Christ directly, the speaker acknowledges the true source of Aethelthryth's tomb miracles. In the previous strophe, the reader experienced Aethelthryth's incorruptible body; now she experiences Aethelthryth's inviolate clothing. An obvious implication is the Aethelthryth has "put on" Christ, as in Romans 13:14, "But put ye on the Lord Jesus Christ, and make not provision for the flesh in its concupiscences." The *vestis Christi* is the glorious majesty of Christ that clothes the body.[33] While Aethelthryth's incorruptible body signifies the Church, her inviolate clothes signify Christ.[34] In these final strophes, Bede will be employing Scriptural and Patristic imagery of the end times. For example, Ambrose describes the shining white garments ("vestimenta") of the resurrected dead, and the light of the Cross that illumines the tombs ("tumulis") of the dead. He speaks of the white clothes of the Word ("vestimenta veri candida").[35]

These appear in this strophe, which begins with <X> in Latin, *Shin* in Hebrew. According to Jerome, the word means *dentis* 'teeth'; Ambrose says it means "super vulnus" (concerning a wound, a disaster). In his commentary on the *Shin* strophe of Psalm 118 (vv. 161–68), Ambrose says that these wounds of the body and the mind are healed by the medicament of Christ.[36] Augustine says that we should not fear such wounds, but instead fear God, whose perfect virtue ensures us of the righteousness of his punishment. How could we not fear and love Christ, the most beautiful, not in body but

---

33. Ambrose, *Lucam*, 10, line 970.
34. Augustine, *Enn.*, *PL* 36:1591A; *Exposition*, 5:488. Augustine writes, "corpus Christi, hoc est sancta Ecclesia." Eddius Stephanus, whose description of Aethelthryth is the earliest extant, calls her uncorrupted body "impollutum"; Eddius Stephanus, *Life of Bishop Wilfrid*, p. 40; see Black, "*Nutrix pia*," pp. 167–90.
35. Ambrose, *Lucam*, p. 288. Compare the "shining white garment" that Christ sends to a naked St. Agnes in pseudo-Ambrose's account; McDaniel, "Agnes among the Anglo-Saxons," p. 227.
36. Ambrose, *Expositio*, §§ 1–2, pp. 474–75.

in virtue ("virtute formosus")?³⁷ Proverbs 31:30 reads, "fallax gratia et vana est pulchritudo mulier timens Dominum ipsa laudabitur" (Favour is deceitful, and beauty is vain: the woman that feareth the Lord, she shall be praised). In his commentary on this *Shin* strophe, Bede notes that the beauty of charity and good works is vain if displayed ("ostentat") without fear of the Lord.³⁸ Fear of the Lord is the beginning of wisdom (Proverbs 9:10). The *mulier fortis*, who is the Church, shines with ardent virtue as she approaches Christ, her *sponsus*, for just praise. Bede uses an image of blazing torches of virtue ("ardentes virtutum lampadas").³⁹ Her ardent virtue shines on account of her love for Christ, as we see Aethelthryth shine in Bede's *Hymn*. Bede's strophe reads, "Xrīstĕ tŭ|(i) ēst ŏpĕ|rīs quĭă | uēstĭs ĕt | īpsă sĕ|pūlchro" (Christ, it is through your doing that the robe itself in the tomb); "īnuĭŏ|lātă nĭ|tēt || Xrīstĕ tŭ|(i) ēst ŏpĕ|rīs" (inviolate shines, Christ it is through your doing).

The appearance of "sepulchro" in relation to Aethelthryth's marble tomb again suggests that Bede may intend a theological point. The term *tumulus* appears only in the Old Testament. New Testament graves and tombs are called sepulchers or *monumenta*. The change in terminology from the previous strophe to this one may suggest to our reader a shift from the royal tombs of the patriarchs to the sepulchers of the saints. Moreover, since *tumulus* means a small hill, we can also imagine our reader associating the term with royal burial mounds of Anglo-Saxon kings. Aethelthryth's move to a sepulcher mirrors changes in Anglo-Saxon royal burial practices over the century prior to Bede's death. We need only think of the royal burial at Sutton Hoo and the tomb of St. Aethelthryth at Ely Cathedral.⁴⁰ Aethelthryth's double burial speaks simultaneously in the languages of Christian typology and Anglo-Saxon mortuary practices. Her

---

37. Augustine, *Enn.*, *PL* 36:1596.
38. Bede, *PL* 91:1053A.
39. In the prose, Aethelthryth suffers a burning sensation ("ardor") from her tumor. *HE*, 4.19, p. 396.
40. See, for example, Williams, "Mortuary Practices in Early Anglo-Saxon England."

tomb also has healing properties. To Bede, this is not only a literal fact but also figurative. In his commentary on Luke, Ambrose writes of Jesus calming the storm on the sea (Luke 8:24); he writes that those whose spirits are similarly troubled and raging are entombed; for what else are deceitful bodies but defunct things in a sepulcher ("sepulchra") which the Word of God does not inhabit?[41] The *Shin* strophes of Scripture speak of the healing, comforting acts of Christ. And Bede's hexameter declares that Christ inhabits Aethelthryth's sepulcher through his own doing.

Christ's presence as a kind of clothing, "vestis Christi," is further implied by the terminology of the invocation ("Christe ... vestis"). Thus, the clothes "nitet" (shine) as Aethelthryth herself does (line 25, "Aedilthryda nitet"). In terms of visual grammar, the image of shining clothes is physically surrounded by the works of Christ in the strophe. The clothes point outwards from the sepulcher towards Christ. The unfolding of the sense of the strophe suggests more. The hexameter addresses Christ, and then simply names clothes and a sepulcher. It separates the clothes and sepulcher from the rest of the verse with a fourth-foot caesura. They are dead, physical, corporeal things as yet to be imbued with divine power. Their spiritual qualities will be suggested by the adjective and verb in the first colon of the pentameter (*c*). Bede ties both verses together in a way we have seen only twice before (strophes <A> and <O>): the verb governing the hexameter lies in the pentameter. The syntax thus suggests that the activity of Christ ("tui est operis") gives the light of life ("nitet") to physical, corporeal bodies ("vestis," "sepulchro"). Bede also ties the verses together with elision, a long $-\bar{o}$ melding with a long $-\bar{\imath}$ and requiring hiatus. But while sound and sense bring the verses together, a metrical shift sets them apart. The strophe's only spondee speaks in its heavy tone of the grave; then the strophe's only adjective, a dactyl, speaks lightly and joyfully of inviolate chastity.[42]

---

41. Ambrose, *Lucam*, p. 250. Prudentius uses the same image to portray Paul calming the gentiles; *Contra Symm.*, 1.7–14.

42. St. Agnes says that Christ keeps secure sacred chastity ("sacrae

22. Even in the Garden of Eden there is a snake. So, too, in Bede's *Hymn*. Just as the victory of the virgin martyr lies in overcoming the turmoil of the world, so the reader will encounter turmoil in the image of a snake. Yet like Magritte's pipe, this snake is not a snake; it is a sign of a snake, of the Devil, of heresy, of evil, and more. Now filled with images of the sanctity of Aethelthryth and conditioned by previous strophes to appreciate the beauty of divine order, our reader has invoked Christ in the voice of the poet and is now prepared to encounter the serpent. Following in the footsteps of the Virgin Mary, our nun of Barking can defeat what Eve did not—something Bede will say outright in the <Z> strophe. Prudentius describes a snake (*vipera*) biting Paul's hand (from Acts 28:3); it does him no harm. Prudentius compares Acts 28 to his own day: the snake signifies slumbering impiety that suddenly bites the right hand of justice.[43] The snake is both real, as in Acts, and figurative, as in *Contra Symmachum*. Similarly, in this strophe Aethelthryth's *hydros* and *morbus* sustain at least two levels of meaning. They represent physical and spiritual death, appropriate to this last letter of the Hebrew alphabet, *Tau*.

The twenty-second strophe begins with <Y> in Latin, *Tau* in Hebrew. According to Jerome, the word means *signa* 'signs'; Ambrose says it means "erravit" (he erred) or "consummavit" (it was finished). As the last strophe of Psalm 118 (vv. 169–76), it signifies the accomplishment of a man ("profectum hominis"), according to Ambrose.[44] "Erravit" is in the perfect tense, he notes, not the present ("errat"). It indicates that a man has come out of error. He cites Titus 3:3–5, which is worth citing in full, as it helps to illuminate the final strophes of Bede's *Hymn*:

> For we ourselves also were some time unwise, incredulous, erring, slaves to divers desires and pleasures, living in malice and envy, hateful, and hating one another. [4] But when the goodness and

---

integritatis"); Prudentius, Hymn 14.34–35 in *Cath*.
43. Prudentius, *Contra Symm.*, 1.56–57.
44. Ambrose, *Expositio*, §1, p. 488.

kindness of God our Savior appeared: [5] Not by the works of justice, which we have done, but according to his mercy, he saved us, by the laver of regeneration, and renovation of the Holy Ghost.

The rejection of that envy and hate can be figured as the rejection of the works of Satan, the serpent. That rejection is discussed by Hilary. The choice to follow the laws of God is not a necessity of nature ("non naturali necessitate"), but an act of pious will.[45] It is a choice for life, not death. Hilary warns, "Nam nasci ad mortem, non vitae est causa, sed mortis" (To be born for death is not a cause for life, but for death).[46] In choosing the laws of God, one chooses to live. Cassiodorus writes that those who draw near the Lord "more eagerly cleanse themselves of vices the more they come to enjoy the proximity of virtue."[47] And Bede imagines that proximity. The last strophe of Proverbs, 31:31, reads, "date ei de fructu manuum suarum et laudent eam in portis opera eius" (Give her of the fruit of her hands: and let her works praise her in the gates). Bede comments that after this life, the Church will be praised. The fruits are those of the spirit: charity, joy, peace, kindness, goodness, modesty, continence, faith (loyalty), and patience.[48] It is this spirit of choosing life through Christ that our reader approaches Bede's strophe: "Ȳdrŏs ĕt | ātĕr ă|bīt sā|crāe prō | uēstĭs hŏ|nōre" (And the deadly serpent departs in honor of your sacred robe); "mōrbī | dīffŭgĭ|ūnt || ȳdrŏs ĕt | ātĕr ă|bīt" (diseases disperse and the deadly serpent departs).

Images of serpents are well known in Virgil, as well. In *Aeneid* 7, the pagan priest Umbro puts them to sleep with music (lines 750–58).[49] He is a snake charmer capable of healing snake bites with his magic. But as Michael Putnam points out, "The injuries which men

---

45. Hilary, *Commentaire*, 2:300.
46. Ibid., 2:298.
47. Cassiodorus, *Explanation*, 3:254–55.
48. Bede, *PL* 91:1052C.
49. Virgil's other snakes include the hissing snakes of the Furies (*Aen.*, 7.447), a dragon (*Georg.*, 2.141), water snakes (*Georg.*, 3.545), and a giant serpent that stops Eurydice (*Georg.*, 4.458). Similar serpents appear in *Beowulf* in Grendel's mere and as the dragon.

inflict upon each other are of a different order and require a different level of sophistication and knowledge to cure, knowledge which the sorcerer Umbro does not possess."[50] Umbro can cause sleep, but he "is unable to cope with death's deeper slumber."[51] In contrast, the snake of Bede's strophe is driven away by Aethelthryth's sacred robe, that is, by her clothing of Christ. And Christ does indeed heal death's deeper slumber. Aethelthryth differs from Umbro as Aaron with his rod and serpent differs from the magicians of Pharaoh's court.[52] Aethelthryth exercises a more profound, if indirect, control over nature. She does not dispel snakes or disease; they leave of their own accord—"abit" and "diffugiunt." In fact, she is absent from this strophe entirely. A reader searching for her will confirm that what was her robe is no longer in her possession; earlier it was "ipsa" (itself, line 41), but now it is "sacrae" (sacred). In other words, her *vestis* has become the clothing of a saint; her clothing now is Christ. During the last three lines, the particular example of her life has become abstracted, dissolving into the honor and glory of Christ.

This abstracted power now sits at the center of the hexameter ("sacrae") and forms the basis of two distinct antitheses. The first is syntactic, formed around the verb "abit." On either side sits an adjective, then a particle/preposition, and then a noun: (N + CNJ + ADJ) + V + (ADJ + PRP + N). The nouns are antithetical: serpent/Devil and robe/Christ. The adjectives, too: deadly and sacred. Beyond this seven-word syntactic parallelism lies "honore," the source of the second major antithesis in the hexameter. The last word of the hexameter, it sits in antithesis to the first, "ydros." The serpent represents evil, yet counter to its nature, it does honor to the saint. The sense unfolds so that a reader experiences in order the serpent, then its departure, then the sacred, then the robe, and then finally honor. By

---

50. Putnam, "Umbro," p. 12.
51. Ibid., p. 13.
52. Exodus 7:10–12. Battles between virgins and serpents are figurative of Eve (see the next strophe) and the serpent in the garden. Margaret of Antioch is an example of such a saint. See Petroff, "Transforming the World."

the end, a reader can thereby compare the serpent that dishonored Eve to the serpent castigated by God in the Apocalypse (20:2–3). Bede will evoke this comparison again in his next strophe when he speaks of the enemy "qui vicerat Evam" (who had defeated Eve). Although there is a spiritual component to these images, there is also an earthly component. The sacred robe is named in heavy spondees, suggesting the world; the only spondee in the pentameter is equally worldly, "morbi" (diseases). Aethelthryth's tomb cures diseases, as Bede says in his prose. Both her terrestrial and heavenly presence are felt in the pentameter. It is arranged in two balanced cola. In the first (*c*), plural diseases disperse; in the second (*d*), a singular deadly serpent departs. Just as the image of Aethelthryth has dissolved into an image of Christ resplendent with his foot on the dragon, so the particularities of Aethelthryth's life have dissolved into a salvific vision of Christ among us.

23. With the Hebrew alphabet at an end, Bede turns to the Christian extensions of the alphabetic ladder of wisdom that he has modified. At this point, he has neither the Psalm nor Proverbs 31 to rely on. Whereas the <Y> strophe focused on the terrestrial defeat of Satan, the next focuses on the heavenly defeat of Satan. The twenty-third strophe begins with <Z> in Latin. This final strophe continues the antithesis of defeated evil and triumphant sanctity of the last strophe. That antithesis is mirrored metrically, with two spondees in the hexameter. But the heavy spondee of the pentameter ("mōrbī") has disappeared. It is replaced by a dactylic, joyful virgin, suggesting a shift from terrestrial to heavenly. The pauses of the two strophes are artfully arranged. There is a fourth-foot word break in both hexameters, which is typical of bucolic verse.[53] Indeed, there is such a break in two-thirds of the strophes. A reader may imagine that the bucolic pause suggests the Garden of Eden. And in the hexameters of the <Y> and <Z> strophes, Bede alludes to the serpent in the Garden,

---

53. Bede, *DAM*, I, xii; Kendall, *Libri II*, p. 113. There seems to be no consistency to the use of heavy or light syllables preceding the pause.

first in the past, and then in the present. Bede's strophe reads, "Zēlŭs ĭn | hōstĕ fŭ|rīt quōn|dām quī | uīcĕrăt | Ēuam" (Jealousy rages in the enemy who once had defeated Eve); "uīrgŏ trĭ|ūmphăt ŏ|uāns || zēlŭs ĭn | hōstĕ fŭ|rīt" (the rejoicing Virgin triumphs, jealousy rages in the enemy).

As the serpent began the previous strophe, so his jealousy begins this one. The reader is transported into the depths of worldly vice, tasting jealousy as her eyes move across the words. She is next invited to imagine the interior of the enemy ("in hoste") and to view there a burning rage ("furit"). Speeding through these feet, she comes slowly and ponderously to the next colon, spondee following spondee. The repeated /k/ of "Quondam Qui" sounds bestial to her, perhaps like the croaking of frogs, another symbol of Satan, the spondees suggesting terrestrial noise. With "vicerat" the reader hears again the bestial croak, but *-erat* in "vicerat" tells her (as Ambrose noticed of "erravit") that the defeat is well past. Diaresis separates the bestial fury of the enemy from Eve. Eve is inflected in the accusative, the trochaic object of the unnamed enemy ("hostis . . . qui"). The enemy is not the subject of the hexameter, but an implied referent of "qui," suggesting that Eve's defeat was not solely his own doing. "Zelus" agrees with "qui," and a reader casting her mind back from the last word to the first can imagine that jealousy itself was the enemy that defeated Eve—jealousy of God. The earlier perspective that looked out from within the bowels of the enemy suddenly becomes a self-reflective perspective, in which the reader casts about within herself for the enemy, jealousy.

As the reader moves to the pentameter, she finds a virgin as its subject. A third shift of perspective now places the reader's eye within the Virgin. With the Virgin, the reader then moves to a present-tense triumph ("triumphat") over jealousy, over the enemy, and over original sin. The tense tells the reader that both she and the Virgin are triumphing at this very moment in the historical present of the reader. With "ovans" (rejoicing), the reader experiences the continuing action of a participle. The temporal complexion of the strophe places a joyful, present-day third colon within a historical setting. At the center of the strophe are Eve and the Virgin: one an object of jealous enmity, the other the subject of joyful triumph. The antithesis is not resolved. Bede offers his reader triumphant joy, but within a sobering view of the toil and turmoil of the world. That same combination of triumph and wariness will characterize the final four strophes.

Now we come to our ending. Bede has progressed through the twenty-three letters of the Latin alphabet. For twenty-two of those letters, he was inspired by the ladder of the Hebrew alphabet. The twenty-third letter spoke of Christianity's triumph, represented by the Virgin. In his *DAM*, Bede noted that Christians use twenty-seven letters. Twenty-three letters with an additional four stanzas in an acrostic give us twenty-seven. The acrostic is a prayerful Christian one: it spells *amen*. That *amen* serves two purposes. First, by bringing the number of stanzas to twenty-seven, it Christianizes the Latin alphabet. In doing so, it offers the reader a further four steps on the ladder (gradus) of wisdom, which is Christ. Second, the acrostic *amen* affirms the lessons in faith acquired during the *Hymn*. Like the "amen" sung during the Mass, these strophes are made for singing. The content of the acrostic concerns choirs of angels and saints. We have already seen how the periods are connected by rhyme (chapter 3), and how the stanzas are also connected by rhyme. Recall the chiastic rhyme of strophe 24, *a-d*, *b-c*. The final three strophes each rhyme cola *a*, *b*, and *d*. And colon 24*a-d* rhymes with colon 26. The final four strophes are as follows:

> [24.] Āspĭcĕ | nūptă Dĕ|ō quae | sīt tĭbĭ | glōrĭă | tērris
>   quāe mănĕ|āt cāe|līs || āspĭcĕ | nūptă Dĕ|ō.
>
> (See what glory is yours among the nations having married God,
>   you who abide in the heavens, see, having married God.)
>
> [25.] Mūnĕră | lāetă că|pīs fē|stĭuīs | fūlgĭdă | tāedis
>   ēccĕ uĕ|nīt spōn|sūs || mūnĕră | lāetă că|pīs.
>
> (You receive joyful gifts gleaming with festive torches,
>   behold, the bridegroom arrives, you receive joyful gifts.)

[26.] Ēt nŏuă | dūlcĭsŏ|nō mŏdŭ|lārīs | cārmĭnă | plēctro
spōns(a) hȳmn(o) | ēxūl|tās || ēt nŏuă | dūlcĭsŏ|nō.

(And new songs you play with sweet-sounding plectrum
and you, the new bride, exult with a sweet-sounding hymn.)

[27.] Nūllŭs ăb | āltĭthrŏ|nī cō|mītătŭ | sēgrĕgăt | Āgni
qu(am) āffē|ctū tŭlĕ|rāt || nūllŭs ăb | āltĭthrŏ|nī.

(No one separates her from the retinue of the high-throned Lamb
she whom no one bore away through passion from the high-throned One.)

We notice immediately the multiple addressees of these strophes. Strophes 24, 25, and 26 are spoken in the second person. "Aspice" (you look on, behold) of strophe 24 (l. 47) seems to address Aethelthryth, although it might address Christ, as in strophe 21 ("Xriste"). The next strophe addresses Aethelthryth ("capis," you receive, take, line 49), although it might as easily address the reader. Strophe 26 addresses Aethelthryth ("modularis," you sing, play, line 51), although it too can also apply to a reader. The final strophe combines these multiple addressees by mixing the masculine form "nullus" with the feminine form "quam." If we were to observe the speaker's eyes, we would see him look about as he intoned strophe 24, then look up to the heavens for strophes 25 and 26, glancing down occasionally, and finally return his eyes to an unnamed woman, likely Aethelthryth ("quam").

24. Strophe 24 instructs the reader to behold. But the next phrase, "nupta deo" (having married God) is not a direct object of "aspice." Our reader infers Aethelthryth from this antonomasia, which "refers to a specific person by his or her attributes."[54] The recent instances of this trope are in the <Y> strophe ("ydros ater") and the <Z> strophe ("hoste," also an epithet). As in the <X> strophe, Aethelthryth is suggested but not directly indicated. Earlier, she was portrayed as a vehicle of Christ's power. Our reader bears in mind Aethelthryth's role

---

54. Bede, *DST* § 5; trans. Kendall, *Libri II*, pp. 186–87.

as she reaches "quae," a feminine singular pronoun (who or which). She is not quite sure whether "quae" refers to the implied bride of the imperative verb, or whether it is proleptic. As she proceeds, she reads "gloria," which is also a feminine singular noun, so "quae" might refer to glory. The grammar of the line thus serves to mix the bride with glory. And a reader is at first unsure of the boundary between them. If "gloria" is taken as a predicate noun, Aethelthryth herself may be an earthly glory to the Lord; but if "gloria" is taken to coordinate with "quae," then the glory is Aethelthryth's. Bede does not require the reader to choose one or the other, since both are at play. They continue to be at play in the pentameter, for both glory and the bride abide ("maneat") with God in Heaven. This complementary pair—glory and the bride—are known in Heaven and on earth. Perhaps to strengthen the parallel and mitigate any desire to separate the two implications, Bede casts both "terris" and "caelis" in the plural. The two verbs aside from "aspice" are both subjunctive, not indicative, so there is no actor to point to (*indicare*), only the presence of activity itself; the reader can occupy two perspectives simultaneously. In the first, she hears the imperative spoken to the person of Christ. She associates "tibi" with Christ—Behold, Christ, what glory is yours in the earth from Aethelthryth's marriage to God. In the second perspective, she hears the imperative spoken to Aethelthryth—Behold, Aethelthryth, what glory is yours in the earth having married God. Colgrave seems to suggest this second perspective in his translation.[55] In this second perspective, which I have also taken, the reader is associated through the imperative mood and the participle with Aethelthryth. The glory of consecrated virginity is offered to her as a glorious goal. Read literally, the strophe implies an audience of nuns and novices. Reader, Bede seems to say, look what glory may be yours in the earth by marrying God, glory which abides in Heaven.

---

55. Bede, *HE,* 4.19, p. 401: "Affianced to the Lamb, now famed on earth! / Soon famed in heaven, affianced to the Lamb."

25. Continuing his apostrophe to the reader through the eyes of Aethelthryth, Bede says that she will receive glad gifts. "Munera" are not only gifts but also duties: she who has married or marries God does joyful service to the Lord. The verb is in the present tense: these gifts are had at this present moment, and these duties are current ones. In the pentameter, the Bridegroom arrives now ("venit"). Bede seems to be speaking of clerical devotion and religious ritual in the present day. The reception of gifts is an annual event. Writing on the feast of Easter, Bede says, "Hic uero uitae UENTURAE et mysteria celebrentur et munera CAPIANTUR" (But in the former case [Easter season] the mysteries of the life TO COME should be celebrated and its gifts RECEIVED).[56] The Bridegroom, who is Christ, may come at any moment, but He is here now, wherever two or three gather in his name (Matthew 3:20). The temporal convolutions of this strophe indicate the multiple presences of Christ. Earthly images are extended next to the heavens. The gifts are "fulgida" (shining, gleaming, glittering). Horace, Ovid, and Virgil speak about fulgent skies and stars. The flames of these torches compare to the flames that would not consume virgin martyrs earlier in the poem. These are the lit lamps of the not-so-foolish virgins, the fires of ardent love for God.[57] Prudentius writes in his *Apotheosis* of the inoffensive flames ("innocuas ... flammas") that refuse to harm martyrs. Citing Daniel 3:25, Prudentius tells his readers to behold the martyrs laughing as they cross unharmed through ardent fires ("ecce, vaporiferos ridens intersecat ignes"). This is the Son of God acting on the *taedae* 'torches'.[58]

The syntax of the hexameter, which associates a word in the second colon with a word in the first, is mirrored in the next strophe ("nova ... carmina"). Meter also associates the two: "fulgida" and "carmina" are dactyls between two spondees. They both reach back from amid a spondaic colon to a dactylic one. "Aspice" of the

---

56. Bede, *De temporibus liber*, 15; trans. Kendall and Wallis, *Bede: On the Nature of Things and On Times*, p. 117.
57. Cf. Prudentius, *Contra Symm.*, 1.263.
58. Prudentius, *Apoth.*, lines 128–36.

previous strophe is further mirrored in "ecce" "behold." Like the rhyme scheme, these cross-references tie the final strophes together. "Ecce," the first word of the pentameter, calls to mind the liturgical formula, "Ecce, Agnus Dei, qui tollit peccata mundi" (behold the Lamb of God who takes away the sins of the world). The imperative of "ecce" will not be fulfilled until the last strophe, however, where the reader experiences "Agni" (line 53). "Ecce" also refers to the arrival of the Bridegroom during the Mass. He becomes available to all during the communion, after the intonation of the *Agnus Dei*. Here, in a metalepsis, is the fulgent gift for a reader dedicated to virginity.

26. Again, a reader is invited to see herself through the eyes of Aethelthryth. As she intones this hymn in praise of the royal virgin, she is literally singing a new song. It is a song in praise of God, not in praise of Aethelthryth. Aethelthryth's glory is reflected light; she gains it through Christ's mercy, which Bede insists upon in the <X> strophe. There, Aethelthryth's clothes shine because of Christ's power. The gifts of strophe 25 shine because of heavenly fire. This strophe's new song earns the designation *hymn* according to Augustine's requirements that a hymn be sung (Bede's "modularis"), in verse ("carmina," "hymno"), and dedicated to God ("sponso"). (Bede seems to have been quite thorough.) It is written in a meter fit for dignified religious themes (*ddds*), and as in strophe 25, the fifth foot of this strophe sits between two spondees (not so in neighboring strophes 24 and 27). This strophe differs from the other four of the acrostic in its third colon, where spondees predominate. The slow, heavy, dignified meter speaks of an exultant hymn. If we turn to our reader, we realize that this hymn is in her mouth. The heavy spondees, used elsewhere to suggest the earthly, here suggest a hymn intoned in the physical world ("os meum," as in Psalms 50:17). Her singing voice is implied by elision in the third colon. In written form the rhymes –*a* and –*o* play no part in making the feet, but in sung form they resonate completely with equivalent vowels in the other three cola. The extreme rhyme connects all four cola closely, as does syntax. Consistent with the golden line, the two adjectives of *a* ("new," "sweet-sounding")

are proleptic, separated by the verb ("play") from their two nouns in *b* ("songs," "plectrum"). The order is reversed in the pentameter. There, the two nouns of *c* ("bride," "hymn") are modified by two adjectives in *d* ("new," "sweet-sounding"), and the pairs here separated by a verb ("exult"). Also connecting the cola are two similar rhetorical tropes: in *b*, "plectrum" is a synecdoche for a harp or cithara. The pick is not sweet-sounding, but the instrument is. In *c*, "nova sponsa" is also a way of naming something or someone without using the name, called antonomasia. The trope invites ambiguity, allowing our reader to imagine herself as the new bride. Again, Bede has put both verbs in the present tense. Our nun of Barking, bride of Christ, is exulting with a new song as she sings this hymn.

27. As our reader in the guise of Aethelthryth begins this last strophe, she may expect *nulla* 'none' in the feminine. Instead, she reads "nullus" in the masculine. Perhaps she thinks back on each of Aethelthryth's two husbands. When she reads "comitatu" she will immediately realize that the military terminology has cast Aethelthryth (and the reader herself) as a *miles*, a masculine word, a soldier of Christ, who serves in the retinue of the high-throned Lamb. We have seen that God acts as a mother and a father, and that virginity is a virtue for both men and women. The speaking voice of the hymn now invites women to take on masculine roles and men to take on feminine roles. At the onset of the pentameter, "quam," a feminine form, invites men and women to imagine how each bears Christ within himself or herself as the Virgin bore the Christ child. Our virgin, Christian nun bears Christ within herself as she intones a new song. That song is further characterized by "altithroni," an allusion to Juvencus. It is his neologism by which he invokes not the Muses, but the Holy Spirit. With that connection, the hymn's opening strophes are brought again to mind. Juvencus speaks in his prologue of the "altithroni genitoris gloria" (glory of the high-throned father).[59] Here, the Father is portrayed as the *genitor*, the

---

59. Green, *Latin Epics of the New Testament*, p. 16. "Comitata" is also found in the same poem by Juvencus (1. 446).

creator, the progenitor, he who *gives birth* to. Bede will pick up on that image of birth with "tulerat" (had borne), which suggests bearing or carrying Christ as the Virgin did literally, or as Aethelthryth did figuratively. As well as bearing Christ within her, our reader bears the image of Aethelthryth, one who was not carried away by means of "affectu" (affection, passion).

The word "affectu" derives from *affectare* 'aspiration, endeavor'. This affection is connected by a kind of ellipsis to Aethelthryth's husbands and to conjugal love. But our virgin nun of Barking knows that passion, which is both worldly and spiritual, is truly sated by God. Perhaps Bede is subtly distinguishing the ultimate aim of his poem—worship of Christ—from the sensuous passion the poem's words might inspire. In other words, Bede may be using conjugal passion to comment on the more orderly poetic passions. We see in these last four strophes a combination of marriage imagery ("nupta," "sponsus," and "affectu") and song ("carmina," "hymno"). To take but one example, "affectu" sits inside the colon's phrase "quam affectu tulerat." As a reader begins the phrase, she might expect passion to be the impetus for Aethelthryth's devotion to Christ. But with "tulerat" our reader likely recalls the hymn's opening "raptus Helenae" by comparison. As in that <C> strophe, this last strophe depends for its force on a negative assessment of worldly passion (recall "luxus erit lubricis"). More prosaically, no one—that is, none of her husbands—bore Aethelthryth away by means of such passion.

But this strophe seems more allusive: as in previous strophes, Aethelthryth is absent. If she is there at all, she is there in a pronoun ("quam"), its referent equally vague ("sponsa," l. 52). As we saw above, the closing four strophes might conceivably be apostrophes to any devoted nun who has passed into Heaven. Rather than record mere history, they put the reader in direct relation to the transcendent reality of Heaven. This widening perspective encompasses the self-referential "new song" of strophe 26, which recalls the "chaste songs" announced by the poet in the <C> strophe. (That self-referentiality recalls Hilary's hymn "Hymnum dicat turba fratrum," above.) Both songs stand in opposition to a negated passion or affection in strophe 27. Bede places them symmetrically: the exultant hymn in 26c and dangerous affection in 27c. Adding to that sense of symmetrical opposition, strophe 26 resonates with /o/, each cola rhyming. But in strophe 27, the very words that indicate being carried away by passion ("affectu tulerat") break the rhyme. In this closing strophe, where one might expect exultant praise, one finds masterfully ordered understatement. In short, Bede seems to be advocating a sober, modulated Christian aesthetic in which one does not get carried away by passion. One is reminded of Pythagoras calming the inner passions of a raging youth with modulated song.

In the hexameter, Bede segregates "Agni" from the "altithroni comitatu" by means of the verb "segregat." The verb is doing precisely what it means, segregating. With that semantic and literal coincidence in a hymn where ambiguity has characterized so many words, we are now at a point where the sign and the signifier are perfectly coincident. It is at this point, moreover, when the act of reading and one's awareness of the act are congruent. Or, the order of language (*Lôgos*) and the movement of one's thoughts are synchronous. The sense of congruity and synchrony are even stronger with the verb "tulerat" (*ferre, tuli, latus*) in the pentameter. It reaches for the preposition *ab* to remind our grammatically trained nun literally of the ablative (*ablativus* < *ab* + *latus*); she might note therein the perfect coincidence of grammatical form and content. As she moves through this ablative moment, she reaches the fourth colon of the strophe. Approaching that colon, there seems to linger a sense of vacuity—an absence implied in "tulerat" and an absence clear in "nullus." That vacuum is filled by the last word of the strophe, which gives the preposition its object. As the grammatical sensation is fulfilled, so is the semantic sense. While "altithroni" echoes in our reader's ears, its rhyme recalls to mind "Agni," which sat at the center of the strophe, and of which "altithroni" is an appositive. Yet both rhymes are instances of antonomasia, leaving our reader looking at epithets rather than at the name of God. They are also inflections, leaving our reader with a sensation of grammatical contingency. The words incline to some other noun, perhaps suggesting a similar, fundamental inclination of readers to move always towards some other meaning. This combined sense of absence and inclination to seek elsewhere is bolstered sonically: a series of /t/ and /l/ tie the last four words together and are interlaced with a series tied together by /u/ ("affectu tulerat nullus"). And it is worth noting again that the poem ends with an allusion, a glance elsewhere in the lyric tradition. Bede does not leave his reader with a sense of unfulfilled contingency. The poem's last syllable, "oni" seems to pun on "uni" (one) as a singular counterpoint to the hymn's triune beginning, "alma Deus Trinitas": the many in the one, the beginning in the end. In this strophe's complex of pronouns, the nun becomes a soldier, the solitary reader becomes part of a retinue, the past becomes present to the reader, and the chaste nun is momentarily filled with passion. In the hymn's closing strophe, we see that all genders, offices, classes, antitheses, and contraries come together; none has been segregated from the retinue of the Lamb. Perhaps with that final thought our nun of Barking puts aside Bede's hymn. Perhaps she saw in it something beautiful.

Works Cited

Primary Sources

Acta sanctorum [*AS*]. Edited by Joannes Bolandus. 68 vols. Paris, 1863–1948.

Aldhelm. *Aldhelm: The Poetic Works*. Translated by Michael Lapidge and James Rosier. Cambridge, 1985.

———. *Aldhelm: The Prose Works*. Translated by Michael Lapidge and Michael Herren. Cambridge, 1979.

———. *Carmen de virginitate* [*CDV*]. Edited by Rudolf Ehwald. MGH AA 15. Berlin, 1919.

———. *De metris et aenigmatibus ac pedum regulis*. Edited by Rudolf Ehwald. MGH AA 15. Berlin, 1919.

———. "Enigma XXX." Edited by Rudolf Ehwald. MGH AA 15. Berlin, 1919.

———. *Prosa de virginitate* [*PDV*]. Edited by Rudolf Ehwald. MGH AA 15. Berlin, 1919.

Ambrose. *De institutione virginis*. PL 16:305–34.

———. *De noe*. Edited by C. Schenkl. CSEL 32.1. Vienna, 1897.

———. *De virginibus ad Marcellinam*. PL 16:187–232.

———. *De virginitate*. PL 16:265–302.

———. *Exhortatio virginitatis*. PL 16:335–64.

———. *Explanatio psalmorum xii*. Edited by M. Petschenig, revised by Michaela Zelzer. CSEL 64. Vienna, 1919 and 1998.

———. *Expositio evangelii secundum Lucam* [*Lucam*]. Edited by C. Schenkl. CCSL 32.4. Vienna, 1902.

———. *Expositio psalmi CLVIII* [*Expositio*]. Edited by M. Petschenig. CSEL 62. Vienna, 1913.

———. *Hymnes*. Edited by Jacques Fontaine. Paris, 2008.

Analecta hymnica medii aevi [*AH*]. Edited by Clemens Blume and Guido Maria Dreves. 55 vols. Leipzig, 1886–1922.

Arator. *De actibus apostolorum*. PL 68:94A.

———. *Epistola ad vigilium*. PL 68:80–81.

Augustine. *Confessiones* [*Conf.*]. Edited by P. Knöll. CSEL 33. Vienna, 1896.

———. *De sancta virginitate*. Edited by J. Zycha. CSEL 41. Vienna, 1900.

———. *Enarrationes in psalmos*. Edited by E. Dekkers. CCSL 39. Turnhout, 1956.

———. *Enarrationes in psalmos* [*Enn.*]. PL 36.

———. *Exposition on the Psalms* [*Exposition*]. Translated by Maria Boulding. 6 vols. Hyde Park, 1999.

———. *On Christian Doctrine*. Translated by D. W. Robertson. New York, 1958.

———. *Retractationum libri duo*. Edited by A. Mutzenbecher. CCSL 57. Turnhout, 1984.

———. *Saint Augustine, Confessions*. Translated by Henry Chadwick. Oxford, 1991.

———. *Sancta Virginitate*. PL 40:397–427.

Avitus. *De virginitate*. Edited by R. Peiper. MGH AA 6.2. Berlin, 1883.

Bede. *Abbots of Wearmouth and Jarrow* [*HA*]. Edited and translated by Christopher Grocock and I. N. Wood. Oxford Medieval Texts. Oxford, 2013.

———. *Cantica canticorum Libri VI*. Edited by D. Hurst. CCSL 119b. Turnhout, 1983.

———. *De arte metrica* [*DAM*]. In *Bede: Libri II De arte metrica et de schematibus et tropis,* edited and translated by Calvin Kendall, pp. 36–167. Saarbrücken, 1991.

———. *De arte metrica et De schematibus et tropis*. Edited by Calvin B. Kendall. CCSL 123a. Turnhout, 1975.

———. *De die iudicii* [*DDI*]. Edited by J. Fraipont. CCSL 122. Turnhout, 1955.

———. *De orthographia* [*DO*]. Edited by Charles W. Jones. CCSL 123a. Turnhout, 1975.

———. *De schematibus et tropis* [*DST*]. In *Bede: Libri II De arte metrica et de schematibus et tropis,* edited and translated by Calvin Kendall, pp. 168–209. Saarbrücken, 1991.

———. *De tabernaculo.* Edited by D. Hurst. CCSL 119a. Turnhout, 1969.

———. *Expositio actuum apostolorum.* Edited by M. L. W. Laistner. CCSL 121. Turnhout, 1983.

———. *Historia ecclesiastica gentis Anglorum* [*HE*]. Edited and translated by Bertram Colgrave and R. A. B. Mynors. Oxford Medieval Texts. Oxford, 1969.

———. "Homily I.13 on Benedict Biscop." In *Abbots of Wearmouth and Jarrow,* edited and translated by Christopher Grocock and I. N. Wood, pp. 1–19. Oxford Medieval Texts. Oxford, 2013.

———. *In epistulas septem catholicas.* Edited by D. Hurst. CCSL 121. Turnhout, 1983.

———. *In Ezram et Neemiam libri iii.* Edited by D. Hurst. CCSL 119a. Turnhout, 1983.

———. In primam partem Samuhelis. Edited by D. Hurst. CCSL 119b. Turnhout, 1962.

———. *In proverbia Salomonis.* Edited by D. Hurst. CCSL 119b. Turnhout, 1983.

———. *In regum librum xxx quaestiones.* Edited by D. Hurst. CCSL 119. Turnhout, 1962.

———. *Liber hymnorum* [*Hymn*]. Edited by J. Fraipont. CCSL 122. Turnhout, 1955.

———. *Martyrology.* Edited by Henri Quentin. Paris, 1908.

———. *Martyrology.* Edited by Jacques DuBois. *Edition pratique des martyrologes de Bède, de l'anonyme lyonnais et de Florus.* Paris, 1976.

———. *On What Isaiah Says.* Translated by Arthur Holder. In *Bede: A Biblical Miscellany,* translated by W. Trent Foley and Arthur G. Holder, 35–51. Liverpool, 1999.

———. *Opera homiletica.* Edited by D. Hurst. CCSL 122. Turnhout, 1955.

———. *Vita S. Felicis*. PL 94:793.

———. *Vita sancti Cuthberti* (prose). In *Two Lives of Saint Cuthbert*, edited and translated by Bertram Colgrave. Cambridge, 1940.

———. *Vita sancti Cuthberti* (verse) [*VSC*]. In *Bedas metrische Vita Sancti Cuthberti*, edited by Werner Jaager. Leipzig, 1935.

Biblia sacra iuxta vulgatam versionem. Edited by Robert Weber et al. Stuttgart, 1969.

Bibliorum sacrorum Latinae versiones antiquae seu Vetus Italica. Edited by D. P. Sabatier. 2 vols. Rheims, 1743.

Bibliotheca Hagiographica Latina. Edited by J. Bollandus. 2 vols. Brussels, 1898–1900.

Cassian, John. *De institutis coenobiorum et de octo principalium uitiorum remediis*. Edited by Michael Petschenig. CSEL 17. Vienna, 1888.

Cassiodorus. *Complexiones in Apocalypsin*. CCSL 107.

———. *Explanation of the Psalms* [*Explanation*]. Translated by P. G. Walsh. 3 vols. Ancient Christian Writers 52. New York, 1991.

———. *Expositio in psalterium* [*Expositio*]. PL 70:9–1056.

Clavis Patrum Latinorum [*CPL*]. Edited by Eligius Dekkers. 3rd ed. Turnhout, 1995.

Cyprian. *De habitu virginum*. PL 4:440–64.

Cyprian of Carthage. *Epistulae*. Edited by G. F. Diercks. CCSL 3B and 3C. Turnhout, 1994–96.

Eddius Stephanus. *The Life of Bishop Wilfrid by Eddius Stephanus*. Edited and translated by Bertram Colgrave. Cambridge, 1927.

Eugenius of Toledo. *Carmina* 20. Edited by F. Vollmer. MGH AA 14. Berlin, 1905.

Eusebius. *Historia Ecclesiastica*. Edited by Theodor Mommsen. Eusebius Werke: Die Kirchengeschichte. 2 vols. Leipzig, 1903.

Fortunatus. *De virginitate*. Ed. F. Leo. MGH AA 4.1. Berlin, 1881.

———. *Poems*. Edited by and translated by Marc Reydellet. *Venance Fortunat: Poèmes*. Collections des universités de France. 3 vols. Paris, 2002.

Gregory the Great. *Moralia in Job*. Edited by M. Adriaen. CCSL 143b. Turnhout, 1985.

Hilarii Pictaviensis Opera. Edited by Alfred Feder. CSEL 65. Vienna, 1916.

Hilary of Poitiers. *Commentaire sur le psaume 118* [*Commentaire*]. Edited and translated by Marc Milhau. Sources Chrétiennes 344. 2 vols. Paris, 1988.

———. *Tractatus super psalmos* [*Commentaire*]. CSEL 22. Vienna, 1891.

Hymnodia hispanica. Edited by J. Castro Sánchez. CCSL 167. Turnhout, 2010.

Ildefonsus of Toledo. *De virginitate perpetua sanctae Mariae*. PL 96:58A.

Isidore of Seville. *Etymologiarum sive originum libri xx* [*Etym.*]. Edited by W. M. Lindsey. 2 vols. Oxford, 1911.

———. *The Etymologies of Isidore of Seville* [*Etym.*]. Translated by Stephen A. Barney et al. Cambridge, 2006.

Jerome. *Commentarioli in psalmos*. Edited by P. Antin. CCSL 72. Turnhout, 1959.

———. Epistle 30. Edited by Isidorus Hilberg. CSEL 54. Leipzig, 1910.

———. *Epistola* 22. Edited and translated by F. A. Wright. Cambridge, 1980.

———. *In librum psalmorum*. Edited by G. Morin. CCSL 78. 2nd ed. Turnhout, 1958.

Liber Eliensis. Edited by E. O. Blake. London, 1962.

Old English Martyrology. Edited by Georg Herzfeld. EETS o.s. 116. London, 1900.

One Hundred Latin Hymns. Edited and translated by Peter G. Walsh et al. Cambridge, MA, 2002.

Ovid. *Amores*. Edited by E. J. Kenney. Oxford, 1961.

Patrologia Latina [*PL*]. Edited by Jacques-Paul Migne. 217 vols. Paris, 1844–64.

Paulinus of Nola. *Carmina*. Edited by W. Hartel. CSEL 30. Vienna, 1894.

Poetria Nova. Edited by Paolo Mastandrea and Luigi Tessarolo. CD-ROM. Florence, 2001.

Prosperi Aquitani: Carmen de ingratis et Epigrammata selecta. Edited by S. Leonis. Rome, 1759.

Prudentius. *Apotheosis* [*Apoth.*]. In Prudentius, *Works*, vol. 2.

———. *Cathemerinon liber* [*Cath.*]. In Prudentius, *Works*, vol. 1.

———. *Contra Symmachum* [*Contra Symm.*]. In Prudentius, *Works*, vol. 3.

———. *Hamartigenia* [*Hamart.*]. In Prudentius, *Works*, vol. 2.

———. *Peristephanon liber* [*Peri.*]. In Prudentius, *Works* , vol. 4.

———. *Psychomachia* [*Psych.*]. In Prudentius, *Works*, vol. 3.

———. *Works*. Edited and translated by M. Lavarenne. *Prudence*. Collections des universités de France. 3rd ed. 4 vols. Paris, 2003.

Sedulius. *Carmen Paschale* [*CP*]. In *Sedulii Opera Omnia*, edited by J. Huemer. CSEL 10. Vienna, 1885.

———. *Carmen Paschale [CP]*. Translated by Carl P. E. Springer. *Sedulius: The Paschal Song and Hymns*. Atlanta, 2013.

Septuaginta. Edited by Robert Hanhart. Stuttgart, 2006.

Servius. *In Vergilii Carmina Commentarii* [*Commentarii*]. Edited by George Thilo and Hermann Hagen. 3 vols. Leipzig, 1884.

Servius' Commentary on Book Four of Virgil's Aeneid. Translated by Christopher McDonough et al. Wauconda, IL, 2004.

Secondary Sources

Abrams, M. H. *The Fourth Dimension of a Poem*. New York, 2012.

Aertsen, Jan A. "The Triad «True-Good-Beautiful». The Place of Beauty in the Middle Ages." In *Intellect et imagination dans la philosophie médiévale*, edited by Maria Cândida Pacheco and José F. Meirinhos, 415–35. Turnhout, 2006.

Allen, Sidney W. *Accent and Rhythm: Prosodic Features of Latin and Greek*. Cambridge, 1973.

———. *Vox Latina: A Guide to the Pronunciation of Classical Latin*. Cambridge, 1965.

Arnou, R.P. "Platonisme des Pères." In *Dictionnarie de théologie catholique*, edited by A. Vacant, E. Mangerot, and É. Amann, 2258–392. Paris, 1935.

Assunto, Rosario. *Die Theorie des Schönen im Mittelalter*. Köln, 1963.

Auerbach, Erich. *Literary Language and its Public in Late Latin Antiquity and in the Middle Ages*. Translated by Ralph Manheim. Princeton, 1965.

———. *Mimesis: The Representation of Reality in Western Literature*. Princeton, 1953.

Beardsley, M. C. *Aesthetics from Classical Greece to the Present*. Tuscaloosa, AL, 1966.

Beare, W. "The Origin of Rhythmic Latin Verse." *Hermathena* 87 (1956): 3–20.

Bede and His World: The Jarrow Lectures 1958–1993. 2 vols. Burlington, VT, 1993.

Bede's Ecclesiastical History. Translated by Rowan Williams and Benedicta Ward. New York, 2012.

Begbie, Jeremy. "Created Beauty." In *The Beauty of God: Theology and the Arts*, edited by Daniel J. Treier et al., 19–44. Downers Grove, IL, 2007.

Bernard, J. H., and R. Atkinson. *The Irish Liber Hymnorum*. 2 vols. London, 1898.

Bestul, Thomas H. "Devotional and Mystical Literature." In Mantello and Rigg, *ML*, 694–701.

Biggs, Frederick M., et al. *Sources of Anglo-Saxon Literary Culture*. Kalamazoo, 2001.

Bischoff, Bernhard, and Michael Lapidge. *Biblical Commentaries from the Canterbury School of Theodore and Hadrian*. CSASE 10. Cambridge, 1994.

Black, John. "Nutrix pia: The flowering of the Cult of St. Aethelthryth in Anglo-Saxon England." In *Writing Women Saints in Anglo-Saxon England*, edited by Paul Szarmach, 167–90. Toronto, 2013.

Blaise, Albert. *A Handbook of Christian Latin: Style, Morphology, and Syntax*. Translated by Grant C. Roti. Turnhout, 1955.

Bonner, Gerald. "Bede and Medieval Civilization." *ASE* 2 (1973): 71–90.

Borinski, Karl. *Die Poetik der Renaissance und die Anfang der literarischen Kritik in Deutschland*. Berlin, 1886.

Breed, Brian W. *Pastoral Inscriptions: Reading and Writing Virgil's Eclogues*. London, 2006.

Brown, George Hardin. *A Companion to Bede*. Cambridge, 2009.

Brunhölzl, Franz. *Histoire de la littérature latine du Moyen Age*. 3 vols. Turnhout, 1990.

Brunk, Gretchen. "Syntactic Glosses in Latin Manuscripts of Anglo-Saxon Origin." Dissertation. Yale University, 1973.

Caillau, D. A. B. *Collectio selecta ss. ecclesiae patrum*. Paris, 1834.

Califf, David J. *A Guide to Latin Meter and Verse Composition*. London, 2002.

Cannon, Christopher. "*Raptus* in the Chaumpaigne Release and a Newly Discovered Document Concerning the Life of Geoffrey Chaucer." *Speculum* 68, no. 1 (1993): 74–94. http://dx.doi.org/10.2307/2863835.

Caridad, M. C. "La poesía rítmica." In *La Filología Latina hoy: actualización y perspectivas*, vol. 2, edited by Ana María Aldama, 627–33. Madrid, 1999.

Carruthers, Mary. *The Experience of Beauty in the Middle Ages*. Oxford, 2013. http://dx.doi.org/10.1093/acprof:osobl/9780199590322.001.0001.

Caviness, Madeline H. "Images of Divine Order and the Third Mode of Seeing." *Gesta* 22, no. 2 (1983): 99–120. http://dx.doi.org/10.2307/766920.

Chardonnens, László Sándor. "Mantic Alphabets in Medieval Western Manuscripts and Early Printed Books." *Modern Philology* 110, no. 3 (2013): 340–66. http://dx.doi.org/10.1086/669251.

Chase, Colin. "Alcuin's Grammar Verse: Poetry and Truth in Carolingian Pedagogy." *Insular Latin Studies* 1 (1981): 135–52.

Christie, Eddie. "By Means of a Secret Alphabet: Dangerous Letters and the Semantics of Gebregdstafas (Solomon and Saturn I, Line 2b)." *Modern Philology* 109, no. 2 (2011): 145–70. http://dx.doi.org/10.1086/663211.

Cipriani, Nello. "Rhetoric." In *Augustine through the Ages: An Encyclopedia*, edited by Allan D. Fitzgerald, 724–26. Grand Rapids, MI, 1999.

Clackson, James, and Geoffrey Horrocks. *The Blackwell History of the Latin Language*. Malden, MA, 2011.

Clark, Anne L. "Medieval Latin Spirituality: Seeking Divine Presence." In *OHMLL*, 465–84.

Clayman, Dee L. "Sigmatism in Greek Poetry." *Transactions of the American Philological Association* 117 (1987): 69–84. http://dx.doi.org/10.2307/283960.

Clayton, Mary. *The Cult of the Virgin Mary in Anglo-Saxon England*. CSASE 2. Cambridge, 1990.

Connolly, Seán. *Bede: On Tobit and on the Canticle of Habakkuk*. Dublin, 1997.

Conte, Gian Biagio. *Latin Literature: A History*. Translated by Joseph B. Solodow. Baltimore, 1987.

Curtius, Ernst Robert. *European Literature and the Latin Middle Ages*. Translated by Willard R. Trask. London, 1953.

Darby, Peter. "Bede's Eschatological Thought." Dissertation. University of Birmingham, 2009.

De Bruyne, Edgar. *Études d'esthétique médiévale*. 2 vols. Paris, 1998.

DeGregorio, Scott. *Bede: On Ezra and Nehemiah*. TTH 47. Liverpool, 2006. http://dx.doi.org/10.3828/978-1-84631-001-0.

———, ed. *The Cambridge Companion to Bede*. Cambridge, 2010. http://dx.doi.org/10.1017/CCOL9780521514958.

———, ed. *Innovation and Tradition in the Writings of the Venerable Bede*. Medieval European Studies 7. Morgantown, WV, 2006.

———. "Monasticism and Reform in Book IV of Bede's 'Ecclesiastical History of the English People.'" *Journal of Ecclesiastical History* 61, no. 4 (2010): 673–87. http://dx.doi.org/10.1017/S002204690999145X.

del Barrio, Susana Bullido. "'Non est in aliquot opera modus nobilior': De muliere forti ein Werk Alberts des Großen?" In *Via Alberti: Texte–Quellen–Interpretationen*, edited by Ludger Honnefelder, Hannes Möhle, and Susana Bullido del Barrio, 385–427. Subsidia Albertina 2. Munster, 2009.

den Boeft, Jan. "Ambrosius Lyricus." In *Early Christian Poetry: A Collection of Essays*, edited by Jan den Boeft and Antonius Hilhorst, 77–90. Leiden, 1993.

Devine, A. M., and D. Laurence Stephens. *Latin Word Order: Structured Meaning & Information*. Oxford, 2006. http://dx.doi.org/10.1093/acprof:oso/9780195181685.001.0001.

The Dialogues of Plato. Translated by Benjamin Jowett. Chicago, 1952.

di Berardino, Angelo. *Patrology*. Allen, 1983.

Dictionary of the Middle Ages. Edited by Joseph L. Strayer. 13 vols. New York, 1982.

Druhan, David Ross. *The Syntax of Bede's Historia Ecclesiastica*. Washington, DC, 1938.

DuCange, D. ed. *Glossarium mediae et infimae latinitatis*. 8 vols. Niort, 1883.

Duckworth, George. "Vergil's Subjective Style and its Relation to Meter." *Vergilius* 12 (1966): 1–10.

Dyer, Joseph. "The Psalms in Monastic Prayer." In *The Place of the Psalms in the Intellectual Culture of the Middle Ages*, edited by Nancy van Deusen, 59–89. Albany, NY, 1999.

Early Latin Hymns, ed. A. S. Walpole. Cambridge, 1922.

Eco, Umberto. *Art and Beauty in the Middle Ages*. New Haven, CT, 1986.

——. *History of Beauty*. New York, 2004.

Ehrismann, Gustav. *Geschichte der deutschen Literatur bis zum Ausgang des Mittelalters*. 4 vols. Munich, 1954.

Eliot, T.S. *On Poets and Poetry*. New York, 1943.

Elliot, Ralph W. V. "Runes, Yews, and Magic." *Speculum* 32, no. 2 (1957): 250–61. http://dx.doi.org/10.2307/2849116.

Evenepoel, W. "The Place of Poetry in Latin Christianity." In *Early Christian Poetry: A Collection of Essays*, edited by Jan den Boeft and Antonius Hilhorst, 35–60. Leiden, 1993.

Fairclough, H. Rushton. *Virgil*. 2 vols. Cambridge, MA, 1942.

Falcon, Andrea. "Aristotle on Causality." In *Stanford Encyclopedia of Philosophy*. Stanford, CA, 2014.

Famulus Christi: Essays in Commemoration of the Thirteenth Centenary of the Birth of the Venerable Bede. Edited by Gerald Bonner. London, 1976.

Farrell, Joseph. *Latin Language and Latin Culture from Ancient to Modern Times*. Cambridge, 2001. http://dx.doi.org/10.1017/CBO9780511613289.

Fell, Christine. "Saint Æðelþryð: A Historical-Hagiographical Dichotomy Revisited." *Nottingham Medieval Studies* 38 (1994): 18–34.

Fitzgerald, William. *How to Read a Latin Poem: If You Can't Read Latin Yet*. Oxford, 2013. http://dx.doi.org/10.1093/acprof:oso/9780199657865.001.0001.

Fleming, Damian. "'The Most Exalted Language': Anglo-Saxon Perceptions of Hebrew." Dissertation. University of Toronto, 2006.

Fokkelman, J. P. *Major Poems of the Hebrew Bible*. 2 vols. Assen, 2000.

Foley, W. Trent, and Arthur G. Holder. *Bede: A Biblical Miscellany*. TTH 28. Liverpool, 1999. http://dx.doi.org/10.3828/978-0-85323-683-2.

Fontaine, Jacques. *Études sur la poésie latine tardive: d'Ausone à Prudence*. Paris, 1980.

———. "Le poète latin chrétien nouveau psalmiste." In *Études sur la poésie latine tardive: d'Ausone à Prudence*, edited by Jacques Fontaine, 131–44. Paris, 1980.

Fränkel, E. *Iktus und Akzent im lateinischen Sprechvers*. Berlin, 1928.

Franklin, C. "The Date and Composition of Bede's De Schematibus et Tropis and De Arte Metrica." *Revue Bénédictine* 110 (2000): 199–203.

Friesen, Bill. "The *Opus Geminatum* and Anglo-Saxon Literature." *Neophilologus* 95, no. 1 (2011): 123–44. http://dx.doi.org/10.1007/s11061-010-9213-5.

Fuchs, Anne, and Sabine Strümper-Krobb, eds. *Sentimente. Gefühle. Empfindungen: Zur Geschichte und Literatur des Affektiven von 1770 bis heute*. Würzburg, 2003.

Gildersleeve, B. L., and Gonzales Lodge. *Latin Grammar*. Bristol. 1895.

Gneuss, Helmut. *A Handlist of Anglo-Saxon Manuscripts*. Tempe, AZ, 2001.

———. *Hymnar und Hymnen im englischen Mittelalter*. Tübingen, 1968. http://dx.doi.org/10.1515/9783110952780.

Hennig, John. "Studies in the Literary Tradition of the 'Martyrologium poeticum.'" *Proceedings of the Royal Irish Academy* C-2 (1954): 197–227.

Godman, Peter. *Alcuin: The Bishops, Kings, and Saints of York*. Oxford, 1982.

———. *Poetry of the Carolingian Renaissance*. Norman, OK, 1985.

Golston, Chris, and Tomas Riad. "The Phonology of Greek Lyric Meter." Journal of Linguistics 41, no. 1 (2005): 77–115. http://dx.doi.org/10.1017/S0022226704003068.

Green, Roger P. H. *Latin Epics of the New Testament: Juvencus, Sedulius, and Arator*. Oxford, 2006. http://dx.doi.org/10.1093/acprof:oso/9780199284573.001.0001.

———. "Proba's Introduction to her Cento." *Classical Quarterly* 47, no. 2 (1997): 548–59. http://dx.doi.org/10.1093/cq/47.2.548.

Greenfield, Stanley. "The Architectonics of Bede's Historia Ecclesiastica." Abstract of Paper. OEN 19, no. 2 (1986): 29–31.

Gunn, Vicky. *Bede's Historiae: Genre, Rhetoric, and the Construction of Anglo-Saxon Church History*. Woodbridge, 2009.

Halporn, James W., Martin Ostwald, and Thomas G. Rosenmeyer. *The Meters of Greek and Latin Poetry*. Indianapolis, 1980.

Harris, Stephen. "The Library of the Venerable Bede." OEN 45, no. 1 (2014): n.p. http://www.oenewsletter.org/OEN/archive/45_1/Harris_LibraryOfBede_OEN45-1.pdf

Hays, Gregory. "Prose Style." In *OHMLL*, 217–38.

Heaney, Seamus. *The Redress of Poetry*. London, 2010.

Heikkinen, Seppo. "Bede's *De Arte metrica* and the Origins of Early Medieval Meter." In *Latin vulgaire–latin tardif VI: Actes de VIe colloque international sur le latin vulgaire et tardif*, edited by Heikki Solin, Martti Leiwo, and Hilla Halla-Aho, 173–82. Hildesheim, 2003.

———. "The Christianization of Latin Meter: A Study of Bede's 'De Arte Metrica.'" Dissertation. University of Helsinki, 2012.

———. "*Quae non habet intellectum*: The Disappearance of Fifth-Foot Spondees from Dactylic Hexameter Verse." In *Interfaces between Language and Culture in Medieval England : A Festschrift for Matti Kilpiö*, edited by Alaric Hall and Matti Kilpiö, et al., 81–98. Leiden, 2010. http://dx.doi.org/10.1163/ej.9789004180116.i-340.21.

———. "Vergilian quotations in Bede's De arte metrica." JML 17 (2007): 101–9.

Henderson, John. *The Medieval World of Isidore of Seville: Truth from Words*. Cambridge, 2007.

Herescu, N. I. *La Poésie latine: étude des structures phoniques*. Paris, 1960.

Herman, Jósef. *Vulgar Latin*. Translated by Roger Wright. University Park, PA, 1967.

Herzog, Reinhart. *Die Bibelepik der lateinischen Spätantike*. Munich, 1975.

Higham, N. J. *(Re-)Reading Bede: The 'Ecclesiastical History' in Context*. New York, 2006.

Holder, Arthur. "The Feminine Christ in Bede's Biblical Commentaries." In *Bède le vénérable entre tradition et postérité*, edited by Stéphane Lebeq et al., 109–18. Lilles, 2005.

———. *The Venerable Bede: On the Song of Songs and Selected Writings*. New York, 2011.

Hollis, Stephanie. "Barking's Monastic School. Late Seventh to Twelfth Century." In *Barking Abbey and Medieval Literary Culture*, edited by Jennifer Brown et al., 33–55. York, 2012.

Holtz, Louis. "Bède et la tradition grammaticale latine." In *Bède le vénérable entre tradition et postérité*, edited by Stéphane Lebeq et al., 9–18. Lilles, 2005.

Huemer, Johannes. *De Sedulii poetae: vita et scriptis commentatio.* Vienna, 1878.

Hunt, R. W. "Manuscript Evidence for Knowledge of the Poems of Venantius Fortunatus in Late Anglo-Saxon England." ASE 8 (1979): 279–87.

Hurst, David. *Bede the Venerable: Excerpts from the Works of Saint Augustine.* Kalamazoo, 1999.

Hwang, Alexander Y. *Intrepid Lover of Perfect Grace: The Life and Thought of Prosper of Aquitaine.* Washington, DC, 2009.

Irvine, Martin. "Bede the Grammarian and the Scope of Grammatical Studies in Eighth-Century Northumbria." ASE 15 (1986): 15–44.

———. *The Making of Textual Culture: 'Grammatica' and Literary Theory, 350–1100.* Cambridge, 1994.

Jackson, Gordon. *The Hymns of Bede.* Lincoln, 1996.

Jauss, Hans Robert. *Towards an Aesthetic of Reception.* Translated by Timothy Bahti. Minneapolis, 1982.

Jeffrey, David L., and Gregory Maillet. *Christianity and Literature: Philosophical Foundations and Critical Practice.* Downers Grove, IL, 2011.

Jones, Charles W. "Bede's Place in Medieval Schools." In *Famulus Christi: Essays in Commemoration of the Thirteenth Centenary of the Birth of the Venerable Bede*, edited by Gerald Bonner, 260–85. London, 1976.

Keil, Heinrich. *Grammatici Latini.* 7 vols. Leipzig, 1857.

———. *Scriptores artis metricae.* Leipzig, 1874.

Kendall, Calvin B. "Bede and Education." In DeGregorio, *CCB*, 99–112. http://dx.doi.org/10.1017/CCOL9780521514958.007.

———. *Bede: On Genesis.* Liverpool: Translated Texts for Historians, 2008. http://dx.doi.org/10.3828/978-1-84631-088-1.

———. "Bede's Historia ecclesiastica: The Rhetoric of Faith." In *Medieval*

Eloquence: Studies in the Theory and Practice of Medieval Rhetoric, edited by James J. Murphy, 145–72. Berkeley, CA, 1978.

———. "The Responsibility of Auctoritas." In *Innovation and Tradition*, 101–19.

———, and Faith Wallis. *Bede: On the Nature of Things and On Times*. TTH 56. Liverpool, 2010. http://dx.doi.org/10.3828/978-1-84631-495-7.

Kerlouégan, François. "Une mode stylistique dans la prose latine des pays celtique." *Études Celtiques* 13 (1972): 275–97.

Kinnavey, Raymond James. *The Vocabulary of St. Hilary of Poitiers*. Washington, DC, 1935.

Kivy, Peter. "Introduction: Aesthetics Today." In *The Blackwell Guide to Aesthetics*, edited by Peter Kivy, 1–11. Oxford, 2004. http://dx.doi.org/10.1002/9780470756645.

Knappe, Gabrielle. "Classical Rhetoric in ASE." ASE 27 (1998): 5–29.

———. *Traditionen der klassischen Rhetorik im angelsächsischen England*. Heidelberg, 1996.

Koutras, Dimitrios N. "The Beautiful According to Dionysius." In *Neoplatonism and Western Aesthetics*, edited by Aphrodite Alexandrakis, 31–40. Albany, NY, 2002.

Laistner, M. L. W. *A Hand-list of Bede Manuscripts*. Ithaca, 1943.

———. "The Library of the Venerable Bede." In *Bede: His Life, Times, and Writings: Essays in Commemoration of the Twelfth Centenary of His Death*, edited by A. Hamilton Thompson, 237–66. Oxford, 1935.

Lanham, Richard A. *A Handlist of Rhetorical Terms*. Berkeley, CA, 1991.

Lapidge, Michael. *Anglo-Latin Literature, 600–899*. 2 vols. London, 1996.

———. *The Anglo-Saxon Library*. Oxford, 2006.

———. "Beda Venerabilis." In *La transmissione dei testi latini del Medioevo*, vol. 3, edited by Paolo Chiesa and Lucia Castaldi, 44–137. 4 vols. Florence, 2004.

———. "Bede's Metrical Life of St. Cuthbert." In *Anglo-Latin Literature, 600–899*, 1:339–55. 2 vols. London, 1996.

———. "The Career of Aldhelm." ASE 36 (2007): 15–69.

———. "Colloquial Latin in the Insular Latin Scholastic *colloquia*?" In *Colloquial and Literary Latin*, edited by Elanor Dickey and Anna Chahoud, 406–18. Cambridge, 2010. http://dx.doi.org/10.1017/CBO9780511763267.025.

———. "The School of Theodore and Hadrian." ASE 15 (1986): 45–72.

———. "Three Latin Poems from Æthelwold's School at Winchester." ASE 1 (1972): 85–137.

Lateinische Lyrik des Mittelalters. Edited and translated by Paul Klopsch. Stuttgart, 1985.

Law, Vivien. *The Insular Latin Grammarians*. Woodbridge, 1982.

Lockett, Leslie. *Anglo-Saxon Psychologies in the Vernacular and Latin Traditions*. Toronto, 2011.

Love, Rosalind. "The World of Latin Learning." In DeGregorio, *CCB*, 40–53. Cambridge, 2010. http://dx.doi.org/10.1017/CCOL9780521514958.003.

Luibheid, Colm. *Pseudo-Dionysius: The Complete Works*. New York, 1987.

Luiselli, Bruno. "Sul perduto Liber epigrammatum di Beda." In *Poesia latina in frammenti*, 367–79. Genova. 1974.

MacIntyre, Alisdair. *After Virtue: A Study in Moral Theory*. Notre Dame, IN, 1984.

Mackay, Thomas. "A Critical Edition of Bede's Vita Felicis." Dissertation. University of Utah, 1971.

Malaspina, Elena. "Tre meditazione salmiche di Beda il Venerabile." In *Studi di poesia latina in onore di Antonio Traglia*, vol. 2, edited by Antonio Traglia, 2:973–87. Raccolta di studi e testi 147. 2 vols. Rome, 1979.

Manitius, Max. *Geschichte der lateinischen Literatur des Mittelalters*. 3 vols. Munich, 1976.

———. *Zu Aldhelm und Beda*. Vienna, 1886.

Mantello, F. A. C., and A. G. Rigg, eds. *Medieval Latin: An Introduction and Bibliographical Guide*. Washington, DC, 1996.

Marouzeau, J. *Traité de stylistique latine*. Paris, 1962.

Martin, Lawrence T., and David Hurst. *Bede the Venerable: Homilies on the Gospels*. Cistercian Studies 110 & 111. 2 vols. Kalamazoo, 1991.

McBrine, Patrick. "The English Inheritance of Biblical Verse." Dissertation. University of Toronto, 2008.

McDaniel, Rhonda L. "Agnes among the Anglo-Saxons." In *Writing Women Saints in Anglo-Saxon England*, edited by Paul Szarmach, 217–48. Toronto, 2013.

McDonough, Christopher J. "Lyric." In Mantello and Rigg, *ML*, 589–96.

Meyer, Wilhelm. *Anfang und Ursprung der lateinischen und greichischen rhythmischen Dichtung*. Munich, 1884.

———. *Gesammelte Abhandlung zur mittellateinischen Rythmik*. 2 vols. Berlin, 1905.

Michell, John, and Christine Rhone. *Twelve-Tribe Nations and the Science of Enchanting the Landscape*. London, 1991.

Milfull, Inge B. *The Hymns of the Anglo-Saxon Church*. CSASE 17. Cambridge, 1996.

Mohrmann, Christine. "Augustine and the Eloquentia." In Mohrmann, 1:351–70.

———. *Études sur le Latin des Chrétiens*. 4 vols. Rome, 1961–77.

———. "La Langue et le style de la poésie latine chrétienne." In Mohrmann, *Études*, 1:151–68.

———. *Liturgical Latin: Its Origins and Character*. Washington, DC, 1957.

Müller, Heinrich. "Die Deutungen der hebräischen Buchstaben bei Ambrosius." Sitzungsberichte der Kaiserlichen Akademie der Wissenschaften 167. Vienna, 1911.

Murphy, James J. *Rhetoric in the Middle Ages*. Berkeley, 1974.

———. "The Rhetorical Lore of the *Boceras* in Byhrtferth's Manual." In *Philological Essays: Studies in Old and Middle English Language and Literature in Honour of Herbert Dean Meritt*, edited by James L. Rosier, 111–24. The Hague, 1970.

Murray, Gilbert. *The Classical Tradition in Poetry*. New York, 1927.

Mustard, Wilfred P. "Tennyson and Virgil." *American Journal of Philology* 20, no. 2 (1899): 186–94. http://dx.doi.org/10.2307/287804.

Newman, John Henry. "Sermon 1: Holiness Necessary for Future Blessedness." In *Parochial and Plain Sermons*, ed. Louis Bouyer, 5–13. San Francisco, 1987.

Noble, Thomas F. X. *Images, Iconoclasm, and the Carolingians*. Philadelphia, 2009.

———, and Thomas Head. *Soldiers of Christ*. University Park, PA, 1995.

Norberg, Dag. *Introduction a l'étude de la versification latine médiévale*. Studia Latina Stockholmiensia. Stockholm, 1958. Translated by Grant C. Roti and Jacqueline de La Chapelle Skubly, *An Introduction to the Study of Medieval Latin Versification*. Edited by Jan Ziolkowski. Washington, DC, 2004.

Norden, Eduard. *Die antike Kunstprosa: vom vi. Jahrhundert v. Chr. bis in die Zeit der Renaissance*. 2 vols. Darmstadt, 1974.

Nussbaum, G. B. *Vergil's Metre*. Bristol, 1986.

O'Briain, Helen Conrad. "Bede's Use of Classical Poetry 'In Genesim, De tempore Ratione' and 'Epistola ad Wicthedum.'" *Hermathena* 161 (1996): 43–51.

O'Brien O'Keeffe, Katherine. *Stealing Obedience*. Toronto, 2012.

———. *Visible Song*. CSASE 4. Cambridge, 1990.

Ó Carragáin, Éamonn. *Ritual and Rood: Liturgical Images and the Old English Poems of the Dream of the Rood Tradition*. London, 2005.

———. "The Wearmouth Icon of the Virgin (A.D. 679): Christological, Liturgical, and Iconographic Contexts." In *Poetry. Place. and Gender: Studies in Honor of Helen Damico*, edited by Catherine E. Karkov, 13–37. Kalamazoo, 2009.

O'Conner, Michael. *Hebrew Verse Structure*. Winona Lake, IN, 1997.

Olmsted, Wendy. *Rhetoric: An Historical Introduction*. Oxford, 2006. http://dx.doi.org/10.1002/9780470776469.

Orchard, Andy. "'Audite omnes amantes': A Hymn in Patrick's Praise." In *St. Patrick, A.D. 493–1993*, edited by David Dumville, 153–73. Woodbridge, 1993.

———. *The Poetic Art of Aldhelm*. CSASE 8. Cambridge, 1994. http://dx.doi.org/10.1017/CBO9780511597558.

O'Sullivan, Sinead. *Early Medieval Glosses on Prudentius' Psychomachia: The Weitz Tradition*. Leiden, 2004.

Oxford Handbook of Medieval Latin Literature. Edited by Ralph J. Hexter and David Townsend. Oxford, 2012. http://dx.doi.org/10.1093/oxfordhb/9780195394016.001.0001.

Palmer, Anne-Marie. *Prudentius on the Martyrs*. Oxford, 1989.

Palmer, Robert B. "Bede as Textbook Writer: A Study of his *De arte metrica*." *Speculum* 34, no. 4 (1959): 573–85. http://dx.doi.org/10.2307/2850658.

Pavlock, Barbara R. "'Frater Ave atque Vale': Tennyson and Catullus." *Victorian Poetry* 4 (1979): 365–76.

Petroff, Elizabeth A. "Transforming the World: The Serpent-Dragon and the Virgin Saint." In *Body and Soul: Essays on Medieval Women and Mysticism*, 97–109. Oxford, 1994.

Platnauer, Maurice. *Latin Elegiac Verse: A Study of the Metrical Usages of Tibullus, Propertius and Ovid*. Hamden, CT, 1971.

Plummer, Charles. ed. V*enerabilis Baedae Opera Historica*. 2 vols. Oxford, 1869.

Putnam, Michael C. J. "Umbro, Nireus and Love's Threnody." *Vergilius* 38 (1992): 12–23.

Quentin, Henri. *Les Martyrologes historiques du Moyen Âge*. Paris, 1908.

Quicherat, L. *Thesaurus Poeticus Linguae Latinae*. 2nd ed. Paris, 1875.

Raby, F. J. E. *Christian Latin Poetry*. 2nd ed. Oxford, 1953.

———. *Secular Latin Poetry*. 2 vols. Oxford, 1934.

Radford, C. A. R. "Saint Peter's Church. Monkwearmouth." *Archaeological Journal* 111–12 (1954): 209–11.

Ramsey, Boniface. *Ambrose*. London, 1997.

Raven, D. S. *Latin Metre*. London, 1965.

Ray, Roger. "Bede and Cicero." ASE 16 (1987): 1–15.

———. "Bede's *Vera Lex Historiae*." *Speculum* 55, no. 1 (1980): 1–21. http://dx.doi.org/10.2307/2855707.

———. "Who Did Bede Think He Was?" In *Innovation and Tradition*, 11–35.

Reichert, Victor E. *Job: Hebrew Text & English Translation*. London, 1946.

Renoux, Christian. "The Origin of the Peace Prayer of St Francis." N.p., n.d. http://www.franciscan-archive.org/franciscana/peace.html.

Riché, Pierre. *Education and Culture in the Barbarian West: Sixth through Eighth Centuries*. Columbia, SC, 1976.

Roberts, Michael. *The Humblest Sparrow: The Poetry of Venantius Fortunatus*. Ann Arbor, MI, 2009.

———. *The Jeweled Style: Poetry and Poetics in Late Antiquity.* Ithaca, NY, 1989.

Robinson, Fred C. "Syntactical Glosses in Latin Manuscripts of Anglo-Saxon Provenance." *Speculum* 48, no. 3 (1973): 443–75. http://dx.doi.org/10.2307/2854443.

Rodriguez-Herrera, Isidoro. *Poeta Christianus: Prudentius' Auffassung vom Wesen und von der Aufgabe des christlichen Dichters.* Speyer, 1936.

Ruff, Carin. "The Place of Metrics in Anglo-Saxon Latin Education: Aldhelm and Bede." *Journal of English and Germanic Philology* 104, no. 2 (2005): 149–70.

Scott, Peter Dale. "Rhetorical and Symbolic Ambiguity: The Riddles of Symphonius and Aldhelm." In *Saints, Scribes, and Heroes: Studies in Medieval Culture in Honor of Charles W. Jones*, edited by Margot H. King and Wesley M. Stevens. 2 vols. Collegeville, MN, 1979.

Sharpe, Richard. "The Varieties of Bede's Prose." In *Aspects of the Language of Latin Prose*, edited by Tobias Reinhardt, Michael Lapidge, and J. N. Adams, 338–56. Oxford, 2005. http://dx.doi.org/10.5871/bacad/9780197263327.003.0017.

Sheets, George A. "Elements of Style in Catullus." In *A Companion to Catullus*, edited by Marilyn B. Skinner, 190–211. Oxford, 2007. http://dx.doi.org/10.1002/9780470751565.ch11.

Shockro, Sally. "Reading Bede as Bede Would Read." Dissertation. Boston College, 2008.

Skeat, Walter W. *Aelfric's Lives of the Saints.* 2 vols. EETS o.s. 76 & 82. Oxford, 1881.

Smart, C. *The Works of Horace.* New York, 1894.

Starr, Raymond. "Vergil's Seventh Eclogue and its Readers: Biographical Allegory as an Interpretative Strategy in Antiquity and Late Antiquity." *Classical Philology* 90, no. 2 (1995): 129–38. http://dx.doi.org/10.1086/367454.

Stevick, Robert D. "Hunting the Anglo-Saxon Aesthetic in Large Forms: A Möbian Quest." In *On the Aesthetics of Beowulf and Other Old English Poems*, edited by John Hill, 135–60. Toronto, 2010.

Stock, Brian. *Augustine the Reader.* Cambridge, MA, 1996.

———. *The Implications of Literacy: Written Language and Models of Interpretation in the Eleventh and Twelfth Centuries.* Princeton, 1983.

Stotz, Peter. "Dichten als Schulfach." Mittellateinisches Jahrbuch 16 (1981): 1–16.

———. *Handbuch zur lateinischen Sprache des Mittelalters*. 5 vols. Munich, 2000.

Szarmach, Paul. "Æðeldreda in the Old English Bede." In *Poetry, Place, and Gender: Studies in Medieval Culture in Honor of Helen Damico*, edited by Catherine E. Karkov, 132–50. Kalamazoo, 2009.

Szövérffy, Josef. *Die Annalen der lateinischen Hymnendichtung*. 2 vols. Berlin, 1964.

———. "Hymnologische Streifzüge." In *Literatur und Sprache im europäischen Mittelalter*, edited by Johannes Rathoffer and Fritz Wagner, 12–38. Darmstadt, 1973.

———. *Latin Hymns*. Turnhout, 1989.

———. "Latin Hymns." In *Dictionary of the Middle Ages*. 12 vols. New York, 1985.

———. *Secular Latin Lyrics and Minor Poetic Forms of the Middle Ages*. 3 vols. Concord, NH, 1992.

Thacker, Alan. "Æthelthryth. d. 679." *Oxford Dictionary of National Biography*. Oxford, 2009. http://www.oxforddnb.com/view/article/8906.

———. "Bede and the Ordering of Understanding." In *Innovation and Tradition*, 37–63.

Thiessen, Gesa Elsbeth, ed. *Theological Aesthetics: A Reader*. Grand Rapids, MI, 2004.

Thompson, Pauline A. "St Æthelthryth: the Making of History from Hagiography." In *'Doubt Wisely': Papers in Honour of E. G. Stanley*, edited by M. J. Toswell and E. M. Tyler, 475–92. London, 1996.

Thornbury, Emily. *Becoming a Poet in Anglo-Saxon England*. Cambridge, 2014. http://dx.doi.org/10.1017/CBO9781107280304.

Threade, Klaus. *Studien zu Sprache und Stil des Prudentius*. Göttingen, 1965.

Tilliette, Jean-Yves. "Verse Style." In *OHMLL*, 239–64.

Townsend, David. "The Current Questions and Future Prospects of Medieval Latin Studies." In *OHMLL*, 3–24. http://dx.doi.org/10.1093/oxfordhb/9780195394016.013.0001.

Trilling, Lionel. *Sincerity and Authenticity*. Cambridge, MA, 1971.

Valentin, L. *Saint Prosper d'Aquitaine*. Paris, 1900.

van der Lugt, Pieter. *Cantos and Strophes in Biblical Hebrew Poetry*. Leiden, 2006.

Vickers, Brian. *In Defence of Rhetoric*. Oxford, 1988.

von Balthasar, Hans Urs. *The Glory of the Lord: A Theological Aesthetics*. 7 vols. San Francisco, 1984.

Waddell, Helen. *More Latin Lyrics*. New York, 1976.

Wallace, Rex E. *An Introduction to Wall Inscriptions from Pompeii and Herculaneum*. Illinois, Wauconda, 2005.

Wallace-Hadrill, Michael. *Bede's Ecclesiastical History: A Historical Commentary*. Oxford, Oxford Medieval Texts, 1988.

Wallis, Faith. *Bede: Commentary on Revelation*. TTH 58. Liverpool, 2013.

——. *Bede: The Reckoning of Time*. TTH 29. Liverpool, 1999.

Wansbrough, Henry. *The Use and Abuse of the Bible: A Brief History of Biblical Interpretation*. New York, 2010.

Ward, Benedicta. *The Venerable Bede*. Harrisburg, PA, 1990.

Wellek, René. *A History of Modern Criticism: 1750–1950*. 7 vols. New Haven, CT, 1955.

Weston, Lisa M. C. "The Saint-Maker and the Saint: Hildelith Creates Ethelberg." In *Barking Abbey and Medieval Literary Culture*, edited by Jennifer W. Brown and Donna Alfano Bussell, 56–72. Woodbridge, 2012.

Wetherbee, W. "Some Implications of Bede's Latin Style." In *Bede and Anglo-Saxon England*, edited by R. T. Farrell, 23–31. Oxford, 1978.

White, Caroline. *Early Christian Latin Poets*. New York, 2000.

Wieland, Gernot. "*Geminus stilus*: Studies in Anglo-Latin Hagiography." In *Insular Latin Studies*, edited by Michael Herren, 113–33. Toronto, 1981.

Wilhelmy, Winfried. "Die Entstehung von *De laudibus* im Spannungsfeld von Bilderstreit und Glaubenswahrheit." In *Raban Maurus*, edited by Hans-Jürgen Kotzur, 23–32. Mainz, 2006.

Wilkinson, L. P. *Golden Latin Artistry*. Cambridge, 1963.

Williams, Howard. "Mortuary Practices in Early Anglo-Saxon England." In *The Oxford Handbook of Anglo-Saxon Archaeology*, edited by Helena Hamerov et al., 238–65. Oxford, 2011.

Williamson, Christine. "Bede's Hymn to St. Agnes of Rome." *Viator* 43, no. 1 (2012): 39–66.

Winbolt, Samuel L. *Latin Hexameter Verse*. New York, 1978.

Winterbottom, Michael. "Aldhelm's Prose Style and its Origins." ASE 6 (1977): 39–76.

Witke, Charles. *Numen Litterarum: The Old and the New in Latin Poetry from Constantine to Gregory the Great*. Leiden, 1971.

Wright, Neil. "Bede and Virgil." *Romanobarbarica* 6 (1981): 361–79.

———. "The Metrical Art(s) of Bede." In *Latin Learning and English Lore: Studies in Anglo-Saxon Literature for Michael Lapidge*, vol. 1, edited by Katherine O'Brien O'Keeffe and Andy Orchard, 150–70. 2 vols. Toronto, 2005.

Yorke, Barbara. *Nunneries and the Anglo-Saxon Royal Houses*. London, 2003.

Young, Arthur M. "Schematized Word Order in Vergil." *Classical Journal* 27 (1932): 515–22.

Zeeman, Nicolette. "The Theory of Passionate Song." In *Medieval Latin and Middle English Literature*, edited by Christopher Canon and Maura Nolan, 231–51. Cambridge, 2011.

Ziolkowski, Jan M. *The Cambridge Songs*. Tempe, AZ, 1998.

———. "Towards a History of Medieval Latin Literature." In *OHMLL*, 505–36.

———, and Michael C. J. Putnam. *The Virgilian Tradition: the First Fifteen Hundred Years*. New Haven, CT, 2008.

Index

Aaron, 261
abbess, 2, 91, 127, 247, 255
abbey, 2, 134, 138, 255
abbot, 154
Abimelech, 75
ablative, 48–49, 210, 230–31, 271
Abraham, 92
Abrams, M. H., 40
accent, 53, 112, 124
accusative, 48–49, 85, 113, 135, 227, 238, 250, 263
acrostic, 22, 45, 146–48, 156, 182, 243–44, 264, 268
Acts of the Apostles, 104, 136, 259
Adalbert, 114
Adamnán, 112, 144
adjective, 35–36, 48, 53, 63–65, 78, 84, 87, 102–3, 112–13, 115, 119–20, 173–75, 186–87, 207, 211, 214–15, 218–19, 226–28, 231, 239, 258, 261, 268–69
adnominatio, 80
adverbs, 48, 242
Aelfric of Eynsham, 39
Aeneas, 72–73, 75–78, 84, 169, 215
Aeneid, 50, 71–73, 75, 78, 84–85, 90, 94–95, 100, 111–12, 145, 169, 172, 174, 176–77, 182, 190, 215, 260
aesthetic, 3–6, 9, 12–13, 20, 22, 25–27, 30, 35, 37, 40, 42–43, 50, 53, 55, 65–66, 86–87, 93–94, 144, 271
Aethelburh, 255
Aethelfrith, 136
Aethelthryth, St., 127, 129, 130, 134, 136–43, 150, 154, 172, 182, 185–86, 188, 191, 197, 202–4, 208, 215–16, 218, 220, 221–23, 225, 228–31, 233–42, 244–59, 261–62, 265–70; Æðeldreda, 127; Æðelþryð, 136, 139; Æthelthryth, 127, 136; Aedildruda, 165; Aedilthryda, 258; Adildrudae, 164
Aethelthryth, Hymn to. *See Hymn to Aethelthryth*
Aethilwald, 81
affricates, 51
Africa, 9, 46, 54, 83, 147
Africanus, Scipio. *See* Scipio
Agatha, St. 141, 155, 159, 165, 204, 209–10, 212–13, 225
Agnes, St. 91, 141, 159, 165, 204, 215–19, 224–25
Ain, 152, 236–37
Alban, St., 103, 250
alcaics, 100
Alcimus Avitus, 88, 124,
Alcuin, 22, 98, 128, 171–72
Aldhelm, 2, 11, 39, 41–42, 45, 48–49, 64–66, 71, 81, 91–93, 98, 105, 108, 112, 114, 139–40, 143–46, 148, 157, 169–71, 173, 182, 188, 192, 200–203, 207, 218
Aleph, 152–53, 167–69, 180
allegory, 17
alliteration, 51, 79–81, 115, 124, 184, 188, 193, 197–98, 207, 238, 242
allusion, 32, 71–72, 89, 104–6, 111, 113, 119–20, 126, 133, 144, 157, 169, 172, 174–77, 179, 181–82, 190, 202, 232, 238, 262, 269–70, 272

295

Alpha, 44, 180
alphabet, 44–45, 83, 148–49, 151–53, 155, 167–68, 178, 180–81, 194, 208–9, 215, 220, 237, 243, 259, 262, 264
alphabetic, 45, 82, 86, 108, 142, 147–48, 152–53, 155–56, 167–68, 185, 199, 208, 239, 262
Altus prosator (by St. Columba), 185
Ambrose, St., 8, 17, 29–30, 41, 43, 89, 101, 105, 117–18, 120–24, 142, 146–47, 149, 151–52, 157, 167–68, 176–77, 179–81, 186, 188, 191, 193–95, 198, 200, 202–3, 216–17, 220–23, 225, 227–28, 231–32, 236–39, 245–47, 249, 251–252, 254, 256, 258–59, 263
Ambrosiaster, 120
amphimacrus, 146
anadiplosis, 69
anapest, 53, 147
anaphora, 69
anastrophe, 73
Andrew, St., 172
Andromache, 76, 78
angel, 5, 91–92, 95, 101, 191, 199, 222, 230, 264
Angles, 127, 227–28, 234
Anglo-Saxon, 2, 12, 31, 34, 38–39, 46, 64–65, 80, 98, 102, 105, 114, 141–42, 204, 213, 226, 257; East Saxons, 255
Anna, King of East Angles 127, 234
Anthony (Emperor), 112
antiphonary, 148; antiphons, 156
antiptosis, 36
antithesis, 63, 110, 113, 123–24, 177, 180, 189, 193, 207, 246–48, 253, 261–62, 264
antonomasia, 189, 265, 269, 271
Apocalypse, Book of, 226, 255, 262; *Commentary on* (by Bede), 247
Apollinaris, Sidonius. *See* Sidonius Apollinaris
Apollo, 8, 11
Apollonius, 72
apostle, 48, 74, 82, 84, 104, 135–36, 138, 187, 200–201, 213, 248, 254

Apostles' Creed, 84, 135–36; Nicene Creed, 241
apostrophe, 128, 208, 236, 239, 243, 256, 267, 270
Aquinas, 22, 25, 229
Aquitaine, Prosper of. *See* Prosper of Aquitaine
Aramaic, 153
Arateus (by Cicero), 200
Arator, 88, 100, 102, 105, 117, 143, 170, 195, 201
Archilochus, 91
Arcite and Palamon, 13
Argonautica (by Apollonius of Rhodes), 72
Aristotle, 14
Artaxerxes, 129
assonance, 51, 82, 193
Assunto, Rosario, 27–28
Athelthryth. *See* Aethelthryth
Auden, W. H., 31
audience, 2, 6, 17, 26, 28, 31, 53, 58, 61–62, 73, 82, 86, 134, 141, 182, 266
Auerbach, Erich, 37, 101, 133
Augustine, St., 12, 17–18, 20, 29–30, 40, 42, 46, 63, 66, 68–70, 74, 83, 89, 113–14, 116–17, 120, 129, 142, 147, 150–51, 155, 157, 167, 175, 179, 183, 185–86, 192, 194, 196, 199–200, 205–6, 240, 246, 256
Augustus Caesar, 95, 223
Aulus Gellius, 56
Ausonius of Bordeaux, 12, 122, 124, 183
Avitus, 88, 124

Babel, 176
Babylon, 77, 176
bacchius, 54, 144
baptism, 157, 168, 175, 236, 254
Barking, 2–3, 9, 26, 61, 88, 90, 100, 104, 130, 138, 179, 182, 197, 244, 255, 259, 269–70, 272
beauty 33, 42, 62, 67, 87–88, 90, 121, 157, 159, 177, 183, 200, 204, 212, 229, 233–37, 249, 252, 257, 259
Bede, St., 1–5, 7–8, 9, 12–13, 17–18, 19, 24–27, 31–52, 56–57, 60–80, 82–93, 95–100, 102–11, 113–14, 116–18,

120–22, 124–34, 136–50, 153–58,
161, 167–97, 199–230, 232–47,
249–64, 266–72
Beethoven, Ludwig von, 119
Beit, 153, 176–80
Benedict Biscop 127, 140
Beowulf, 13, 220
Beta, 180
Beth, 152. *See also* Beit
Bethel, 149
Beverley, John of. *See* John of Beverley
Bible, 5, 42, 44, 72, 88, 122, 147–48,
178–79. *See also* Scripture
Biscop, Benedict. *See* Benedict Biscop
Blume, Clemens, 156
Boeft, Jan den, 123
Boethius, 36
Boisil, 213
Bonner, Gerald, 96, 100
Bordeaux, Ausonius of. *See* Ausonius
of Bordeaux
Borinski, Karl, 29
Breviary, 6
bridal, 204
bride, 5, 129, 139, 160, 226, 231, 234,
236, 255, 265–66, 269
bridegroom, 160, 193, 238, 264,
267–68
Brigit, St., 148
Britain, 2, 6, 19, 24, 34, 118, 134, 136,
139–40, 190–91, 203, 213, 225; British, 65, 148, 213; brittania, 132
Bruyne, Edgar de, 43
Bucolics (by Virgil), 111; bucolic verse,
108, 262
Byzantium, 225

Caedmon, 49, 126, 134, 140, 193
Caedmon's Hymn (by Caedmon), 120,
126
Caesar, Julius. *See* Julius Caesar
caesura, 82, 107–8, 111, 115, 119, 145,
176–77, 193, 197, 206, 243, 258
Califf, David, 107
Canaan, 233
Canterbury, school of, 61
Canticle of Canticles, 104
Canticle of Habakkuk. *See* Habakkuk

canticles, 101
Caph, 152
Carmen paschale (by Sedulius), 91, 108
Carolingians, 22, 82, 97, 105
Carragáin, Éamonn Ó, 140
Carruthers, Mary, 65
Carthage, St. Felicity of. *See* Felicity
of Carthage
Cassian, John. *See* John Cassian
Cassiodorus, 61, 66, 69, 73–74, 99,
114, 120, 151, 155, 167, 170, 187, 189,
191, 196, 199, 204–5, 209, 215, 217,
245, 249, 260
Castro, Eva, 35
catalectic, 91, 96, 118, 145
catalogue (rhetorical device), 62–64,
123, 203
Catania. *See* Agatha 141
Catholic Church. *See* Church
Catholicism, 5–6, 10, 28, 32, 37, 77,
106, 136, 142, 156, 168, 178, 204,
226, 246, 253
Catullus, 19, 40, 58, 94, 200, 223
Cecilia, St., 141, 159, 165, 204, 216–18,
224–25, 234
Cecily of Chaumpaigne, 185
Celestine I, Pope, 114
Ceolwulf, King, 137
Ceres, 169
chant, 10, 223
charity, 20, 48, 139, 209, 215, 220,
222, 257, 260
Chaucer, Geoffrey, 13, 86, 185, 218
chiasmus, 14, 88, 123–24, 175, 180,
189, 214, 224, 231–32, 235
choir, 57, 91–92, 102, 109, 122, 173,
190–91, 217, 264
chorus, 119, 187, 199, 205, 249
Christ, Jesus. *See* Jesus Christ
Christie, E. J., 155
Chrysostom, John. *See* John
Chrysostom
Church (Catholic), 5–6, 37, 54, 76–77,
101, 121, 126, 134, 136–37, 139–41,
153–54, 156–57, 168, 170, 178, 180,
187–88, 199–200, 204, 206, 209,
212–13, 218, 226–28, 236, 246, 250,
253–57, 260. *See also* Catholicism

Index 297

church, 14, 140, 192, 195, 227
Cicero, 9, 50–51, 54, 56, 61, 67, 200
Circe, 177
circumlocutions, 48
cithara, 11–12, 269
Cleopatra, 183
Clio, 223
cloister, 2, 26, 67, 191
clothing, 16, 188, 204, 218, 222, 225–26, 237, 241, 256, 258, 261
coffin, 142, 222, 254–55
cola, 63, 243–44, 262, 264, 268–69, 271
Colgrave, Bertram, 154, 161, 266
Colloquy (by Aelfric), 39
colon, 243, 247–48, 250, 258, 263–64, 267–68, 270–71
Columba, St. 185
Columban, Life of (by Adamnan) 144
Comgall, 148
commata, 170
Commentary on the Tabernacle (by Bede), 247; commentaries also listed under book of Scripture
Commodian, 54, 147
communion, 141, 241, 251, 268
conexio, 168, 194, 208, 215, 220, 226, 237, 249
confession, 188, 249
consonant, 44–47, 51, 56, 112, 144–45, 173, 198
Constantine, 141
continuant, 47, 57, 197, 231
Contra Symmachum (by Augustine), 259
Coph, 153. *See also* Koph
Corinthians, St. Paul's Epistle to, 7, 11, 120, 141, 153, 178
Cornelius Severus, 105
couplet, 83, 91, 96, 115–16, 142, 145, 175–77, 184, 219
creed. *See* Apostles' Creed
cretics, 48
Crucifixion, 94, 219
Cuchuimne, 81
Cupid, 172
Curtius, Ernst Robert, 97, 173
Cuthberg of Wimborne, 182

Cuthbert, St., 49–50, 56, 67, 78–79, 117, 125, 128, 130, 146, 171, 213
cyclopes, 94
Cyprian of Gaul, 74–75; also called Cyprianus Gallus, 105, 124

dactyl, 10, 45–46, 49, 51, 92–93, 95, 99, 107, 110–11, 122, 132, 144–45, 147, 173, 182, 186, 188, 201, 206, 211, 219, 228, 236, 248, 258, 262, 267
dactylic hexameter verse, 62, 65, 80, 90, 92–93, 95, 107, 116, 180, 193, 251, 255, 267
Daleth, 186–87, 189
Damasus, Pope, 29
dative, 210–11, 230–31, 250
ddds (metrical pattern), 95, 173, 193, 268
ddsd (metrical pattern), 173
ddss (metrical pattern), 111, 236
deacon, 85, 144
decorum, 61–62, 67, 88, 242
De orthographia (by Bede), 40
Degregorio, Scott, 126, 134
Deleth, 152
demons, 178
De re publica (by Cicero), 9
Deuteronomy, 99, 131, 147
Devil. *See* Satan
devotion, 5, 13–14, 30–32, 66, 84, 104, 114, 133, 135, 140, 143, 170, 195, 205, 209, 245–47, 250–51, 267, 270
dialyton, 69
diaresis, 263
Dickinson, Emily, 122, 142
Dido, 72, 84, 215
dimeter, 89–91, 122, 142, 146
Dionysus, 8
Dionysius of Halicarnassus, 87
Dionysius, pseudo-, 26
diphthong, 46–47, 50
dipody, 118, 122
disciple, 154, 189, 213, 232
distichs, 114–15
Donatus, 34, 39, 44, 69, 72, 75, 79–80, 148
Dracontius, 124

Dream of the Rood, 194
ds (metrical pattern), 95, 189
dsds (metrical pattern), 111
dsss (metrical pattern), 95, 173
dsssdc (metrical pattern), 95
Duckworth, George, 94–95
Durham, 8

Eadfrith, 78
Eanflaed of Whitby, 182
Easter, 135, 267
Ebert, Adolf, 31
Ecclesiastes, 100
Ecgfrith, 127, 134, 136
eclogue, 100, 111–12
Eco, Umberto, 7, 10, 23
ecthlipsis, 50
Eden, Garden of, 259, 262
Ehrismann, Gustav, 29
eiron, 13
elegy, 42, 89, 91–92, 96, 98–100, 108, 114, 117, 124–25, 128–129, 131, 142–43, 145, 149, 172, 174, 176–77
Elijah, 104
Eliot, T. S., 27, 31, 53, 96
elision, 50–51, 108, 111, 116, 145, 173, 228, 231–32, 238, 258, 268
ellipsis, 75, 270
Ely, 127, 250–51, 257
England, 2, 38–39, 58, 80, 98, 105, 114, 140, 142
enjambment, 58, 78–79, 102, 108, 110, 116, 207
Ennius, 80, 184
Eorcenwold, St. (*also spelled* Erkenwald), 255
epanalepsis, 69, 108, 115, 174, 176, 178, 207, 209, 243, 250
Ephesians, 76–77, 101
Ephesus, 76
epic, 47, 74, 86, 96, 97–98, 100–101, 104–6, 111, 180, 190, 269
epideictic, 62
epigram, 29, 113–116
epilogue, 63, 99
Epirus, kingdom of, 76
epistle, 17, 129, 136, 152, 181
epitaph, 228
epithet, 110, 169, 174, 201, 236, 265, 271
epitome, 113
epizeuxis, 69
Eriugena. *See* John Scotus Eriugena
Erkenwald, St. *See* Eorcenwold
Ermoldus Nigellus, 98
Ethelburg, Abbess of Barking, 138
Eucharist, 195
Eugenius of Toledo, 228
Eugippius, 68
Eulalia, St., 141, 155, 159, 165, 204, 209–10, 212–13, 225
Euphemia, St., 141, 159, 204, 213–15, 225; *also spelled* Eufemia, 162, 165, 213
euphemism, 216
euphony, 45, 53, 55, 215
Europe, 18, 38, 98, 225
Eurydice, 58
Eusebius, 17, 151, 153
Eve, 156, 160, 259, 261–64
evangelists, 17
Exameron (by Ambrose), 200
exempla, 18
Exodus, Book of, 25, 240, 252
extrametrical, 58
eyesight, 253
Ezra, 117, 129

faith, 5, 15, 25, 29, 43, 67, 135–37, 140, 147, 151, 156–57, 168, 178, 187, 198, 200, 206, 215, 217, 237, 239–41, 246, 249–50, 253–54, 260, 264
Farrell, Joseph, 51
Fasti (by Ovid), 169
fasting, 149, 253
February, 210
Felgeldus, 171
Felicity of Carthage, St., 141
Felix, Minucius. *See* Minucius Felix
Fell, Christine, 176
female, 2, 38, 126, 138–41, 150, 156–57, 170, 184, 191, 203–4, 246
feminine (grammatical gender), 36, 139, 146, 152, 157, 169, 170, 174, 182, 198, 211, 223, 226, 238, 251, 265, 266, 269; feminine Christ, 204

Fitzgerald, William, 36, 85, 112–13, 143
flax, 187–88
Fontaine, Jacques, 15, 121
formalism, 28
formula, 35, 79, 122, 144, 154, 187, 268
Fortunatus, Venantius. *See* Venantius Fortunatus
Foucault, Michel, 26
fountain, 63, 152, 175, 236
Francis, St., 29; *Prayer to St. Francis*, 31
fricatives, 51
Fursa, St., 210

Galatians, St. Paul's Epistle to, 188
Gall, St., monastery of, 44, 145, 164, 243–44
Gallus, Cyprianus. *See* Cyprian of Gaul
Gamma, 180
garment, 188, 215, 218, 222, 225, 256
gate, 158, 170, 194–96, 198, 223
Gellius, Aulus. *See* Aulus Gellius
Geminatum. *See opus geminatum*
geminus stilus, 127, 130. *See also* Koph
gender, 36–37, 174, 272
Genesis, Book of, 5, 75, 132, 149, 177, 199; *Commentary on* (by Bede), 247
genitive, 35, 51, 238
genre, 15, 61, 86, 88–89, 96, 98–100, 112, 127, 143, 179
Geoffrey of Vinsauf, 21
geometry, 25
Georgics (by Virgil), 49, 57, 100, 111, 177
Germain, St., Abbey of, 91
Germany, 29, 81; germanic, 79
gerunds, 48
Gimal, 180; also spelled gimel, 152, 180–83
gloss, 61, 65, 98, 102, 119, 120, 170
goddess, 169
Godman, Peter, 106
gold, 3, 5, 17, 36, 64, 65, 79, 102, 103, 108, 111, 218, 224, 268
Gospel, 14, 16, 67, 86, 101, 107, 136, 175, 197, 200, 224
Gottschalk of Orbais, 82, 84
grace, 20, 67, 68, 115, 168, 171, 187–89, 192–93, 209, 233, 246, 252

grammar, 18, 37, 59, 64, 66, 69–70, 72, 78, 84, 92, 113, 116, 135, 173, 175, 198, 210, 227, 250, 258, 266; grammarian, 66, 97, 143
gravity of tone, 56, 258
Greece, 6, 42, 64, 76, 190; Greek language and literature, 6–10, 13, 15, 17–18, 40, 42, 44, 50, 54, 56, 80, 104, 180–81, 184
Gregorian chant, 10
Gregory, Pope (the Great), 12, 15, 62, 124, 129, 185, 227
Gregory Nazianus, 36
Gregory of Tours, 97, 170

Habakkuk, 77
Hadrian (Roman Emperor), 14
Hadrian (Archbishop of Canterbury), 61
Hamman, Adalbert, 114
handmaidens, 141
happiness, 150, 209
harmony, 7–13, 25, 42–43, 57, 125, 223, 231, 251, 253
harp, 101, 110, 269
He, 191
Heaney, Seamus, 12
Heaven, 64, 91–92, 139, 154, 160, 170–71, 185, 187–88, 193, 198, 201, 218–20, 226, 229, 233–34, 237–38, 241–42, 244, 247–51, 266, 270; heavenly city, 73–74, 172, 195, 228; heavenly father, 230, 232–33, 235; heavenly gifts, 158, 186, 188–89, 191; heavenly home, 76–77, 236, 246; heavenly justice, 245; heavenly life, 227, 239, 241; heavenly light, 7; heavenly mysteries, 236–37; heavenly power, 204; heavenly protectors, 8, 200, 237; heavenly queenship, 248; heavenly reward, 208–9, 212, 229, 233, 235; heavenly things, 109
Hebrew, 42, 44, 80, 99–101, 132, 146, 149, 151, 153, 156, 167–68, 170, 176, 180–81, 186, 191, 194, 198, 205, 208–9, 212, 215, 220, 225, 228, 232, 236, 239, 245, 249, 252, 256,

259, 262, 264. *See also* Ain; Beit; Daleth; Gimel; He; Heth; Iod; Kaph; Lamed; Mem; Nun; Phe; Resh; Sade; Samech; Shin; Tau; Teth; Vav; Zain
Hebrew Questions in Genesis (by Jerome), 132
Heikkinen, Seppo, 42, 90, 92–93
Helena, 141
Helenus, 76, 78
hemistich, 14, 174, 179, 186, 189, 193, 197–98, 207, 224
Henry of Avranche, 24
Heptateuch, 74
Herculaneum, 54
Herescu, N. I., 57–58, 219
heresy, 182, 259; heretics, 253
heroic verses. *See* hexameter
Heth, 152, 205–6, 208
hexameter, 5, 14, 42, 45, 47–51, 53, 65, 79–80, 89–93, 95–103, 107–8, 111, 111–17, 123, 125, 128, 143–47, 149, 158, 169, 172–73, 175–77, 184, 189, 193, 195–97, 201, 206–7, 211, 214, 217, 219, 224, 227, 230, 235, 238–39, 241–44, 248, 258, 261–63, 267, 271; heroic verses, 50, 62, 92, 96–98, 100–101, 113, 128, 132, 172, 180
hiatus, 50–51, 80, 111, 210, 215, 231, 258
Hilary of Poitiers, 18, 67, 101, 105, 114, 117–21, 148, 151, 167, 178, 181, 187, 191, 195, 198, 205, 208–9, 212, 220, 228–29, 232–33, 237, 239, 245–46, 249, 252, 260, 270
Hild of Whitby, 134, 138–40, 182
Hildelith, Abbess of Barking, 2, 138, 182
hirmus, 64, 69
Hisperic style, 18
Hisperica Famina, 65
hiss, 93, 211
Historia apostolica (by Arator), 195
Historia ecclesiastica (Bede), 1–2, 39, 57, 60, 71, 74, 103, 107, 117, 126–29, 132, 136–37, 153, 164, 177, 185, 202, 210, 213, 218, 221–22, 227, 234–35, 240, 250, 252, 254–55, 257, 266
Historia ecclesiastica (Eusebius), 227
Historia monarchum Rufinus),141
holocaust, 210
holy, 42, 69, 73–74, 91–92, 100, 109, 114, 135–37, 139, 142, 168, 170–71, 175–76, 180, 189, 196, 205, 209, 213–14, 250, 260, 269
Holy Spirit, 76, 135–36, 157, 168, 170–71, 175–76, 189, 196, 269
Homer, 86, 90, 189
homily, 6, 219
homoeoptoton, 69, 82, 193, 243
homoeoteleuton, 69, 82, 228, 232, 239, 242–43
homophony, 197, 231, 252
Honorius of Autun, 11
Horace, 17, 42, 64, 85, 105, 120, 122, 177, 223, 267
Host, the (Eucharist), 154, 195–96
Hraban Maur, 22, 98, 127
Huemer, Johannes, 97, 108
humility, 27, 187, 191, 196, 248, 251–52
hymn, 31, 57, 80, 82–83, 86, 108, 113–14, 117–29, 142–43, 145–48, 150, 153, 224, 244, 268; "A solis ortus cardine" (by Sedulius), 108, 199; "Adesto Christe uocibus" (by Bede), 140; "Aeterna Christi munera" (by Ambrose), 121–23, 179; "Aeterne rerum conditor" (by Ambrose), 146; "Agnes beatae uirginis" (by Ambrose), 170, 216, 218; "Altus Prosator" (by Columba), 185; "Ante saecula qui manes" (by Hilary), 148; "Apostolorum gloriam" (by Bede), 82–83, 171; "Audites omnes amantes" (by St. Patrick), 80, 142, 148; "Cum surgit Xristus tumulo," 254; "Hymnum dicat turba fratrum" (by Hilary), 118–19, 270; "Illuxit alma saeculis" (by Bede), 141, 217–18; "In Ascensione Domini" (by Bede), 219; "Inter quos igitur uirgo egregria," 227; "Nunc Andreae" (by Bede), 172; "O Stella maris," 170; "Primo Deus" (by Bede), 48–49, 57, 169; "Splendor paternae gloriae" (by Ambrose), 8

Hymn to Aethelthryth (by Bede), 2, 19, 43, 45, 47, 74, 84, 89, 103–5, 107–8, 110, 113–14, 117, 122, 124–26, 128–31, 133, 137–48, 150, 153–272
hyperbaton, 36, 73, 78–79, 102, 108, 111, 189
hypophrygian mode, 10–11
hypozeuxis, 69

iamb, 11, 48–49, 89, 96, 101, 107, 122, 143, 146, 152, 182
icon, 22, 139, 140, 195
ictus, 53, 58
idiom, 17, 38, 79, 99–100, 118
Iliad (by Homer), 190
imbalance, 25, 117, 214, 224
Imma, 153–54
Incarnation, 101, 168, 190–91, 193–94, 196
India, 201
infinitive, 123, 144
insular, 24, 38, 81, 98, 154
Iod, 152, 208, 212–13
Ireland, 18, 43, 65, 86, 112, 119, 142
irony, 13, 84, 251
Irvine, Martin, 38, 60–61, 97
Isaac, 75
Isaiah, Book of, 104, 170, 187, 216
Isidore of Seville, 44–45, 60, 69, 72, 97, 118, 127, 148, 180, 211
isocolon, 110
Israel, 77, 239–40, 248
Italy, 51, 54, 76, 108

Jacob, 139, 149, 235
Jarrow, 2–4, 27, 140, 170, 195
Jeremiah, Book of, 100, 200, 235
Jerome, St., 15, 17–18, 42, 72, 80, 89, 99–100, 106, 113, 132, 146, 149–53, 155, 167–68, 170, 176–78, 181, 186, 191, 194, 198, 205, 208–9, 212, 215, 220–21, 225–26, 228, 232, 236–37, 239, 245, 249, 252, 256, 259
Jerusalem, 172, 239
Jesus Christ, 77, 154, 172, 208, 256, 258; the Savior, 73, 109, 196, 205, 260
jeweled style, 13, 88, 124–25, 244

Jews, 74, 155–56
John the Baptist, 171, 203, 218, 254
John of Beverley, 39
John Cassian, 101, 157
John Chrysostom, 17
John Scotus Eriugena, 11, 23, 26, 43
John, St. (evangelist), 117, 157, 173, 175, 189, 208, 229; *iohannem*, 228; *iohannis*, 117
Johnson, Samuel, 58
Jordan River, 175
Joseph, St., 194
Josephus, 149
Joshua (prophet), 77
joy, 119, 122, 159–60, 170, 173, 179, 193, 200, 205, 209, 215–18, 225, 249, 251, 256, 258, 260, 262–64, 267
Judas, 189
Judea, 77
Julius Caesar 79, 103
July, 203
June, 203
Junius Philagurius, 112
Juno, 73
Jupiter, 110, 174, 201
Juturna, 73
Juvenal, 65
Juvencus, 9, 16, 88, 96, 103, 105–7, 117, 124, 143, 175, 269
juxtaposition, 62, 110, 131, 169, 174, 186, 219, 223, 238

Kant, Immanuel, 4
Kaph. *See* Koph
Katherine, St., 156
Keats, John, 58
Kendall, Calvin, 21
Knappe, Gabrielle, 64
Koph, 208, 215, 217, 248–49. *See also* Coph

Lactantius, 17, 101
lamb, 160, 181, 213, 216, 226, 242, 265, 268, 272
Lamed, 152, 208, 215, 220–21, 223, 247
Lamentations, 99–100, 147, 152, 232, 239

Lapidge, Michael, 27, 42, 48, 50, 104
Latin Anthology (Codex Salmasianus), 81
Lavarenne, M., 106
length (of syllables and vowels), 35, 40, 45–49, 51–54, 108, 110, 112, 116, 119, 124, 248, 255; of words, 197
Lent, 149
Leonardo da Vinci, 9
leonine rhyme, 82–83, 177, 243–44
Lérins, 113
letter (of the alphabet), 34–35, 39–41, 43–45, 47, 56, 71, 82–83, 87, 102, 146, 148–49, 151–56, 167, 168, 176, 178, 179, 180, 181, 191, 194, 205, 208, 209, 215, 235, 237, 245, 249, 259, 264
Letter to Arcircum (by Aldhelm), 146
Letter of Artaxerxes, 129
Liber Hymnorum, 118–19
Life of Saint Felix (by Bede), 238
Life of Saint Felix (by Paulinus of Nola), 96, 128
Life of Saint Martin (by Fortunatus), 93, 97
lightness (of syllable), 93, 193, 219, 225
Lindisfarne, 78
Lindsey (shire), 170
litany, 150, 191, 204, 215–16
liturgy, 5–6, 15, 100, 118, 126, 133, 135; liturgical, 15, 17–18, 23, 31, 42, 72, 101, 117, 120, 125, 127, 134–35, 140, 268
Lôgos, 11, 25–26, 32, 140, 271. See also Jesus Christ
London, 2, 36, 141, 255
Love Song of J. Alfred Prufrock (by T. S. Eliot), 96
Lucan, 65, 85, 102–3, 105, 183, 201
Lucretius, 15, 100, 105, 200
Lucy, St. 141
Luke, St., 17, 101, 142, 232–33, 240, 252, 254; *Commentary on* (by Ambrose), 258; *Commentary on* (by Bede), 62, 157; *Sermon on* (by Bede), 76
Luther, Martin, 108

Lycidas (by Milton), 190
lyre, 8–9, 11–12, 109–10
lyric, 28, 29, 31, 101, 115, 118, 120, 123, 131, 147, 190, 272

Macintyre, Alisadir, 28
Mackay, Tom, 128
Macrobius, 9
Magi, 9
Magritte, Réné, 259
maiden, 170, 196, 237
Manitius, Max, 31, 108
mantic alphabet, 155
Marcellus (nephew to Augustus), 223
Marouzeau, J., 55, 80, 106, 184
marriage, 134, 139, 141, 182, 225, 236, 238, 245, 266, 270
Marseilles, 113
Martha, St., 142
martyr, 29, 121, 123, 126, 141, 149–51, 179–80, 187, 191, 203–4, 209, 213–14, 217–18, 233, 250, 259, 267; virgin martyrs, 141, 157, 203, 208, 210, 213–14, 216, 219, 221, 225, 241, 267
Mary, Blessed Virgin, 92, 140, 142, 157–58, 170, 172, 191, 194–98, 200, 202, 205–6, 208, 219–21, 223, 225, 242, 259; chapel to, 140
masculine (grammatical gender), 36, 169–71, 174, 238, 265, 269
Matthew, Gospel of, 103, 154, 187, 189, 192, 197, 205, 212, 220–21, 229–30, 240, 252–54, 267
Maur, (H)raban. See Hraban Maur
Medea, 72
melancholy, 185
Meliboeus, 112–13
mercy, 187, 195, 239–40, 245, 260, 268
metalepsis, 268
metaphor, 8, 20, 23, 56, 68, 79, 120, 123, 174, 197, 205
meter, 5, 10–11, 14, 24–25, 32–33, 39, 41–43, 45–51, 53, 55, 65–66, 79, 80, 87, 89–103, 106–8, 111–18, 122–25, 128–29, 131–33, 137, 142–47, 149, 152, 158, 161, 169, 172–77, 179, 182, 184, 189, 192–93, 195–97, 201–2,

Index 303

meter (cont.)
206–7, 210–11, 214–15, 217, 219, 224, 227, 230, 235–36, 238–39, 241–44, 248, 250, 252, 255, 258, 261–63, 266–69, 271
metonymy, 68, 134, 188
Milan, Ambrose of. *See* Ambrose of Milan
Milton, John, 10, 58, 88, 190
minster, 127, 134, 136, 204, 250
Minucius Felix, 17,
miracle, 109, 142, 239, 255–56
Mohrmann, Christine, 84
monasteries, 2, 5, 113
monastery, 2, 4–6, 18, 32, 38, 100–101, 113, 116, 133–34, 137, 150, 154, 159, 246, 248, 251, 255
monk, 8, 22, 32, 38, 66, 101, 125–26, 148, 156–57, 171, 189, 255
Monkwearmouth, 195
monosyllable, 143, 231
mora, 45–46, 143, 146, 255
Moralia in Job (by Pope Gregory the Great), 185
Moses, 92, 99, 191, 239, 247
motif, 13, 77, 144
Müller, Heinrich, 151, 153
muse, 37, 170–71, 189, 223, 269
Mynors, R. A. B., 161

Nazianzus, St. Gregory, 36
necklaces, 204, 218, 241
Nehemiah, 117
neologism, 107, 119, 269
Neoplatonists, 10
neuter (grammatical gender), 174, 226
Nicene Creed, 241
Nietzsche, Freidrich, 8
Niclas von Wyle, 29
Nigellus, Ermoldius. *See* Ermoldius Nigellus
Noah, 254
Nola, Paulinus of, 12, 17, 49, 96, 98, 105, 117, 128, 145, 175, 238
nominative, 48, 51, 113, 119, 211–12, 251, 253
Norberg, Dag, 83
Northumbria, 127

noun, 35–36, 48–49, 51, 63–65, 85, 102–3, 112, 120, 139, 146, 169, 173–76, 182, 186, 211, 214, 219, 224, 227, 238, 261, 266, 269, 271
November, 160, 203, 253–55
novice, 140, 183, 266
numbers, 8–10, 23, 42, 48, 180
nun, 2–4, 9, 26, 32, 38, 61, 88–90, 100, 104, 130, 152, 179, 186, 197, 202, 204, 226, 228–31, 244–45, 247, 250, 259, 266, 269–72

October, 111, 203, 254
octosyllables, 53
ode, 16, 85, 100–101, 119, 120, 223
Odyssey (by Homer), 100
O'Keeffe, Katherine O'Brien, 116, 155
Omega, 44
onomaton, 69
onset, 32, 143, 145, 269
Opus (by Sedulius), 108
opus geminatum, 127–28
Orbais, Gottschalk. *See* Gottschalk of Orbais
Orchard, Andy, 71, 80, 98, 114
Origen, 17, 151
Orleans, Theodulf of. *See* Theodulf of Orleans
Orpheus, 57–58, 223
Orthographia, De. See De Orthographia
O'Sullivan, Sinead, 105–6
Ovid, 17, 34, 89, 105, 115, 143, 169, 172, 177, 200, 227, 267

pagan, 14–19, 42, 69–70, 74, 78, 89, 95–96, 102, 105, 109–11, 125–26, 134, 147, 150, 170, 172–75, 178, 189, 216, 235, 260
Palamon, 13
Palmer, Anne-Marie, 122
Palmer, Robert, 43–44
Pan, 15
paradise, 190
paradoxes, 176, 205, 208, 223
parallelism, 63, 84, 106, 124, 207–8, 261
paranomasia, 69
paraphrase, 74, 155, 175

paregmenon, 81
paromoeon, 69, 79–80, 184
participle, 48, 111, 135, 144, 194, 211, 263, 266
particle (grammatical), 186, 261
pastoral (genre), 15, 111–13, 190; role as pastor, 71, 221
Pastoral Care (by Pope Gregory the Great), 12
Patrick, St., hymn to. *See* hymn, "Audites omnes amantes"
Paul, St., 7, 11, 17, 76, 85, 88, 101, 171, 190–91, 213, 259; Church of, London, 255; chapel of, Monkwearmouth, 244. *See also Corinthians*; *Ephesians*; *Romans*
Paul the Deacon, 85, 144
Paulinus of Nola, 11–12, 17, 49, 96, 98, 105, 117, 128, 145, 175, 238
penance, 236, 240
pentameter, 90, 91, 96, 99, 100, 114–16, 143, 145, 147, 149, 158, 172, 174, 176, 179, 182, 184, 189, 192–93, 196, 197, 207, 211, 214–15, 217, 219, 224, 227, 230, 235–36, 243, 244, 248, 250, 252, 255, 258, 262–63, 266–69, 271
Pentecost, 210
penthemimer, 115
penultimate syllable, 102, 121, 145
Periphyseon (by John Scotus Eriugena), 43; also P*eriphysion*, 11
Peristephanon (by Prudentius), 32
Peter, St., 54, 82, 92, 139, 171, 218; *Book of 1 Peter*, 254
Phaedrus (by Plato), 7
phalaecean meter, 90
Pharsalia (by Lucan), 102, 183
Philagurius. *See* Junius Philagurius
Phoebus, 75
Picts, 213
Plato, 7, 10, 88; platonism, 175
Plautus, 184
pluperfect, 248
plural (grammatical), 25, 49, 111, 119–20, 123, 177, 210–11, 238, 251, 262, 266
Poitiers, Hilary of. *See* Hilary of Poitiers

polyptoton, 69, 80–81, 123
polysyndeton, 69
Pompeii, 54
Pompey, 103
pope, 204. *See also* Celestine I; Damasus; Gregory the Great
Pope, Alexander, 58
Praxiteles, 7
prayer, 5, 31–32, 79, 83–84, 120, 123, 133, 135–36, 139, 151, 154, 157, 173, 187, 241, 253
prefix, 47
preposition, 224, 261, 271
priest, 38, 66, 77, 106, 108, 117, 125, 154, 204, 260
Proba, 14, 86, 179
prolepsis, 63, 69, 72–75, 207, 232, 266, 269
pronoun, 48, 63, 85, 113, 173, 186, 266, 270, 272
Propertius, 89, 120
prophet, 73, 101, 252; prophecy, 76, 107, 142, 252
Prosper of Aquitaine, 96, 98, 102–3, 105, 113–17
proverbs, 79, 151
Proverbs, Book of, 79, 100, 139, 147, 151–52, 156–57, 167–69, 178, 181–82, 187, 189–90, 192, 196, 199, 206, 209, 212–13, 215, 222, 226, 229–30, 233, 237, 240, 246, 249, 253, 257, 260, 262
Prudentius, 8, 11–12, 31, 71, 89, 105–6, 117, 124, 143, 155, 183–84, 216–18, 259, 267
Psalms, Book of, 73, 74, 99, 100–101, 109–11, 113, 117, 120, 131, 181, 187, 188, 194, 198, 245, 268; study of, 101; *Psalm 1*, 72; *Psalm 9*, 216; *Psalm 14*, 78; *Psalm 44*, 226; *Psalm 50*, 156; *Psalm 57*, 184; *Psalm 84*, 77; *Psalm 86*, 73–74; *Psalm 90*, 185; *Psalm 117*, 81, 184; *Psalm 118*, 86, 117, 137, 147, 149–151, 167–272; *Psalm 125*, 240; *Psalm 138*, 40; *Psalm 144*, 110. *See also Song on Psalm 112* (by Bede)
Psalmus contra partem Donati (by Augustine), 148

Psalmus responsorius, 147
Psalter, 100–101, 118, 148, 155
Psychomachia (by Prudentius), 12, 155, 184
pun, 272
Putnam, Michael 260
Pyrrha, 85
pyrrhic, 48, 143
Pythagoras, 8–10, 94, 271

quantitative verse, 25, 34–35, 46–47, 53, 55, 58, 142
quantity (of syllables), 46, 51, 112, 146
queen, 125, 129, 141, 159, 186, 218, 226, 233–34, 236, 241, 245–48; virgin queen, 140–41, 246–47. *See also* Aethelthryth, Helen
Quintilian, 34, 56, 64

Raby, F. J. E., 28–31, 52, 97, 106, 115, 117, 145
Radegund, 141
Ravenna, 81, 87
reform, 126–27, 133–34, 137, 142–43, 145, 147, 170, 173, 178, 190
Resh, 251–53
Resurrection, 136, 254
Revelation, Book of, 44, 67; *Commentary on* (by Bede), 8, 103
rhetoric, 17, 36–37, 59, 60–71, 73, 75, 77, 79, 81–83, 85, 87, 89, 97, 106, 109, 122–24, 184, 186, 207, 208, 214, 231, 236, 269
Rho, 56
rhyme, 41, 80, 82–84, 112, 115–16, 123, 135, 158, 177, 180, 186, 188–189, 193, 197, 211, 215, 238, 243–44, 248, 251–52, 256, 264, 268, 271
rhythm, 10–11, 24, 30, 34–35, 41, 54–55, 107, 112, 119, 122, 132, 142, 180, 224, 238; rhythmic verse, 34–35, 51, 122, 142,
riddle, 148
righteousness, 78, 150, 256
Roberts, Michael, 12, 37, 74, 124
Romans, St. Paul's Epistle to, 191, 252, 256
Rome, 10, 74, 78, 95–96, 111, 113, 122, 141, 175, 190, 225

Rood, Dream of the. *See* Dream of the Rood
rood screen, 195
Rufinus, 14, 141
rune, 153–55
Ruodlieb, 81
Ruotger, 106
Ruthwell, 194

Sade, 153, 237, 245–46
saint, 8, 52, 79, 126, 134, 141–42, 150, 156–57, 191, 201, 203–4, 211–12, 214, 216, 219, 220–21, 224–27, 236, 241, 251–52, 257, 261, 264
Salmasianus. *See* Latin Anthology
salvation, 20, 26, 74, 104, 110–11, 139, 141, 153–54, 156–57, 195–97, 209, 215, 219–21, 225, 232, 245, 249–50, 262
Samech, 152, 226, 232–33
Samuel, Book of, 77, 136; *Commentary on* (by Bede), 68, 155
sapphic verse, 100, 128, 90, 152
Sappho, 7, 87
Saragossa, 105
Satan, 15, 185, 260, 262–63; the Devil, 155, 189, 245, 259, 261; devils, 178, 253
satire, 177
Saturn, 155
Saul, 136
Savior. *See* Jesus Christ
Saxons. *See* Anglo-Saxons
schesis, 69
Scipio Africanus, 9
Scott, Peter Dale, 20
Scotus, John Eriugena. *See* John Scotus Eriugena
Scripture, 1, 5–6, 10–11, 17–18, 26, 28, 37, 42, 60, 66, 68–69, 70–72, 74–75, 77–78, 80, 87–88, 100, 105, 110, 126, 129, 132, 134, 136, 139, 142, 148, 149, 153, 155, 167–68, 181–82, 195, 198, 200, 206, 221, 226, 245, 252, 258
Scyld Scefing, 13
Seaxburh, 138
Sebbi, 255

Sechnall, 142
Sedulius, 88, 91, 94, 96–98, 100, 102–6, 108–11, 113, 143, 147, 199, 202
Seneca, 17, 85, 122
September, 203, 213
septenarius, 90, 118, 120
Septuagint, 180–181
Sergius, 44, 105
sermo humilis, 67, 101
sermo purus, 184
sermo simplex, 17, 67, 124, 184, 197, 224
sermon, 17, 76, 83, 140, 150, 247
Servius, 72–73, 80, 174
Severus, Cornelius. *See* Cornelius Severus
Seville, Isidore of. *See* Isidore of Seville
Shakespeare, William, 10, 58, 88, 96, 111
Sharpe, Richard, 27
Shelley, Percy, 58
sibilant, 45, 56–57, 235, 238
Sicily, 225
Sidney, Philip 58
Sidonius Apolliaris, 65, 89, 124
sin, 29, 77, 114, 117, 140, 155, 178, 181, 183, 188, 193, 196, 212, 214, 233, 254, 263, 268
Smaragdus, 98
smoothness (rhetorical effect), 231
Socrates, 55
Solomon, 101, 155, 157
Song on Psalm 112 (by Bede), 201
soul, 7–8, 10–11, 77, 115, 149, 154, 160, 182, 186–88, 190, 192, 196, 215, 219, 237, 249–51, 254
Spain, 9, 65, 105–6, 142, 225, 227, 254
spirants, 231
Spirit, Holy. *See* Holy Spirit
spondee, 10–11, 45–46, 92–95, 99, 115–16, 118, 122, 143–45, 180, 182, 186, 188, 197, 206, 211, 219, 228, 248, 251, 258, 262–63, 267–68
Springer, Carl, 94, 109–10
ssdsdc (metrical pattern), 146
Statius, 49, 86
Stevick, Robert, 24
stophe, 197

Stotz, Peter, 38, 54
Strauss, Johann, 197
subjunctive, 120, 178, 241, 266
substantives, 64, 78, 119, 174, 207
superlative (grammatical), 119
Sutton Hoo, 257
swelling. *See* tumor
syllable, 34–35, 39–40, 44–51, 53, 57, 66, 92–93, 99, 107–8, 111–12, 115–16, 119, 123–24, 143, 144–46, 176, 197, 219, 224, 231–32, 236, 255, 272
syllepsis, 69
symbol, 21, 28, 122, 139, 151, 155, 173, 263
synchisis, 36
synchrony, 271
syncopation, 34–35
syndeton, 62
synecdoche, 176, 190, 216, 269
Synodis, De (by Hilary of Poitiers), 118
synonyms, 119, 123–24, 215, 254
syntactic, 49, 54, 58, 75, 84, 102–3, 123, 125, 131, 135, 161, 175, 177, 215, 261
Szövérffy, Josef, 119, 121

Tau, 153, 259
temple, 9, 151, 176, 178, 210
Tennyson, Alfred, 56, 58
Tennyson, Hallam, 58
tense (grammatical), 191, 211, 248, 252, 254, 259, 263, 267, 269
Terence, 110
Tertullian, 17, 188
Teth, 152, 208–9
tetracolon, 83
tetrameter, 107, 118, 122, 152
tetrasyllables, 197
Thecla, St., 141, 159, 204, 213–14, 222, 225
Theocritus, 15, 113, 190
Theodore, Archbishop of Canterbury, 53, 61
Theodulf of Orleans, 98
Thomas, St., 201
Thornbury, Emily, 42
Tilliette, Jean-Yves, 20, 51–52, 128
Timothy, Epistle of St. Paul to, 181

Titus, Epistle of St. Paul to, 259
Titus Tatius (the tyrant), 80
Tohdbehrt, 234
Toledo, Eugenius of. *See* Eugenius of Toledo
tomb, 8, 142, 160, 203, 222, 225, 240, 253–58, 262
torture, 204, 214, 229
Tours, Gregory of. *See* Gregory of Tours
Townsend, David, 86
tradition, 5–6, 14–15, 18, 32, 39, 47, 58, 61, 64–65, 68–70, 72, 91, 98, 113, 120, 125, 142, 155, 167, 171, 183, 190, 204, 221, 225, 272
tribrach, 47, 122
tricolon, 81–82
trimeter, 152
Trinity, the, 48, 136, 158, 169–72, 174–76, 190, 236, 253
trisyllables, 176, 197
trivium, 2
trochee, 11, 45, 92, 118, 143, 201, 263
Troilus and Criseyde (by Chaucer), 86, 218
Troy, 75–78, 158, 182, 186–190, 204; Trojan, 76, 78, 84, 102, 184
tumor, 216, 218, 255; swelling, 119, 46, 229
Tunna, 153–54
Turin, 121
Turnus, 73

Valentin, L., 114–15
Vav, 152, 194–96
Venantius Fortunatus, 62–64, 81, 89, 91–93, 95–100, 102–3, 105–6, 117, 143, 146, 148, 173, 177, 193, 197
Venus, 169
verb, 47–48, 50, 63–65, 75–76, 78–79, 84–85, 87, 102–3, 111, 113, 116, 119–20, 135, 144, 173–77, 186, 188, 194, 196–97, 200, 210, 212, 224, 227, 242, 248, 250, 258, 261, 266–67, 269, 271
Vergil. *See* Virgil
vernacular, 6, 46, 80, 86

Vexilla regis proderunt (by Forunatus), 91
Victorinus, 39, 103
Vinsauf, Geoffrey of. *See* Geoffrey of Vinsauf
Virgil, 14–15, 17, 19, 34, 42, 47–49, 53, 56–58, 60, 65, 71–76, 78, 84–86, 90–91, 95, 97–98, 102–5, 111–13, 115, 119, 123, 144–46, 158, 169, 172–80, 182, 189, 191, 200, 202, 204, 223, 260, 267; virgilian, 58, 72, 74, 104, 106, 113, 183; spelled Vergil, 53, 94–95, 98, 100, 102, 112
virgin, 2, 49, 62, 91–93, 96, 98, 103, 129, 137, 139, 140–42, 144–46, 157–60, 164, 168–72, 178, 182, 187, 190–98, 200–208, 210–14, 216, 218–19, 221, 223–28, 234, 238, 241–42, 246–47, 250, 253, 255, 259, 262–64, 266–70. *See also* martyr; virgin
Virginitate, de (by Aldhelm), prose and verse, 2, 49, 93, 144, 146, 157, 170–71, 201, 203
Virginitate, de (by Fortunatus), 62, 91, 98, 103
Virginitate, de sancta (by Augustine), 246
virginity, 96, 129, 137, 139, 142, 145, 157, 159, 172, 182, 185, 190, 192, 195, 200–201, 203–5, 207, 212–13, 228, 234, 247, 253, 266, 268–69
Vitruvius, 9
vocative, 51
vowel, 34, 35, 40, 44–50, 52–57, 90, 93, 143–44, 173, 193, 197–98, 210, 217, 231, 244, 268
Vulgate, 75, 169

Waddell, Helen, 107
Wallace-Hadrill, J. M., 130
Walpole, A. S., 121
Wearmouth, 2–3, 127, 140, 195
Wearside, 38, 43, 59
weaving, 204
Wellek, René, 28
Weston, Lisa 157
Whitby, 182

widow, 181–82
Wilkinson, L. P., 53, 64, 94
Wimborne, 182
Winterbottom, Michael, 65, 80
wisdom, 22, 24, 36, 62, 195, 220, 240, 252, 257, 262, 264
wool, 187–88, 204, 212–13, 215, 218, 222
Wordsworth, William, 83, 107

Yodh, 212
York, 22

Zain, 198, 237; Zai, 152
Zephaniah, Book of, 28
zeugma, 63–64, 69, 75–79, 214
Zeus, 9
Zion, 74, 77
Zorobabel, 77

Latin Words

ab, 49–50, 102, 138, 163, 166, 171–72, 265, 271
abimelus, 75
abit, 165, 261
ablativus, 271
abstentia, 149
ac, 48, 65, 82, 92, 102, 129, 131, 156, 209, 234
accinxit, 206
acta, 216
actibus, 201
actis, 162, 250
actis, 165, 250–51, 253
actuum, 104
acumen, 63
acuminum, 62
ad, 29, 44, 56, 61, 75, 81, 88, 91, 100, 112–13, 130, 185, 201, 203, 212, 215–16, 260
adest, 237–38
adesto, 120
adhesit, 186
adhuc, 63
adire, 194
adit, 164, 193, 196–97
adiunxit, 206
adiutorium, 152, 232
adnue, 145, 161, 164, 174–75
adnuntiabit, 156
adoret, 222
adprehenderunt, 212
adversa, 168
aedes, 51
aedificata, 81
aedil, 162, 226

aegis, 67
aegyptiae, 50
aenigmatibus, 92
aequaliter, 233
aetate, 246
aetatibus, 247
aetatis, 62
aeterna, 121, 179
aeternae, 249
aeternales, 221
aeterne, 43, 123, 146, 176
aeternorum, 198
aeternum, 78, 222
aethere, 162, 241
aetherei, 165, 242
aethram, 82
aevo, 171
aevum, 82
affectare, 270
affectu, 166, 270–72
affectus, 30
agmen, 91, 92
agmina, 91–92, 172
agminis, 92
agna, 216
agne, 216
agnetis, 217
agni, 163, 242, 265, 268, 271
agnorum, 216
agnus, 216, 268
agri, 209
agrum, 199
alba, 183
albo, 222
alii, 229

311

aliis, 165
aliqua, 252
aliquam, 70
aliquot, 156
aliquoties, 132
alit, 80
aliter, 132
alma, 107, 143, 145–46, 158, 161–62,
    164–65, 169–74, 176, 217, 223, 228,
    236–39, 253, 272
alme, 170
almi, 166, 171
almus, 171–72
alphabeti, 156
alta, 146
altera, 147
alterius, 147
alternans, 62
altertum, 52
altissimus, 119
altithroni, 166, 269, 271
altithronum, 201
altithronus, 107, 175
alto, 119, 172, 194
altus, 119, 161, 164, 193–98
aluum, 161, 164, 193, 198
amantes, 71, 80, 148
amaritudo, 76
amatoris, 81
amica, 164
amicus, 75, 199
amor, 165, 222–24
amore, 192
amores, 143, 172
amplo, 114–17
ancillis, 196
angeli, 199
angelico, 185
angelorum, 199
anglorum, 2, 139, 157
ani, 162, 250
anima, 36, 157, 165, 182, 186, 223,
    249
animabus, 156
animae, 156, 229, 237, 254
animam, 249, 251–52
animata, 103

animis, 70
anni, 85
annis, 162, 165, 248
ante, 148
aperi, 156, 240
aperies, 156
aperui, 239
aperuit, 215, 240
apologistes, 66
apostolicae, 201
apostolo, 213
apostolorum, 82, 104, 201
apta, 50
apud, 40
aqua, 56
aquas, 85, 172
aquitani, 114
arbor, 146
arce, 170
ardentes, 257
argivae, 183
arma, 172, 174, 176–77
ars, 40, 64, 66, 69
arte, 33, 35, 41–42, 44, 46–47, 51, 99,
    109–10, 223
artes, 35
artis, 40, 85
ascendit, 135
ascensione, 219
aspectibus, 82–83
aspice, 163, 165, 249, 264–67
assuetus, 109
astra, 162, 165, 233, 235
astris, 165, 230, 235
athleta, 150
atque, 58, 170, 234, 252
auctor, 170
auctorem, 61
auctores, 97
auctoritas, 21, 105
audacibus, 174
audi, 232
audire, 67, 239
audite, 71, 80, 148, 239
auit, 162, 226
aulus, 56
aurea, 83

auream, 219
auribus, 30
auso, 62
austris, 78
aut, 70
autem, 70, 185, 226
ave, 58, 170

baptistam, 228
barbarus, 112–13
beata, 146, 170
beati, 128
beatissimam, 249
beatitudes, 229
beatitudinem, 171
beatus, 72
beauit, 165
bella, 158, 161, 164, 176, 179–80
belli, 85, 180
bello, 230
bene, 30, 41, 64
benediximus, 81
benignus, 83, 228
bernas, 143, 161, 169
bestias, 213
biblia, 99
bibliorum, 81, 168
biblis, 109
bis, 162, 246, 248, 253
blasphemia, 76
boatu, 109
boceras, 61
bona, 137–38, 195, 209
boni, 134
bonis, 137–38, 249
bonitate, 229
bonum, 152, 208–9
bonus, 116
bracchia, 94
brachium, 206
brevisque, 147
britannia, 57
brittania, 132
bucinae, 201

cacumine, 81
cada, 243

caecili, 162, 217
caeco, 80
caeleste, 80
caelestia, 109, 249
caelestibus, 80
caelestis, 237
caelestium, 199
caeli, 57, 64, 82, 172, 233, 247
caelis, 165, 228, 266
caelius, 88, 108
caelo, 154
caesarius, 101
calce, 63
calentia, 216
campum, 94
canamus, 121, 123, 164, 179–80
canant, 109
candida, 172, 256
candidum, 226
candor, 81, 188, 249
canebat, 57
canendi, 109–10
canentes, 63
canere, 67, 176
canina, 56
cano, 172
canora, 222
canorus, 82
cantare, 111
cantatae, 199
cantate, 120
cantemus, 81
cantibus, 109
cantica, 104
canticorum, 104
canticum, 120
cantu, 177
cantus, 67, 119–20
canunt, 149, 199
capiantur, 267
capis, 166, 265
capite, 252
capitis, 40, 153
caram, 227
cardine, 108, 147, 199
cari, 171
caritas, 48, 131, 146, 204, 222

Latin Words 313

carmen, 91, 97, 108, 114, 120, 144, 164, 170, 175, 182, 192, 238
carmina, 12, 49, 67, 81, 103, 121, 129, 131, 133, 146, 161, 163–64, 166, 175, 182–84, 186, 189, 197, 207, 214, 227–28, 244, 265, 267–68, 270
carmine, 63
carminibus, 129
carminis, 62
carminum, 16
carnalibus, 70, 188, 217
carnalis, 114
carne, 63, 101
carnem, 252
carnis, 253–54
caro, 165, 254
carpitur, 80
casta, 161, 164–65, 182, 185–86, 197, 207, 214–15, 253
castae, 182
castimoniae, 83
castissimo, 205
castitas, 36, 182
castitatis, 237
casto, 164, 207–8, 211, 250
castos, 182–83
castus, 205, 222
catenis, 80
caterua, 91
catholica, 156, 253
catholicas, 184
causa, 67, 132, 231, 260
causam, 229
cave, 84
caveat, 18
cecidit, 206
cecinisse, 179
cedes, 51
celebraturi, 63
celebrentur, 267
cęli, 170
celsa, 91
celsis, 165, 249–51
celsiusque, 90
celui, 133
cento, 86, 179, 183
cernenes, 81
certe, 63

cessit, 162, 165, 210, 212
ceteris, 90
ceu, 82
chananeo, 233
charitatis, 209
chordarum, 109, 111
choris, 91–92, 199
choro, 109, 111, 200
chorus, 82, 199
christe, 84, 120, 258
christi, 109, 117, 129, 141, 150, 175, 179–80, 189, 191, 213, 234, 256, 258
christiana, 68, 70, 97
christianus, 24
christum, 84, 101, 135, 188
christus, 79, 237–39
cibaria, 196
cinge, 83
cingulum, 233
cinxit, 218
circumda, 62
cis, 161, 182
civitas, 48, 146, 172
civitatis, 229
clamaverunt, 130
clamavi, 249
clamor, 76, 249
clara, 109, 111, 162, 165, 226, 229, 230–31
clarii, 75
claris, 230
claritas, 48, 146, 229
clarius, 230
clarus, 114
classici, 15
claudentur, 85
clausa, 195
claves, 51
clementiae, 240
clienti, 144
coaxare, 56
coelesti, 204
coelestibus, 249
coelestis, 171, 229
coelestium, 199
coeli, 48
coelumque, 201
coenobiorum, 157

coepti, 164
coeptis, 145, 174
cogito, 31
cohortatur, 201
colla, 80
collectio, 148
collum, 218
comedet, 246
comitata, 269
comitatu, 166, 269, 271
commate, 63
communionem, 84
compagibus, 85
complent, 91–92, 95
complexiones, 120
compositione, 87
conceptus, 135
concinant, 222–23
concinere, 119, 223
concinna, 223
concinnentes, 119
conclusio, 249
concrepans, 201
concrepet, 222
concretas, 85
condere, 169
condis, 64, 81
conditor, 43, 123, 146, 169, 176
conditoris, 168
confessione, 213
confessoris, 128
confidit, 178
confossus, 146
confusio, 152, 176
congregant, 195
congregaverunt, 253
coniugare, 77
coniunctio, 77
coniunx, 57
conjugis, 114
conjunx, 234
conposita, 129
conpositus, 129
considerat, 246
consideravit, 199
consilio, 187
consilium, 72
consolabor, 200

consolatio, 245
consolatione, 36
consolemur, 198
consonet, 82
conspici, 252
constat, 129
consuetudes, 133
consummavit, 259
contagia, 109
contemnat, 93
contemnit, 168
contemplantur, 23
contentant, 219
convellere, 123
conveniens, 50
convertam, 200
cor, 30, 153, 178, 220–23
corda, 162, 165, 215, 221–22, 224, 228
corde, 85, 109, 130, 178, 228, 249
cordi, 222
cordis, 152, 220, 222, 240
coronati, 63
corporis, 185, 222
corpus, 86, 183–84, 252, 256
coruscante, 200
coturnati, 63
cras, 162, 213
crata, 162, 250
cratera, 84
creata, 138
creatione, 212
creatorem, 135
credantur, 63
credendi, 151
credere, 85
credidisti, 157
credimus, 135
credo, 135, 162, 165, 173, 175, 240–42
cristi, 121
cristo, 119
cristo, 120
cristus, 119
crocitare, 56
cruces, 12
crucifixus, 135
crudelissimum, 149
crux, 146
cui, 81, 237

Latin Words

cuius, 70, 129, 131, 156
cuiusque, 156
cul, 146
culmen, 81, 213
culmina, 64, 81–82, 91, 95
culmine, 162, 165, 172, 213, 215, 222
culta, 112
cultum, 201
cum, 30, 41, 75–76, 78, 109–10, 114, 229, 254
cuncta, 70, 81, 107, 143–44, 161, 164, 168–69, 173, 204
cur, 109–11
curatura, 62
currebant, 30
currens, 99

da, 185, 235
dactilo, 99
dactilus, 92
dactyli, 65
dare, 120, 211
das, 52
dat, 230
data, 93
datas, 54
daviticis, 109
debitas, 119, 121, 179
decedente, 57
decem, 109
deciderit, 212
decore, 121, 157, 252
decori, 103
decoris, 67, 132
decreta, 85
decurrat, 183
decus, 165, 233, 235, 237
dederit, 144
dederunt, 63–64
dedi, 71
dedita, 114, 162, 165, 237–39
deditque, 196
defecerunt, 216
defectus, 216
defessus, 50
defetisci, 50
dei, 67, 120, 170, 172, 195–96, 198, 229, 237, 268

deitatis, 171
delectatur, 245
delectet, 109
delicias, 16
demus, 119–20
dentis, 256
dentium, 153
deo, 12, 81, 157, 171, 199, 220, 238, 246–47, 265
deosculor, 47
depositio, 254
derisus, 219
descendit, 135
describantur, 156
deseruisti, 81
dest, 162, 237
det, 161–62, 189, 217
devenient, 84
deum, 135, 151, 223
deus, 48, 57, 81, 143–44, 169–70, 172, 174–75, 194, 197–98, 222–23, 235, 247, 272
deus, 161, 193
devicit, 213
devota, 164, 197
devotarum, 202
devotas, 201
devoto, 144
dextram, 218
diabolum, 245
dialectica, 36
dicat, 118–119, 270
dicata, 165, 246–47
dicati, 247
dicendi, 64, 66, 132
dicere, 119–20
dicimus, 82–83, 182
dicione, 144, 169
dicit, 157
dicitur, 119
dico, 66, 192
dicta, 165, 220
dictamina, 156
die, 49, 57
diebus, 49
diemque, 49
dieresis, 107–8, 111, 115
dierum, 49

316   Latin Words

dies, 48–49
diesque, 49
diffugi, 163, 260
diffugiunt, 165, 261
digiti, 212
digna, 81, 220
dignetur, 172
dignitas, 48, 146
dignitate, 246
dignus, 196
diligat, 222
diligit, 73
dirae, 85
discendens, 81
disciplina, 16, 153, 209
disciplinae, 152, 220
discrepare, 151
dispositionem, 221
distributione, 63
divum, 75
diversis, 149
divina, 71, 128
divinae, 23, 192
divinitus, 70
divinorum, 153
divisi, 102
divitias, 253
docens, 194
doceretur, 151
docet, 168
doctiloquus, 98
doctrina, 68, 70, 97, 152–53, 167–68, 228
doctrinae, 151
doctrinam, 209
dolore, 200
dolorous, 228
domestici, 221
domesticis, 196
domina, 234
dominans, 234
dominante, 114
dominator, 233
dominatrix, 234
domine, 156, 196
domini, 81, 91, 149, 216, 219, 234
domino, 81, 231
dominum, 84, 109–10, 135, 185, 196, 257

dominus, 73, 79, 81, 178, 196, 205, 229, 231–32
domitilla, 156
domo, 81
domui, 221
domus, 81, 152–53, 177, 246
dona, 144, 161, 164, 176, 186–92, 194–95
donare, 194
donati, 148
decor, 67, 237
donavit, 79
donum, 175
draconem, 103
dubia, 147
duces, 180
dulcibus, 82
dulcis, 57, 97
dulcisono, 163, 166, 244, 265
dum, 138
duo, 227
duodecim, 48
duplicibus, 221
dura, 56
durare, 227
durum, 93–94, 208
dux, 84

ea, 80, 178
eam, 249, 260
eandem, 84
ecce, 163, 166, 264, 267–68
ecclesia, 139–40, 156–57, 178, 253, 256
ecclesiae, 62, 79, 148, 153, 156
ecclesiarum, 180
ecclesiastica, 49, 60, 103, 132, 157, 227
ecclesiasticae, 194
ecclesiasticus, 138
edomandi, 70
effusa, 147
ego, 25, 109–11, 119, 135
egregia, 162, 165, 226–27, 231
egressi, 102
ei, 120, 260
eis, 30
eius, 73, 84, 168, 209, 212, 221, 226, 229, 237, 240, 249, 260
eiusdem, 164, 234

electis, 156
elevamini, 221
eliensis, 127
eliquabatur, 30
eloquentia, 64, 70, 83–84
eloquio, 114, 246
eminentiores, 69
emundet, 188
en, 161, 164, 193, 201
enarrationes, 138
enigmatibus, 48
enim, 70, 221–22
eo, 132
eorum, 200
eos, 200
epichirematibus, 63
epigrammata, 113–14, 116
epigrammatum, 100
epilogiorum, 63
episcopum, 81
epistola, 100, 203
epistulae, 240
epistulas, 184
erat, 30, 263
ergo, 31, 120, 209, 229, 232, 249
erit, 164, 175, 183, 270
errat, 259
erravi, 239
erravit, 259, 263
erudiendi, 151
erudiendos, 61
erula, 102
erunt, 154
esau, 149
esse, 23, 25, 129
est, 24, 41, 65, 67, 70–71, 80–81, 85, 90, 92, 99, 103, 114, 132, 134–35, 149, 151, 156–57, 162–63, 165, 168, 185, 187, 191–92, 194, 209, 217, 222, 226, 229–31, 237, 246–47, 252–53, 256–58, 260
esto, 157
et, 16, 24, 30, 33, 47–48, 50, 60, 62–63, 67, 75–76, 78, 80–81, 84–85, 91–93, 109, 114, 117, 119–20, 129–30, 138, 147, 151–53, 156–57, 162–68, 170–71, 178–79, 187, 194, 196, 199–200, 204, 206, 210–13, 215, 218, 220–21, 226, 228–31, 233–34, 237, 240, 244, 246–47, 249, 253, 257, 260, 265, 267
eta, 44
etenim, 252
etiam, 70, 254
etsi, 63
etymologiae, 44–45, 69, 127
euisdem, 129
eum, 199
evangeliorum, 107
evangelium, 117
evertere, 123
ex, 47
exaestuabat, 30
exametro, 99
excedere, 123
excelsa, 220
excepit, 172
exhilarant, 164
exhortatio, 203
eximio, 165, 230–31
eximius, 231
explanatio, 41, 101, 222
expositio, 61, 73, 100, 104, 187, 196, 199, 220–23, 232, 237–39, 245, 247, 249, 251–52, 256, 259
exquisivi, 178
extendit, 215
extinctus, 85
extinguetur, 209
exultas, 166, 244
exulto, 216

faceret, 206
facit, 78
facta, 192
facunda, 81
fallax, 257
falsitas, 48, 146
faltonia, 179
familia, 138, 230
familiae, 138
famina, 65
famularum, 141
famuli, 171
famulus, 114, 115, 117
fastidium, 102

fateri, 109
fecit, 226, 233
fedae, 186
fedus, 47
felici, 228
felicis, 128, 217, 238
felix, 101, 170, 218
femina, 161, 164, 196–98, 205, 253
feminae, 50
fera, 213
feras, 165, 213–14, 217
ferentes, 121
ferentes, 179
feris, 165, 211, 213, 217, 235
ferre, 211, 271
ferreas, 218
ferro, 85, 165, 216–17, 219
ferrum, 216
fert, 162, 210
feruidi, 62
ferulas, 147
ferus, 211
festiui, 63
festiuis, 166
fide, 168, 171, 253
fidei, 79, 147, 217, 222, 246, 249
fidelem, 178
fidelis, 156
fides, 228
figmenta, 109
figuratus, 132
fili, 81
filiae, 253
filias, 253
filii, 249
filiorum, 77
filium, 84, 135
filius, 152
finem, 191
finesse, 106
finibus, 168
firmamentum, 232
flamma, 78, 222
flammas, 204, 267
flore, 172
flores, 164, 206–8, 217
floruit, 165, 250
foedae, 184

foedo, 192
foedus, 46, 184
foemina, 141
fons, 152, 175, 236
fonte, 63
forma, 62, 134
formas, 23
formator, 170
formosus, 257
fortem, 157, 168, 178
fortia, 212
fortiorem, 204
fortis, 139, 156–57, 168–69, 182, 187–88, 196, 200, 204, 206, 238, 257
fortitude, 157
fortitudine, 157, 206
fortitudo, 237
fortium, 132
fove, 146
fragore, 201
frater, 58
fratres, 91
fratrum, 118–19, 270
freti, 62
frigore, 85
frigoribus, 81, 221
fructu, 199, 206, 260
fructum, 206
frui, 82
fuit, 199
fulgescere, 79
fulgida, 163, 166, 264, 267
fulgidi, 62
fumam, 81
fundamenta, 73
funde, 81
furentibus, 78
furit, 165, 263
furuam, 81
fusa, 146
fusum, 212

gaudebunt, 199
gaudens, 199
gaudent, 199
gaudere, 193
gaudet, 162, 164, 197, 199–200, 205
gaudia, 156, 183, 200, 218

gaudio, 199
gaudium, 91, 200
generis, 106
genitor, 144, 169, 269
genitoris, 269
genitrix, 172
gens, 2
gentem, 123
gentiles, 109
gentis, 139
gentium, 171
genuit, 164, 207–8
genus, 15
geraris, 75
germina, 82
germine, 162, 164, 206–8, 250
gesta, 175, 220
geta, 109–10
gladios, 162, 165, 204, 217, 220
gladium, 219
gladius, 216
glebae, 82
glescunt, 81
globum, 48, 57
gloria, 163, 165, 264, 266, 269
gloriae, 8, 221, 229
gracilis, 85
gradibus, 149
gradum, 149
gradus, 149, 181, 191, 264
grammaticale, 68–69
grammatici, 68
grammaticus, 41, 60, 68
grandisonis, 109
granum, 206
gratia, 252, 257
gratiae, 171, 192, 246
gratissima, 102
gratum, 103
gravia, 56
gregis, 228
gregori, 170
gregorius, 227
grex, 227
gubernans, 144, 169, 172, 221
gubernare, 144
gubernas, 144, 164

gubernator, 169–70
gubernatur, 221
gustavit, 209

habebit, 112–13
habet, 90, 92–93, 120, 132
habitare, 254
habitasse, 254
habitu, 203
habitus, 226
haec, 67, 78, 85, 112, 129, 146, 152–53, 198–99
harena, 102
haurit, 80
helenae, 164, 183, 270
heroicum, 132
heroum, 132
hi, 161, 182
hic, 82, 156, 228, 267
hispanus, 106
historia, 131
historiae, 129, 131
hoc, 67, 70, 132, 192, 198, 256
homilia, 140
hominem, 62, 149, 229
homines, 164
hominis, 259
hominum, 91
homo, 70
honore, 165, 261
horrens, 93
hors, 162, 200
horum, 82
hoste, 163, 263
hoste, 165, 263, 265
hostiae, 154
hostis, 263
huc, 198
huius, 162, 164, 206–8, 247
humanae, 209, 252
humilis, 67, 101, 228
humilitatem, 251–52
hydros, 259
hymnis, 101
hymno, 163, 244, 265, 268, 270
hymnodia, 227, 254
hymnorum, 81, 118–19

hymnos, 182
hymnum, 118–19, 129, 270
hymnus, 120, 142

iactantiae, 252
iam, 145, 161–62, 164–65, 174, 225–26, 228, 231, 236–37, 241–42, 248
idiotes, 17
ieiunium, 149
ieiunius, 149
iesum, 84, 135
igitur, 227, 252
igne, 200
ignem, 216
ignes, 213, 267
igni, 80
ignibus, 162, 165, 210–11, 213, 235
ignis, 209, 225
ignobilis, 229
illa, 70, 157, 227
illae, 30
ille, 194
illecebris, 188
illi, 63, 94
illius, 75, 209
illo, 199
illos, 254
illud, 70
illustribus, 97
illuxit, 170, 217
imaginationes, 23
imitari, 129
imitatio, 134
imperii, 134
impius, 112–13
impollutum, 256
in, 162–65, 222, 253, 263
inardescit, 222
incarnatus, 254
incidit, 78
incipit, 164
incomparabilis, 141
inconsulti, 233
inde, 162, 233
indicare, 266
indigebit, 178
indignatio, 76

indita, 129, 131
indoctus, 85
induistis, 188
indumentum, 226, 237
induta, 157
inferros, 165
infers, 251, 265
influebant, 30
ingenia, 62–63
ingenti, 72
ingratis, 114
ingreditur, 78
initio, 138
inlustrat, 249
inluxit, 81
inmerito, 254
inmitem, 103
inmortale, 107
innere, 16
innocuas, 267
innuitur, 156
innumeris, 12
inopi, 215
inorbe, 165
inque, 162, 246
inquinet, 183
institoris, 192
institutione, 195, 203
institutis, 157
institutum, 70
instructa, 213
insuauissima, 55
insula, 57, 132
integritatis, 201, 259
intellectum, 90, 92–93
intellegentiae, 181
intellegit, 70
inter, 94, 132, 172, 227
interea, 72, 75
intermissione, 199
interpres, 75
interpretandi, 60
interpretatio, 124
intersecat, 267
intimis, 225
intres, 196
introibit, 221

Latin Words

intulit, 228
inueniet, 157
inuentione, 63
inuiolata, 163, 257
inuiolate, 165
inuisibilis, 23
inveniet, 168
inveniri, 132
inveniuntur, 69
investiture, 91
inviolata, 224
invitae, 85
ipsa, 163, 165, 257, 261
ipsis, 152, 225
ipso, 206
ipsum, 25
ira, 76
ista, 120, 152–53, 191
istiusmodi, 253
istus, 165
italia, 47
italiam, 47
itaque, 67
iubilamen, 49
iucundi, 63
iucundum, 67
iudici, 207
iudicii, 172
iugiter, 172
iugo, 70
iugum, 77
iulianum, 138
iuppiter, 174
iustitia, 245
iustitiae, 153
iustitiam, 78
iuvenes, 200
iuxta, 99

kasta, 162, 165, 213–14, 217, 219, 224

labes, 51
labia, 156
lacrimae, 30
laeta, 162–63, 165–66, 215, 217–19, 224, 264
laetabitur, 200
laetanturque, 91

laetare, 218
laetificabo, 200
laetior, 216
laetis, 122, 179
laetum, 228
lampadas, 257
lana, 188
lanam, 187
laneis, 218
lapidibus, 168, 218, 248
lapis, 195
lapsu, 185
larem, 81
largitor, 171
laris, 163, 265
lata, 162–63, 253, 257
latina, 40, 81
latinae, 81, 92
latine, 55, 57–58, 68–69, 219, 231
latinus, 73
latus, 271
laudabitur, 257
laudanda, 63
laudate, 201
laudavit, 249
laudem, 120, 129, 142, 156
laudent, 260
laudes, 67, 82, 119–21, 149, 179
laudibus, 22, 82–83
laurus, 75
lectio, 128
lecto, 177
lege, 151
legere, 105
leges, 147
legis, 191
lenae, 161, 182, 186
lenis, 93
letis, 121–22
lex, 131, 240
libellus, 2, 129, 139
liber, 2, 46, 65, 70, 81, 99–100, 118–19, 127, 267
liberat, 192
liberet, 161, 164, 192–93
libidini, 184
libidinis, 222
libra, 143

librant, 81
librati, 63
libri, 33, 35, 40–42, 45–47, 50–51,
    56–57, 62, 76, 80, 89–90, 100,
    102, 104, 107, 114, 116, 118–19, 122,
    147–48, 227, 247, 262, 265
libris, 105
libro, 99
librorum, 153
librum, 104, 149
licet, 114, 116
lingua, 80, 91, 183, 240
linguae, 92
linguis, 12
linum, 187–88
liquoribus, 81
lira, 133
literarum, 15
litore, 57
littera, 39, 55–56
litterarum, 106
litteras, 154
locetur, 147
loci, 15
locum, 75
locus, 5
locutus, 189
longa, 147
longe, 192
loquar, 164, 179
loquendi, 60, 66
loqui, 109
loquor, 188
lubrica, 183
lubrici, 183
lubricis, 164, 182–83, 270
lucem, 229, 235
lucerna, 209
lucernae, 79
lucida, 64
lucidis, 82
lucificat, 229
lucifluam, 81
lucis, 249
luctum, 200
luculenta, 62–63
lugubri, 185
lumbos, 206

lumen, 217, 235
lumina, 79, 180
lumine, 91–92, 95, 217, 237
lutosam, 81
lux, 79, 84, 206, 229
luxuriosus, 183
luxus, 161, 164, 182–84, 270
lyricus, 43, 120, 123–24

magis, 16
magistro, 109
magno, 199
magnum, 84
magnus, 36
mala, 138
male, 114, 116, 140, 157, 185, 203–4
malis, 138
malitia, 76, 91
malus, 117
mane, 163, 264
maneat, 165, 266
manens, 165, 235
manes, 148
manifesta, 109
mansionibus, 77
manum, 212, 215
manus, 152–53, 183, 215
manuum, 187, 199, 260
maria, 81, 164, 172, 195, 197–98
mariae, 199, 234
maris, 170
marmore, 222
martyrum, 121
martyrum, 179
mater, 40, 81, 165, 170, 172, 202, 234,
    242
materna, 223
matre, 162, 164, 200–201
matrem, 165, 242
matrique, 182
matris, 81
maxime, 132
maximus, 121
me, 162
mea, 47, 156, 186, 205, 234
meam, 218
mearum, 84
medio, 185–86

meditandis, 71
meditate, 42
meditazione, 100, 130
medius, 145, 243
mei, 187, 234
meis, 30
mella, 53
membra, 170, 185
membrum, 185
memorare, 81
mendacia, 109
mendax, 183
mens, 114, 157, 222
mensura, 24
mente, 228
mentes, 201
mentibus, 121, 179
mentis, 165, 213, 215, 222, 249
meo, 85, 178, 249
mercedem, 193
metrum, 24, 53
metuens, 84
meum, 30, 156, 196, 218, 239, 251, 268
metro, 129, 131
mi, 81, 161–62, 182, 186, 200
mica, 162, 200
micans, 164, 199–201
micant, 200
micantes, 201
micare, 171
micat, 171
mihi, 30, 164, 175, 182, 197, 234–35
milites, 180
miracula, 109, 227
mise, 161, 188
miser, 114
miserae, 164, 186, 189
misere, 81
miserere, 187
misit, 212
mitatu, 163, 265
mitis, 103
modi, 168
modis, 109
modulamine, 12
modulandi, 41
modularis, 166, 244, 265, 268
modulatio, 41

modulatione, 41
modus, 156
mole, 73
monarchiam, 172
monarchum, 141
monasterio, 165, 224, 250
montibus, 73
monumenta, 109, 257
monumentis, 254
monumentum, 254
mor, 162, 222
morari, 50
morbi, 163, 165, 260, 262
morbus, 259
morem, 129
moribus, 114
mors, 233
mortalibus, 219
mortem, 260
mortificatum, 206
mortis, 260
mortuus, 135
movebitur, 78
mox, 47
mulier, 139, 156–57, 168–69, 182, 187–88, 196, 200, 204, 206, 238, 257
mulierem, 157, 168
mulieris, 236
mulierum, 192
multa, 79, 85, 91, 94–95
multae, 253
multi, 12, 16, 101
multorum, 129, 222
multos, 165
multum, 206
multus, 162, 165, 220, 222, 224
mundi, 164, 170–71, 180, 188, 195, 197, 198, 212, 268
mundo, 101, 192
mundum, 144, 169
munera, 121, 161, 163–64, 166, 179–80, 189, 191, 264, 267
muneris, 171
munia, 147
munus, 182, 187, 195
musa, 36
musas, 170
musica, 41

musicale, 55
mysteria, 267
mysterio, 194

naevius, 184
nam, 46, 175, 260
namque, 104
narramen, 49
nasci, 260
nativitas, 186
natura, 23, 62, 100, 200
naturae, 237
naturali, 260
natus, 135, 199, 229–30
navis, 192
ne, 55, 66, 116, 183
nec, 47, 162, 165, 227, 253–54
necessaria, 69
nefandarum, 109
negotiatio, 209
neque, 81
neruis, 12
nesciens, 70
nigram, 81
niliacis, 109
nimium, 114
nitens, 228, 230
nitere, 226
nitet, 165, 228, 230, 258
nitoribus, 81
nivis, 221
nobili, 162, 230
nobilior, 156, 165, 230–31, 237
nobilis, 229–30
nobilissimi, 106
nobilissimus, 8
nobilitatem, 237
nobis, 56, 81, 171, 238
nocent, 81
nocte, 196, 209
noctem, 81
nolverunt, 239
nomine, 228
non, 161–62, 182, 188, 210
nondum, 70
nos, 82–83, 161, 164, 176, 179–80, 247
noster, 82, 155, 178
nostra, 162, 165, 225–27

nostrae, 245
nostri, 81, 227
nostro, 63
nostrum, 84, 134, 172
novembres, 165
nova, 12, 21, 79, 82, 121, 163, 166, 244, 265, 267, 269
novalia, 112
novalis, 115
novissimo, 237
novum, 120
novus, 246
noxa, 183
nubes, 51
nubiculis, 81
nubs, 51
nulla, 222, 269
nullus, 163, 166, 265, 269, 271–72
numen, 106
numero, 24
numerus, 24
numina, 75
nupta, 163, 165, 238, 264–65, 270
nuptialis, 183
nur, 106
nutrix, 256

obilior, 231
oblectat, 16
occisa, 216
octo, 162, 165, 203, 253–55
oculi, 200
oculis, 217
oculus, 152, 236
odas, 109
oderit, 232
odilia, 156
odium, 233
oleum, 209
omne, 216
omnem, 71, 229
omnes, 71, 80, 148, 221, 253
omni, 76, 81
omnibus, 90, 156, 204
omnipotens, 144, 169, 174
omnis, 76
omnium, 172, 222–23
opera, 139, 148, 156, 260

Latin Words

operam, 71
operata, 187
operatur, 70, 78
opere, 67, 253
operibus, 63
operis, 165, 258
opes, 252
oportet, 70
optata, 102
optima, 62, 65
orantem, 171
orateur, 115
oratio, 99
oratore, 50
orbe, 162, 165, 220, 222
orbem, 49
orbis, 146, 223, 227
orbitas, 48, 146
ordine, 70–71, 156
ordo, 132, 181
ore, 40, 62
organi, 101
originis, 229
origo, 73
ornata, 56
ornatus, 183
ornavit, 49
orta, 162, 165, 230–31
orti, 230
ortus, 108, 147, 199, 230
os, 40, 47, 152, 156, 162, 206, 217, 239–40, 268
oscula, 183
ostentat, 257
otiosa, 246
ovans, 165, 263
ovantes, 82

pacis, 161, 164, 176, 180, 191
palma, 170
palmas, 215
panem, 192, 246
pange, 91
papillas, 216
paradisum, 83
parens, 169, 195
parentem, 164, 193, 197
parentis, 199
paribus, 12
parit, 164, 193, 197–98, 205
pariter, 63
partem, 77, 93, 148, 248
partitione, 63
passio, 217, 225
passione, 209
passus, 135
pater, 40, 155, 229, 231–32
paternae, 8
patientiae, 245
patre, 165, 230–31
patrem, 135
patria, 246
patriae, 229
patribus, 230
patrum, 148
patuerunt, 102
paulo, 213
pauperem, 215
pavimento, 186–87
peccata, 268
peccator, 114
peccatores, 233
peccatorum, 84
peccent, 183
pedum, 48, 92
penetrat, 249
per, 162, 210, 222
percepti, 234
percipere, 234
percipit, 162, 165, 233–34
percussa, 216–17
perdere, 227
perduto, 100
perennis, 200
perfecta, 253
perfectissimo, 156
perfectoris, 247
perfectus, 151
perfert, 165, 211, 212
perficitur, 156
perfidiae, 221
peri, 217, 236
periodis, 63
permissa, 227
perpetes, 83
perpetua, 141, 234

perplurium, 202
personabant, 120
personarum, 171
personet, 119, 120
pervia, 102
pervulgatis, 220
pes, 92
petis, 162, 165, 237, 239
philosophia, 36
philosophiae, 36
pia, 156, 172, 179, 256
pictor, 81
pictorem, 81
pietatis, 30
piis, 91–92
piorum, 91
pius, 228
placent, 22
placidis, 109–10
placidus, 228
plaga, 46
plantavit, 199
plectro, 163, 166, 244, 265
plectrum, 160, 265, 269
plectuntur, 80
plenissime, 156
plenitudine, 153
plenitudo, 152–53, 181
plures, 162, 164, 206–7
plurima, 109, 129, 131
plus, 162, 233
pocula, 172
poema, 114
poesia, 35
poeta, 24
poetae, 48, 108–9
poeticas, 16
poeticum, 171
poeticus, 92, 182
poetria, 21, 82
pollens, 228
polo, 165, 249–51
polos, 91, 95
pompare, 109
pompeius, 44
pondere, 24, 85
ponti, 102
pontifex, 48, 146

populus, 46, 132, 246
porta, 161, 164, 170, 195–98
portas, 73, 85, 218, 221
portat, 192
portio, 205
portis, 229, 260
positio, 65–66
positione, 66
possim, 109
posteris, 63
posthabui, 147
postumi, 63
potestates, 43–44
potiuntur, 102
potius, 70
praecedit, 246
praecepti, 233
praecessor, 171
praecipit, 247
praeclaris, 63
praeconia, 170
praeconium, 129, 142
praedam, 196
praedicaverunt, 249
praeeminet, 66
praefatio, 63
praemia, 156
precamur, 82
precantes, 146
precatur, 252
precor, 81
pretiosior, 168
pretiosis, 168, 218, 248
pretiosissima, 195
pretium, 168
prima, 104
primae, 230
primam, 77, 248
primatus, 252
primo, 48, 57, 169, 171, 247
primum, 149
primus, 101
principes, 180, 221
principium, 56, 152–53, 212
pro, 162–163, 213, 260
procul, 168
proelia, 161, 164, 188–89
proelium, 188–189

Latin Words

profectum, 259
proflui, 63
proles, 51
prologus, 99
prolumine, 165
promissorum, 198
propheta, 101
prophetae, 199, 252
propositi, 134
propres, 85
propter, 199
prosa, 99
prospere, 168
prosperi, 114
protulerim, 85
prouidi, 63
proverbia, 156
prudenter, 228
psallere, 109
psalmis, 82
psalmorum, 41, 61, 101, 149, 222
psalmos, 18, 149, 185
psalmum, 149
psalmus, 147–48
pubes, 51
publica, 9
publius, 111
puellae, 92
puellam, 81, 237
puer, 85
pueri, 201, 230
puero, 85
pueros, 61
pulcher, 5, 235
pulcherrima, 65
pulcherrime, 222
pulcherrimo, 121
pulcherrimus, 118
pulchra, 22
pulchre, 66
pulchritudinem, 236
pulchritudinis, 23
pulchritudo, 257
pulchrius, 90
pulchro, 163, 257
pulsa, 177
purpura, 226
purus, 184

putet, 162, 253–54
puto, 147
putrem, 94

quadrupedante, 94
quae, 22, 67, 85, 90, 92–93, 107, 153, 156–57, 161, 163–65, 168–69, 172, 204, 213, 221, 253, 264, 266
quaecumque, 154
quaemundum, 164
quaesivit, 187
quaestiones, 104
qualibet, 109
qualis, 157
quam, 81, 132, 156, 166, 265, 269–70
quamuis, 56
quando, 229
quanta, 144
quantitas, 48, 146
quaris, 162, 241
quatit, 94
quattuordecim, 48
quem, 75, 81, 228
qui, 25, 62, 64, 70, 75, 78, 80, 85, 114, 148, 161, 163, 165, 189, 192, 194, 199, 229, 246, 262–63, 268
quia, 165, 168, 178, 209, 234, 246
quibus, 82–83, 164, 197
quibusdam, 254
quid, 70, 162, 165, 237–38
quidem, 62, 149, 216
quintam, 93
quintus, 92
quis, 85, 92, 157, 168
quo, 5, 70, 138, 162, 226
quod, 70, 85, 132, 221, 229, 235
quonda, 165
quondam, 263
quoque, 162, 165, 225, 227, 239, 241–42
quorum, 70
quos, 16, 105, 182, 227
quot, 114

radianti, 91, 95
raptus, 161, 182, 184–86, 228, 270
ratio, 41, 60, 151
ratione, 41

rationem, 229
recepero, 216
receperunt, 192
recesserat, 131
recesserunt, 130
recte, 60
recubat, 228
reddere, 250
reddidit, 162, 165, 250
redemptor, 178
redemptoris, 253
referat, 137–138
referenda, 70
referens, 228
referent, 63, 263, 270
refrigescet, 222
regali, 165, 231
regalia, 226, 231
regalis, 231
reges, 72, 75
regi, 119
regiam, 219
regina, 141
reginae, 129, 164–65, 234
regis, 91, 162, 165, 241–42
regitur, 221
regna, 201
regnant, 26, 124, 148
regnator, 170
regnauerat, 162, 165, 246, 248
regni, 252
regno, 114–17
regnum, 134
regulis, 48, 92
regum, 104
rei, 146
religio, 47
reliquere, 63–64
rem, 70, 227
remissionem, 84
renouent, 109
rentem, 161, 196
repellas, 178
repperiatur, 153
reproborum, 221
rerum, 23, 43, 100, 109, 123, 146, 176, 200
res, 162, 206

resonare, 109, 176–77
resonat, 177
resonet, 161, 164, 177, 179
respondentque, 12
responsiorium, 129
responsorius, 147
restitui, 138
resurrexit, 135
retractationum, 227
retributio, 181
retribuuntur, 138
revelari, 70
reverentia, 237
revolumen, 49
rex, 221, 231
ridebit, 237
ridens, 267
ridet, 165, 218
ridiculoue, 109–10
rigati, 81
rigentia, 221
rithmus, 24, 41, 53
ritmica, 35
rituque, 109
rivulo, 81
roboravit, 206
robustior, 165, 217, 219
romanae, 73
romanitas, 184
romanus, 211
roris, 81
rosa, 85
roscidi, 81
rubentis, 172
ruminabant, 130
rupit, 85
ruricolas, 170
ruris, 81
rusticitas, 108

sacerdos, 228
sacra, 99, 215
sacrae, 129, 165, 182, 258, 261
sacram, 237
sacramentis, 23
sacramentorum, 199
sacras, 165, 214, 217
sacrata, 165, 251–52

sacri, 17
sacrior, 165
sacro, 246
sacrorum, 81, 168
saeclis, 79
saecula, 79, 148, 161, 169, 173, 198, 221
saecularium, 16
saeculi, 168–69, 229, 233, 247
saeculis, 170, 217
saeculorum, 79
saeculum, 198, 222
saeva, 80, 109–10
salmiche, 100, 130
salomon, 157
salomonis, 156
salus, 195
salutantis, 199
salutarem, 196
salutaris, 154
salutem, 78
salutiferi, 109, 111
salutis, 104
salva, 147
salvator, 196
samuhelis, 77, 248
sancta, 91–92, 170, 203–4, 246–47, 256
sanctae, 156, 171, 199, 234
sancti, 78, 99, 128, 199, 213
sanctis, 73
sanctissimis, 23
sanctitas, 48, 146
sanctorum, 84, 216
sanctus, 151, 254
santoque, 109
sapiens, 157, 228
sapientia, 36, 62
sapientiae, 240
saporem, 82
satanique, 15
satorem, 81
saxonum gens, 2
scelerum, 109
scelus, 147
sceptra, 162, 165, 188, 233, 235
sceptris, 114
scientia, 41, 60

scientiae, 229
scolastici, 128
scolasticus, 8
scribendi, 56, 60
scriptores, 40, 45
scriptura, 80
scripturae, 23, 129
scripturis, 71, 132
se, 25, 60–61, 84, 133, 162–63, 241, 252, 257
sectatur, 253
secula, 164
secum, 57, 146
secunda, 49
secundius, 142
secundum, 186, 221, 252
securi, 62
secutus, 206
sed, 70, 81, 84, 130, 149, 165, 216, 246, 252–53, 260
sederit, 229
sedes, 51
sedet, 135
sedulii, 108
sedulo, 81
segetem, 78
segetes, 112–113
segregat, 163, 166, 265, 271
semitas, 246
semper, 170
sempiternum, 152, 228
senarius, 101
senatoribus, 229
senes, 200
sensibus, 109
sentis, 75
sepelitur, 252
septem, 184
sepulchra, 258
sepulchro, 165, 257–58
sepulchrorum, 254
sepulchrum, 254
sepultus, 135
sequaris, 165, 242
sequens, 242
sequi, 239
sequitur, 246
serii, 63

sermones, 157
sermonis, 67
serpens, 184
servanda, 212
serviana, 112
servire, 201
servit, 70, 114, 116
servitutis, 70
servo, 220
servus, 116–17
sese, 94
seu, 109
severitatis, 209
servus bonus, 116
servus malus, 117
sex, 162, 246, 248
si, 67, 147, 222
sibi, 63, 226
sic, 82, 183
sicut, 81
sidera, 75
signa, 70, 153, 259
signavit, 254
significantem, 70
significet, 70
signo, 70
signum, 70
sillaba, 93
silvam, 123
simplex, 228
simplici, 99
simpliciter, 228
simul, 168, 172, 200
sindonem, 233
sine, 41, 78, 199, 252
sint, 56
sion, 73
siquidem, 254
sis, 162, 165, 241–42, 250
sit, 163, 264
sive, 23, 152, 220, 236
sobria, 162, 222
sobrie, 162, 222
sobrietas, 222
sobrietatis, 165, 223–24
socia, 67
solebas, 56
solent, 227

solet, 132
solia, 81
solis, 108, 147, 199
solo, 57
solum, 218
solus, 114–15
soluta, 154
solutorias, 154
solveretur, 154
solveritis, 154
sonitu, 94
sonus, 249
sordium, 254
sorte, 15, 55, 228
spargens, 53
spe, 198
speluncam, 84
spem, 85
spiritalis, 70
spiritualiter, 232
spiritum, 252
spiritus, 146
splendens, 226
spoliis, 178
spolium, 178
spondaei, 93
spondeoque, 99
sponsa, 129, 139, 162, 165–66, 234, 237, 244–47, 269–70
sponsae, 234
sponsi, 199
sponso, 238, 268
sponsus, 162, 165–66, 193, 237–38, 244, 257, 270
stant, 149
stare, 109
statione, 147
statui, 85
stella, 170
stellas, 201
stelligeri, 64
stemma, 230
stemmate, 162, 230–31
stili, 17
stilo, 17
stilus, 127, 130
stirpis, 73
strages, 51

stragulam, 226
strepitu, 177
studeant, 109
studio, 114
studiorum, 16
stultus, 195
stupore, 63
sua, 109–11, 199
suae, 221, 229, 246
suam, 193, 212, 215
suarum, 187, 199, 260
suas, 215
suauitatis, 231
suavibus, 82
sub, 56, 70, 162, 165, 196, 233, 235
sublima, 56
sublimibus, 82
subsistentia, 171
substantia, 171
subtilitas, 72
succiso, 63
sucorum, 82
sui, 63, 168, 178, 253
suis, 79, 130, 196
sum, 25, 31, 119, 196
summo, 54, 162, 165, 237, 238
summum, 81
sumpsisti, 81
sumunt, 82
sunt, 16, 22, 62, 70, 138, 221, 227, 247
suo, 130, 200–201, 252
suorum, 62, 185–86
suos, 206
super, 162, 233
superans, 216
superat, 165
supergreditur, 253
supergressa, 253
superna, 164, 186–90, 195
superpositis, 80
surgit, 254
surrexerunt, 249
surrexit, 196
susceptaculum, 131
susperat, 204
suum, 192, 206, 240
syllaba, 147
saecula, 107, 143, 169

tabes, 51
tabulae, 186
tabularum, 152–53
taceam, 109, 111
taedae, 267
taedis, 163, 166, 264
tale, 63, 107
tali, 81
talia, 70
talis, 70
talium, 254
tam, 112
tanta, 80
te, 17, 57, 83, 85, 107, 178, 222–23, 231, 235
tecla, 162, 165, 213, 219, 224
tectum, 196
tedis, 166
tegebat, 84
temperans, 222
temperantia, 222
tempora, 43, 45, 162, 165, 225–28
tempore, 63, 70
temporibus, 267
temporum, 43
tempus, 43, 123
tenebrarum, 84
terra, 123, 161, 164, 189, 197–98
terrae, 85, 229, 233
terram, 154, 206
terris, 50, 163, 165, 220, 264, 266
tertium, 15
tibi, 62, 80, 163, 165, 264, 266
timebit, 221
timens, 257
timor, 186
tirones, 183
tite, 80
tollatur, 76
tollit, 268
tollite, 221
tollunt, 94
tonans, 201
tonantem, 109–10, 201
tonanti, 201
tonantis, 164, 201
tonitruali, 201
tormentis, 204

torpore, 221
torrentibus, 81
tot, 114
tota, 162, 165, 183, 249–50, 251–252
totius, 156, 171
toto, 109, 178, 249
tractare, 220
tractatus, 18, 117
tradant, 109
tradidit, 233
tragico, 109–10
trahit, 172
transcendit, 204
transcends, 43
translatio, 15
transtulit, 172
tremet, 81
tria, 120
tribulatione, 209
trina, 171
trinitas, 48, 143, 145, 146–47, 164, 171, 174, 223, 272
trinitate, 43, 118
trinus, 170
tripodas, 75
tristia, 227
triti, 62
triticum, 130
triumphales, 180
triumphat, 165, 263
triumphus, 165, 220, 223–24
troes, 102
troiae, 161, 164, 174, 186, 188–89
troianus, 84
troiugena, 75
tu, 119, 162–63, 165, 241–42, 253, 257
tuam, 156
tueri, 172
tui, 165, 258
tuis, 83, 178
tule, 163, 265
tulerat, 166, 211, 270–72
tuli, 271
tulisti, 80
tum, 114
tument, 229
tumere, 229
tumet, 46

tumulata, 255
tumulis, 254, 256
tumulo, 165, 254–55
tumulus, 254–55, 257
tunc, 200
turba, 118–19, 270
tute, 80
tuum, 156, 186, 240
typice, 156
typus, 194
tyranne, 80
tyranno, 114, 116

ubi, 62, 162, 165, 250
ulterius, 184
ultimis, 168, 225
ululabant, 130
umbro, 260–61
umida, 53
umulata, 165
uni, 272
unica, 146
unici, 134
unicum, 84
unicus, 228
unique, 4, 134, 231
unitas, 48, 146
universas, 253
universorum, 233
uno, 12
unum, 149
urbes, 56
urbis, 56
usta, 162, 165, 210–11, 235
ustor, 210
ustus, 210
usu, 62
ut, 50, 63, 81–83, 119, 161–62, 164–65, 193, 196, 206, 241
utatur, 114
utile, 70
utilitate, 71
uxor, 234

vacemus, 83
vale, 58, 77
vales, 107
vana, 257

Latin Words 333

vanitas, 48, 146
vaporiferos, 267
vasis, 80
vates, 24, 36, 48, 76
vatorum, 48
vel, 63, 156–57
vel, 71, 220
velandis, 203
velut, 201
veluti, 78
vena, 72
vendidit, 233
venenum, 72
venerabile, 100
venerabilis, 81, 127, 141
venerandae, 164
venerandae, 193, 197
veneratur, 70
veneratus, 194
veni, 62, 80
veniente, 57
venis, 80
venissent, 75
venit, 166
venit, 267
veniunt, 75
venturae, 267
venustatem, 236
venustatis, 252
venusti, 63
vepallida, 177
vera, 67, 131, 180, 206, 229
veraciter, 234
verae, 233
verba, 81
verbi, 175, 221
verbis, 109
verbis, 110
verbo, 173
verborum, 87, 132
verbum, 173, 175, 186
verenter, 109
vergilium, 179
veri, 256
veritas, 30
veritas, 30, 119, 146
veritas, 48
vero, 267

vero, 70
versionem, 99
verum, 235
vestem, 226
vestigia, 253
vestigia, 63
vestimenta, 256
vestimentis, 218
vestis, 163, 165, 257, 260
vestis, 256, 258, 261
vestiti, 221
vestra, 134
vestram, 171
vestri, 221
veteres, 53
veteris, 53
veteris, 62
vetus, 53, 81
vibrer, 115
vicerat, 163, 165, 263
vicerat, 262–63
vici, 62, 80
victorias, 121
victorias, 179
vide, 251
videam, 235
videantur, 254
vident, 138
videntes, 83
videtur, 70
vidi, 62, 80
vigere, 223
viget, 165
viget, 224
vigilium, 100
vigor, 252
vim, 70
vinci, 245
vincit, 204
vinculo, 83
vineam, 199
vini, 172
vinum, 44, 130
vinum, 44, 80
vipera, 259
vir, 72, 114, 178, 204, 229, 238, 249
virga, 103
virgine, 162, 164, 200, 206

virgine, 199
virgineo, 172
virgineos, 164, 207–8
virgines, 199
virgini, 162, 200
virgini, 182
virginibus, 203, 216, 227
virginis, 161–62, 164–65, 193, 253
virginis, 162, 253
virginis, 170, 193, 195, 198, 203, 255
virginitate, 164, 228
virginitate, 2, 49, 62, 91, 93, 98, 103, 130, 139–40, 144, 146, 157, 164, 170–71, 173, 192, 195, 201, 203–4, 212, 224, 228, 234–35, 246–47
virginitatis, 129
virginitatis, 203, 207
virginum, 201–3, 230
virgo, 161–65, 172, 196, 226–27, 263
virgo, 81, 170, 172, 194, 198, 200, 202, 211, 218, 227, 253
viri, 178
viris, 97
virorum, 132
virtus, 146
virtute, 62, 147, 170, 204, 257
virtutes, 156
virtutibus, 245
virtutis, 67
virtutum, 257
virum, 165
virum, 174, 238
virumque, 172
visa, 22
visceribus, 199
visibiles, 23
vitae, 252, 267
vitalem, 81

vitalia, 175
vitia, 212
vitiis, 114
vivait, 66
vivendi, 151
vivere, 63
vivifica, 186
vivo, 191
vobis, 76
vobis, 81, 85, 192
vocales, 44
vocatio, 153, 249
vocatur, 132, 156
voces, 30
vocibus, 120, 199
vocis, 249
voluptas, 67
voluptates, 16
vos, 81
vota, 161, 196–97
vox, 39–40, 222
vox, 62
vulgaris, 132
vulgatam, 99
vulgus, 132
vulnus, 80, 256
vulpes, 51
vultu, 228

xriste, 82, 163, 168, 257, 265
xristus, 254

ydros, 163, 165, 260–61, 265
ymnis, 82
ymno, 166

zelus, 163, 165, 245, 263
zona, 83

www.ingramcontent.com/pod-product-compliance
Lightning Source LLC
Chambersburg PA
CBHW021817300426
44114CB00009BA/209